When Political Transitions Work

STUDIES IN STRATEGIC PEACEBUILDING

Series Editors:
R. Scott Appleby, John Paul Lederach, and Daniel Philpott
The Joan B. Kroc Institute for International Peace Studies,
University of Notre Dame

STRATEGIES OF PEACE
Edited by Daniel Philpott and Gerard F. Powers

UNIONISTS, LOYALISTS, AND CONFLICT TRANSFORMATION IN
NORTHERN IRELAND
Lee A. Smithey

JUST AND UNJUST PEACE: AN ETHIC OF POLITICAL RECONCILIATION
Daniel Philpott

COUNTING CIVILIAN CASUALTIES: AN INTRODUCTION TO
RECORDING AND ESTIMATING NONMILITARY DEATHS IN CONFLICT
Edited by Taylor B. Seybolt, Jay D. Aronson, and Baruch Fischhoff

RESTORATIVE JUSTICE, RECONCILIATION, AND PEACEBUILDING
Edited by Jennifer J. Llewellyn and Daniel Philpott

QUALITY PEACE: PEACEBUILDING, VICTORY AND WORLD ORDER
Peter Wallensteen

THE PEACE CONTINUUM: WHAT IT IS AND HOW TO STUDY IT
Christian Davenport, Erik Melander, and Patrick M. Regan

WHEN POLITICAL TRANSITIONS WORK: RECONCILIATION AS
INTERDEPENDENCE
Fanie du Toit

When Political Transitions Work

Reconciliation as Interdependence

FANIE DU TOIT

OXFORD
UNIVERSITY PRESS

OXFORD
UNIVERSITY PRESS

Oxford University Press is a department of the University of Oxford. It furthers
the University's objective of excellence in research, scholarship, and education
by publishing worldwide. Oxford is a registered trade mark of Oxford University
Press in the UK and certain other countries.

Published in the United States of America by Oxford University Press
198 Madison Avenue, New York, NY 10016, United States of America.

Library of Congress Cataloging-in-Publication Data
Names: Du Toit, Fanie, author.
Title: When political transitions work : reconciliation as interdependence /
Fanie du Toit.
Description: New York, NY : Oxford University Press, 2018. |
Series: Studies in strategic peacebuilding
Identifiers: LCCN 2017056471 (print) | LCCN 2017058077 (ebook) |
ISBN 9780190881863 (updf) | ISBN 9780190881870 (epub) |
ISBN 9780190881856 (hardcover)
Subjects: LCSH: Post-apartheid era—South Africa. | South Africa—Politics
and government—1994– | Reconciliation—Political aspects—South Africa. |
Transitional justice—South Africa.
Classification: LCC DT1971 (ebook) | LCC DT1971 .D8 2018 (print) |
DDC 968.07—dc23
LC record available at https://lccn.loc.gov/2017056471

1 3 5 7 9 8 6 4 2

Printed by Sheridan Books, Inc., United States of America

CONTENTS

FOREWORD

Fanie du Toit brings to this book his deep knowledge and experience of having lived through the South African transition to democracy from before and after the historic elections of April 27, 1994. Convinced by, and believing in, Nelson Mandela's efforts to work toward reconciliation after a difficult history in which the "white" part of the population colonized and systematically oppressed the "black" part, South Africans have to ask how far they have come in the twenty-three years since embracing democracy?

Du Toit asks the question more directly. How can we reevaluate "South Africa's transition now, twenty-four years after formal apartheid ended"? This question calls up an ability to sense and hopefully observe a trajectory of social, cultural, political, and economic events and how South Africans have responded to them and understood their implications for their project of reconciliation. Were they able to converge with some consistency toward a shared sense of common citizenship, or have they tended to diverge from it? What insights does du Toit distill from his rigorous attempt to answer such questions?

President Nelson Mandela's inaugural one-term tenure of office began a people's precarious journey into a future armed with untested optimism. It took off through the extraordinary trust South Africans were willing to invest in a leader who convinced them "to have a go at it." It was a working optimism that had enabled them to avert the nightmare of a racial civil war. It provided an environment in which the South African constitution, backed by the legitimacy of extensive public participation, was approved by parliament. A system of institutions of democracy was conceived and set up, and a plethora of policies and laws promulgated with a genuine intention to work toward a democratic and just society. It all happened under the rubric of reconciliation. Intangible, and therefore susceptible, just under the skin, to the cynical charge of emotionalism, the appeal of reconciliation bore a persuasive, and even functionally cohesive appeal.

President Thabo Mbeki's tenure of two terms, begun in 1999, was preceded by the decision as to whether Mandela's successor would be Mbeki himself or Cyril Ramaphosa, whose turn to serve as president occurred nineteen years later. What drove Nelson Mandela's preference for the latter was the symbolic, yet constitutional significance of Ramaphosa's origins from the Venda people, a relatively small ethnic group in the northeastern parts of South Africa. A Ramaphosa presidency immediately after Mandela's would signal an intent to ensure a democratic distribution of the sources of power across the land.

While Mbeki had solid credentials within the African National Congress in exile, and came from Mandela's own, large and politically dominant ethnic group, internally he was more "known of" than known. Ramaphosa's in-country political currency had been proven in the trade union movement and in the United Democratic Front during the buildup to the end of apartheid. But whatever the case might be, the post-Mandela succession of either of them was certain to come with some measure of public uncertainty. How solid and reassuring would the immediate post-Mandela presidency be? Would it enhance the project of reconciliation?

It is historically significant that President Mbeki chose Jacob Zuma to serve as his deputy president. Respectively they represent astute political rationality and astute political populism. Where Mbeki would critically deploy reason transparently, Zuma would deploy emotion through song and dance. This does not mean that behind the song and dance there was no political logic: just that whatever that logic was he would never declare transparently. Thus, song and dance would be a choreography for hidden intentions.

Yet human rationality and human emotion coexist to influence the ebbs and flows of human history. At play is how either of them, sometimes in delicate interplay, influenced the making of historic choices. Between transparency and secrecy, human values have their playground. In a constitutional democracy that playground should always be the focus of public attention. It provides space for the public to confront the full and complex reality of how their past and their future converge in their present.

Indeed, ten years of President Zuma's presidency saw the visible decline of state institutions and the rule of law as a result of the spread and consolidation of systemic corruption. This happened in the face of bold government anti-corruption proclamations and its declared continued commitment to empowering the masses. The gap in meaning between the two realities resulted in a large measure of public disaffection and anguish. Historical political mass support enjoyed by the African National Congress and the expected public benefits of that support were seen not to coincide. Because the message of the Zuma presidency's intention to defraud the state could never be openly proclaimed, cumulative public disaffection would be its legacy. There was the real prospect that South Africa could succumb to the rule of institutionalized criminality. The question is: What kind of political dynamics would emerge to confront such a situation?

The rats of race and racism, glaring and growing inequality in wealth and educational opportunity, rising unemployment, and the resilience of apartheid spatial planning began to scramble to the surface of a ship with a major leak taking in seawater. The most visible emblem of the "afterlife of the empire" was the #RhodesMustFall student movement, followed by the @FeesMustFall movement, which flew the flag of "decolonization." The movements highlighted the question: Did "white" South Africans maintain, in their behavior if not in their intention, a vested interest in being beneficiaries of an extractive economic system still oriented in its business perspectives toward Europe and North America and to the collateral benefit of their structural and cultural clients in South Africa: "white" South Africa?

This is the trap of "white" South Africans' history. Where do their social, cultural, and economic loyalties now lie? The order in which I have listed the orientations of loyalties is deliberate. The social and the cultural are about the grounding of existential purpose and the extent to which the economic is derived from that purpose, serves it, and sustains it. For "white" South Africans, existential purpose may have to be extracted from being "white" toward being "un-raced" new South Africans. But then what does it mean to be an "un-raced" new South African? The answer is not an easy one, and it has to be earned.

Fanie du Toit feels the terrain of reconciliation with the hands of his searching mind. He recognizes the contours of reconciliation "as political beginning, as institutionalized transfer of power, and as social change." In these, as the student movements strongly point to, social change may be the greatest challenge of the South African state in 2018 and beyond. In this connection, du Toit brings up a major flaw in the tendency of South Africans to see the Truth and Reconciliation Commission as the "silver bullet" to South Africa's transition. This tendency has drawn attention away from the more pervasive aspects of "transitional reconciliation" which would have given the process of transition a more systemic feel, such as "the National Peace Accord (NPA), the Multi-Party Negotiation Process (MPNP), and the Transitional Executive Council (TEC)." The challenge is for South Africans is to endeavor to keep in full view the coherence of the transitional evolution of the South African state both in its formal systemic nature and in its informal social processes.

This speaks, as Fanie du Toit compellingly points out, to "how then the transfer of actual power is institutionalized in processes that go beyond agreements, declarations and high-profile meetings." "Going beyond" is crucially about giving life to agreements and declarations. It is about "reconciliation's implicit normativity," by which I understand du Toit to mean how constitutional democracy, one outcome of transitional reconciliation, is actualized in the social conditions of the vast majority of South African citizens in such a way that new norms of social living emerge and evolve across the largest, most extensive human space in South Africa: the millions of unracialized "blacks" of South Africa.

Indeed, the pivot away from racialized thinking is how a particular perspective of human living renders racial thinking ultimately irrelevant. In this connection, the enabling conditions of true reconciliation may be more present than absent, if only they could be acknowledged. In my opinion, the greatest human convergence in South Africa has been among the conquered and dispossessed. They were able to "reconcile" far more over time and in a social process deep enough to be the very foundations of a reconciliation across "race" when that convergence becomes the new gravitational pull toward a broader social cohesion. Then "race" ceases to be the fulcrum around which a national consensus is established. "Race" will be placed in its proper historical role and isolated as a factor of injustice in colonial and apartheid history without becoming the foundation of the solution to the problems it created.

Indeed, if the resilience of race is caused by entrenched economic privilege and assets of land and capital concentrated in the hands of "white" South Africans, then a potentially compelling solution to the distribution of the opportunities and benefits of such historical accumulation and concentration of the "white" privilege seems tied up with the possibilities of how the now enfranchised "blacks" have access to such opportunities and benefits. Initially it is about how the state uses collected taxes to change the material conditions of "blacks." It will be about wages, salaries, productivity, and a professionalized civil service and how the integrity of the state is derived from its ability to empower the broadest population with a new economy oriented toward it.

The focusing on the prosecution of individuals arising from the Truth and Reconciliation Commission's recommendations diverted attention from systemic culpability, in the same way that the focusing of reparations on individual victims of gross violations of human rights diverted attention from apartheid as systemic gross violations of human rights. The aberrations of systemic injustice can properly be corrected at the level of the state galvanized by not only a corrective but also a transformative purpose. The processes of the state, therefore, are critical in bringing about systemic social justice. This imposes a communal approach to social and economic practice that could come with more deeply structured social reconciliation.

Fanie du Toit's contribution to this complex challenge is to approach it with a fresh theoretical rigor. It is an approach to be savored.

Njabulo S. Ndebele

ACKNOWLEDGMENTS

During a hearty lunch, Professor Scott Appleby, the then director of the Kroc Institute for International Peace Studies at Notre Dame University where I was visiting research fellow, invited me to turn a lecture I gave on campus into a manuscript. This book is the end result. I am grateful to Scott, as well as the Kroc Institute and all the colleagues I met and worked with there, for the space for reflection and stimulating conversations, away from the hurly-burly of being "in the field."

Subsequently, Scott has been the primary reader of the manuscript, a confidant and guide who kept me going through the process of writing this book.

The book would have been unthinkable without the experiences and collegiality that have marked my life as part of the Institute for Justice and Reconciliation (IJR) over the past decade and a half. It has been a remarkable journey working alongside many talented and committed colleagues, too numerous to mention here by name, and with many partners across the African continent.

It would be wrong not to single out Archbishop Desmond Tutu, IJR's beloved patron, who has been a constant source of inspiration, love, and wisdom to me, as indeed he has been to so many others; or Charles Villa-Vicencio, who was founding director of IJR and taught me much of what I came to know as the space of reflective practice. Indeed, today I find it hard to imagine working in any other way.

The many hours spent thinking through various aspects of the argument developed here with Erik Doxtader have been crucial to project. Without abusing our friendship in this way quite systematically over the past few years, this book could not have emerged.

I am deeply indebted too to several secondary readers of parts or the whole text that follows. These include, in no particular order, Alice Nderitu, Ozonnia Ojielo, Kenneth Lukuko, Eleanor du Plooy, Samar Ali, Lino Owor Ogora, George Lopez,

Mac Maharaj, Roelf Meyer, Piers Pigou, Peter Gastrouw, Patrick Hajayandi, Kelly-Jo Bluen, Jan Hofmeyr, Fidi Bubenzer, Louise du Toit, Leon Wessels, Phil Clark, Andre du Toit, Annette Seegers, Christopher Saunders, and Lillian Umubyeye.

Mary Ralphs did sterling work in editing the penultimate draft of this work, whereas Elizabeth Lacey provided important support at the onset.

Finally, I dedicate this book to my wife Sarah, and children, Jennifer, Daniel, and Eloise, who have had to do too many river walks while I had my head in the clouds. This book, in the final instance, is a conversation with them about their future—and how we are struggling together to overcome a past that continues to project its (hopefully fading) shadow onto our aspirations and hopes.

ABBREVIATIONS

ANC	African National Congress
CODESA	Convention for a Democratic South Africa
COSATU	Congress of South African Trade Unions
ICC	International Criminal Court
IFP	Inkatha Freedom Party
IJR	Institute for Justice and Reconciliation
LRA	Lord's Resistance Army
MPNF	Multi-Party Negotiating Forum
MPNP	Multi-Party Negotiation Process
NGO	nongovernmental organization
NP	National Party
NPA	National Peace Accord
TRC	Truth and Reconciliation Commission
UN	United Nations
USIP	United States Institute for Peace

When Political Transitions Work

Introducing the Argument

Reconciliation emphasizes relationships as a crucial ingredient of political transition. This book builds an argument for the importance of such a relational focus in crafting sustainable political transitions. The goal of this exercise ultimately, is to develop a consistent yet flexible theoretical approach to political reconciliation rooted in the central idea of a pervasive, unavoidable interdependence between groups in conflict.

But why another theory on reconciliation? And why build this, in part, on a re-evaluation of South Africa's transition *now*, twenty-four years after formal apartheid ended? We know that bibliographies of studies on South Africa's political change run into hundreds of pages and that the process has been discussed, debated, and analyzed endlessly around the world. Is there anything fresh that remains unsaid?

It turns out much remains unsaid, if South Africans are to be taken as a yard stick. If reconciliation was indeed no longer important, then someone indeed forgot to tell them. Mandela's death on December 5, 2013, saw a massive outpouring of grief, but also yet another round of intense debates about reconciliation. It clearly continued to matter—a lot. Citizens waged protracted and heated arguments about the merits and failures of Mandela's legacy—and by extension, of their country that had been founded amid so much promise two decades earlier. In trying to find answers, some commentators focused on Mandela's style of leadership as compared to his political counterpart, F. W. de Klerk. Others evaluated achievements of the ANC government after two decades in power. Some developed conspiracy theories to the left, others suspected foul play to the right. Some blamed "white monopoly capital," others viewed political corruption with its concomitant lack of delivery to mainly poor, black communities as the main problem. Whatever the many different views, one crosscutting sentiment prevailed: that reconciliation remained at the very heart of what South Africa stood for, but had not yet, achieved.

I would argue that not much has changed since those days when South Africans were coming to terms with the passing of their founding father. Today reconciliation remains an issue of critical importance to citizens from all walks of life—an unfinished national conversation that continues unabated, for some by decrying "rainbowism" as a ruse for maintaining vested interest, and for others as a call to return to a politics of inclusion, compromise and racial cooperation.

This book makes its own limited contribution to these conversations, by evaluating reconciliation from three angles: as political beginning, as peaceful transfer of power, and as social change. The aim is to understand how reconciliation begins as political settlement (often despite conditions which seem to militate against its possibility), how then the transfer of actual power is embodied and institutionalized in processes that go beyond agreements, declarations and high-profile meetings and finally what reconciliation promises, and is able, to deliver in terms of actual change in society, once the new dispensation gets underway.

One often hears that the time is "not yet right" for reconciliation, for talking to the enemy or for settling historical scores. Depending on who is making the claim, or where it is made, reasons proffered to substantiate this assessment may include a lack of the "right" leadership, or a "bad neighborhood," poor economic conditions, or low levels of historic precedent for peaceful transitions, etc. And yet, of course, time is seldom, if indeed ever, "right" for reconciliation. Rather, reconciliation processes that prove both transformative and sustainable display remarkable resilience against often "insurmountable" odds.

Much like a young sapling taking root and beginning life, only to find itself perilously balanced on some exposed rocky outcrop, or protruding from a crevice in a sheer cliff face, reconciliation too, needs to battle hostile and harsh conditions—often so daunting that they seem to rule out reconciliation very *possibility* even before it gets a chance to develop—like a rock face appears to rule out the possibility of a healthy tree thriving with it as its foundation. And yet some trees manage to do just that, seemingly against all odds. As their stubborn roots weave their way around the rocks, and into whichever narrow crevices they can find to extract all available nutrients and moisture, these searching roots entwine with one another and the rocks to which they cling to form an unshakeable foundation for a tree that should never have been able to stand there in the first place. Trees can surprise one with their will to survive. And so do reconciliation processes that achieve their goals under the most unlikely conditions.

In the coming pages, I hope to show that reconciliation processes that "work" are not all that different from trees who manage to survive, grow and ultimately thrive, where they should never have been able to do so.

And so the three angles of my investigation of reconciliation—beginning transition, transformation—shape the discussions right through the book: in Section I, where the focus is on re-evaluating the South African case; Section II, which tracks the field's broader theoretical approaches; and, finally, Section III, where I explain the theory of reconciliation that emerges from these discussions.

In Section I, I draw attention to aspects of South Africa's history that are in danger of being forgotten, or that may not yet have been considered adequately.

By looking at how South Africa's reconciliation process began, then extended into an institutionalized handover of power, and finally led, or depending on one's perspective, *failed* to lead, to a transformed society, several broad themes emerge. When, for example, is reconciliation a ruse of powerful elites to hide their interests? When does it constitute truly transformative leadership? When does it become a betrayal of justice, and when it is a visionary opening of a new dawn? How do we judge its failure, and under which conditions would we be prepared to admit to its success? Exactly which criteria ought we to use in these judgments, and over what time span?

In the second section of the book, these questions are taken up in a discussion on ways in which reconciliation is being theorized.

To compare approaches, I develop typologies for three different kinds of reconciliation theories. Liberals, restorative justice advocates, and agonists, I claim, each have a distinct approach to framing the messy, uneven, and disjointed affairs which we call "political transition" or "political reconciliation." A key focus throughout in these discussions remains on how relationships which form the core of reconciliation are viewed to be initiated, institutionalized and socialized within each of these different theoretical approaches.

Drawing on the findings from the first two sections in the book, I conclude in the third section that relationships created through political reconciliation, between top leaders as well as between ordinary citizens, are illuminated in interesting and productive ways when understood as an expression of a comprehensive (pervasive) and fundamental (unavoidable) "interdependence" that precedes, and long outlives, any formal peace process between enemies.

Such interdependence is illustrated by the kind of relationship that may develop between sworn enemies stuck in the same lifeboat following a shipping disaster many miles offshore. To begin, trust and hope would be low, and animosity high. Some will choose a dual to death with their fellow survivor or swimming for the shore, rather than having to cooperate with the very person they have learnt to hate so passionately. But should sanity prevail, there would eventually be a gradual, perhaps grudging acknowledgment that chances of survival are greatly improved first by remaining inside the boat; and furthermore if the boat is rowed by two rowers rather than one, working in rhythm toward the shore line.

In political terms, this acceptance of the need to achieve common goals with the enemy and making a sincere effort to do so, no more and no less, constitutes reconciliation's inception. It is set in motion not when the "shore" of peace is reached, but when the oars are first picked up together to get there in the acknowledgment of interdependence.

During the process of rowing together, gradually, conversations might begin and understanding might grow, first of how to row most effectively, and later perhaps about how to survive together on the life-boat. Gradually, the survivors will get to know one another. As the boat moves ahead, possibilities for more effective cooperation might emerge, producing hope for life beyond the crisis, and eventually, though perhaps only at the journey's end, the promise of some measure of acceptance of someone now no longer simply the enemy of old, but a fellow survivor of a life-threatening crisis. It is this shared determination to reach the shore that keeps the process going through all the difficulties and challenges.

Linking reconciliation so closely with the acknowledgment of interdependence seeks to convey that enemies have little choice but to reconcile, should they wish to reach the "shore" alive. It conveys the sobering fact that without ensuring the conditions in which an enemy can survive and eventually flourish, one's own community is unlikely to prosper sustainably. The theoretical approach that develops from this discussion locates the deepest motivation for reconciliation in choosing mutual well-being above the one-sided fight for exclusive survival at the other's cost.

This is not necessarily the kind of news that is popular in an era of resurgent nationalism and crude power politics. We would much rather row our own boats, than risk the arduous task of learning to row with our enemies. To those who have fought one another over years, decades, and even centuries, this message almost certainly would require painful compromises, which some could see as betrayal of their historic struggle for justice. This means that reconciliation is often as much resented and feared as it is desired. Interdependence between fighting groups, when first acknowledged, appear therefore as a daunting, even unwelcome, imposition. Yet the promise of reconciliation to deliver transitions "that work" lies precisely in its ability to turn this *imposition* of interdependence into an *aspiration*, into hope, and into a set of possibilities with concrete benefits for those on both sides of the conflict. From an existential threat to my well-being and freedom, the enemy and his presence in my world develops into a unique opportunity to attain these aspirations, even as I become the gateway toward my enemy's future—without necessarily accepting to "like," "forgive," or "befriend" the enemy in any of the commonly accepted senses of these words. This tightrope that hovers so precipitously between the violence of betrayal and the violence of self-defeating struggle appears often the only way to reach a desired future in many intractable conflicts.

Apart from conveying this risky inevitability, the concept of reconciliation-as-interdependence also seeks to introduce a "workmanlike" dimension to reconciliation agendas. Rather than a primarily emotional journey of finding peace of mind, or closure, reconciliation is understood as more about what we *do* together (at least initially) than what we feel about one another. Of key importance, therefore, given these limitations, is to manage expectations about the levels of intimacy and trust one can expect from reconciliation once the fighting stops, whether around negotiation tables, or in community halls, schools, food markets, or board rooms.

Political leaders who want to lead their people to peace, must muster the tenacity of a tree hanging from a cliff face. They will also need the pragmatism of enemies surviving together in a life-boat on the open ocean.

South Africa's Transition: An Ongoing Debate

In anticipation of the Israeli elections of March 2015, the journalist Marwan Bishara wrote that it was high time that Israel adapted to a changing region and globe, and urgently reconsider its belligerent stance on Palestine. Yet, he concluded, the chances of this happening were slim because none of the main presidential candidates was likely to provide the leadership Israel requires. Bishara argued that Israel urgently needs an Israeli equivalent of F. W. de Klerk— a political leader willing to forge a historic agreement with the Palestinians as the South African leader did in the final days of apartheid. As it turned out, the Israeli electorate returned the hawkish Benjamin Netanyahu to power in 2015. Bishara anticipated this outcome, but suggested nevertheless that in the event that Israel does one day opt to elect a De Klerk of its own, that there would be no shortage of Palestinian Mandelas on the other side. Israelis would only need to "look in their jails or in the occupied territories" to find an inspirational Palestinian leader such as Mandela.[1]

Bishara's linking of the South African case with that of Israel and Palestine is interesting—not so much because of the accuracy or otherwise of his political assertions, but because his article illustrates how the South African transition continues to be held in esteem as an example of reconciliation. Why, one may ask, does the South African example still get cited in this manner? And why would Bishara assume that it holds relevance for such a vastly different conflict? Why too extol De Klerk's virtues when he remains controversial in his own country? And why invoke the concept of reconciliation as a possible solution?

At face value, some of the answers may be found in the fact that South Africa's political transition is still viewed by many as a moment of historic importance or, as historian Leonard Thompson called it, "one of the finest achievements of the twentieth century."[2] It may also have to do with growing disappointment over other potentially historic moments that failed to materialize. The high hopes for rapid democratization in Africa, for example, like those for a democratic and stable Middle East after the "Arab Spring," have all but disappeared.

On the gloomy international stage where it is hard to find more recent examples of countries that have dealt with a violent or repressive past peacefully and sustainably, South Africa stands out as one of the few relative success stories (even if, ironically, South Africans themselves appear to be losing faith in a unified country).[3] And yet apart from these well-known assumptions, there may also be less obvious reasons for South Africa's ongoing relevance, some of which have come into focus for me during the past two decades.

The Institute for Justice and Reconciliation (IJR)—the organization I worked for since 2000—emerged in the wake of the South African Truth and Reconciliation Commission (TRC). The organization is often asked to assist countries undergoing processes of political transition, reconciliation, and transitional justice.[4] In these conversations questions arise such as how to make a start to reconciliation when conditions seem set against it, how to enable a sustainable and peaceful transfer of power, and how to deliver concretely to society against their inevitably high expectations, all with reference to how South Africa had done it.

These conversations extend not only beyond South Africa and into a more general political sphere, but also into deeply existential, personal dimensions. Reconciliation can sometimes seem to mean all things to all people, so another important question is, what is specific to reconciliation, and how is it different to other forms of political transition? Moreover, how can its processes be evaluated as successful or not, both as a promise at inception and as time goes by? Do some kinds of processes in fact fail to qualify as reconciliatory even if some claim that they are, or do such judgments constitute a form of moral imperialism? What is the role of the observer/researcher in all this, not least as in my case, when his history is one of deriving incalculable benefit from apartheid and colonialism? How does one balance one's own position "within" the story with "telling" the story?

Through many years of wrestling with questions such as these and trying to distill lessons, insights, and warnings from cases like South Africa and others, I have increasingly become convinced of the need for a coherent and versatile theory of reconciliation to address questions such as these. And so, the idea for a book like this was gradually born. In these pages, I try to explain political reconciliation from three angles and, by doing so, build a concept of reconciliation that corresponds largely with the South African experience itself as judged with the benefit of hindsight. The concept also explains some of the larger universal insights at stake.

Thus, in the first section of the book comprising the first four chapters, I revisit certain dimensions of the South African case to try to explain its ongoing allure for so many international observers, and its durability twenty-four years on (while at the same time not assuming that these gains are permanent or indeed irreversible), and to point out a few stubborn but important misconceptions about the process.

In the book's second section, I map out the international theoretical landscape on reconciliation, identifying some strengths and weaknesses in current theories, which I spell out in more detail.

In the final section, I attempt to draw together a coherent yet versatile approach to reconciliation that can be used to make sense of and guide the processes often involved in political transitions.

Chapter 1 analyzes the key role that the kind of political leadership Bishara called for plays in initiating reconciliation processes. One can almost hear the clamor of incredulous responses to Bishara's claim that Palestine has many Mandelas. A claim often heard about groups like the Palestinians is precisely that peace would be more achievable if only they *did* have a leader like Mandela. And yet I am unsure which Mandela is being referred to in assertions like these—the real, historical figure, flaws and strengths included, or an idealized, even fictional, figure. Mandela was undoubtedly a giant of his time, but his reputation posthumously seems to have grown even larger, perhaps too much so. He now seems to enjoy a kind of secular beatification that makes it virtually impossible for any contemporary leader to claim to emulate him, let alone improve on his ideas. I believe this would have horrified the real Mandela.

To substantiate the argument developed through the course of the book I refer to some of the best published histories as well as a careful selection of interviews with principal actors during this era, therefore not making the entire historical case myself. There is simply not enough space to do this here, and it would be distracting to the main objective, which is to work toward a coherent approach to political reconciliation, articulated in the concluding section of the book.

In Chapters 2 and 3, I turn from Mandela and De Klerk as individual leaders to introduce another line of inquiry that remains relevant throughout the book, namely, how to understand reconciliation's unfolding over time into a real but peaceful transfer of power, both through different waves of negotiations and various transitional justice processes, the one overlapping with and building on the other. Once the inspiring words had been spoken, and the years of off-the-record meetings had run its course, how then did reconciliation shape and inform the actual political processes intended to achieve the effective transfer of political power from an entrenched white elite to a democratic majority of South Africans?

In societies such as South Africa where the past dominates every aspect of society, it takes special resolve to articulate, let alone pursue, a new future. If the inception of South Africa's reconciliation process depended crucially on political leadership, then its subsequent enactment and sustainable moves toward a new future depended equally crucially on the range of platforms, mechanisms, institutions, organizations, and initiatives that emerged in its name. Arguing that reconciliation is morally or strategically desirable is one thing, but to convince a divided nation that it is actually possible and practically workable—that a new future is around the corner—is quite another. And it was this burden, more than any other, that a range of transitional institutions in South Africa carried as they set out to put reconciliation into practice in a country that had never before experienced black and white citizens working together in intentionally reciprocal and mutually beneficial ways.

Despite this resolve to move forward in realizing a common future, South African leaders quickly found that seeking a basis for working together toward a desired future in a context of deep mistrust and historical enmity, and with the specter of protracted violence hanging over society, unavoidably raises the question of transitional justice, which I take up in more detail below.[5] While finding ways to build trust between former enemies is crucial, the new elite must directly address the wrongdoings of the past and the lingering resentments these have created. Otherwise, peace is likely to be temporary,[6] even if some countries prefer to encourage citizens deliberately to forget the past through what Andrew Rigby calls a "pact with oblivion."[7]

Against this background, Chapter 4 focuses on such normative and empirical questions related specifically to South Africa's reconciliation processes. First, I investigate reconciliation's implicit normative implications by asking which social goods had in fact been promised as outcomes of reconciliation—and therefore by which normative criteria reconciliation ought to be evaluated. Clearly, the architects of reconciliation did not promise the solution of all social problems and challenges overnight. What in fact then did they promise? And consequently which normative guidelines should we use to judge progress toward reconciliation? The first aim in Chapter 4 is therefore to explore reconciliation's implicit normativity, in the rhetoric of its chief political advocates, but also in the ways that it was first enacted and made concrete in the various mechanisms and platforms that followed. This is important, because South Africans' experience of reconciliation was decisively shaped by these institutions.

After exploring reconciliation's promise, the second half of Chapter 4 explores whether reconciliation did or did not deliver on this promise. Looking back on what has occurred since the late 1980s, I draw on public-opinion surveys conducted in South Africa, as well as victim and perpetrator interviews, and data tracking the implementation of TRC recommendations.

So, re-reading this history, produces a set of conclusions about why South Africa's transition from apartheid to democracy was able to put an end to political violence, if not *all* forms of violence; why it produced democratic institutions that, amid growing executive impunity, have appeared reasonably effective; and why, after four hundred years of colonialism and apartheid, South African society is finally taking concrete steps toward racial justice, even if these steps have not been fast or decisive enough, not least as a result of a toxic mix of public and private sector corruption and nepotism which swept across the country during the Zuma era.

What is new here are the normative criteria against which the claim that South Africa's transition "worked" is made. If a transition is meant to deliver, within a matter of years, the complete erasure and closure of an evil past, then clearly South Africa's transition did *not* work, either in the Marxist sense of a class revolution, or in the restorative justice sense of forgiveness. However, the book builds a different set of criteria against which South Africa and political transitions, more broadly, ought to be judged.

Judged by these criteria, I argue that the South African transition "worked." Political violence was replaced by largely nonviolent political contestation; the apartheid state was replaced by a constitutional democracy with institutions that since 1994 have acted at least partially effectively in curbing executive impunity (not least with increasing conviction during the Zuma presidency), and a vast array of policies and measures have been undertaken to improve the lives of poor South Africans, which has led to the gradual but steady increase in the life expectancy of all South Africans. This story is not, as the ANC's campaign slogans during the 2014 elections glibly proclaimed, simply a "good story to tell" (there are too many missed chances and squandered opportunities along the way), but despite this, the story does go a long way in dispelling the Afro-pessimism so typical of many "critical" studies of South Africa.

I do acknowledge, through the course of the discussion, the deep disappointment of many South Africans who feel that, in the light of the escalating inequality and pervasive corruption, not enough has been done. But this disappointment should not blind us to the fact that the 1994 transition did away effectively and peacefully with "apartheid" as a political dispensation and set South Africa on the road toward social transformation.

More on the relationship between Reconciliation and Transitional Justice

Before moving on to outlining the next section of the book, it is important to revisit an important underlying relationship which, depending on how it is understood, profoundly impacts the rest of the discussion—namely the relationship between transitional justice and reconciliation. These are two adjacent, partially overlapping, but ultimately distinct fields of study, practice and normative debate. Too often these terms are used inter-changeably, or in vague, ill-defined consort—whereas it is important to be precise about how they differ and where they do overlap.

The single-minded pursuit of a shared future in the context of deep division often means, at least initially, that there is little room for settling old scores; and yet it is increasingly clear that this willingness to forgo vengeance or even forms of legalized retribution does not equate with ignoring the past. Indeed, in many cases, dealing with the past appears necessary to overcome lingering resentments and achieve the desired future. Transitional justice correctly insists therefore that reconciliatory spaces need to be concerned, in principle and from the outset, with justice and accountability. It is therefore wholly understandable that a prominent emphasis in the enactment of reconciliation is on transitional justice mechanisms and processes.

Transitional justice scholars tend to have three main concerns. First, they examine the concrete practices and processes through which transitional or post-conflict societies deal with past political atrocities. The second focus is on normative debates about what ought to be the aims of these processes, and the third focus is on empirical studies to measure their impact. Distinguishing between these three broadly differentiated definitions of transitional justice—first as a practice, second as normative discourse on this practice, and third as empirical investigation of the outcomes and impact—is not only useful for structuring the discussion of the South African case, but it also clarifies the relationship between reconciliation practices and transitional justice as they are treated throughout this book.

The generic concept of "dealing with the past" naturally includes a diverse range of interventions that address past atrocities in ways that seek to promote reconciliation and democracy.[8] Institutional arrangements typically, but not exclusively, include bringing past political perpetrators to account through criminal prosecution and punishment, vetting and lustration, structured processes of public truth-telling, the production of publicly accessible archives about past political crimes, public apologies or other formal opportunities for reconciliation between former political and military opponents, and reparations for those who had fallen victim to gross human rights violations.[9]

As explained earlier, a key focus in Chapter 2 and 3 is on identifying and investigating some of the cross-cutting traits that characterized the various platforms for reconciliation and transitional justice in South Africa, those which were tasked to anticipate a shared future (in Chapter 2) as well as those tasked to deal with the past (in Chapter 3).

To understand how the transitional arrangements in South Africa balanced the struggle between the future and the past, more is needed than an individualized study of each mechanism. Absolutely central to the success of achieving a correct balance between moving on and facing the past is how the various mechanisms and organizations themselves work together and build on one another.

This, in turn, raises the concern of how the various mechanisms, platforms, and institutions contributed to a larger, more comprehensive political transition that was framed by the concept of reconciliation. The alternative—thinking of transitional justice in isolation from political transition and reconciliation—often results in transitional justice mechanisms misfiring or even undermining one another in ways that were never foreseen. Too often, transitional justice mechanisms are then viewed as "silver bullets," able to operate in isolation from one another, and from the processes they are meant to serve. Unrealistically, such processes are habitually required to address shortcomings in the political transition, without the process itself being corrected. Importantly, this is not only an unfortunate tendency of transitional justice practice, but also a fairly marked blind spot in transitional justice literature.

In South Africa's case, this kind of "silver bullet" analysis has led to a disproportionate focus on the TRC as the sole platform for reconciliation and transitional justice, while crucial platforms and mechanisms that preceded, surrounded, and followed on from it, and on which it depended heavily for its own impact, have been largely ignored. I therefore aim to correct this bias by discussing additional reconciliation platforms to the TRC, namely the National Peace Accord (NPA), the Multi-Party Negotiation Process (MPNP), and the Transitional Executive Council (TEC)—as well as importantly the important ways in which they related to, paved the way for, and limited the possibilities for what the TRC could and did achieve.

The focus on the political integration of transitional justice institutions highlights important concerns about how to move from a violent past in genuinely transformative ways to a desired, shared future. For example, isolating and prosecuting individual criminals may deliver some benefits, but this does not address wider issues of accountability for the past, and contributes little to the need to balance credible levels of accountability with ongoing inclusivity.[10] Equally, reparations can, at best, provide some sense of emotional and very limited material relief for a small group of victims (even smaller when court trials are chosen over TRCs), but they do not address the structural issues related to social justice, either historically or as communities live into the future. Likewise, public truth-telling often amounts to an obscuring rather than a revealing of truth if these exercises are not conducted within a range of support mechanisms, not least a functioning legal system and agencies with proper investigative powers and political independence. In the absence of a rights-based gender policy, traditional reconciliation practices have the potential to simply reinforce hegemonies and power relations that might have been major contributing factors to the conflict in the first place.[11] These dangers and risks associated with transitional justice all demand careful reflection on how mechanisms, processes, and platforms are integrated and allowed to complement one another.

In addition to this, and as mentioned earlier, the term "transitional justice" can also refer to normative discourses and debates about what ought to constitute the aims of measures and mechanisms for dealing with past political atrocities.[12] These debates are conducted in academic discourse as well as popular political debates, with one arguably feeding off the other.

As explained further in Chapter 4, these questions are taken up with reference to South Africa: how and why reconciliation and related transitional justice initiatives were undertaken; how they were justified or on what grounds they were opposed; and how they purportedly contributed to outcomes such as justice or peace. Far beyond the South African case, these concerns have given rise to a widespread and prolific academic discourse, with specific terminologies that emerged in parallel to the operational history of political transition. Paige Arthur has described how a series of international conferences in the late 1980s and early 1990s launched the term "transitional justice" into the policy environment, and how this was aided by the publication of seminal works by authors such as Neil Kritz, Ruti Teitel, and Guillermo O'Donnell.[13] Arthur also described how a range of NGOs, some with international reach, others much more modest, adopted the notion of "transitional justice" as their mandate. Erik Doxtader, in turn, explained how transitional justice became standard UN parlance.[14] Meanwhile, bibliographies on transitional justice relating only to the South African case already run to hundreds of pages.[15] Transitional justice debates often range from polemical and partisan commentaries to more even-handed reports, grounded justifications, and sustained analyses. Insofar as transitional justice institutions publish written outputs (such as the proceedings of tribunals or truth commissions), these are often closely associated with the normative discourses and debates.

In addition to normative debates, transitional justice and reconciliation are increasingly also the focus of empirical analyses and investigation. In the second half of Chapter 4 I show how in seeking to evaluate South Africa's transition, such studies have begun to challenge the key assumptions and conclusions of some of the normative assumptions made at the onset.[16] Thus, empirical investigations of various kinds, such as public opinion surveys, smaller-sample surveys focusing on specific stakeholder groups like victims or perpetrators, as well as detailed analysis of the impact of reconciliation programmes such as reparations, have led to an interdisciplinary literature including comparative and theoretical analyses of case studies and global trends.[17] This subfield of research on transitional justice is of course closely related to the study of democratic transitions, and have provided a rich body of literature that helps us make sense of how to judge whether or not, or what ways, the South African transition "worked."[18]

Theories of Reconciliation

In the second section of this book, I turn away from the focus on South Africa specifically to chart the landscape of international theorizing on political reconciliation since the mid-1990s. Chapters 5, 6, and 7 each describe a family or cluster of theories on reconciliation prevalent in academic debates internationally. I outline the same three core questions in relation to each cluster of theories that I considered regarding the South African experience—that is, about reconciliation's inception, its progressive enactment, and its promise. This section is meant to chart current thinking on political reconciliation, and to discuss what I consider to be some of the weaknesses and strengths of each position. A comparative table summarizing the main points in these typologies, and comparing them to reconciliation-as-interdependence, is found in the appendix (pages 237–239).

The first group of theories are discussed in Chapter 5, under the title of "the forgiving embrace" (after the work of the Croatian theologian Miroslav Volf).[19] This group of theories cluster around the theme of social restoration, viewing restored *personal* relations (variously defined) as reconciliation's key outcome. These theories overlap considerably with those that place forgiveness at the heart of reconciliation processes, and see this as the key to social change.

In Chapter 6, I then develop a different typology based on liberal approaches to reconciliation. These approaches overlap significantly with current UN-sponsored transitional justice discourses and practices globally, which view the promotion of the rule of law and accountability for political crime as a key feature of reconciliation's theory of change, and increased levels of civic trust as its main outcome.

In Chapter 7, I outline a third approach, the agonist paradigm of reconciliation, in which nonviolent political contestation is seen as the surest sign of progress toward reconciliation. For agonists, reconciliation is a goal that is never fully reachable, while conflict is seen as inevitable and indeed a sign of a healthy political life.

Reconciliation as Interdependence

In Chapter 8 and the Conclusion which comprise the third section, I attempt to draw these many lines of study, practice, and reflection together in a coherent, progressively realized, and nonexclusive approach to reconciliation based on the notion of interdependence: *coherent* because this kind of reconciliation develops a recognizable quality as the basis for comparative analysis between contexts; *progressively realized* because the same core idea is politically, institutionally, *and* socially relevant and productive over the course of an entire political transition, and is thus able to frame a transition process from its fragile political inception during "talks about talks" to its eventual social enactment, a process that may last decades; and *nonexclusive* because it does not claim to be the only way or the final word on how to conceptualize or implement reconciliation.

Indeed, ongoing reconciliation processes require that theoretical positions be reviewed continuously. At the same time, the approaches followed in different contexts themselves need to be constantly re-evaluated in light of ongoing critical analysis and reflection. Obviously no case study could ever be a "model," nor should any theory ever exude any pretense of permanence. I nevertheless proceed on the assumption that comparative analyses that remain sufficiently sensitive to the particularities and peculiarities of each context, are in fact able to yield cross-cutting insights and lessons, and can contribute to reasonably coherent, if always provisional, approaches to reconciliation. For this reason I am not proposing a particular *method* of reconciliation, but rather the outlines of a theoretical *approach* that remains open-ended.

This is not to say that reconciliation has universal application—that it is the answer for every context or any conflict. For the concept to have integrity, I contend, one needs to be able to acknowledge and identify situations and contexts in which reconciliation is *not* appropriate. For example, I am not sure how one applies reconciliation as a framework for transitioning beyond the classic scenario of interstate warfare, or indeed where states or coalitions of states fight terror groups such as the Islamic State or Al-Qaeda. By contrast, I argue that reconciliation *does* have particular relevance in conflicts in which enemies live in proximity and are contesting key levers of power, rights, and resources within a particular territory, whether through civil war, liberation struggle, or civic rights movements. Reconciliation also has relevance in ideological conflicts that may spread over regions or even globally, but where reasonably coherent religious or cultural groups clash, less for control over physical territories than for control of moral or religio-cultural landscapes. Moreover, reconciliation can conceivably also apply where political transitions signal the end of an era of oppression and a move toward a more inclusive, open and fair society.

Essentially, my aim is to develop a relevant concept of reconciliation in terms of which the outcomes of political transitions can be promoted, pursued, and, ultimately, accounted for. Peacemaking, transitional justice, and social transformation all form crucial elements of an approach to reconciliation based on the central idea of social and political interdependence.

We now turn to the question of how South African leaders articulated realistic possibilities for reconciliation at a time and in a society where it was considered a pipe dream.

SECTION ONE

MOMENTS IN TRANSITION

1

Making the Case for Reconciliation

Today we no longer vow our mutual destruction but solemnly acknowledge our interdependence as free and equal citizens of our common Motherland.

—Nelson Mandela, Reconciliation Day, 1995

After Nelson Mandela's death in December 2013, and before South Africa's fifth round of national elections in May 2014, heated debates erupted around the country over what reconciliation meant nearly twenty years after democratization, and who needed to shoulder the blame for the many shortcomings the process still faced. Across the political spectrum, individuals and organizations scrambled to claim Mandela as their own, while at the same time denouncing their competitors' claims to Mandela's legacy as insincere or even fraudulent. With his memorial service barely concluded, "owning Mandela" became one of the hottest issues on the campaign trail.

Some of those who supported Mandela's 27 years incarceration as a "terrorist," now proclaimed him, with little or no irony, as their leader. Others, who fought for his release, or were born during his presidency with high hopes of benefiting from a new South Africa, decried reconciliation as a sellout of black rights in favour of white interest.

It was ironic, even distressing, to see the dignified Mandela being laid claim to, whether by being superficially praised or denounced, in these ways. Yet, beyond the irony, the contestation illustrated a deeper need, prevalent to this day, to understand the ways in which South Africa's experience of reconciliation matters, both domestically and internationally.

I begin the effort (charted across the next four chapters) to make sense of reconciliation, the South African way, by focusing on a question that often features in discussions on the topic. What made it possible for political reconciliation to make a start—even if not an entirely new start amid the violence and hostility that was tearing South Africa apart in the 1980s? Perhaps this question remains of interest, because it is felt intuitively that, to understand reconciliation *now*, it is important to understand reconciliation *then*—to understand in more detail, and more precisely, the motives, promises and strategies which enabled reconciliation to gain such a prominent foothold on South Africa's political landscape. This part of the motivation for revisiting reconciliation's inception becomes all the more important as, with the passage of time, memories of the era appear to begin to obscure as much as they reveal about what in fact had happened.

Memory is never simple, pure, or politically unbiased, so it is telling to consider why some parts of the story are falling by the wayside, or have fallen victim to misrepresentation, while other aspects remain vivid. Nowadays, the story of the ending of apartheid is told in many different ways, not infrequently exaggerating the role of the particular storyteller or plied in ways that conveniently justify a preexisting theory or political agenda. But the question is important for reasons beyond South Africa too: when and how does political reconciliation begin, and what marks such a transition as "reconciliation" as opposed to some other kind of political change? These broader questions provide for another, different but equally vibrant and ongoing engagement with the question of reconciliation's beginnings in South Africa.

The standard answer to this question is of course well-known: that a complex set of historical realities, well documented and analyzed, combined to bring about apartheid's demise. The fall of the Berlin wall in 1989 marking the end of the Cold War in its peculiar racialized manifestation in southern Africa, certainly contributed, as did increasing international isolation and condemnation of the regime, as well as sustained waves of domestic protest, pressure, and sabotage from a mix of civil society and other interest groups as well as underground resistance movements.

Yet, it is also true—and that is the particular angle that this chapter will explore—that historic opportunities have to be *seized* by leaders of certain ilk, for them to lead to desired outcomes. Too often, a lack of precisely such leadership means that historic opportunities for turning a nation or country away from cyclical conflict and towards better future are missed. The assumption which I will explore in more depth, is that in South Africa's case, the *inception* of reconciliation, depended critically on political leadership of a particular kind that came, for better and worse, to be exemplified by Nelson Mandela, and to some degree as well, by his counterpart, Frederik Willem de Klerk.

This first chapter therefore examines afresh the kind of leadership that enabled reconciliation to take root in South Africa. And because our concern *is* reconciliation, I will examine not only their individual contributions, but also the relationship between them. Importantly, I will search for historical evidence for the popular claim that forgiveness had been a crucial factor between Mandela and De Klerk, and by extension within the broader transitional period.

To find meaningful answers to these questions, it is important too to move beyond the popular imagery which have come to dominate popular memory about this era, and which is endlessly repeated in documentaries, plays, and films. These images have become an important source for those seeking to understand what reconciliation is, or should be, about, including about what kind of leadership Mandela and De Klerk offered, and what role forgiveness played in their relationship. Mandela with his fist raised, leaving prison; Mandela being sworn in as South Africa's first democratic president and waving to the crowd standing next to De Klerk; Mandela enjoying a cup of tea with Betsie Verwoerd, widow of apartheid's chief architect; Mandela in a Springbok rugby jersey (a symbol of Afrikaner national aspiration) at the 1995 Rugby World Cup final; or Mandela and De Klerk receiving the Nobel Peace Prize together in Oslo.

But these somewhat rosy portraits hide important aspects of South Africa's reconciliation story and the leaders who helped to enable it when it seemed a complete impossibility. Fortunately, in addition to popular memory, there exists several excellent histories of this period outlining the country's reconciliation journey in the context of the centuries-old struggle against colonialism and casting its main characters in a believable, and perhaps therefore, even more inspirational light.[1] It is from these sources that I develop the arguments in this and following chapters.

It is important to emphasise two further issues: first, by focusing on Mandela and De Klerk side by side, the aim is not to imply moral equivalence between their respective political positions. Apartheid was an egregious crime against humanity and the struggle against it a justified, defensive war for basic human rights. But, it is my position, that although De Klerk remains controversial and in some ways the "lesser partner" in the reconciliation story, even his staunchest critics today must admit that he too played a key role. Without De Klerk, it is difficult to imagine a nonviolent end to apartheid.

And second, it is important to acknowledge too, before moving on, that Mandela and De Klerk were by no means the only actors who influenced reconciliation's inception. But their actions contributed in very fundamental ways to enable reconciliation to get off the ground. Analyzing these leaders, and the many complicated features of their working relationship might be a responsible way of learning from them, and from this remarkable era in South Africa's history, as time moves on.

Reconciliation at Apartheid's End

Amid the anger and confusion of the late 1980s and the early 1990s, Mandela and De Klerk faced a farrago of competing voices clamoring for their own solutions to questions about how to kick start what was at the time a thoroughly moribund peace process. After Mandela's sensational release from prison, the momentum seemed lost. It was by no means obvious to important constituencies on either side that the path of political settlement was desirable, or feasible.

The stakes were high and so were the potential cost of embracing reconciliation. Both sides faced the prospect of having to accede to deep cutting compromises that would seem to border on betrayal, certainly from the perspective of many of followers—Afrikaners had fought for self-determination for over two hundred years, and Africans had fought for basic rights and dignity, and a return of what many regarded as stolen livelihoods, in the land of their birth for even longer.[2]

And so, when it became known that Mandela and De Klerk were seriously considering reconciliation, both leaders became frequent targets of accusations of betrayal. These accusations persist to this day, admittedly in the main from fringe groups, but there are many who still feel let down, betrayed even, by the outcomes of the reconciliation process that Mandela and De Klerk had set in motion.

How did Mandela and De Klerk negotiate this fine line between reconciliation and betrayal? How did Mandela evolve from the first commander of the underground armed resistance to someone who was prepared to meet the President of the regime what was keeping him imprisoned and his people in bonds. And how did De Klerk explain *his* change of heart after occupying leadership positions as Afrikaner politician from as early as 1969, for almost the entire duration of statutory apartheid? As Mandela somehow managed to convince his comrades to lay down arms, how did De Klerk manage to convince his frightened white supporters to vote in favour of the negotiations in the country's last all-white referendum in 1992, even if they stood to lose their historic privilege?[3]

In their autobiographies, both leaders stress the slow and incremental growth of their own convictions regarding the need for inclusivity rather than a narrow, parochial form of nationalism. Interestingly, for both these leaders, awakening never required renouncing their original communal or political identities. Mandela remained a steadfast ANC member, and a loyal Xhosa Chief all his life. De Klerk remained equally firmly a member of the NP until the party's final demise, and since then has turned into a strong advocate for Afrikaner rights, particularly linguistic rights. Thus, it was within the confines of their own cultural and political loyalties that their perspectives gradually expanded. Rooted as it was in their respective identities, it was the intellectual and political expansion which set them apart from so many leaders in conflict zones who appear on the opposite trajectory, towards an increasingly parochial or tribalistic hardline stance which sees the world in terms of insiders and outsiders, of those either for or against "us."

Mandela attributed his driving force towards the horizon—his quest to be free—to his experiences as a Xhosa child growing up in the deeply rural, peaceful hills of the Eastern Cape of South Africa. As a boy there, herding cattle across the rolling fields of the Transkei, he wrote of feeling free in every way—free to swim in the streams that criss-crossed the local village, to roast mealies (corn) under the stars, and to ride the oxen he guided along the narrow footpaths.[4]

When he moved to Johannesburg as a young lawyer some years later, Mandela discovered that his boyhood freedom had in fact been limited to those idyllic childhood days, and that the freedom to be a professional adult simply did not exist for him as he set out to start a career in law. Thus began his fight for basic individual freedoms: to marry, to earn a decent living, and to have a family at a place and in a manner of his choice. In time, after he experienced first hand the incalcitrance and racism of the regime, he joined the ANC and eventually turned freedom fighter, beginning a new clandestine life in pursuit of rights for "his people." This commitment, he reflected later, turned a roaming, playful boy into an undercover revolutionary, a law-abiding attorney into a "criminal," a family-loving husband into a fugitive, a life-loving man into a monk.

Remarkably, in another revealing turn, during his prison time, his struggle for the freedom of his own people morphed into a quest for the freedom of all people, including his captors. He wrote, "I knew as well as I knew anything that the oppressor must be liberated just as surely as the oppressed."[5] And even more remarkably, as South Africa's first democratically elected president, he was able to preside over the first stages of the fulfilment of that dream.

From roaming young herder to lawyer, freedom fighter to prisoner, president to international icon, Mandela's personal history coincided with his incremental acknowledgment of ever-wider circles of inclusion and solidarity. Leaving the intimacy of his rural village, he joined a political movement to fight for the freedom of his fellow South Africans. As a leader (and later an imprisoned leader) of an underground armed struggle, he worked with comrades across the world; eventually he helped to bring an end to the armed struggle, and became the president of a democracy that guarantees the rights of all who live in it, including those of his erstwhile enemies and persecutors. And finally, as an international leader, he worked with activists across the globe in the fight against HIV and AIDS, poverty and injustice, and put his weight behind numerous other worthy causes.[6]

Importantly, Mandela seemed to be able to adopt ever-wider allegiances and causes, yet it is equally clear that he never renounced the traditional loyalties and deeply held beliefs that first prompted him to join the liberation struggle. Tellingly, upon his death, Mandela's official wake began with his lying in state in Pretoria, where hundreds of thousands of South Africans filed past to pay homage to the man they regarded as the father of their nation; but the final night before his burial was spent in a private family ceremony in his home village in the Xhosa heartland of the Transkei, where the elders gathered around the deceased in a night-long vigil of reflection and prayer. Perhaps it can be argued that by the time Mandela was grappling with the notion of national reconciliation, he had already had to reconcile the tribal and the universal within himself. By not abandoning his identity as a Xhosa and an African, and by valuing the universal dimensions reflected in his local identity,[7] he was able to demonstrate how the universal should be anchored in, and justified in terms of, the local and the particular. In other words, it is possible to conclude that his embrace of the fight for the rights of *all* South Africans while drawing on his particular identity and heritage to do so, played some role in his decision to pursue reconciliation as political strategy.

But there is a second, different set of characteristics to which he attributes equal importance in his memoirs. Mandela combined his commitment to a humanistic values with a shrewd political realism. An inclusive and progressive figure, Mandela at the same time was no naïve political push over. It was his keen appreciation for concrete opportunities to further the struggle for justice, alongside his hard-fought convictions, which led him to reconciliation. Mandela began to defend the idea that reconciliation was not only possible given the broader climate in South Africa, but that it might present very real opportunities to benefit the struggle for black liberation:

> Many people on both sides had already died. The enemy was strong and resolute. Yet, even with all their bombers and tanks, they must have sensed they were on the wrong side of history. We had the right on our side, but not yet the might. It was clear to me that a military victory was a distant if not impossible dream. It simply did not make sense for both sides to lose thousands if not millions of lives in a conflict that was unnecessary. They must have known this as well. It was time to talk.[8]

Mandela later admitted that, at this time, he moved ahead of his constituency, which undoubtedly put pressure on his supporters and increased concerns about him selling out, of having become "soft" in prison, rather than remaining supportive of the armed struggle. But, he later remarked "there are times when a leader must move out ahead of the flock and go off in a new direction, confident that he is leading his people in the right way."[9] In 1985, after publicly declining the state's offer to release him on condition that he renounced violence,[10] he took a bold first step. He agreed to hold secret talks with then minister of justice Kobie Coetsee while remaining in prison. In 1987, South African president P. W. Botha set up a committee of top officials to facilitate further talks, and in 1989, Mandela secretly met the hard-line apartheid leader at his official residence in Cape Town.

But in Mandela's mind, these secret meetings had no impact on, or relevance to, his loyalty to the struggle. To the contrary, in a note prepared for the meeting with Botha, he wrote:

At the outset, I must point out that I make this move without consultation with the ANC. I am a loyal and disciplined member of the ANC, my political loyalty is owed primarily, if not exclusively, to this organisation and particularly to our Lusaka Headquarters where the official leadership is stationed and from where affairs are directed. In the normal course of events, I would put my views to the organisation first, and if these views were accepted, the organisation would then decide on who were the best qualified members to handle the matter on its behalf and on exactly when to make the move. But in my current circumstances I cannot follow this course, and this is the only reason why I am acting on my own initiative, in the hope that the organisation will, in due course, endorse my action.[11]

Soon afterwards, and without revealing to his comrades that he had already taken the first steps in this direction, Mandela began to lobby for embracing the idea of negotiation with the enemy. Reading Mandela's correspondence from prison, it is striking how patient and painstaking his arguments in favor of reconciliation were, and how they always assume the intimacy of shared convictions with his comrades in the liberation movement.[12] Never moralizing or condescending, Mandela argued in favor of political strategies that he believed would best serve the interests of black South Africans, even if those strategies initially demanded compromises and adjustments.

His interlocutors included key figures among exiled ANC leaders in Lusaka, Zambia, such as Oliver Tambo and Thabo Mbeki, as well as leaders of its armed wing, Umkhonto we Sizwe, who were continuing to operate undercover inside the republic and in neighboring states. In addition, he engaged various formations within the popular resistance movements inside South Africa.[13]

Ironically, it was none other than Mandela himself who, nearly thirty years before, had persuaded his colleagues to relinquish the principle of nonviolence in favour of armed struggle. After serving as first commander of the ANC's military wing, Mandela now argued for the suspension of its activities. Mandela's lobbying for a peaceful end to apartheid received a major boost in 1989. That year, at a meeting in Harare, the Organisation of African Unity adopted the ANC-drafted Harare Declaration that outlined conditions for a peaceful end to apartheid.[14]

The liberation movement had long been a broad church that accommodated several different ideological leanings, some of which made this move towards reconciliation less contradictory than what many assume today. At times, multiracialism was dominant, and those who proposed non-racialism were in the minority. At other times, the opposite was true. But a central theme was always that it should, in principle, be possible for any South African to be part of the movement—including white South Africans who supported these ideals.[15] It was, after all, precisely for the realization of an integrated and equal South Africa that the ANC was established on January 8, 1912. As far back as 1943, the ANC had produced a document titled *The Africans' Claims in South Africa*, which asserted the notion of human rights (including political *and* socioeconomic rights, women's rights, and other rights). Published in response to the Atlantic Charter, which was drawn up by Allied forces in the midst of the Second World War, the *African Claims* document was, in some ways, ahead of international developments, including as it did, a full bill of rights well before the adoption of the Universal Declaration of Human Rights in 1948.[16] Subsequently, the Freedom Charter, adopted in 1956, began with the famous phrase that "South Africa belongs to all who live in it, black and white." All these documents helped to form the foundations for Mandela's appeal to his comrades to embrace reconciliation, not only because it was an opportune moment, but because there was strong grounds for such a move within the intellectual tradition of the movement itself.

All this meant that, powerful though Mandela's influence was, his reconciliation agenda was not the result of his private convictions alone. Mandela had much to work with in terms of the ideological traditions of the liberation movement and did so consultatively and persistently. And in this, he was not as much of an outlier to the movement as is often assumed today. In fact, his undoubted loyalty to the movement stood him in great stead.

It was therefore important to him to make the case for reconciliation within its various structures. His was the ability to read the signs of the times clearly— including the global political and economic changes that helped to propel the unraveling of apartheid in the 1980s—and then foreground the particular legacies within his movement that could help him galvanize the response he favoured as strategically the wisest. Of course, it did not happen overnight. Mandela reached out to the apartheid leadership in 1985, and soon thereafter began to lobby his comrades to accept reconciliation as the preferred route. But it took five more years before he was released, and he was only elected president four years after that.

In turning across the aisle to Mandela's "enemy", F. W. de Klerk also wrote about his incremental and gradual acceptance of the need for reconciliation, albeit initially on terms markedly different from those of Mandela. But like Mandela, De Klerk maintained that he never had "a Damascus Road experience."[17] Instead, the changing political landscape of the late 1980s, including increased international pressure, the end of the Cold War, and escalating internal unrest, convinced him that the military stalemate was becoming too costly and that a change of strategy would be wise.

Reconciliation was a familiar term in white political circles decades before apartheid's demise. Erik Doxtader has written compellingly about how reconciliation evolved, and how, in various guises, it had served different agendas across the years.[18] For example, the notion featured in attempts to mend relations between Afrikaners and the British after the Anglo-Boer War at the onset of the twentieth century,[19] and in the subsequent founding of the Union of South Africa in 1910, but to the exclusion of black South Africans.

Ironically, the concept of reconciliation was also used to justify apartheid, and its forceful subjugation of different racial groups. Apartheid apologists professed a kind of "reconciliation" achieved through the creation of a commonwealth of (ethnic) nations that would coexist in mutual respect and prosperity—but, tellingly, always under white patronage. The deeper implication of their stance was that black and white were inherently irreconcilable within a single society.[20] Apartheid's notion of reconciliation, like that which produced the Union of South Africa, not only assumed white supremacy, but also racial and ethnic homogeneity—both sets of ideas which have been thoroughly discredited since on scientific as well as moral grounds.

For a variety of geo-political reasons other than a fundamental ideological shift, some of which I mentioned above, the need to move beyond apartheid to a system of power sharing between white and black within a unitary state had been gaining support in Afrikaner circles since the mid-1980s. And it was in the late 1980s, when political leaders realized that apartheid was nearing its end, that a potentially transformative notion of reconciliation eventually began to emerge within white circles. In heated debates between the so-called verligtes (progressives) and verkramptes (conservatives) within the Afrikaner intelligentsia, the verligtes advocated "strategies that sought to play into the reformist possibilities offered by the system" while the verkramptes felt that very little adjustment was necessary.[21] De Klerk, by his own admission, had spent most of his life on the verkrampte side,[22] although his brother Willem was a well-known verligte. Willem played an important role in swaying F. W.'s mind, and eventually he switched sides.

The intelligentsia were not the only Afrikaners who began to question the workability of apartheid. In 1985, for example, after a disastrous speech by president P. W. Botha, in which he made it clear that his government was not open to real reform, Afrikaner businessman Anton Rupert wrote to Botha, warning him that, "apartheid is crucifying us; it is destroying our language; it is degrading for a once heroic nation to be the lepers of the world."[23]

At the same time, various interest groups within the white establishment began to reach out to ANC counterparts, secretly at first and then more openly, inside and outside the country.[24] This included meetings organized by civil society, sports bodies, business, religious organizations, musicians, writers, and other artists, many of whom identified with the Afrikaner community. The secretive and influential Afrikaner organization the "Broederbond" (Brotherhood) also saw the writing on the wall. In fact, as early as 1986, the Broederbond, which until then had acted as one of apartheid's informal propaganda machines, circulated a communiqué to its members titled "Basic Constitutional Values for the Survival of the Afrikaners," which challenged many of apartheid's core assumptions. As Hermann Giliomee explains, the communiqué "projected the exclusion of blacks at the highest decision-making level as a threat to the survival of whites."[25] The inclusion of blacks would require "talking to the ANC" unconditionally (at that point the official position in government and Afrikaner circles was to demand the laying down of arms by the ANC before talks could be considered), and even the changing of symbols, such as the national anthem and the national flag.

A third of the Broederbond resigned after the communiqué was circulated to branches for discussion, but while Botha continued to present a hard-line, anti-reformist face to the world, the possibility of a black head of state was being discussed by Afrikaner leaders in secret meetings held across the country. Admitting that such changes were highly risky, and arguing for a range of political models that could provide minority guarantees, Broederbond chairperson Piet de Lange nevertheless told members: "The greatest risk we run is not to take any risks."[26]

By 1987, spurred on by their intelligence agencies and growing internal and international pressures, politicians on both sides too began a series of secret talks. Whereas correctional services minister Kobie Coetsee and others met with Mandela while he was still in prison, secret-service agent Niel Barnard and others opened direct channels of communication with both Mandela and the exiled ANC leadership in Britain and Lusaka.[27]

In September 1989, De Klerk became president after ousting the ailing Botha in a dramatic vote of no confidence during a special Cabinet meeting. Once in power, De Klerk sought an explicit political mandate from white South Africans for reconciliation. De Klerk, like Mandela, then had to engage his colleagues and their followers in extended arguments about the merits and demerits of switching from a rigid policy based on military security to one that would enable negotiations to take place. What was new about De Klerk's agenda, as opposed to those of his predecessors, was his linking of the concept of reconciliation with the prospect of meaningful power-sharing and "justice for all," even if his initial vision did not match up to African demands for full equality.

One can therefore conclude that, when De Klerk released Mandela in February 1990, he did not override his constituency as a result of external pressure, or because of any personal moral "conversion," but because he could see no other way forward which did not contain unreasonably high risks to survival of his clan and because he believed that he had sufficient support from mainstream Afrikaner circles to do so. In short, as Mandela, he too was not as much of an outlier to his political movement, as is often assumed today. His views were vindicated in 1992, when he sought and received an overwhelming political mandate in South Africa's last all-white referendum: 69 percent of whites voted in favor of talks and a negotiated settlement with the ANC.

Thus, both De Klerk and Mandela gradually and cleverly built support for reconciliation within their own constituencies. Neither developed his own political positions in isolation but based his actions on concrete political and intellectual traditions established on both sides. Both men received clear political mandates to proceed with "talks about talks," even though there were still plenty of doubters in both camps and many reasons to keep fighting—not least the fear of betraying the historical struggles of their respective peoples. Turning the tables on apartheid, the national reconciliation agenda of the late 1980s and the early-to-mid-1990s was based on the premise that apartheid, *not reconciliation*, was unrealistic and unworkable. In direct and deliberate contrast to apartheid, the inherent *reconcilability* of black and white was assumed, along with the fundamental *equality* of all human beings.

In embarking on the path to reconciliation, Mandela and De Klerk had to contend with the entrenched and mutually exclusive ambitions that drove both Afrikaner and African nationalism. Both men had to convince hotheads around them, who doubted the wisdom or desirability of peace, that a pragmatic approach would benefit everyone in the long run. In this process, hawks on both sides, who prided themselves on being arch realists, were shown to be utopian and unrealistic to the extent that a mutually exclusive solution driven unilaterally by either the ANC or the NP would inevitably fail. Although ridiculed in some quarters as "pie in the sky," reconciliation emerged as the most realistic way forward, notwithstanding disagreements over how radical its implications would be.[28]

The power of a new visionary realism challenged the hawks' insistence on a politics based on threats by "the other side." This became evident in the way that arguments for a new kind of reconciliation linked to "justice for all" gained steady ascendency under Mandela's and, for different reasons, De Klerk's guidance. For Mandela, this meant convincing black comrades that re-establishing relations with white South Africans not only would serve their best interests, but could also be reformulated on terms that would be fundamentally different from those on which apartheid and colonialism were based. For De Klerk, this meant convincing skeptical white business executives, generals, and politicians that it was in their long-term interests to engage with their black counterparts as equals.

For anti-apartheid forces, Mandela's message meant abandoning the idea of an outright military victory, and of being able to make a fresh start unencumbered by painful compromises. It meant negotiating for, rather than reclaiming by force, their rights, their land, and the country's wealth of which they had been deprived for so long. It meant learning to live with white people, rather than driving them (literally or metaphorically) into the sea whence they had come with such violent consequences centuries before. And, importantly, it required the invoking of earlier struggle traditions. Those in the liberation movement who supported Mandela's line of thinking leaned heavily on the ANC's long tradition of nonviolence and inclusivity to build consensus that some form of cooperation with Pretoria was the best way forward.

For apartheid's beneficiaries, in turn, De Klerk's message implied letting go of the notion of their inherent superiority justifying their stunning levels of privilege, and relinquishing their exclusive right to resources to which they had been entitled. It meant letting go of the two-hundred-year-old dream of an Afrikaner state where ethnic self-determination would be safeguarded. It meant assuming a radically new vulnerability as minority citizens in a majority black country, cutting their emotional and other ties with Europe and throwing in their lot, for better or for worse, with Africa.

With leaders on both sides taking calculated risks, and relinquishing dogmatic positions up front on what reconciliation might mean, the process gained important momentum by retrieving various traditions inherent in both sets of opposing nationalisms that seemed to suggest possibilities for accommodation, inclusion, and non-racialism.

Despite having carefully cultivated and won the support of their comrades and colleagues, Mandela and, to a lesser degree, De Klerk are often presented as radical exceptions within their own ranks—as leaders who stood up against existing political trends, forgave one another against all odds, and miraculously convinced others to lay down their weapons. In this version, theirs was a brief moment of greatness (or, to some, of deception) that flickered momentarily and died down as soon as the country returned to "normal."

Besides being at odds with historical evidence, the larger problem with interpreting the South African transition as wholly exceptional prevents its lessons from being applied in other contexts. It absolves leaders elsewhere from taking genuine reconciliation seriously, with its radical implications for their political and economic interests, because they are "not Mandela." At best, the transition becomes a quaint moral lesson, a unique event to be admired from afar, but inapplicable elsewhere. At worst, the "South Africa problem," as Reed Brody of Human Rights Watch once termed it, has to be dismissed and ignored as quickly as possible.[29]

Those embroiled in conflict, many of whom have paid a high personal price for their involvement, often see reconciliation as impossibly unrealistic, so perhaps it is understandable that they are tempted to romanticize examples of genuine reconciliatory leadership. However, romanticizing reconciliation by depicting it as miraculous is little more than a way of "othering" reconciliatory leaders. In this way, reconciliatory leaders such as Mohandas Gandhi, Martin Luther King, and now Nelson Mandela have been cast as political "others." While ostensibly honoring these figures for taking reconciliation seriously, the very act can imply that, while reconciliation is admirable, it is the preserve of those with exceptional moral qualities. This conveniently makes reconciliation seem inapplicable in (presumably less exceptional) situations dominated by realpolitik, and serves to justify ongoing conflict.

Exceptionalism also denies the gradualism evident in both De Klerk's and Mandela's memoirs of how and why they came to see things as they did. It ignores the painstaking work that both leaders undertook to build sufficient support within their own ranks to enable them to move into reconciliation politics while taking their constituencies with them.

Guided by a basic realism that acknowledged the fundamental *interdependence* instead of the fundamental *apartheid* of black and white South Africans, Mandela, De Klerk, and others crafted a successful path away from apartheid and into a dispensation that acknowledged their interdependence on a more just and sustainable basis. Romanticising reconciliation is thus a crucial mistake that strips the concept of its relevance in conflict resolution. In my view, it relies on a superficial understanding of the leadership that enabled the South African transition to take place. It can be argued that the actions taken by Mandela and De Klerk, and the myriad of other leaders who backed them up, were in fact better attuned to the realities facing them, than those of leaders who choose to continue "fighting fire with fire," often losing touch with the real suffering and destruction of communities in the process.

A Radical Realist Meets a Cautious Pragmatist

Having tracked the emergence of reconciliation in each of the opposing camps and how this was enabled by the principal leaders on either side, is it possible now to trace the nature of the *collaboration*—and the nature of the actual relationship—between these leaders more precisely? In the eulogies that followed Mandela's death, commentators inside the country and across the world spoke about the greatness of his capacity to forgive. This, too, has become a theme closely related to memories of Mandela—a catch-all explanation for both his exceptionality and the nature of his relationship with his former enemies. Yet there may be more to this. How, for example, did Mandela manage to balance his realism and his rootedness in the ANC, as well as his abiding anger at the ongoing state violence in black areas even as negotiations were ongoing, with his gradual acceptance of interdependence with, and acceptance of, a sworn enemy? How did this play out concretely?

A large literature has developed around efforts to understand and promote the concept of political forgiveness. Daniel Philpott, for example, refers to "the Mandela factor" as a model of political forgiveness. He references the fact Mandela "forgave" De Klerk.[30] Moreover, Mandela "practiced forgiveness even during the twenty-seven years that he was imprisoned on South Africa's Robben Island," and Mandela made "reconciliation and forgiveness" major themes of his presidency.[31] Indeed, for Philpott, Mandela might be the most paradigmatic case of political forgiveness, given the ways in which he restored his enemies to citizens in good standing.

One can easily agree with Philpott that Mandela's obvious lack of bitterness toward his erstwhile oppressors was striking, as was his politics of grace toward minorities who had benefited systematically from the very policies that had subjugated him and his fellow black South Africans. But to be sure, these observations make a series of assumptions about the nature of the link between reconciliation and forgiveness for which there is not a lot of historical backup. As it turns out, a careful consideration of the available historical evidence does not seem to point toward forgiveness, at least as it is outlined by theorists like Philpott and others, as a key catalyst of reconciliation, and certainly not for Mandela or De Klerk. To illustrate this, it is perhaps best to look at the start of the formal negotiations process.

On December 21, 1991, the Convention for a Democratic South Africa (CODESA) convened for the first time. Delegations from nineteen political organizations met with the apartheid government to plan for the creation of a transitional government and a representative parliament. The meeting took place in Johannesburg and proceedings were broadcast live via national radio and television.[32] On the first day, in what was to have been the closing speech, De Klerk chastised the ANC for not "coming into line with other political parties and movements."[33] The heart of the problem, said De Klerk, was that the ANC had not yet "terminated what it itself defined as the 'armed struggle.'"[34] Mandela had not been scheduled to speak after De Klerk, but he stood up, walked to the podium, and made the following statement:

> I am gravely concerned about the behaviour of Mr de Klerk today. He has launched an attack on the African National Congress, and in doing so he has been less than frank. Even the head of an illegitimate, discredited, minority regime as his, has certain moral standards to uphold. He has no excuse, because he is a representative of a discredited regime, not to uphold moral standards. Let him not persuade us that he

should be the last speaker—because he wants to abuse that privilege and to attack us—in the hope that he will get no reply.[35]

After this, Mandela assured those listening that he was nevertheless still "prepared to work with [De Klerk] in spite of all his mistakes" and even though De Klerk had "sometimes very little idea what democracy means." Mandela then concluded that

> [De Klerk] doesn't represent us. He can't talk to us in that language . . . we can only succeed if we are candid and open with one another. This type of thing, of trying to take advantage of the co-operation which we are giving him, willingly, is something extremely dangerous and I hope this is last time he will do so.[36]

In his memoirs, De Klerk recalls his intense anger at what he regarded as an unwarranted personal attack. He writes that he refrained from retaliating in equal measure because he knew it would "place all the reform initiatives for which my team and I had worked so hard at risk if I followed my natural political instincts and paid back Mandela in equally insulting terms."[37] The next morning, Mandela crossed the negotiating chamber to shake De Klerk's hand. Although he accepted Mandela's gesture, De Klerk says he suspected that "good relations between us would never again be possible."[38]

Over the next few years, Mandela regularly and publicly voiced his reservations about De Klerk's bona fides, refusing, for example, to appear with De Klerk at a media conference on the White House lawn as guests of President Clinton. Tensions were evident on several other occasions, including when they both received the Nobel Peace Prize in Oslo in 1993, belying the impressive photographs of the two unlikely co-laureates together. For his part, De Klerk accused Mandela of being less than honest and forthright throughout the period they worked together, and he reiterated this in his memoirs published in 1998. In 1994, Mandela invited De Klerk to be one of two deputy presidents in the Government of National Unity. Two years later, De Klerk walked out of Mandela's Cabinet, citing disagreements over the Constitution and opting instead to play a role in opposition politics; soon after this, he left party politics to become active in civil society.

While Mandela appeared not to hold historical grudges against the white community in general, his relationship with De Klerk seems to have been much more conflicted than even a nuanced understanding of the concept of forgiveness might imply. (In Chapter 5 I analyze forgiveness in more detail.) Although formally cordial, the Mandela/De Klerk relationship never really blossomed. Rather than a relationship based on forgiveness, it is perhaps more accurate to speak about tough but cordial relations, rooted in a steely determination on both sides to "get the job done" in a context in which there was no other choice. In other words, they had to depend on one another to be able to deliver what they had promised to their respective constituencies.

Interpersonal forgiveness, at least as popularly understood, may foster inaccurate conclusions as to why these men were able to cooperate as they did. Rather than offering De Klerk "forgiveness," Mandela demanded a new kind of politics from all representatives of the old establishment—the politics of engagement and cooperation.

De Klerk, too, seems to have never understood his own politics as a response to political forgiveness. Indeed, it is doubtful that De Klerk ever felt the need to receive political forgiveness or even to show remorse. "My hands are clean and my conscience is clear!" he exclaimed after a TRC hearing in which one of the commissioners, Alex Boraine, criticized him for denying any knowledge of apartheid security forces' dirty tricks campaigns.[39]

If Not Forgiveness, Then What?

If forgiveness is not the most appropriate term, what was the relationship between Mandela and De Klerk based on? In light of the evidence and arguments so far presented, it is likely that a growing sense of their interdependence—the indispensable role of their adversary in realizing the aspirations of their respective struggles —provided a firm platform for cooperation. Indeed, they were "in this together." In addressing the CODESA talks, De Klerk described reconciliation along these lines as "trying to find mutually acceptable solutions together, to together discussing what the new South Africa should look like, of constitutional negotiations that would lead to a lasting mutual understanding."[40]

In his early attempts to develop a political case for reconciliation, Mandela developed a similar idea of the way beyond apartheid as the acknowledgment and gradual enactment of racial interdependence. Mandela argued that racial interdependence was a realistic and desirable political option because of how strongly interwoven South Africans' interests are, despite myriad attempts by proponents of apartheid and colonial social engineering to achieve the opposite. As Mandela said in a speech to the European Parliament in 1990:

As we watched the staring eyes of the oppressors and the torturers, year in and year out, and felt the pain of their cruelty, year in and year out, we understood that we could not end the nightmare by surrendering ourselves to the passion of hatred and the spirit of vengeance and retribution. We understood that were we to succumb to these elemental instincts, we would turn ourselves into a new cabal of oppressors, the instrument for the destruction of our people.[41]

Put simply, whereas apartheid aimed at what Archbishop Desmond Tutu described as "unscrambling the racial omelette,"[42] reconciliation represented a political agenda that, as its point of departure, admitted to the fundamental (unchangeable) and comprehensive (political, economic, social, and moral) interdependence of all citizens. Interdependence was acknowledged, not only as a given fact, but as a possible norm for how society ought to organize itself in future, and as a promise of justice to come.

In his inaugural address as president of South Africa in September 1989, De Klerk hinted at a similar embrace of racial interdependence that would be fundamentally more just than what had gone before when he said:

[T]here is but one way to peace, to justice for all: that is the way of reconciliation, of together seeking mutually acceptable solutions, of together discussing what the new South Africa should look like, of constitutional negotiation with a view to a permanent understanding.[43]

Three months later, in December 1989, in a letter written to De Klerk from prison, Mandela quoted De Klerk's own words back to him, and then went on to add:

The cornerstone of that address was the idea of reconciliation. . . . By reconciliation in this context, was understood the situation where opponents, and even enemies for that matter, would sink their differences and lay down arms for the purpose of working out a peaceful solution.[44]

Thus reconciliation—as an acknowledgment of interdependence—became a framework for *non-violent engagement between sworn enemies stuck in a political and military dead-end.* Eventually, even the more militant ANC members began to see reconciliation as an unavoidable reality.

Two factors helped reconciliation gain further traction, eventually beyond the political elites. First, an awareness grew that interdependence was not peripheral or incidental to apartheid society, but *fundamental* to it. Despite a long history of denying this fact, racial interdependence was recognized as self-evident and unalterable. Second, the realization dawned of just how *comprehensive* interdependence was; that, in fact, it covered not only political aspirations, but every level of existence.

It is worth elaborating on this a little more since apartheid sought, with a fair amount of success, to emphasize black people's reliance on white "civilization," while denying entirely the dependence of white people on the black population. In reality, whites depended on black tolerance and cooperation for even their most basic sense of security. This became abundantly clear during the uprisings of the 1970s and 1980s, when many white people lived in desperate fear that black people armed with sticks and knives would invade areas reserved for whites. This never happened. Of course, white communities had always depended on black labor too to extract gold and coal from the mines, to grow and harvest food, to build roads and railways, and even to clean their homes and mind their children. "Unscrambling" the racial omelette proved impossible, precisely because of the comprehensive nature of interdependence between black and white. What apartheid legislation succeeded in doing for white South Africans was to create a false sense of independence and superiority, as if there was no connection between the ways in which white communities flourished while black communities floundered.

While the politicians argued back and forth, and gradually arrived at a value-based, and workable, definition of reconciliation, initially they differed on how to achieve this. For De Klerk, reconciliation included minority veto rights on both political and economic change. For Mandela, reconciliation implied a much more radical change to a fully democratic "one-person-one-vote" system in tandem with strong economic redress.

They differed in other ways too. In terms of leverage, De Klerk was obviously and understandably reluctant to relinquish control over his biggest resource—South Africa's strong and well-armed state machinery. Roelf Meyer, the regime's chief negotiator, later admitted that "we always thought we could tell the other side what to do, because we were in government. It was only when we realised that this was not the way to resolve things that things started to move forward."[45] But it took time—the best part of two years after Mandela's release—for this realization to dawn. Mandela, in turn, had to rely largely on public pressure for his own leverage at the negotiating table.

In style, De Klerk favored a guarded, cautious, and tightly controlled negotiating style, whereas Mandela took a more inclusive, open-ended approach that encouraged wider public engagement. These differences in style might have had more fundamental causes than their respective positions as president and leader of the liberation movement, and been rooted in their personalities to some degree. De Klerk can perhaps best be characterized as a cautious pragmatist and Mandela as a radical realist. De Klerk was also a realist but a cautious one, and although no one can doubt the courage it took to release Mandela and begin a negotiations process that would almost inevitably require him to hand over power, he favored a slow transition with some kind of veto to retain some of the social and economic assets of the white community. As he wrote later, "My natural instinct was to take a step-by-step approach." In a message to his comrades in Lusaka, smuggled out of prison, Mandela wrote: "My assessment of Mr De Klerk is that of a strong, cautious but flexible man who is prepared to adapt to new ideas and to meet new challenges."[46] In De Klerk's own words:

> Those who espouse absolute moral rectitude are unlikely to become successful political leaders—since their principles will require them to resign at the first moral test that their party fails . . . the political art is to acquire power and then to direct public affairs toward a more just and morally acceptable outcome. One cannot achieve political leadership without caution, pragmatism and realism. By the same token, leaders must be prepared to take risks and never lose sight of the vision or principles for which they are working—however unrealistic this might appear to be.[47]

Mandela was realistic in that he accepted the presence of white South Africans as a permanent political fact, and took steps to overcome apartheid in favor of a dispensation that could include even his former oppressors' aspirations and rights. At the same time, he was decidedly pragmatic about what such a "reconciled relationship" might entail, and all the limitations it might carry. He certainly did not hold his breath and wait for any profound moral conversion from his enemies. He was sensible about what could be expected in the short to medium term. From this point of view, Mandela was not a revolutionary who advocated abrupt and violent change, but rather a leader who pushed for bold, yet carefully managed, transformation.

Yet Mandela was also a radical. He made it plain from the start that reconciliation could never entail any form of black subservience, however subtle. Instead, at the heart of the new dispensation would be an acknowledgment of human dignity, and all sociopolitical institutions had to alter radically to reflect this. This was the basis of his attack on De Klerk at CODESA's opening meeting (and perhaps subsequently), when De Klerk failed to address the ANC as an equal and thus, more important, failed to signal his acceptance of a sociopolitical dispensation that would reflect the dignity of all. At that stage, in late 1991, De Klerk still seemed to think that he and his allies could control both the process and the outcome of the negotiations, and that this would include entrenching both a political veto and the economic assets controlled by white South Africans, thus jettisoning any real prospects of black empowerment and redress.[48] De Klerk made it clear initially that his party would not be willing to scrap South Africa's apartheid-era constitution but would seek a gradual revision of that document.

Reining in the Extremists

While building consensus across the main political divide, each side had an additional task: namely, to contain potential spoilers outside the fold. Philpott writes that although impossible to prove, it is entirely plausible that "Mandela's acts of forgiveness and general spirit of reconciliation helped to avert a violent backlash among conservative whites in South Africa and a corresponding counter-retaliation among blacks."[49]

De Klerk did outstanding work in unifying a large majority of white South Africans behind him while entering into and completing the negotiations that put their interests at risk at least to some degree, but he was less effective in convincing radical groups to the right of his party. Ironically, Mandela had more influence over the Afrikaner right wing than De Klerk.

Ominously, in 1993 several white military leaders founded a "Committee of Generals" to support Afrikaner demands for self-determination that they felt were being sold out at the negotiation table. General Groenewald, who led the group along with the former head of the Defence Force, General Viljoen, warned of the possibility of secession backed by an informal, militia-style army of potentially five hundred thousand young white men. In a series of telephone conversations after a botched attempt to deploy some of these militias in early 1994, President-in-Waiting Nelson Mandela admitted to Viljoen that the ANC was not in a position to defeat the South African military or indeed Viljoen's militias, but, he argued, "you cannot kill all black people in South Africa either." Implying that they would have to talk sooner or later, Mandela asked Viljoen, "why not now, before we destroy the country and one another and end up having very little to negotiate over?" Viljoen took this to heart, swapped his fatigues for a suit, and led the Afrikaner right wing into the political process,[50] thereby averting major bloodshed and contributing at the same time a significant building block in South Africa's process of national reconciliation.

Reflecting on this conversation twenty years later, Viljoen acknowledged that Mandela had played a major role in his decision not to continue to pursue a military strategy.[51] Yet his relationship with Mandela was not about forgiveness either. Viljoen, like De Klerk, never believed he needed to be forgiven. Mandela's integrity and trustworthiness, and his ability to understand and appreciate military power, as well as its limits, made Viljoen realize that Mandela was, in fact, someone he, as a soldier, would be able to talk to and learn to trust. It was then, on the basis of Mandela's invitation, that he accepted the reality of the ANC's presence in the country, and the consequences of his own political interdependence on Mandela, and on others like him. At the same time, Viljoen also accepted that the survival of his kith and kin depended on finding ways to coexist with black South Africans, and he began to engage in the political process in a sustained and meaningful way.

Meanwhile, De Klerk seemed to have more influence over another potential spoiler of the peace process—the Inkatha Freedom Party (IFP) led by Mangosuthu Buthelezi. In the 1980s and early 1990s, the apartheid security apparatus worked closely with the IFP to destabilize parts of South Africa, particularly the province of Natal (subsequently renamed KwaZulu-Natal). ANC supporters often retaliated in kind, making the province by far the most violent in the country at that time.

In the context of increasingly lethal clashes between ANC and IFP supporters, Mandela and Buthelezi struggled to establish sufficient trust to work together. The fighting arguably culminated in a standoff in April 1994 after several IFP members were shot dead by ANC security personnel during a protest march to the ANC's headquarters in Johannesburg.

With ANC–IFP relations at an all-time low, De Klerk organized a mediation meeting in the Kruger National Park, including Mandela, Buthelezi, and the Zulu king, Goodwill Zwelithini. This led to several further attempts (including by Henry Kissinger and Lord Carrington) to convince Buthelezi to participate in the first democratic elections. Eventually, Kenyan academic professor Washington Okumu persuaded Buthelezi to bring the IFP into the elections less than a week before voting took place on April 27, 1994.

Conclusion

Reconciliation in South Africa was made possible through a particular kind of political leadership that emerged when larger geopolitical conditions favored a settlement of a historic conflict caused by the injustices of colonialism and apartheid. This political leadership was based on a gradual acceptance by both sides of their interdependence, and of consequent need to find a dispensation that acknowledged this.

There is little doubt that Mandela, De Klerk, and others offered visionary leadership. Yet it is possible, indeed probable, that reconciliation arose not out of any notion of personal forgiveness but from a pragmatic acknowledgment of the intractability of a military stalemate, and of the power of reconciliation to change things fundamentally.

For this and other reasons, it is not helpful to see Mandela, De Klerk, or any other political leaders as moral exceptions who stand apart from their communities, their political movements, and from humanity in general. While models of reconciliation based on idealized notions of political forgiveness amidst the unfinished and deeply messy middle ground of transition, might well require a Mandela-type figure, they require an idealized version of Mandela, not the visionary and principled pragmatist that he was. And such models make it all too easy for warring parties to see reconciliation as impossible in their own contexts.

This does not mean that forgiveness played no role, or was wholly absent. Even being in the same room as one's former oppressor is remarkably difficult, and it requires the politics of grace that rightly earned Mandela his reputation. And yet it seems that what convinced apartheid and ANC leaders to turn to reconciliation as a means to end apartheid was not an individualized or generalized sense of forgiveness but a political realism that faced reality as it was. Apartheid was ending, and a new beginning, crafted with the enemy, was the only viable, responsible, and moral way forward.

Leaders on both sides of the apartheid divide showed courageous realism when they faced the need to work with their former enemies to further the interests of their own constituencies. Once this need was acknowledged, both groups began to put in place measures that would enable lasting change. And in this commitment to genuine change, the promise of a more just, inclusive, and fair society was a nascent presence.

Both Mandela and De Klerk recognized the possibility of combining realpolitik with deeply held conviction, and, crucially, they acted on it. Each extended an olive branch to his enemy and won the chance of a better life for the majority of South Africans. The fact that so many South Africans still live in abject poverty, a sense of exclusion, and perhaps a growing sense of unfairness is not the fault of the leaders who argued for reconciliation. It is the fault of those of us who expected the process to be over before it had really begun.

2

Settling on a Shared Future

In this chapter, the focus shifts from reconciliation's inception, as articulated by its principal leaders, toward its concrete enactment across South Africa's political and institutional landscape in the years which followed Mandela's release. It is often precisely here where conflict transformation runs into serious difficulties. Having crossed a first, important hurdle when the leadership on both sides realize and acknowledge a historic opportunity for peace, and their reliance on one another to achieve that peace, the next challenge is to set in motion concrete processes that take the country forward towards that vision. But what drives such a vast transition, what are its key characteristics, and how does one ensure coherence and some measure of integration among its many constituent processes?

In the South African context, this raises the question about whether and how the idea that black and white shared an interdependent future, once articulated by Nelson Mandela, F. W. de Klerk, and their respective parties, was allowed to shape the transitional processes that followed.[1] If it was a crucial part of the argument for reconciliation in the first place, did the idea of racial interdependence continue to play an important role, or did it fade as time went on? This question obviously demands an understanding of initiatives, movements, and institutions involving leaders and ordinary citizens in many different spheres of society.[2] It also demands insight into how the various initiatives and platforms operated together, complemented one another, and ultimately became part of a comprehensive political transition. In seeking to learn how this process was managed in South Africa, the aim is to identify insights that might be considered helpful in the context of other political transitions.

As in the previous chapter, my argument leans heavily on several of the more credible published historical assessments of the period, while fresh material includes interviews with people who were key role players during the transition. The discussion focuses on the period from 1987, when P. W. Botha and Mandela first established contact, to 1998, when the TRC handed in its final report to President Mandela.[3] During this time, a significant number of faith-based, political, and civic organizations all helped to turn reconciliation from idea to an evolving reality (albeit imperfect and unfinished). Today, however, the TRC is virtually the only mechanism that receives any real attention as having deliberately sought to further reconciliation. Not only does this provide a skewed picture of the TRC itself, it also means that we run the risk of fundamentally misunderstanding the dynamics that led to political reconciliation being concretized to the degree that it was.[4]

Among the many organizations, initiatives, individuals, and mechanisms that contributed to securing a common future for South Africa, I highlight four that I consider the most important and relevant to reconciliation specifically. These platforms—the National Peace Accord (NPA), the Convention for a Democratic South Africa (CODESA), the Multi-Party Negotiating Forum (MPNF), and the TRC—carried out vitally important work, expanding the political transition across lines of political conflict and, beyond the political elite, encouraging civic and sectoral organizations to join the quest to establish a common basis for the future.

The NPA was especially influential during the initial period of struggle after Mandela's release. It helped to create an important *civic* space, amid increasing political assassinations and street battles, where politicians could convene to renounce violence and try to build trust so that "talks about talks" could resume. I show that, as a civic initiative, the NPA helped to prepare the ground for constructive political negotiations and, ultimately, for efforts to deal with the apartheid past. For at least these reasons it strengthened the reconciliation process that followed.

The formal multi-party negotiations evolved through various incarnations, as CODESA I, CODESA II, and finally the MPNF. When referring to the multi-party negotiation process (MPNP), I include this whole stop-start process in all its various incarnations as well as the elaborate structures that constituted the negotiating forum, the various technical and planning committees, and the Transitional Executive Council (TEC). The MPNP was especially important during the middle period of the transition—that is, from 1991, when political parties first convened, until 1993, when the interim Constitution was adopted.

It is important to note that the NPA and MPNP were primarily concerned with articulating and agreeing on modalities for a shared, constitutional *future*. Only after having agreed on the basic constitutional principles in the interim constitution, did the country develop the confidence formally to turn to its past through the work of the TRC. This chapter focuses on the former, forward-looking dimension of reconciliation's institutional course, whereas as the next chapter focuses more squarely on the TRC and "dealing with the past."

Carving Out Space for a National Peace Process

The year 1989 was a violent one for South Africa; approximately 1,403 people lost their lives in political clashes and hope for a change under the new President De Klerk was fading fast. The next year, after De Klerk caught everyone by surprise in his historic speech at the opening of Parliament, and after Mandela's release some nine days later, the ANC and NP prepared to meet officially for the first time. Yet, political violence only increased *further*, and approximately 3,699 people died that year. Two and a half years later, by September 1993, just before the negotiations concluded, a total of 10,495 people had died in political violence since the day Mandela walked free.

As a result of this escalating instability, Mandela and De Klerk both appeared isolated and weak, and the idea of a negotiated settlement increasingly unattainable.

Concerned by the emergence of this power vacuum (the central government was apparently losing control, and evidently the liberation movement was not yet in a position to take its place), an umbrella body representing business interests, the Consultative Business Movement, together with leaders of the Mass Democratic Movement and certain unions, began to mobilize instead. Their first priority, after seeking out one another, was to arrange a series of low-key, but crucial meetings with political leaders on all sides to discuss ways forward.[5] First this impromptu civic leadership group approached senior MPs in the white-dominated parliament. In March 1991, they met with ANC leaders as well. Later they met with the South African Communist Party and Congress of South African Trade Unions (COSATU), and soon thereafter with the Zulu-dominated Inkatha Freedom Party (IFP).

During the same period, in a parallel development with potentially serious consequences, the ANC presented the government with a seven-point ultimatum to be answered before May 9, 1991. After an acceptable response failed to materialize, the ANC threatened to break off contact with the government indefinitely. In the memorandum it was apparent that the ANC was particularly appalled by what they believed to be the government's ongoing "dirty tricks campaign" which fomented violence within black communitieas.

Instead of responding to the detailed ultimatum, the NP called a two-day "all-in" peace summit. While IFP welcomed the initiative, the ANC on the one hand, and the Afrikaner right wing on the other, rejected it outright. Both sides saw De Klerk, a leader whose moral standing they questioned, as an inappropriate host for such a conference.

As the ANC's deadline approached with no compromise in sight, shuttle diplomacy by civic leaders, who understood the calamitous potential of an indefinite postponement of negotiations, intensified. These individuals, all well-known personalities in their own right, met on an almost daily basis to monitor developments and nudge the politicians toward compromise. The ANC deadline eventually passed without a major incident—and observers attributed this largely to the ongoing, intense diplomacy behind the scenes initiated and driven by a deeply committed and concerned civic leadership.

But such gains are seldom permanent. As the date of De Klerk's proposed peace summit approached, tensions escalated again. The South African Council of Churches, which had earlier publicly committed itself to facilitating a peace process, announced that an alternative summit would be held in the province of Natal—where incidents of violence were highest. Mandela gave his support to the latter move, while De Klerk and the IFP immediately questioned the credentials of the Council of Churches to host such an event. At the same time, business leaders who supported De Klerk's summit found relations between themselves and the ANC growing tense.

Normally, when opposing parties propose different peace processes, international mediators are called in to rescue the situation. South Africans, however, responded differently to the crisis. Instead of calling on international mediation, civic leaders again took the initiative. The Consultative Business Movement and the South African Council of Churches called a meeting of civic organizations and trade unions to discuss the opposing peace processes and ways to bring them together. At the meeting, trade union leader Jay Naidoo suggested that the ANC might consider attending De Klerk's summit if De Klerk would agree to the appointment of an independent chairperson, and if a representative committee could be established to draw up the agenda. When the suggestion was sent to De Klerk's office, a positive reply was issued almost immediately. De Klerk also agreed that the summit could form part of an ongoing process, thus opening the door for ANC-initiated events down the line. In turn, although the ANC eventually declined their invitation to attend De Klerk's summit, they accepted that the event would form part of a larger process. De Klerk's summit went ahead without further complications, but it was clear to delegates that a more representative summit would follow.

In this way, civic leaders provided political parties with an opportunity to regain momentum toward creating a joint platform for negotiations. The ANC and the NP both agreed to consider signing multilateral agreements containing mutual obligations regarding the escalating violence, and the NP agreed to attend a subsequent peace conference facilitated by the churches.

The task of calling the next event was delegated to Louw Alberts, a respected scientist who had the ear of both camps. Despite some opposition from De

Klerk and others, Alberts began to build a representative committee that could organize another peace summit. De Klerk thought that the event should include the major leaders only, and that his government would play a leading role. Louw, by contrast, thought there was a better chance of compromise if the meeting included second- and third-tier leaders, and was hosted by civic rather than political figures. Importantly, it was during this standoff that it gradually became clear that President De Klerk was no longer unilaterally able to determine the shape of the process. In a series of meetings in May, and in direct opposition to De Klerk's wishes, business and church leaders debated a wide range of names for possible inclusion in the summit. They also designed a process that would lead to what they identified as their primary goal: the convening of an all-inclusive national peace conference.

The next major step was to get buy-in for this peace conference from all the political organizations. The civic leaders organized a preparatory meeting in June 1991 to which they invited all the political organizations.[6] With this, it appears that the initiative shifted from the state to a group that was made up essentially of concerned citizens. Almost all parties accepted the invitation, except for three white extremist groups.[7] Marking the first time in South African history that such an inclusive group of mandated political leaders had ever convened in one meeting, individuals representing twenty organizations met on June 22, 1991, to discuss peace, violence, and security.[8] The goal was to brainstorm key issues and practical solutions to the violence. With the consent of participants, the meeting was chaired by representatives of the religious fraternity and the business community—individuals with track records of inclusive and credible leadership, such as Archbishop Desmond Tutu and others. Not surprisingly, given its historic significance, the atmosphere was decidedly strained, so the organizers decided initially to allow discussions on relatively noncontentious matters only.[9] The meeting made some progress toward drafting a code of conduct for members of political organizations and the security forces. When discussions moved on to the shape that possible enforcement mechanisms might take, arguments began to escalate into heated exchanges and accusations.[10]

To ease the tensions, Tutu, who was chairing a particularly difficult session, suggested an adjournment during which the NP, ANC, and IFP brokered a joint proposal. It suggested that a new organizing committee consisting of the existing committee plus delegates from each of the three main parties should plan an "all-in" National Peace Convention.[11]

With momentum re-established, the newly constituted committee was asked to establish working groups that would prepare for the proposed convention. The reports from each working group were then collated into a document which later became known as the NPA (and which gave birth to an organization with the same name). Thus, by the time that all the parties met for South Africa's first all-inclusive peace conference in September 1991, much of the tough negotiating had already taken place—and an impressive civic coalition representing a wide range of cross-sectional interests had pledged their support to the potential accord to flow from the meeting.

Of significant symbolic importance too was the fact that the NPA enabled De Klerk, Mandela, and Buthelezi—for the first time in unison from the same stage—to renounce political violence forcefully and unambiguously. Until that moment, all three leaders presided over movements with armed wings which continued activities in their respective names.

Just as important, the platform from where this historic announcement was made, was a *civic* platform; none of the political leaders could take the credit. The merger of the disparate peace processes into a truly inclusive one, when it finally happened was manifestly a *civic* achievement, not one that belonged to one or another political initiative. Traditional leaders, trade unionists, media, business, religion, and the diplomatic corps all attended; the only political leaders missing were from three extreme-right-wing Afrikaner parties that had opted out from the start. The attendees all signed the accord, except the Pan African Congress and the Azanian People's Organisation, which supported the accord but were unable to sign it owing to their principled commitment to non-collaboration.

In reflecting on these early stages of South Africa's national reconciliation history, it is clear that, by taking the initiative in an understated but organized way, civic leaders established themselves as credible facilitators in what subsequently became a substantially more inclusive and credible reconciliation process. It was more inclusive because a wider range of political and civic actors became involved, and more credible because it was now possible to argue that reconciliation belonged neither to the government nor to the ANC, but essentially to the citizens of South Africa; and that it would be them that would ultimately stand in judgement of whatever the politicians would agree on and implement. This was later corroborated by the last all-white referendum that offered De Klerk a strong mandate to continue with negotiations (despite Afrikaner extremists' resistance), as well as the groundswell of popular black support for the unbanned ANC, which enabled it to win a runaway victory in the first democratic elections. The first signs of this popular support for reconciliation were captured in the obvious convening power that civic leaders were able to demonstrate in staging the NPA as South Africa's most inclusive political gathering ever. These characteristics played an important role in shaping South Africa's understanding and expectation of what reconciliation could be, what it promised, and ultimately how it would seek to direct social transformation. It was when civic leaders, from a range of interest groups—faith, business, unions—joined forces that sustained change became a real prospect. After the NPA's success, its civic leadership continued to meet frequently to plan, strategize, and lobby for inclusive, nonpartisan, and credible, processes.

The fact that the NPA enabled talks to resume was symbolically important for another reason: when the tough, highly charged political negotiations subsequently ensued, only to break off again repeatedly each time political violence escalated, the NPA stood as a firm reminder to politicians of the civic involvement, leverage, and interests that were integral to the process. Thus, the NPA arguably helped to imbue the subsequent negotiations with a resilience they might not have had, had it been solely a government and/or ANC initiative driven at the political level alone. That the MPNP proceeded in this context, therefore contributed to its stability, and the intent displayed by civic leaders, together with the political inclusivity they cultivated, added credibility and a moral reference point to the ongoing negotiations process. Peter Gastrow, who had been intimately involved in the NPA process, confirms that the NPA played a significant role in smoothing the way toward constitutional negotiations:

> What is also important is that even before negotiations for a new constitution had commenced, the NPA contained key principles that underpin a democracy and the rule of law. It was therefore not necessary for CODESA to start from scratch—it could hit the ground running because large areas had already been discussed and agreed upon in the NPA. In addition, it provided a channel for communication and a platform to meet, at times when the NP and ANC were in deadlock over constitutional negotiations. National leaders who could not be seen near their political opponents during such times had no problem in meeting with them in the National Peace Committee. NPA structures were generally regarded as neutral territory, and played a key role in keeping lines of communications open and in building trust despite the occasional rough rapids of constitutional negotiations.[12]

This does not mean that civic leaders acted unilaterally or without regard for political leadership. Instead, they carefully dovetailed their actions with political initiatives. Civic leaders were, after all, significantly dependent on political leadership by De Klerk and Mandela, who had already acknowledged the interdependence of their respective political aspirations and the need for negotiations. And yet, when the Mandela–De Klerk axis ran out of steam, civic leaders reignited reconciliation as a significantly more inclusive process. Moreover, the De Klerk government relinquished real control to civic leaders after it acknowledged, to its credit, that it could no longer act as the sole or even a primary sponsor of the peace process, and that it needed to assume the role of participant. This further deepened the credibility of the reconciliation process because the space it helped to create was manifestly fairer than what had preceded it, not least because now so many parties were in the same room and the government, as just one interested party to the negotiations, was no longer afforded control of the process.

Importantly too, the NPA developed a national network of peace mediators who were tasked with managing community tensions across the country. This infrastructure included a National Peace Secretariat, eleven regional peace committees, and two hundred local peace committees. In addition, fifteen thousand peace mediators were recruited from all sectors of society, trained and deployed in communities around the country during the 1994 elections. To give just one example of the NPA's on-the-ground drive to help ensure free, credible, and inclusive elections: on election day in April 1994, in the town of Stellenbosch, near Cape Town, a multiracial NPA task force of volunteers escorted black voters into the heart of the town to cast their ballots for the first time. The task force literally carved a route for black residents through the apprehensive white crowds lining the streets. This multiracial human chain in brightly colored clothing literally stood between those voting for the first time and those who had to share their vote for the first time. Then, despite the newly elected government withdrawing funding for the NPA soon after the elections, the local Stellenbosch Peace Committee, an offshoot of the NPA task force, continued to operate for several years.

Often overlooked by reconciliation theorists, the story of the NPA illustrates the profound difficulties involved in building the trust between political opponents needed to produce meaningful progress toward sustainable reconciliation in climates of profound mistrust that routinely linger in the wake of deep conflicts.[13] The NPA also illustrates the important mediating role that strong and credible civic leaders can play in convening sufficiently credible and ever more inclusive processes in the wake of formal declarations and political commitments to reconciliation—and the role this plays in enabling the beginnings of trust to develop between historic enemies.

First steps towards a Fair and Inclusive Future

The nature of the negotiations process that followed the signing of the NPA was one of ebb and flow, of opening and closure, of transition and consolidation. At least twice more, talks would be suspended or broken off indefinitely, but each time another round of negotiations was pulled together. And, at each new beginning, invitations were re-extended to all political parties. Eventually, the will to reach a settlement outlasted the incentives for delaying or blocking one. The result was an interim constitution, signed by all parties in November 1993 with the proviso that, once in power, a democratically elected government would draft a final constitution honoring the basic principles of the interim document but also fully canvassing and representing the aspirations of ordinary South Africans.

Throughout this time, ongoing political violence, and parties' reaction to it, was a key challenge to the sustainability of the negotiations. After the signing of the NPA in late 1991, for example, tensions in the streets remained at breaking point. Violence erupted daily. Smoke billowed from cities, towns, and villages across the country. Highways were lined with soldiers. In the Natal midlands, tit-for-tat killings had reached the level of a low-key civil war. A state of emergency, granting special powers to the police, was in place and there was repeated references to "no-go zones," where the government were said to have effectively ceded control to local militias. .[14]

Throughout all this, the NP kept challenging the ANC to suspend its underground activities and disarm its militias. The ANC, in turn, kept accusing the government of being complicit in the violence through their own "dirty tricks campaigns." Both the NP and the ANC leaders also faced criticism from within their own ranks, and were accused of fraternizing with the enemy while their frustrated rank-and-file members were bearing the brunt of the violence. All this combined to motivate the respective leadership groupings to break off negotiations at various points. Roelf Meyer, the government's chief negotiator, recalls one such moment:

> After the massacre of shack-dwellers on 22 June 1992, the ANC said it was finished talking with government, that it was in fact cutting all ties with government. No further talks. I remember Mr Mandela announcing this on the evening television news. And I said to myself, "Oh damn it. There we go." All the hard work up to that point appeared to be over. It seemed everything had been done for nothing. Then a few minutes later, Cyril [Ramaphosa] phoned me at my home in Pretoria. And I said, "What the hell are you doing?" And his response was, "When can we talk?" ... For the next three months, the two of us, Cyril and myself, were locked in by our principals ... to find a way to end the deadlock. We had to come up with something and we did. It became known as the Record of Understanding, an agreement between the ANC and the National Party government that formed the basis ... for all further negotiations.[15]

Eventually, the trust generated through Meyer and Ramaphosa's work on a range of contentious issues, led to the resumption of the MPNP toward the end of 1992. This time, a more urgent timetable was followed, and a commitment to universal franchise within a constitutional democracy based on individual human rights was strongly articulated. Several historians point to September 1992 as the point at which De Klerk finally relinquished not only his quest to control the talks but also his longer-term ideal of entrenching some form of group rights that could safeguard minority white interests.[16]

Another critical juncture occurred six months later, when Chris Hani, one of the liberation movement's most influential and popular leaders, was assassinated by right wingers. Anger among those pushing for more radical change at a faster pace reached boiling point, and the country faced the real prospect of an all-out war. De Klerk realized that, of the two of them, Mandela had more popular authority, and facilitated Mandela's unscheduled appearance on national television during which he appealed for calm and noted that while white people had committed the horrendous crime, it was also a white person who provided the information that led to the speedy arrest of the perpetrators. At that point, a much emboldened Mandela was every bit the president in waiting, and able, against the odds, to unite black and white South Africans against the threat of escalating political violence.

Mandela's leadership added impetus to another important development, namely the establishment of the TEC, a body that represented the first grip on state power for the liberation movement and, concomitantly, the first real abdication of some areas of authority by the apartheid government.[17] Comprising one member from each of the parties in the MPNP (with the Freedom Alliance and the Pan African Congress again declining membership), the Council was established by an Act of Parliament, with the goal of preparing for and promoting the transition to democracy.[18] Both the Council and its sub-councils received wide powers to curtail actions of the apartheid regime that it deemed might have an adverse effect on the attainment of democratic elections. It could, for example, instruct the regime to halt proposed legislation, and the regime would be obliged to comply.

In addition to the involvement of civic, labor, and business organizations mentioned earlier, the conviction of the main parties that they had "no choice" but to honor their interdependence seems to have played a decisive role, time and again, in driving the negotiations beyond disappointment and conflict, into renewed engagement, and ultimately toward the concrete transfer of power. Ramaphosa recalled that

> both of us [ANC and NP] failed in our original objectives. We could not obliterate, wipe each other off the face of the earth. So we were left with no alternatives: there had to be an accommodation, a compromise, and the compromise had to be a win–win type of situation.[19]

Across the negotiating table, Meyer agreed that

the threat of the abyss played an important role; the fact that we knew there was actually no alternative but to find a negotiated settlement. That was an important driving force for all the parties.[20]

This acknowledgment of mutual political interdependence—of having "no alternative" mentioned above by both Ramaphosa and Meyer—proved strong enough to overcome the threats associated with violence. It produced a process of inclusive debate, fresh thinking, and open discussion, together with a technocratic determination to find solutions to pressing problems, to move ahead, and to make the country work. The process involved engaging in tough questions that cut to the root of the South African conflict.

Despite the profound challenges this opened up, the pragmatic will to succeed was complemented by a series of smart negotiating techniques. For example, momentum was maintained by the negotiators agreeing to acknowledge every agreement, however tentative, as progress. In this way, adequate, rather than complete, consensus was sought, with a view to maintaining dialogue rather than stalling at every disagreement. As has been well documented, embracing the concept of "sufficient consensus" allowed the process to proceed even when full agreement was not reached. Ramaphosa explained that "sufficient consensus was defined as a process of reaching agreement that would take us to the next step."[21] A key element of "sufficient consensus" was the notion that disappointment forms an inevitable part of the process. This meant, among other ramifications, that no issue was vetoed outright, nor was any party barred from taking a seat. Yet, if a particular party was unable or unwilling to talk, despite formal invitations, the process continued without them.[22]

Mac Maharaj, who participated centrally in the talks, described a simple formula that was used during the negotiations to implement the idea of sufficient consensus. As issues arose, they were placed in one of three boxes: the first contained issues the parties agreed on; the second box, issues they differed on; and the third box, issues they partially agreed on. Gradually, issues were moved into the "agreement box," on condition that all agreements would be reviewed again before finalization. He remembers that "In this way, we were able to keep the process going. It was the secret of our success. The more we agreed on issues, the easier it was to handle more contentious issues which we began to see within the context of the broader agreements."[23]

The negotiators' willingness to embrace the notion of sufficient consensus stands in contrast to the dictum often heard during peace talks, namely that "nothing is agreed until everything is agreed." Ramaphosa explains that "sufficient consensus was defined as a process of reaching agreement that would take us to the next step."[24] And Meyer notes, "if you come to a point where those around the table in a plenary session can't make progress on a particular point, then the best option is to take whatever the matter in dispute is off the table, re-move it from the agenda for a while. Take it to a bilateral discussion."[25]

The Question of persistent Political Violence

To illustrate how the MPNP managed to proceed while containing the impact of potentially divisive issues, the question of political violence is instructive. How were issues related to accountability for violent political crimes, which were so crucial to the credibility of the process, handled without derailing the process's hard-won inclusivity?

Political violence was the main reason for the MPNP breaking up so often. On one occasion in June 1993, the negotiators themselves were directly threatened when a group of heavily armed right-wing extremists from the Afrikaner Weerstandsbeweging (AWB) invaded Johannesburg's World Trade Centre, where the negotiations were under way. The group drove an armored vehicle through the plate-glass windows of the complex and into the foyer. Douglas McClure, a security adviser to one of the NP ministers, recalls seeing khaki-clad men pouring into the huge vestibule while, upstairs in the negotiating chamber, the high-level ANC and Communist Party delegations were quickly hustled into a strong room:

> An AWB mob, armed to the teeth, appeared at the top of the landing and demanded in Afrikaans that a young officer get out of the way. The young officer raised his rifle and said in nervous Afrikaans (his first language was Spanish) to the apparent leader of the group, "*Asseblief, meneer,* (please sir) go back down the stairs. There are more of you than me, but I will shoot you and take as many of you with me as I can if I have to. Please, sir, I beg you, do not force me to do that. You have made your point by coming here, and no one has been hurt yet, so please go back down the stairs. Please, sir."[26]

Inexplicably, and thanks to his bravery, the gang backed off and returned to the foyer. Eventually, the politicians returned to their tables and the talks continued, but this incident brought home the reality of political violence to the negotiators in a most immediate way.

Obviously, such political violence posed a grave threat to political reconcilia-tion. Over the next four years during which formal talks dragged on, two indem-nity laws and several investigative commissions were created—all to address the issue of political violence within the context of limited trust and a still open-ended transition.[27] Most historians agree that the first indemnity law favored the liberation movement, freeing many of its members who had been held prisoner by the apartheid state, while the second broadly favored government operatives who had been captured by the ANC.[28] In principle at least, these laws had the effect of allowing for the inclusion of more political players within the MPNP, rather than leaving them on the outside as potential spoilers. The indemnity laws were later revoked, but by then they had served to build inclusivity and to reassure all players that they were at least in principle welcome at the table.

In addition, a series of introspective truth-seeking exercises was conducted in the face of mounting accusations about ongoing human rights abuses on both sides of the political divide. However, uncovering human rights abuses could of course lead to perpetrators being held accountable instead of receiving indemnity, so the objectives of the indemnity and truth-seeking processes came into tension. At a deeper level, the quest for credibility (facilitated by a more truthful and accountable approach) created tensions in relation to the quest for inclusivity (to keep everyone around the table). The Goldstone Commission, for example, appointed by De Klerk during the latter part of 1991, effectively confirmed the existence of collusion and death squads in the security establishment. Its findings were released only weeks before the elections in 1994, and led De Klerk to fire twenty-three members of the South African Defense Force, including various brigadiers and generals. This action heightened anxiety within the security branches, conceivably increasing the risk of spoilers disrupting the elections.

To investigate human rights abuses that had occurred within its own ranks, the ANC on the other hand appointed three commissions of inquiry. The Stuart, Skweyiya, and Motsuenyane Commissions all examined events in ANC military training camps outside South Africa; the last arguably produced the most credible findings.[29]

It was in their official response to the Motsuenyane Commission that the ANC's national executive first proposed the idea of a truth commission. This was done while criticizing the Further Indemnity Act, which, the ANC claimed, "failed to investigate thoroughly allegations of abuses" and had "not made available information on security force activity or collusion into activities that have resulted in torture, disappearances, detentions without trial, etc." The ANC went on to say that "substantial evidence exists that the government had consciously destroyed materials necessary for a full disclosure of the past" and that no effort at reparations had been made.[30] Expressing "profound regret and apology for each and every transgression" in its own ranks, the ANC then called for the establishment of a "Commission of Truth" with the aim of investigating all violations of human rights across the board. "This will not be a Nuremberg Tribunal," they insisted. Instead, the role of such a commission would be to identify abuses across the political spectrum, to propose a future code of conduct for all public servants, to ensure appropriate compensation to the victims, and to work out the best basis for reconciliation, thereby providing a moral basis for justice and preventing future abuse. Finally, the ANC called for compensation "across the board," a task that could only be carried out by a legitimate government following the identification of the truth: "Partial punishment or partial reparations is unfair to the perpetrators and victims alike."[31]

These ongoing initiatives enabled the different parties to signal their intentions of dealing with sources of violence dispassionately and fairly. But each process was tentative and piecemeal, deliberately forestalling a more thorough engagement with these deeply unsettling issues until a political settlement could be reached. Effectively, agreements on stopping generalized political violence and institutionalizing democracy were prioritized during this period over securing accountability for past political crimes, but without allowing for total amnesia or blanket amnesty. By signaling the possibility for future processes of accountability, the negotiators maintained a delicate balance between credibility and inclusivity on an issue that revealed the decidedly fragile nature of this particular reconciliation process, a fragility that is in fact experienced widely elsewhere too. In so doing, they kept reconciliation's promise of justice alive, but recognized that this was little more than a promise at the time.

Thus it was particularly the Motsuenyane and Goldstone Commissions that signaled the intentions of both sides to establish a TRC that would offer a much more thorough engagement with the specter of political violence. During the MPNP, though, a keen sense of what could be done without scuppering the fragile reconciliation process developed. In this regard, there was agreement among the negotiators. As the deputy chair of the TRC, Alex Boraine, recalled: "the past was all too present with us, and our major focus was on how to confront the present and transform it rather than to look back to the past."[32]

Roelf Meyer argued that if the negotiating parties had themselves tried to establish more systematic ways of dealing with the past *at that time*, there might not have been a settlement at all; it might have been too difficult for them to reach agreement on how to address the past before agreeing where the country as a whole should be heading. Meyer explained that "the basic argument was that it was better to deal first with the future and decide a settlement on that."[33] Only once the broad outline of a political and economic plan for South Africa had been agreed on did delegates begin to consider how to deal with the past. In practice, this meant accepting that amnesty in one form or another would form part of the interim settlement.

The MPNP' finally resulted in the adoption of the Interim Constitution, formally signed by all members of the MPNF on December 18, 1993, binding them to a new political dispensation based on human rights and the rule of law, to be formally inaugurated after democratic elections scheduled for April 1994.

It is often possible to judge the quality of a negotiations process by the parties and issues excluded from formal talks. For all its imperfections, the MPNP developed into what can be called an "all-in; all-on" process—almost all the parties were "in" and almost every difficult issue was "on" the table. In other words, the MPNP was sufficiently *inclusive* and sufficiently *credible*, a forum in which all the crucial parties had a stake and a place (even if some refused to take their seats at times), and from which no issue was excluded.

The realization and acknowledgment of interdependence, which became such an important driver of the reconciliation process, occurred prior to either side having had to make moral choices about the transition but was perhaps foundational to those choices. As the realization of their de facto interdependence grew, the political "other" was gradually acknowledged as indispensable—as a requirement for, rather than an obstacle to, each side achieving its own political objectives. Gradually it became evident that each side's own self-interests demanded strong and credible negotiating partners.

Building on this, the MPNP was able to capitalize on the space provided by the NPA to produce a framework for political inclusivity and fairness that satisfied all parties involved. In doing so, it understood and acknowledged its own limits. Dealing with the past was left up to the democratic government, in the hope that the confidence and credibility that constitutional democracy brings would place it in a better position to deal with the past. The only aspect of accountability for past violations that the MPNP did determine was that any mechanism chosen by the future government would have to include some form of amnesty, to be administered in the spirit, not of victor's justice or legalized revenge, but of ubuntu, inclusion, and national reconciliation. Ubuntu is discussed in more detail later, but for now it is sufficient to note that it is a cultural ideal, popular throughout Sub-Sahara Africa, that emphasizes social interconnectedness as the most basic reality that shapes both individuals and society.

Conclusion

The "art of strategic peace-building," wrote Lederach and Appleby, is closely related to realizing interdependence and the need for an integrated, comprehensive approach. "We are encouraged," they said, "by the growing realization by powerful actors . . . that smart investment in carefully planned and coordinated peace-building operations is 'in their own interests' given the increasingly interdependent environment."[34]

In my view, and not altogether dissimilar to the well-known philosophy of ubuntu (discussed in more detail in Chapter 8), the acknowledgment that an "interdependent environment" is a feature of deeply divided societies can provide a major impetus to the sustained institutionalization of reconcilia-tion across political transitions—not only to its inception, as discussed in the previous chapter. Building on the realization of the fundamental and compre-hensive interdependence of all of South Africa's communities, major political parties increasingly came to view themselves, too, as mirrors of society, and as fundamentally interdependent in their quest to deliver what they had promised to their respective constituencies. Political enemies thus learned to rely on and trust one another in limited but sufficient ways in order to achieve what was necessary. And when trust broke down at times, as it invariably would, not least after horrific incidences of political violence, it was their awareness of "having no choice" that drove them back to the negotiating table.

But even the most resolute commitment to getting things done eventually loses credibility in the eyes of both participants and onlookers if the process fails to deliver tangible outcomes. South Africa's process delivered early on a series of platforms that helped to concretize reconciliation beyond rhetor-ical commitments, and also helped to shape expectations around what recon-ciliation would eventually be able to deliver. Put differently, it was crucial that the core features, traits, or characteristics of these transitional arrangements foreshadowed, albeit in limited and provisional ways, the changes they were aiming to bring about (such as their increasing inclusivity and fairness), thereby creating confidence that such change was not only possible but was to some de-gree inevitable. In (yet) other words, the organizations and mechanisms that emerged in the name of reconciliation had to take steps to deliver on the promise of justice, both in how they operated and in what they achieved.

Thus, the question of how reconciliation expands, concretizes, and lives on in concrete mechanisms and platforms is inextricably linked to the traits evident in the key arrangements that facilitate the transition. When reconciliation began in South Africa, no one had a clear idea of where it would lead or how it would take shape, beyond a commitment that the new state would be fundamentally more just. And this is where the NPA and the MPNP played crucial roles. Each in their own way made it clear to a skeptical public, and their uncertain leaders, how rec-onciliation as a just form of interdependence could work. I hope I have shown that the NPA and MPNP shared two important traits—the ability to widen polit-ical and civic inclusivity, and to deepen the credibility of reconciliation, insofar as this was linked to delivering on the promise of fairness in the eyes of participants and direct stakeholders (as distinct from those of international observers).

The NPA extended political inclusivity beyond the main parties to include a range of other important role players, some political but other civic, including traditional leaders, religious and cultural leaders, trade unionists, and business leaders. Civic leadership thus contributed to determining the criteria against which genuine objections to unfairness could be differentiated from objections offered in bad faith or with the intention of prolonging violent conflict. Most important among these criteria was the rejection of violence as a legitimate form of political action. Phrased in South African parlance, the work of the NPA marked the point at which both sides turned away from the "violence of apartheid and struggle politics" toward "a politics of reconciliation." Moreover, after the formation of the NPA, neither the apartheid state nor the liberation movement could present themselves as the sole guarantor of reconciliation's inclusivity and credibility, as this was firmly underwritten by an impressively cross-sectional (though not universal) civic engagement. The MPNP maintained this political inclusivity, and eventually produced an agreement on how to extend this inclusivity to the whole of society in the form of the Interim Constitution, democratic elections, political representation, and a nascent amnesty regime.[35]

Closely related to the widening of *inclusivity* was the deepening of a sense of the *credible fairness* of the transition process. This sense also emerged through the various reconciliation platforms. Thus, in a deeply divided and contested environment rife with political violence, mistrust, and parallel "peace processes" initiated by the NP and the ANC, the NPA provided the first nonpartisan civic platform on which political leaders could agree to renounce violence. This imbued the NPA process with a sense of fairness that neither a regime-sponsored nor an ANC-driven process would have been able to rival. Then, the MPNP developed protocols and processes that involved a clear sense of fairness in terms of how issues were dealt with, and through the TEC, produced the first real power-sharing platform in South African history. This power-sharing deepened the sense of credible fairness, as did various signals exchanged between the NP and ANC that they were serious about dealing with political violence, but that they also agreed that the time for addressing the full scope of past violations had not yet arrived. That would have to wait for the stability only a democratic government could bring.

Seeing these efforts as part of a larger, more comprehensive political transition, with the promise of deepening credibility and widening inclusivity over time, was absolutely critical in finding the right balance between inclusivity and fairness at key moments during the transition. If there had been no efforts to get at the truth behind political violence at this point, for example, a truth commission later on may have had very little to go by, and perhaps not enough political support. It may have felt even more like an imposition foreign to the spirit of the negotiations. As it happened, the ANC's call for a truth commission sometime down the line, together with initiatives such as the Goldstone Commission, prepared crucial ground for an eventual TRC. If, on the other hand, inclusivity would have been compromised by a hard-line prosecutorial approach during the negotiation period, South Africa may quite possibly never have seen democracy. It may well have scuppered inclusivity and undermined constitutional negotiations to the point of a resumption of hostility. In my view, this nuanced approach seeking to balance inclusivity and credible fairness, so often lacking in other contexts, helped to ensure that South Africa's transition remained broadly credible while retaining all the major role players on board.

My primary aim in recalling this history is to counter the revisionism inherent in the ways in which the South African example continues to be invoked today as foundational to transitional justice and reconciliation discourse. Such revisionism occurs when the South African reconciliation process is romanticized as one of political forgiveness shown by key leaders such as Mandela and Tutu or by the TRC, at the expense of acknowledging the far more nuanced and painstaking process of building inclusivity and credibility that they undertook in a context of abiding mistrust and compromise. It occurs, too, when liberal critiques of South Africa's process equate its outcomes with impunity for perpetrators, or when social justice critiques accuse the authorities of selling out the poor under guise of granting political rights to all. These powerful critiques and commentaries, while not without value, do not do justice to the careful and determined ways in which reconciliation was expanded beyond an elite pact and into a national movement for durable and radical change, and which made it possible for political leaders to credibly promise political and socioeconomic inclusion to all citizens. Unfortunately, whereas the Constitution guaranteed and has delivered on the former, it could not do so on the latter, and South Africa remains a deeply divided society caught within a painfully incomplete reconciliation process.

3

Dealing with a Violent Past

The negotiations culminated in free, fair, and largely peaceful elections in April 1994. The constitutional assembly, made up of the newly elected national assembly together with the senate, immediately set about drafting a final constitution. For all their insistence on moving ahead and looking to a shared future, the South African political leaders understood that their country's troubled past could not be ignored. Desmond Tutu captured the public mood at the time when he exclaimed, "bygones are never simply bygones. No one has the power to say: 'Bygones be gone!' They never go. They almost always return to haunt us."[1] So, under the auspices of a democratically elected government of national unity, and having secured a national consensus on the way ahead via a widely accepted constitution outlining a shared future, South Africans turned to face their past.[2]

The TRC came about in a context influenced by the NPA and the MPNP but also by the newly formed democratic institutions—notably the Constitutional Court. The TRC placed reconciliation squarely on the new nation's political agenda, making it a topic of conversation in the living rooms of ordinary South Africans, not only in the corridors of power or of civic leadership. Central questions were regarding who should take responsibility for the past, and whether answering this question would help to undo some of the damage caused by apartheid, thus enabling society to move forward more rapidly than if the question remained unaddressed.

An unspoken assumption was that any accounting for the past would have to be public—an event or process that would have an impact on how South Africans spoke and thought about themselves, about the past, about one another, and about how they could learn to live together as equals. Despite this conviction, it was immediately clear that finding an inclusive and credible process to deal with the past was far easier said than done. Significant obstacles were obvious. The fledging social compact that formed the basis of the newfound relative stability and enabled even the *possibility* of engagement with the past remained an exceptionally delicate balancing act between white insecurity and black aspiration. Get that balance wrong, it was felt, and reconciliation's national momentum could be lost overnight. Further, massive evidence gaps existed; the apartheid regime had systematically destroyed as many of the records of its activities as possible before leaving office, thus covering a significant number of tracks.[3]

In addition, the legal system was under siege. Political violence quickly morphed into extraordinarily high levels of criminal violence, earning the new South Africa a new kind of infamy as of one of the world's most violent societies.[4] Tasked with containing the escalating crime figures was a criminal justice system that contained large numbers of security officials and magistrates who only a year or two before had enforced apartheid laws.[5] A further imposing obstacle was the amnesty agreement of November 1993, which promised amnesty for political crimes without going into detail about how that was to be done, was captured in a postscript to the Interim Constitution.

Despite these obstacles, the world's first-ever truth *and reconciliation* commission emerged—an initiative that generated unprecedented international and local interest, both during and after its life. In what follows, I briefly sketch the basic operational history, outcomes, and some of the main arguments about the TRC, but I have tried not to add to the recycled truisms, denunciations, and clichéd praise on the subject. My focus remains, here as before, on discerning those activities of the TRC that can be associated with the broader reconciliation agenda that originated with political leadership in the 1980s, and then was widened and deepened between when Mandela was released and when he was elected South Africa's first democratic president through initiatives like the NPA and the MPNP. So, in what ways did the TRC build on this process, and in which ways did it deviate from it? First, the focus falls on claims by various influential observers (mainly from abroad) who argued that that the TRC was neither inclusive nor credible (that it actually compromised reconciliation in possibly disastrous ways). Then, I attempt to show that, in fact, the TRC successfully deepened reconciliation's credibility and widened its inclusivity.

Brief Background

Operationally, it was not long after Mandela took office in May 1994—a time rife with challenges and obstacles—that civil society and government officials began to prioritize discussions about how to deal with the past. As explained earlier, thinking about a possible TRC had begun long before this. Building on those initial thoughts, formal consultations led by the democratic government eventually led to the passage of the National Unity and Reconciliation Act in 1995, which sought to restore the "human and civil dignity" of victims of gross human rights violations committed in the course of political violence during the apartheid era. The act tasked the TRC with establishing "as complete a picture as possible of the nature, causes and extent of violations of human rights committed." This included determining "the fate or whereabouts of the victims of such violations"; affording victims "an opportunity to relate the violations they suffered"; taking "measures aimed at the granting of reparation" for those who suffered from these violations; and granting amnesty to perpetrators who revealed the full extent of their wrongdoing, could prove a political motive, and show that their deeds were proportional to the political aim of the crimes in question.[6] Finally, the TRC had to deliver a report detailing its work and findings to the new president, Nelson Mandela.

Three separate processes were meant to run in parallel, namely: human rights violation hearings, amnesty hearings, and a report-writing process, with the last culminating in a series of recommendations for reparations, reform, and redress.[7] Mandela appointed the charismatic Nobel laureate Desmond Tutu as chairperson, along with sixteen other commissioners from a cross section of society after a public recruitment process.[8] The commissioners were spread across the three committees, and several support staff were recruited additionally, including a highly experienced research unit that was expected to produce the final report and a robust investigation unit that had to verify information gathered during the hearings as well as the written statements submitted to the commission.

The Human Rights Violations Committee conducted public hearings across South Africa over a period of eighteen months. Proceedings were broadcast on public radio and television, and conducted in all of South Africa's eleven official languages. The TRC received statements from 21,290 individuals, of whom more than 19,050 were found to be victims of gross violations of human rights. A further 2,975 victims were identified via testimonies delivered during the amnesty process. Of the victims identified, approximately 2,000 were given an opportunity to make statements at public hearings. Importantly, the TRC's final report acknowledges that hundreds, possibly thousands, of victims were unable to access the TRC for a variety of reasons, including their inability to access hearings from remote rural villages and their being subjected to political pressure; the IFP, for example, discouraged its members from participating in the TRC.[9]

The Amnesty Committee gave the perpetrators of political violence an opportunity to apply for amnesty. The criteria for amnesty, such as whether the crime was politically motivated and disclosure was complete, ensured that political "criminals" could walk free, but simply applying for amnesty did not guarantee that it would be granted.[10] Of the 7,116 amnesty applications, 1,167 were successful and 5,644 were rejected.[11] The essence of this moral trade-off

demanded that unsuccessful applicants and perpetrators who failed to participate would be prosecuted. Failure to follow through on this policy would not
only play into the hands of those who opposed the TRC process, but would
leave the process dangerously unfinished in the eyes of victims. To avoid this
scenario, the TRC's *Final Report* called for perpetrators who did not comply
with the TRC process to be prosecuted. Accordingly, the TRC handed over 300
names to the National Prosecution Authority, but this body subsequently chose
not to pursue these prosecutions.[12]

In the first five volumes of the *TRC Report*, published in 1998, the Reparation
and Rehabilitation Committee proposed that the new government implement
a broad-ranging reparations policy. Government's unconscionably long delays
in responding to these recommendations, aspects of which have still not been
attended to by 2018, have led to widespread disappointment and have undone
some of work done by the TRC with victims and victim communities.

The TRC as neither Inclusive nor Credible: A Liberal Critique

Soon after its inception, the first analyses of the TRC's work began to emerge,
with many seeking to make sense of this unique experiment in post-conflict reconciliation. Heated debates ensued, with TRC supporters and critics squaring
off on a range of issues, including its inclusivity and credibility.

Richard Wilson, perhaps before anyone else, floated the idea that South
Africa's politics of truth and reconciliation was an elite and ultimately misguided
project to manufacture legitimacy for the post-apartheid state. The project, he
claimed, had failed, and he argued that it was misguided to attach human rights
to "a religious notion of reconciliation-forgiveness, a regrettable amnesty law
and an elite project of nation-building."[13] But Wilson went further, stating that
amnesty-as-ubuntu also ran dead against the values and sensibilities of ordinary
South Africans. If evidence he gathered during field studies of vigilante justice
in Sharpeville (a township south of Johannesburg) was to be believed, black
South Africans preferred retributive justice as means of addressing crime. At
the time in which Wilson gathered his evidence, vigilante justice in townships
was indeed closely associated with "kangaroo courts," a phenomenon that
originated in areas where the apartheid regime had failed to provide credible
law enforcement. For Wilson, the TRC was therefore a coercive process that
diminished the agency of victims and depleted their freedom, forcing them to
accept forgiveness and reconciliation. It is morally objectionable, wrote David
Crocker, another analyst who agreed with Wilson, to "force people to agree
about the past."[14]

For liberals, especially, the democratic deficit in the TRC was most vividly evident in the "top-down" manner in which restorative justice appeared to have been chosen as the preferred mode of justice—ostensibly to placate the apartheid security establishment. Along these lines, Amy Gutmann and Dennis Thompson claimed that a post-apartheid state that forgave apartheid crimes could not credibly claim to be committed to the most basic democratic principles, which include treating all adults as free and equal citizens. Timothy Garton-Ash famously wrote that, taken to extremes, the reconciliation of all with all would be a deeply illiberal idea.[15] Gutmann and Thompson agreed: reconciliation would indeed be illiberal if it expected an entire society to subscribe to a single comprehensive moral perspective. These critical analyses derive primarily from a principled commitment to various variations of political liberalism.

Other observers and practitioners within the international justice system criticized the TRC retrospectively along similar lines, especially after the signing and ratification of the Rome Statute by scores of countries (including thirty-three African states) in early 1998 just as the commission was entering the final phase of its work. A historic achievement, the Rome Statute proclaimed that there shall be no impunity for serious international crimes, and established the International Criminal Court (ICC) to prosecute such cases. The approach taken to prosecutions by signatories to the Rome Statute further underlined the suspicion that the TRC's approach to amnesty (which was equated with impunity) failed to meet basic standards of justice.[16]

Desmond Tutu, whose irrepressible persona had a massive influence on how the TRC shaped its mission, also came in for a fair amount of criticism. For Gutmann and Thompson, the problem was that many victims might not have shared Tutu's beliefs or value system. Even those who professed to be Christians, these commentators observed, may have had different views about the appropriateness of forgiveness in such situations.[17] From a slightly different angle, Michael Ignatieff took Tutu to task for equating nations with individuals when concluding that nations can be healed by arriving at "the truth."[18] It was alleged that Tutu not only lacked democratic credentials, but was also misguided in promising "closure" following "healing" after apartheid. Crocker agreed, arguing that "ultimately reconciliation trades on empty promises contained in a veil of ambiguity with no means or plans to make good on these promises."[19]

In the liberal view, it seems that reconciliation should exclude the seeking of social harmony.[20] Instead of delivering on its promise of closure, Wilson detects enough evidence "in the crime statistics and wild justice in places like Sharpeville" to assert that criminality has been exacerbated by the TRC's inability to deliver "full accountability for human rights offenders."[21] For these commentators, when political leaders fail to observe strict limits between public affairs and private sentiments, as Tutu is alleged to have done, a democratic deficit and renewed injustice arises. South Africa, for these analysts, illustrates perfectly how the dangers of charismatic leadership outweigh its benefits.

Against this background, the standard liberal critique of the TRC can be summarized as that the TRC was neither inclusive nor credibly fair. For liberals, the TRC was fundamentally *unjust* on the one hand in offering amnesty for un-pardonable crimes, and justifying this by moralistic references to restorative jus-tice. It was furthermore *illiberal* in preaching ubuntu and political forgiveness as universal forms of public morality, and it was finally also *irresponsibly utopian* in promising national healing.[22] For such critics, the TRC represents a setback for South Africa's reconciliation process since it undermined human rights and the rule of law, and raised unrealistic expectations. This, they argue, led to the regrettable fact that the TRC did not deepen the inclusivity or credibility of South Africa's efforts to reconcile after apartheid, but instead achieved some-thing close to its opposite. This appears to place the TRC in sharp contrast to my earlier observation that preceding reconciliation-related institutions such as the MPNP and the NPA were both sufficiently inclusive and fair. In what follows, I engage these angles of critique to substantiate my position that, like the NPA and MPNP before it, the TRC in fact succeeded in significantly broadening the inclusivity *and* deepening the credibility of South Africa's reconciliation process, thus extending the achievements of the two preceding reconciliation initiatives to new levels.[23] It is important to note, however, that my counterarguments do *not* assume a flawless commission. The TRC clearly made errors, particularly when it took impulsive decisions, and when it trusted the new government to implement its recommendations. Yet the TRC contributed positively to making reconciliation more inclusive and credible in South Africa, in ways that some liberal critics do not yet seem to appreciate fully.

The Negotiated Amnesty: Security-Sector Blackmail or Political Dexterity?

An account of how the amnesty provision in the TRC Act came about offers important clues about how the politics of reconciliation began to concretize through a growing but carefully managed focus on transitional justice.

Academic and former national-intelligence operative Willie Esterhuyse recalls that ANC leader and future president Thabo Mbeki raised the issue of amnesty directly with him as early as 1988. "It will have to be top of the agenda for dialogue with the South African government," Mbeki reportedly said then already, and he apparently repeated the point on several occasions thereafter.[24] In 1990, when the ANC entered into formal negotiations with the government, the release of political prisoners and the lifting of restrictions to enable liberation movement fighters to return home topped their list of demands. But towards the final stretch, when an end to the negotiations was in sight, and the Interim Constitution was about to be signed, the details of precisely how past human rights abuses would be dealt with, remained shrouded in vagueness.

The story goes that, just before the looming deadline for the Interim Constitution in November 1993, a postscript was hastily drawn up by a small ANC/NP committee to determine how past violations would be dealt with. While the last-minute inclusion of the amnesty clause invokes romantic images of smoky back rooms and eleventh-hour whiskey-fueled deals,[25] the politics of this clause has motivated several serious studies,[26] some of which are still underway.[27]

The wording of the eventual agreement reflected much the same spirit as the ANC's formal response to the Motsuenyane Commission's report. Recognizing "the need for understanding but not for vengeance, a need for reparation but not for retaliation, a need for ubuntu but not for victimisation" and, "in order to advance such reconciliation and reconstruction," the postscript to the Interim Constitution prescribed that amnesty would be granted in respect of acts, omissions, and offences associated with political objectives and committed in "the court of the conflicts of the past."[28] To this end, it was agreed that the democratically elected parliament would determine the relevant time period, as well as the "mechanisms, criteria and procedures, including tribunals if any, through which such amnesty shall be dealt with at any time after the law has been passed." The postscript concluded that with "this Constitution and these commitments we, the people of South Africa, open a new chapter in the history of our country."[29]

Some critics of the TRC alleged that this amnesty clause came about as a result of the apartheid security sector's blackmailing of ANC politicians. The suspicion is that some of the most powerful individuals in South Africa—those in charge of the apartheid army, police, and security agencies—were willing to ensure a free and safe election, and to then hand over power, in exchange for immunity from any criminal prosecutions that might have arisen from their past actions.

A story told by Mac Maharaj, a senior ANC leader who played an important role in drafting the amnesty clause, seems to bear this out. Maharaj recalls receiving a telephone call late one night about a month before the 1994 elections. The person on the line was Mo Shaik, a comrade from the ANC's security division whom he knew and trusted. Shaik, who later became South Africa's intelligence chief, asked Maharaj to meet him on a deserted street in downtown Pretoria sometime after midnight. Maharaj agreed, and upon arrival was ushered by Shaik up a fire escape and into a back room of a derelict building where a selection of the apartheid regime's top security chiefs was waiting for them. After a

cordial exchange of greetings, Maharaj and Shaik sat down. Among the security
chiefs Maharaj recognized two men who had tortured him severely when he was
in detention. One by one, the chiefs produced crude homemade weapons from
their briefcases: explosives, a booby-trapped videotape, a handmade shotgun,
a laser-guided pistol, and so on. "Why are you showing this to me?" Maharaj
asked. Then one of the generals spoke:

> Mr Maharaj, we understand you are a close confidante to Mr Mandela.
> Please tell him that we have confiscated these weapons from the right
> wing, but do not worry. We will act so as to ensure that there are
> peaceful elections next month.[30]

Maharaj remembers being on the verge of asking what they expected in return,
what the quid pro quo would be, but he refrained from doing so. Instead he po-
litely excused himself from the meeting and left. One Sunday morning about
eighteen months later, he remembers reading in a news report that one Captain
Roelf Venter, who was one of the men who had tortured him and had been present that evening in the secret mid-night hour meeting with the outgoing security chiefs in downtown Pretoria, was applying for amnesty through the TRC. As
he put the paper down, he reflected that the unspoken quid pro quo of meeting
with the security chiefs must have been that, post-transition, the books on the
past would be closed.[31]

While this reality must have played some role, analysts have increasingly
questioned whether security-sector blackmail was the *only* or even the *main*
reason for the inclusion of the amnesty clause in the TRC legislation. South
African political scientist Annette Seegers argues that, for most of the period of
the MPNP, amnesty was seen as relatively unimportant.[32] This was, in part, because of the view that "the basics" of the agreement had already been hammered
out behind closed doors in September 1992, during the Meyer-Ramaphosa-
initiated talks that led to the Record of Understanding, when the ANC and
the government had agreed to release all political prisoners unconditionally.[33]
Furthermore, Seegers argues that some agents of the apartheid state with records
of human rights violations fell out with their cohorts and entered into plea
bargains with the new state, while "other covert operators, arguably the worst of
the perpetrators, believed either that amnesty was irrelevant because they had
erased their tracks or taken refuge in a witness protection programme."[34]

By contrast, Maharaj's account presents amnesty as the result of a bitter compromise with a dangerous enemy, and liberal critics of the TRC seem to have
accepted this perspective—rather than seeing amnesty as a source of political
agreement between the NP and the ANC. They, therefore, tend to view the
TRC process as the moralistic sugar coating on an unpalatable compromise,

a Faustian pact that led to victims of gross human rights violations having their rights derogated once more and then being expected to forgive their perpetrators. However, if Seegers's argument holds, the amnesty clause in the Interim Constitution was perhaps a compromise as far as retributive justice is concerned, but was decidedly not the result of the blackmailing of ANC politicians by apartheid operatives. In fact, it may have been, at least partly, a strategic political agreement that developed gradually across party lines even before formal talks began. After all, both the ANC and the NP had strong vested interests in this, with the exception, initially and ironically, of De Klerk and his justice minister, Kobie Coetsee, who seem not to have believed that the rot in their own ranks was as widespread as it was. They claimed to have discovered otherwise as late as 1992, as a result of the Goldstone Commission's revelations, and they then signed the Record of Understanding, which set out the basic position on amnesty and was later reiterated in the Interim Constitution.

Along similar lines, former TRC investigator Piers Pigou comments that the ANC's participation in the amnesty process can hardly be described as "principally reticent" or "politically magnanimous."[35] After all, as Seegers pointed out too, several high-level ANC leaders needed amnesty. In this light, Maharaj's story can be read differently. Perhaps the securocrats who met Maharaj were less concerned about creating a theatrical performance of a purported blackmail "deal," and were in fact sending Mandela a reminder based on an agreement long since reached—issuing a signal to confirm that both sides still "understood one another."

Framed more positively, both parties might have chosen to attain stability first, and deal with accountability later, under the guidance of a democratic government. If this was the case, amnesty was a price they were prepared, and in fact perhaps needed, to pay. To the degree that this is correct, or at least partially correct, liberal critics will have to amend their views. If the process was less a crude form of blackmail of one party by another, and more an example of political dexterity across enemy lines, the amnesty clause would have been an important component of the larger political settlement that enabled the country to move decisively toward democracy, and in the longer run, to a fuller, more inclusive justice for all.

A Second Amnesty Process: Civics Push for More Inclusion and Fairness

South Africa's amnesty process was even more complex in ways that, if ignored, would lead to further important misunderstandings.

A subsequent process of public consultation largely distinct from the constitutional negotiations which produced the Interim Constitution, also greatly influenced the TRC's amnesty regime. These two processes, the negotiations and the subsequent public consultations, produced two different kinds of outcomes each containing somewhat different conceptions of amnesty. Whereas the agreement that formed part of the Interim Constitution occurred as a result of sensitive, behind-the-scenes consensus building (as illustrated by the Maharaj narrative), the other was the result of a public process of democratic deliberation and engagement and was made possible only once the country had made it safely through the first democratic elections. Once the newly elected government of national unity was in firm control, and security-sector reform had begun in earnest, did civil society enter the fray to debate how to handle the thorny issue of the past in light of both the amnesty clause in the Interim Constitution and the desperate need to afford victims meaningful recognition and redress.

Thus, in the period between the signing of the Interim Constitution in 1993 and the inauguration of the TRC in 1996, a second amnesty agreement emerged, largely from within the newly constituted democratic parliament. The story of its evolution, almost entirely ignored in the main sources of liberal critique on the TRC, helps to explain why it was hoped that amnesty would begin to function as a limited but significant aspect of a larger process of accounting for the crimes of the past. Those who pushed strongly for the establishment of this second amnesty agreement included civil society groups inside the country, the human rights community internationally, and, crucially, progressive thinkers within the ANC. Once again, like during the period of the NPA, the civic presence within South Africa's reconciliation process would prove the decisive factor.

In 1992, a year before the ANC first called for the establishment of the TRC, Kader Asmal, a law professor and key ANC member, fleshed out a proposal for a truth commission in his inaugural lecture at the University of the Western Cape.[36] Asmal had earlier worked on preparing a legal case against apartheid crimes in case of a possible UN tribunal. However, with the political transition in progress, Asmal's thinking began to shift. He was aware, for example, that Alex Boraine, a Methodist minister who had played a leading role in the struggle against apartheid, had chaired an international conference on alternative ways to deal with South Africa's past, and in 1994, Asmal and Albie Sachs, another leading ANC lawyer, approached Boraine and asked him to write to the new government outlining his proposals for a truth commission.[37] Boraine then wrote to Mandela, Mbeki, and Dullah Omar, the newly appointed justice minister, briefing them about the conference, and making a set of proposals about how the new government could implement the ANC's call for a truth commission. Omar responded that amnesty ought not to be allowed to dominate ways of dealing with the past but that "victims, reparations and truth" ought to be the focus.[38] And so began the movement away from the notion of amnesty as a kind of blanket impunity that informed the first agreement contained in the postscript to the Interim Constitution.[39]

On May 27, 1994, a month after the ANC had been elected into power, Dullah Omar addressed the new parliament about the government's decision to set up a truth and reconciliation commission to enable South Africa to come to terms with its past:

> We cannot forgive on behalf of victims, nor do we have the moral right to do so. It is the victims themselves who must speak. Their voices need to be heard. The fundamental issue for all South Africans is therefore to come to terms with our past on the only moral basis possible, namely that the truth be told and that the truth be acknowledged.[40]

Omar's poetic, profoundly moving speech stressed that the framework for amnesty would be national unity and reconciliation, as indeed the Interim Constitution had determined, but that the emphasis would be primarily on the needs and interests of victims, not perpetrators. Despite agreeing with the Interim Constitution on national unity as framework for amnesty, this new conception constituted a material shift away from the ways in which the connections between amnesty, national unity, and reconciliation had previously been understood.

Nearing the end of the grueling four-year negotiation process in November 1993, reconciliation meant for key protagonists within the negotiations a fresh start within a fundamentally futuristic orientation, and that implied closing the books on the past once and for all. Only a few months later, however, with the newly elected government firmly established, the conversation broadened to include civil society and human rights groups. In this conversation, reconciliation's meaning, as it functioned during the negotiations, began to develop to include specific civic groups and their interests as opposed to protecting firstly the interest of the political elite who had brokered the settlement. More specifically, those citizens who had suffered gross human rights violations began to receive more sustained focus. An agenda thus emerged that sought to deal with the past by seeking to restore the dignity of those who suffered most, but without dishonouring the agreement that made democracy possible or excluding those who had been responsible for inflicting that suffering, and their kith and kin, from participating in the new society. For many of the politicians who took part in the MPNP, amnesty implied excusing those who were guilty of acts, omissions, and offenses committed in the course of the conflicts of the past. Essentially their plea was for a blanket amnesty. For civil society and more principled political leaders in the new government, impunity was unacceptable, principally because of what this would do to the dignity of victims, but also because it would violate important Constitutional principles. And so a certain tension developed within the South African reconciliation process, a tension that exists to this day, between those more concerned with individual human rights and those who favored the importance of political settlement.

Given that democracy was now in play, however, the new process was able to give voice to ordinary citizens in ways that had been inconceivable before, enabling this tension to emerge more publicly and more honestly. This shift, towards listening to victims, brought the aspect of accountability to the foreground, because for each victim there would presumably be one or more perpetrators, and perhaps even a whole chain of command.

The suggestion of a TRC, initially provoked a strong reaction from De Klerk, who declared that "the TRC could undermine the goodwill and sense of national unity that has begun to take root since Mandela's inauguration."[41] Constand Viljoen, the former army chief, warned that the TRC would turn into a witch-hunt against Afrikaners.[42]

Nevertheless, after the announcement by the government, and when the early parliamentary debates on the topic had been completed, a draft bill was circulated countrywide. In a systematic attempt to get the citizenry involved beyond the confines of parliament, NGOs and other civic bodies were invited to seminars and workshops to elicit input from specific professional groupings on various technical aspects of the bill. Hundreds of thousands of booklets presenting the basic ideas behind the bill were then distributed in six languages throughout the country, and radio programs were used to get South Africans debating the topic.[43] The Parliamentary Portfolio Committee on Justice duly received submissions from numerous human rights organizations and other interested parties, and publicly debated the issues. Further submissions were called for from institutions, organizations, or individuals who were either deemed to be able to make a special contribution or felt the need to do so, including faith-based organizations, Amnesty International, and many others.[44]

The TRC Bill, formally titled the Promotion of National Unity and Reconciliation Bill, was published in November 1994. Introducing the bill to parliament for debate on May 17, 1995, Omar noted that

> Merely granting amnesty to perpetrators without addressing our international obligations, dealing with wounds of the past and our duty to victims will undermine the process of reconciliation. It is necessary therefore, to deal with South Africa's past, including the question of amnesty, on a morally acceptable basis.[45]

The longest debate yet in the new democratic parliament followed Omar's submission, but eventually virtually all parties represented in Parliament voted on the bill. The IFP abstained, and the right-wing Afrikaner party, the Freedom Front, voted against because the cutoff date for crimes to be considered had not been brought forward (mainly to accommodate rightwing violence during the election time) as they had requested.[46] All other parties voted in favor, and the Promotion of National Unity and Reconciliation Act (No. 34 of 1995) was signed into law on July 19, 1995. And so a second amnesty agreement, this time significantly more inclusively debated than the first, took effect. On the one hand, the act pushed for some form of accountability for past political crimes, thus deepening the credibility of the transition, while on the other hand, it respected the agreed-upon guarantee of amnesty for the sake of future coexistence and inclusivity.

With the law in place, a public selection process ensued, run by a specifically appointed committee consisting of parliamentarians from across the political spectrum. In December 1995, the first commissioners were appointed. They began work almost immediately, and the TRC's first victim hearings commenced on April 16, 1996, in East London, in the Eastern Cape, a province that had endured and fought apartheid oppression for decades.

Drawing strongly on the so-called Norgaard Principles,[47] the TRC Act eventually settled on a form of amnesty that depended on the condition that applicants made full disclosure, established political motive and demonstrated proportionality of the crime to the stated political objective.[48] The conditionality of the South African amnesty provisions meant that no blanket amnesties were granted. If apartheid-era political criminals could convince the TRC that they had made a full disclosure of all their actions, had been driven by bona fide political motives shared by the political organization of which they were proven members, and that the crime was in proportion to their stated political aims, they would receive amnesty. Alex Boraine, who served as deputy chair of the TRC, argued therefore that "the South African decision not to prosecute does not in any respect put it in breach of international law."[49]

Neil Kritz, one of the key thinkers in the transitional-justice debate, described South Africa's conditional amnesty as profoundly distinct from earlier amnesties in Latin America and elsewhere, noting that

> Overall, the amnesty programme was successful in establishing individual accountability and in facilitating the construction of a far more complete record and analysis of the patterns and institutions of abuse under apartheid than would have been possible without these individual confessions.[50]

Kritz reminds us, though, that the TRC process would in all likelihood not have been able to generate so many amnesty applications if the threat of prosecution had not been maintained against those who chose to remain outside the process. Clearly both amnesties, the one that emerged from the political negotiations, and the one that emerged from the Parliamentary process, were crucial in cementing the shift from apartheid to democracy.

There appears therefore some case to be made for amnesty to be used, as long as it can be shown to be part of an effort to curtail the kinds of gross impunity typically associated with civil war and political oppression whilst helping to smooth the way to a fairer and more inclusive national dispensation. Exactly where this balance ought to be struck remains deeply context-specific. If amnesties are too easily obtained, unconditional or collective, they can amount to impunity and worsen a situation in profound ways. If, on the other hand, amnesties are tied to clear conditions designed to benefit victims—such that the burden of proof rests on the perpetrator not on the victim, and that this proof has to be provided *individually*—amnesties might help to provide a bridge between a divided past and a more humane future, as turned out to be the case in South Africa.

The eventual TRC policy on amnesty, once announced, enjoyed widespread support among South Africans, even after the TRC had completed its formal hearings, although some whites specifically remained skeptical. In a public opinion survey conducted in 2001, 72 percent of black South Africans approved of amnesty being given to those who committed atrocities in the struggle, and 39 percent of white South Africans supported this notion.[51] These findings were corroborated in a study by David Backer, who interviewed victims in 2003 and again in 2008, producing a result, "contrary to intuition," that a majority of respondents (57.5%) were in favor of amnesty. Backer noted that analogous surveys he conducted in Ghana, Nigeria, Liberia, and Sierra Leone produced similar results. His results also show, however, that approval of amnesty declined quite dramatically in South Africa between 2003 and 2008. According to Backer, this shift was due mainly to the inaction of the government in response to the TRC's recommendations.[52] However, Piers Pigou pointed out that victims' needs and desires also evolved:

> for most, as we saw at the TRC, "truth" and acknowledgement were primary objectives. Amnesty, without doubt, shed important light on a number of cases in a very public and symbolic way. But in the bigger picture it dealt with only a handful of cases. Most victims were left with the possibility and sometimes the promise of further investigation. This was simply dropped by government, a situation that fed into [as Backer points out] growing unhappiness with the amnesty process. In South Africa, we are faced with the rather unpleasant reality of a de facto general amnesty ... a reneging on the second settlement and a de facto return to the first.[53]

I return to this comment later. For now it is important to note that the measure of inclusivity achieved by the second amnesty process, notably during the debates about the TRC mandate, added to its credibility and to the sense of fairness that undoubtedly made the reconciliation process more sustainable than if it had included a blanket amnesty and been administered solely by politicians, with no public participation, scrutiny, or debate.

Clearly, the process that led to the adoption of the National Unity and Reconciliation Act was *inclusive* in significant ways, and it pushed back against the idea of impunity associated with a general or blanket amnesty, as some interpreted the Interim Constitution's amnesty provision to determine. Of course, as things turned out, the process had weaknesses, and citizens ought to have been encouraged to get more involved, but at the time it did represent a largely successful attempt to deepen the credibility and inclusivity of the amnesty component inherent in the South African reconciliation process.

An Inclusive TRC? A Passionate Bishop and His Flock

Another issue that led to accusations of heavy-handed illiberal moral overreach relates to the role of Desmond Tutu and his pleas for forgiveness to victims who appeared before the TRC. Richard Wilson, for example, asserted that "reconciliation was the Trojan horse used to smuggle an unpleasant aspect of the past (that is, impunity) into the present political order, to transform political compromises into transcendental moral principles." For Wilson, talk of reconciliation "structures a field of discourse to render commonsensical and acceptable the abjuring of legal retribution against past offenders."[54] He quoted Tutu as saying that "forgiveness will follow confession and healing will happen, and so contribute to national unity and reconciliation,"[55] and concluded that the TRC ascribed to a highly individualized (therefore presumably unjustifiable) notion of reconciliation at the expense of retributive accountability.

I have discussed the issues of impunity and amnesty within the context of the TRC's politico-legal background, and suggest that my arguments invalidate Wilson's observations, at least as far as a wholesale "smuggling of impunity" into the present political order is concerned. Admittedly, the TRC processes were less than perfect, and I return to some of its "design faults" later in this chapter. But the TRC did promote accountability and truth-telling as critical underpinnings of reconciliation, and thus removed impunity from the agenda, at least as far as its own mandate was concerned.

Wilson's argument, however, also concerns Tutu more personally, and specifically his choice of language. To Wilson, the TRC's liberal deficit was most clearly demonstrated by its appropriation of Tutu's use of the notion of ubuntu, with its religio-cultural undertones, as a way of justifying the unjustifiable, including amnesty for those who committed crimes against humanity.

In post-apartheid South Africa, Wilson argued, ubuntu became an "Africanist wrapping used to sell a reconciliatory version of human rights talk to black South Africans."[56]In sharp contrast, journalist and poet Antjie Krog who covered the TRC process believed the process would have been unthinkable without Tutu and the ways in which he used words. "Whatever role others may play, it is Tutu who is the compass. He guides us in several ways, the most important of which is language. It is he who finds the language for what is happening."[57]

So was Tutu's reconciliation-talk a Trojan horse smuggling impunity into a future political order, or a moral compass that guided society, developing a vocabulary when words were all but impossible to find, articulating an interdependent future, and coming to terms with a divided past? In my view, Tutu's actions reflect the latter not the former. Despite Wilson's claims, Tutu almost always advocated forgiveness or ubuntu only after careful consideration of specific situations and of the need for accountability. For example, in his foreword to the TRC's *Final Report*, Tutu commented on the inherent difficulties and contradictions between forgiveness and accountability, noting that

> there are erroneous notions of what reconciliation is all about. Reconciliation is not about being cosy; it is not about pretending that things are other than they were. Reconciliation based on falsehood, not facing reality, is not true reconciliation and will not last.[58]

There is a mischaracterization that underlies much of Wilson's critique: namely, that the TRC was mainly about political forgiveness. Even a cursory reading of the TRC mandate reveals that it was never intended to be a platform for white and black South Africans to express remorse and forgiveness. Nor was it meant, as others may have expected, to humiliate and punish perpetrators. Its credibility relied as much on rejecting "victors" justice as it did on avoiding "cheap forgiveness." In fact, even if restorative-justice principles were inspirational to many via Tutu's use of rhetoric, the TRC processes were not designed to bring perpetrators and victims face-to-face to express remorse or forgiveness. If interpersonal forgiveness did take place, it was almost always a byproduct of a process that deliberately refrained from what the TRC's research director Charles Villa-Vicencio termed "legislating emotions." Indeed, many restorative-justice supporters were disappointed at the lack of tangible examples of interpersonal forgiveness.[59]

As a man of faith, Tutu made no secret of the fact that he acted from deeply held personal beliefs, and his moral credibility made him an ideal candidate to head up the commission.[60] As a pastor, Tutu probably reacted instinctively to try to comfort those who appeared before the commission in distress; more than once, he cried when heart-rending testimony was delivered. His ability to reach out to individual witnesses was powerfully bolstered, not by moral reprimand, exclusion, or intolerance, but by a language of acceptance, embrace, and inclusion. Few South Africans were surprised that Tutu acted in this way. After all, as he pointed out with characteristic humor, "the president knew that I was an archbishop when he appointed me!"[61]

Tutu's occasional exhortations to forgive ought to be understood, therefore, not only as exceptions to the rule but also as motivated by his desire to include and embrace. Arguably, the occasions on which he did exert moral pressure (such as during the hearings involving Winnie Mandela) were few and isolated.[62] More important, Tutu used language that was familiar to the vast majority of South Africans, and intimately so to most of the victims. Tutu used language to articulate complex processes, and to bring to light narratives of deep emotive force that had never been publicly discussed in quite this way in South Africa, or indeed anywhere else. In so doing, Tutu powerfully demonstrated the role that accessible and inclusive language can play in making transitional-justice processes genuinely credible to ordinary citizens.[63]

While international human rights discourses remain indispensable to ensuring fairness across deeply entrenched and unjust power relations, *truth-telling processes need to be rendered familiar in terms that are meaningful to victims and their communities.* This requires reaching out to victims and perpetrators on their own terms. For example, a hearing about victims of sexual assault in Tunisia under the Ben Ali regime, or Aleppo under ISIS rule, would look and sound very different from a meeting with identical aims in Gugulethu, South Africa, or Greensboro, North Carolina.

By using the culturally resonant language of forgiveness and ubuntu, Tutu opened up the human rights discourse to victims from every community and background in South Africa. By the very act that some liberal critics see as exclusionary (that is, using the language of one particular faith and cultural group), the TRC, in fact, *broadened* its inclusivity (and credibility) in the eyes of those who should take priority—the victims. It is therefore possible that, in this instance too, liberal critics got things wrong.

This was, after all, the same vocabulary that had carried, consoled, and guided the struggling masses in their fight against apartheid.[64] At many of the funerals during the 1980s, when murdered activists were laid to rest, thousands of ordinary South Africans would turn up, defiant in the face of police tear gas and rubber bullets. Almost always, Tutu would be there, conducting the service and exhorting mourners to keep believing in their cause of unity and ubuntu. When the same people marched on state institutions, Tutu marched with them. When angry mobs turned on their own, threatening to kill suspected informants, Tutu was often there, rescuing the suspects and bustling them off to safety. When the country's first democratically elected president was inaugurated, Tutu held

Mandela's hand high. It was only natural that he would be there when South Africa turned to face its traumatic past.

It is difficult to argue convincingly therefore, in light of the democratic nature of the second amnesty agreement, and a more nuanced reading of Tutu's role, that the TRC's restorative justice agenda was a wholly undemocratic imposition. Rather, it is more credible to assume that it helped to broaden reconciliation in ways that involved South African citizens more directly than ever before on the issue of political crime, facilitating a broadening of support for reconciliation among ordinary citizens.

A Credible TRC? Restorative and Retributive Justice in the Balance

In addition to questioning its inclusivity and democratic credentials, critics have also expressed doubts about the TRC's credibility in terms of being fair and just. Some analysts see the TRC as an exercise in which accountability and fairness (understood in strictly judicial terms) slipped away, taking the credibility of the entire reconciliation process along with it. Apart from overemphasizing the role of the TRC and largely ignoring the role of the NPA and MPNP, this allegation is based on an unjustifiably narrow understanding of the relationship between restorative and retributive justice, and of the profound way in which both modes of justice were relied upon in rebuilding a democratically inclusive and credibly fair dispensation after apartheid.

As explained earlier, this critique implies that restorative justice is a kind of "second-best" option that does not pass muster against the (supposedly higher) standards of due process as developed in classic liberal jurisprudence. If justice is seen exclusively in these terms, the TRC does seem to come up short, and more so if the TRC is viewed as an experiment in political forgiveness. But this reading of the TRC bases a questionable conclusion on an equally questionable assumption. Whether liberal notions of justice are inherently superior to other systems of justice, and whether the TRC was in fact a classic restorative-justice exercise in political forgiveness, are both questions fairly easily debunked. These twin errors, the one compounding the other, render the core of the liberal critique inaccurate and misleading.

In my view, the TRC was not only a credibly fair exercise in itself, but also advanced the fairness and credibility of the *larger* reconciliation process by helping to build conditions for the rule of law in a context where the rule of law itself had been thoroughly discredited and was struggling to reassert itself (and arguably continues to struggle even today). Casting aside the metaphorical (and I suspect unanswerable) question of whether retributive or restorative justice is superior, it is important to note that the TRC exercise was a careful and pragmatic combination of *both* forms of justice, and that the combination worked so that both forms enhanced one another. For this reason, I believe that the TRC (initially at least) contributed to legitimizing the rule of law rather undermining it, as many have claimed.

The TRC was conceived and designed in a manner that enabled restorative and retributive justice processes to operate interdependently. And with its emphasis on truth-telling, institutional introspection, reparations, and so on, the TRC was *crucially* dependent on the law courts in at least four distinct ways: for administration, for the adjudication of internal disagreements within the TRC, to strengthen the accountability of perpetrators, and to provide a constitutional mandate for truth-telling as justice. I take each of these areas in turn to illustrate that the TRC depended as much on retributive justice as it did on restorative justice—that the experiment was therefore never intended to designate the moral superiority of one mode of justice over another (a misunderstanding which got the liberals up in arms) but much rather as a wise combination of the strengths of both forms of justice—institutionalized in a mechanism tailor-made for what South Africa faced at the end of apartheid.

The Administration of Justice

The interdependence of the two modes of justice was made plain in the composition of the TRC's Amnesty Committee, which was made up of three judges and two commissioners.[65] Initially, judges were included largely at the insistence of the NP, who did not fully trust the impartiality of the TRC commissioners. Later, the presence of judges in the commission was seen as helping ensure that amnesty decisions were more consistent and legally sound. However, the justices also created a number of complications. Alex Boraine recalls that the Amnesty Committee seemed to lack urgency and operated far too slowly. It eventually remained operational for five years after the official two-year period of the commission's life had expired in 1998. This not only had a negative impact on the amnesty regime and on perceptions of its fairness to those most directly affected, but crucially also delayed the payment of reparations, which had a significantly negative impact on the victim-centered approach that initially won the commission so much admiration.

Adjudicating Internal Disputes

The courts played an important, albeit limited, background role as arbiter, primarily of contested amnesty decisions. In one such intervention, the TRC was compelled by the courts to issue so-called Section 30 notes to perpetrators who were going to be named by victims in the TRC's Victim Hearings to make the process fairer to the perpetrators. Piers Pigou recalls that this had massive logistical and resource implications for the TRC's work.

In another instance, the TRC took its own Amnesty Committee to court, and won. This was after the ANC leadership applied for amnesty en masse, to demonstrate solidarity with their foot soldiers, and astonishingly were granted amnesty by the Amnesty Committee, who decided to use their prerogative as a semi-independent committee of the TRC. In this case, despite the presence of judges, the ruling clearly flouted the TRC's mandate, which, based on its commitment to establishing some form of individual accountability (as opposed to potentially rendering an entire ethnic or political group guilty or innocent) could offer individualized amnesty *only*. The Amnesty Committee's decision to grant amnesty to the ANC leadership forced Tutu to contest his own committee's decision in court—this time opting for a more "retributive justice" stance than what could arguably be described as a "restorative justice" compromise assumed in the ANC application.

But Tutu would have none of it. The TRC won the case and the decision was set aside.[66] In effect, the justices in the Amnesty Committee were overruled by their colleagues in the courts for being too lenient on the amnesty provisions. Eventually, quite a few more amnesty cases landed in court, most notably those associated with the IFP. These cases dragged on well beyond the official life of the TRC. In retrospect, it is hard to imagine how the TRC would have operated without such judicial arbitration.

Strengthening Perpetrator Accountability

Earlier, I noted that the TRC needed the courts to provide a credible threat of prosecution as a means of convincing perpetrators to apply for amnesty and account for what they had done. According to Kritz, the TRC would never have received the more than seven thousand applications for amnesty that it did, had it not been for what was believed, at least initially, to be a credible threat of prosecution.[67] Without the "stick" of retributive justice, the "carrot" of restorative justice would not have been pursued.[68]

However, an important caveat applies to the "successful" collaboration between courts and the TRC. When scrutinizing the records, it is clear that very few amnesty applications came from top politicians or army generals in the apartheid state. This may have been related to the fact that South Africa's criminal justice system was then still largely untransformed (apart from the newly established Constitutional Court), and so a number of those individuals might well have retained some influence over judicial officials. This meant that, in terms of bringing high-profile cases to trial, the courts did not act as effectively in support of the TRC as they might have done had they been less severely compromised during the apartheid years.

This lackluster support for the TRC by the courts became apparent in certain famous cases.[69] For example, the cases of both former defense minister Magnus Malan, and the former head of the country's secret chemical and biological warfare program Dr. Wouter Basson, failed to produce convictions.[70] To see individuals like Malan and Basson simply walk away strengthened the perception that the law was being manipulated, and thus undermined the quest for credible reconciliation. Such cases also strengthened the tendency for other senior apartheid officials to stay away from the TRC and bide their time, hoping that criminal charges would never be laid against them.

But what happened when the top leadership appeared in front of the TRC's Amnesty Commission? How did the TRC model of combined retribution and restorative justice work out political and moral culpability in cases where orders were given, but no direct violence committed? It seems clear that the TRC experienced difficulties at this level. The fact that individuals' status within the chain of command was never linked to appropriate forms of either amnesty or punishment prevented the Amnesty Commission from adopting a consistent approach. The exact nature of how restorative and retributive justice could be combined in a single morally defensible accountability matrix was therefore not sufficiently developed, in either the mandate or the practices of the Amnesty Commission. This must be acknowledged as a key weakness of South Africa's TRC model.

The appearance of De Klerk at the TRC was a case in point. Political parties were invited to submit their versions of the conflict in special hearings.[71] Like most parties, the NP was allocated two hearings. During the first hearing, De Klerk submitted a history of apartheid from the NP perspective, together with a list of alleged ANC atrocities, and an explanation of the role that his government had played in initiating the transition. He also acknowledged that things went wrong and that millions suffered as a result. For this he issued an apology:

> I should like to express my deepest sympathy with all those on all sides who suffered during the conflict. I, and many other leading figures, have already publicly apologized for the pain and suffering caused by the former policies of the National Party. I reiterate these apologies today.[72]

But this apology failed to convince the TRC. In fact, it drew immediate and sharp criticism from both Tutu and Boraine. This hostile reaction to his presentation, echoed by civil society and political opponents alike, apparently shocked

De Klerk. The ANC and civil society organizations, including victim groups and the South African Council of Churches, reacted with outrage at what they perceived to be a self-justifying and insincere "taking of responsibility" style of apology.[73] The point they were making is that political apologies that admit to general failures of government without admitting personal responsibility can of course be manipulated for political advantage, at little or no cost to the leader issuing the apology. He or she tends to appear generous and essentially innocent, whilst admitting to no real transgression or taking no effective steps that require concrete action or effective redress of wrongs committed.

At the TRC hearing, Boraine's suggestion that De Klerk should apply for amnesty further incensed the ex-president. He replied:

> Amnesty is there to get pardon for a crime of which you believe you could be found guilty if you were charged in court. . . . It is not the correct channel in which to express your sorrow, your acceptance of responsibility, your repentance for things which are not crimes.[74]

Boraine responded to De Klerk that in terms of "accepting moral and political responsibility for [the severe ill-treatment of millions of South Africans] I would have thought that the amnesty process was the exact place."[75]

De Klerk clearly interpreted amnesty in its narrower retributive-justice sense, arguing that unless there was evidence that linked him directly to a criminal act, he needed not to apply for amnesty, even though he was a senior leader in the apartheid regime. After all, he reminded the commission, the act offered amnesty from criminal prosecution, based on evidence of actual wrongdoing. Casting amnesty within a more restorative-justice context, Boraine argued that applying for amnesty would have provided De Klerk with an opportunity to make the reconciliation process more credible to victims of apartheid especially. By applying for amnesty, De Klerk would have indicated his personal responsibility for perpetuating apartheid, whether or not his guilt was linked to a specific crime. Arguably, this might have deepened the TRC's credibility for many. That this did not happen, Boraine viewed as a lost opportunity.

Using somewhat different terms to those of De Klerk, his deputy minister of justice, Leon Wessels issued a confession to the TRC that was far more warmly received. He said:

> I further do not believe that the political defence of "I did not know" is available to me, because in many respects I believe I did not want to know.[76]

Evidently the victim community felt that Wessels admitted his own moral indifference honestly and sincerely, and for this he won respect. He was later appointed as a commissioner to the newly established Human Rights Commission under the ANC government.

In retrospect, and although individual culpability was one of the TRC's core principles, it may have been better if the amnesty regime had made provision for applications based on the acceptance of moral guilt and collective responsibility, as slippery as these concepts can be. Such a provision might have strengthened the TRC's claim to fairness and credibility by helping to prevent a sense that most of the commanders who issued orders got away scot-free, while only a few of the foot soldiers accounted for their misdeeds.[77] As it happened, it was never clear how the TRC resolved this tension internally, or how "moral accountability" was understood to relate to individual criminal liability or to notions of "command responsibility" that have since become much more prominent in international jurisprudence. Despite strong circumstantial evidence to the contrary, De Klerk claimed not to have known of illegal activities. Given that it was unlikely that he would face any legal accountability outside the TRC process, it is difficult to avoid the conclusion that the TRC's findings about De Klerk in its final report were an effort to apportion some measure of quasi-legal accountability to the apartheid government's most senior figure.[78]

Ultimately, it must be conceded that a degree of impunity did characterize the South African process but, crucially, *not* because restorative justice components were part of the process. In fact, as in the case of De Klerk, *the accountability bar was, at times, set higher by those thinking from a restorative justice angle than it was by those whose views were based on retributive justice.* The impunity that occurred resulted from a failure to think through systematically how a combination of court action *and* TRC hearings could have prevented so many big fish from swimming away.[79] Whatever one thinks of the TRC's performance at this level, it remains therefore unlikely that the courts, on their own, would have fared any better in establishing accountability at the top levels of command for apartheid-era crimes, given their own poor track record in holding top politicians accountable.

Providing a Constitutional Mandate for Truth-Telling as Justice

The legality of the TRC's truth-telling agenda of course had to be tested against the country's new constitution, and the newly established Constitutional Court was the only institution that could pronounce on that. The opportunity for the TRC to obtain constitutional legitimacy came relatively early on in the process when its mandate and the related legislation was challenged by families of deceased victims, Griffiths Mxenge and Steve Biko, who felt that their right to due process was being infringed upon by the TRC. The Constitutional Court upheld the legality of the TRC, thus adding very significantly to its credibility in the eyes of South Africans and the world.

Yet, in so doing, the court, through the ruling made by the deputy-judge-president Ismail Mohamed, stunningly turned the tables on the interdependence of restorative and retributive justice as set out so far in this discussion.[80] My argument has been that, in order to function properly, restorative justice needed the expertise, force, powers of arbitration, and the official sanction of the criminal justice system. But Justice Mohamed turned this causality on its head by arguing that the criminal justice system in fact also needed the TRC to "deal with the past", lest this very past became the proverbial elephant in every court room in the country—thereby undermining the new dispensation's attempt to build a political system based on respect for the rule of law.

Its relationship with judicial institutions was a mixed blessing for the TRC; the criminal justice system helped in some ways but as explained undermined the TRC's work in others. Justice Mohamed's ruling made it clear that the opposite was also true: the judicial system, and the agenda of establishing the rule of law after apartheid, needed the TRC in profound ways.[81] Mohamed's ruling therefore endorsed the TRC, despite the fact that the amnesty clause appeared to contradict more-established criminal justice principles. In fact, Mohamed acknowledged this fundamental tension, noting that "every decent human being must feel grave discomfort in living with a consequence which might allow the perpetrators of evil acts to walk the streets of this land with impunity, protected in their freedom by an amnesty immune from constitutional attack."[82] But despite this discomfort, his ruling made it clear that the TRC exercise was an essential step in building the rule of law. Truth-telling, he claimed, was a *necessary condition* for establishing the rule of law, and for restoring judicial credibility. This implied that rebuilding the rule of law depended crucially on an exercise in restorative justice that had the potential to restore the "legitimacy of law itself which had been deeply wounded as the country haemorrhaged dangerously in the face of this tragic conflict."[83]

This claim, that restorative justice was a precondition for rebuilding the rule of law in the post-apartheid state, and therefore for retributive justice, is carefully explained in Mohamed's ruling in terms of truth-telling.[84] Mohamed's rationale for presenting truth-telling as the heart of the restorative justice agenda, and (thereby) of rebuilding the rule of law after apartheid, is worth repeating in detail. Most of what transpired in South Africa's shameful history, Mohamed wrote, is shrouded in secrecy because agents of

> authoritarianism have concealed the truth in little crevices of obscurity in our history. Records are not easily accessible; witnesses are often unknown, dead, unavailable or unwilling. All that often effectively remains is the truth of wounded memories of loved ones sharing instinctive suspicions.[85]

The TRC Act addresses this massive problem, the ruling continues, by encouraging survivors, and the dependents of the tortured and the wounded, the maimed and the dead, to publicly unburden themselves of their grief, to receive the collective recognition of a new nation that they were wronged, and crucially,

> to help them discover what did in truth happen to their loved ones.
> That truth, which the victims of repression seek so desperately to know
> is, in the circumstances, much more likely to be forthcoming if those
> responsible for such monstrous deeds are encouraged to disclose the
> whole truth with the incentive that they will not receive the punish-
> ment which they undoubtedly deserve if they do ... with that incentive,
> what might unfold, are objectives fundamental to the ethos of a new
> constitutional order.[86]

By contrast, the reasoning continues, upholding the abstract right to prosecution, without the evidence to ensure convictions, keeps many dependents of such victims substantially ignorant about what happened to their loved ones. This in turn perpetuates grief and resentment while allowing the culprits freedom. Mohamed concluded:

> Both the victims and the culprits who walk on the historic bridge ... [of
> the Interim Constitution] will hobble more than walk into the future
> with heavy and dragged steps delaying and impeding a rapid and enthu-
> siastic transition to the new society at the end of the bridge.[87]

And in unequivocal terms, restorative justice is then presented as the condition for the rule of law:

> [E]ven more crucially, but for a mechanism providing for amnesty, the
> "historic bridge" itself might never have been erected. For a successfully
> negotiated transition, the terms of the transition *required* not only the
> agreement of those victimised by abuse but also those threatened by
> the transition ... the result, at all levels, is a difficult, sensitive, perhaps
> even agonising balancing act between the need for justice to victims of
> past abuse and the need for reconciliation and rapid transition to a new
> future.[88]

Thus, as much as the agenda of truth-telling, conditional amnesty, and reparations depended on the courts, the agenda of rebuilding the rule of law and of strengthening retributive justice needed the TRC. Restoring the credibility of a deeply compromised legal system depended in vital ways on addressing

political crimes of the past. Without such a reckoning with South Africa's unjust past, every subsequent court case, every legal process, and every judicial appointment would arguably have struggled a lot more to establish their
credentials as legitimate arbiters of justice.

And yet despite the overwhelming and obvious need to deal with gross
human rights violations, the justice system would have been fundamentally unable to do so. The TRC took on this vital task and dealt with a backlog of heinous crimes, which if left unaddressed would have cast serious doubts on the
credibility of efforts to re-establish the rule of law. In this way, South Africa's
legal system was imbued with a measure of credibility that it would otherwise
lack, and it can now more convincingly portray itself as an instrument of the
Constitution—a document in which the notion of redress for past injustice
occupies pride of place.

The TRC brought home to South Africans the importance of pausing to listen
to victims' stories and affording these victims the human and civic dignity of acknowledgment. It also demonstrated that not all political compromises have to
be void of accountability for past atrocities, that not all forms of accountability
reside in the law courts, and that not all forms of punishment entail the incarceration of perpetrators.

Ironically, rather than the TRC letting down the criminal justice system, as liberal critics have alleged, the criminal justice system failed to adequately support
the TRC. In some of these failures, the classic weaknesses of the criminal-justice
system in a post-conflict transitional justice context were all too clear—to a degree, it can be argued that these have not done enough not combat a growing
culture of impunity in South Africa ever since.

One can conclude that the TRC's mandate was written largely from a human
rights perspective, but with certain key restorative-justice values pragmatically
incorporated alongside retributive elements. From the start, the process was intended to be a hybrid initiative, with a pragmatic combination of *both* retributive
and restorative justice elements crucially dependent on one another. Therefore
both sets of one-sided criticisms popular readings of the TRC—whether liberal
rejection or the naïve insistence on forgiveness at all costs—ought therefore to
be questioned.

Conclusion

The Interim Constitution provided the basis for fair and credible elections that
led to the election of Nelson Mandela as president. This provided a historic vindication of the liberation struggle without unduly humiliating the outgoing leadership and risking a potential backlash. This seemed fair at the time, as did the

assurance of an offer of amnesty to those involved in bona fide political crimes. However, this sense of fairness was considerably deepened through the "second" amnesty process that led to the passing of the TRC Act in 1995. Enacted by a representative and democratically elected parliament after significant (if not comprehensive) public participation, this legislation was thereby imbued with a sense of fairness that a presidential decree, for example, would have lacked. Moreover, at least in principle, the sense of fairness was further strengthened by the ways in which the TRC and the wider legal system collaborated, and in the ways that the TRC mandate could, again in principle, be applied to both perpetrators and victims alike. That the newly elected government failed to follow up on the TRC's recommendations did, at the same time, detract from the commission's impact in countering the hard-won sense shared by many South Africans, that fairness was an inherent characteristic of institutionalized reconciliation.

The widening of inclusivity and the deepening of credibility were key traits of the succession of reconciliation platforms that I have discussed so far. Whereas the argument is reasonably straightforward in the case of the NPA and the MPNP, the TRC has often been accused of a lack of both inclusivity and credible levels of fairness towards all. In refuting criticisms that maintain that the TRC was neither inclusive nor credibly fair, I am not arguing that the South African TRC was a perfect model, nor that it alone was responsible for what was achieved in terms of reconciliation. But I *am* stating that it constituted a sufficient next step, given what had gone before it, what was happening around it, and what had been planned to follow from it.

Moreover, the disproportionate focus on the TRC has obscured the fact that it was only one in a series of reconciliation and transitional justice measures, and formed part of a much more comprehensive transition process. Each initiative depended heavily on the preceding ones for their efforts to widen inclusivity and deepen credibility. In fact, if the TRC had come before the MPNP, it may have derailed the process. Thus the sequencing was crucial, and in the South African case, dealing with the future first (by negotiating the Interim Constitution and the final Constitution) helped to pave the way for dealing with the past. Dealing with the past in a reasonably inclusive and fair manner became possible only once Mandela was safely in power and reforms of the apartheid security sector were irreversible. It is significant that what is arguably the world's most successful TRC so far, emerged *after* a credible political transition; that is, after free and fair and inclusive elections, after an inclusive public debate about its mandate, and after a public selection process for its various office bearers. Despite serious obstacles, the TRC began its work in 1996, less than two years after the first elections. This was only possible because important foundations had been laid in the preceding years, and because the leaders of the TRC knew they could depend on the criminal justice system to provide crucial support when needed.

By acknowledging and restoring the dignity of victims, establishing account-ability, and producing a public record of violations to act as a permanent re-minder, the TRC aimed to contribute toward building a shared resolve for such atrocities to never happen again. The measure to which the initiative caught the public's imagination worldwide came as a surprise. It elevated the concept of reconciliation to a higher level of public consciousness than before, and attracted intense analytical scrutiny, resulting in both high praise and searing critique.

In South Africa, the TRC constituted a deliberate step toward creating the *conditions* in which human rights could be meaningfully applied from the low base offered by a deeply compromised past.

4

Justice Promised or Just a Promise?

> At the end of the day, the yardstick that we shall all be judged by is one
> and one only: and that is, are we, through our endeavours here, creating
> the basis to better the lives of all South Africans!
> —Nelson Mandela, August 18, 1994, address to the South African
> parliament

Thus far my argument has been that reconciliation in South Africa was made possible by a growing sense of interdependence between those who upheld apartheid, and those who fought against it. This awareness opened avenues for change, and once articulated, it was embodied in a succession of movements and organizations that, to varying degrees, succeeded in embodying the change they foreshadowed, namely the development of a more inclusive and fair society.

In this chapter, while still focusing on South Africa's reconciliation history, I turn to the question of whether the decision to opt for reconciliation proved justified, or turned out to be an empty promise.[1] The implicit or explicit promises made in reconciliation's name and that contributed to its acceptance provides a handy normative framework for evaluating reconciliation, for determining whether or not it achieved its goals, and thus for deciding whether it was a justifiable route to follow. In the first half of the chapter I revisit the debate about whether the South African reconciliation process had broken its justice promise during the MPNP, as some critics claim. This discussion includes a preliminary effort to conceptualize justice (insofar as it is enacted as a response to reconciliation's promise) as inclusivity *and* fairness. In the second half of the chapter, I discuss various empirical questions and arguments raised about whether or not South Africa had indeed been able to make good on its promise in terms of forging a fundamentally more just society in the years since Mandela took office, or whether South Africans are justified in feeling let down by a political era that began in the name of reconciliation.

Reconciliation, of course, resists any simplistic or formulaic impact assessment. Not only are reconciliation's goals difficult to determine, their realization is necessarily intergenerational, multisectoral, and risky. Reconciliation's aim is nothing less than to address the social challenges that cut to the historic roots of conflict. In addition, reconciliation resists instrumentalization because this would require imposing normative frameworks on the process itself. By contrast, experience seems to suggest that, to be successful, reconciliation has to be built, owned, and driven by those who themselves live in a conflict, and, for the most part, it also has to be implemented and enacted "on the hoof," so to speak—with a normative framework gradually emerging as the result of a joint effort across erstwhile enemy lines. Of necessity, no reconciliation process can be prescribed or predetermined, and especially not by anyone who is not part of it.

In fact, when efforts are made to pre- or over-determine them, reconciliation processes can become counterproductive. Then, instead of bringing freedom and self-determination, reconciliation can even become a symbol of renewed subjection, adding insult to injury for those emerging from war or oppression, who are often desperate for a sense of self-determination. Processes determined by those who do not have to live with the consequences of decisions taken, or who are unfamiliar with conditions on the ground, run the danger of being calibrated against abstract and unrealistic ideals. And without local ownership, the resulting rapprochement has every chance of being superficial. Such superficial exercises tend to leave exploitative or violent relations intact, thereby turning reconciliation into little more than a political ruse that hides lingering injustice, rather than illuminating a pathway to a more inclusive and fairer social system.

This is not to say that the international community, third party mediators, and advisers from beyond the conflict do not have a role to play. As in South Africa, support from the outside is often vital to keep processes on course. Such support may arrive in the form of political pressure (to contain spoilers and urge the powerful and belligerents to play by the rules), but also as technical advice, comparative analysis to offer some insights gained elsewhere, training and capacity-building, or even facilitated discussions and dialogues. These are all necessary and important and can help to further faltering processes at crucial moments. At the same time, my argument is that engagement by external supporters ought to feed into processes that are locally determined and managed.

But with these observations firmly in mind, normativity can also not be ignored at reconciliation's inception. In some way or another, the nascent promise that restored relations would also entail a fairer more inclusive society needs to be present in sufficient degrees to motivate parties to participate in the realistic hope of a better tomorrow. Reconciliation as a *completely* open-ended and undetermined engagement risks renewed manipulation in favor of the powerful and resources, thereby incorporating the seeds of the next conflict into the peace process itself. So inevitably the question of promise—of what is offered and to be expected—arises early on in reconciliation processes.

Asking what reconciliation promises, challenges the notion that reconciliation is a purely regulative ideal, as an ideal that is always out of reach.
Reconciliation defined as an ever-elusive goal may motivate people for a while,
but sooner or later they realize that they are chasing an impossible dream and
give up. In South Africa, with its history of injustice, inequality, and ongoing radical acts of violence and discrimination against the majority of the population,
it was clear from the outset that reconciliation had to promise but also *produce*
tangible and concrete results lest it be rejected as little more than a sop to those
who had little left to lose.

One such concrete outcome associated with South Africa's earliest efforts at
reconciliation concerned the quality of promised relationships. Many in other
situations too would agree that, at a minimum, reconciled (or reconciling)
relationships ought to promise not only greater levels of trust and respect, but
also increased fairness or equality. It is not enough merely to cease hostile relations after a conflict—new relations ought to be formed that are of such a quality
that they interrupt established patterns of hostility, subjugation, and estrange-
ment. Indeed, the quality of these relations determines whether or not a political change can be considered reconciliatory. In short, in addition to establishing
peace, reconciliation has to promise and deliver lasting and concrete relational
dividends. And to guarantee such dividends, reconciliation has to be credible
and inclusive, presenting a fair deal to all parties across society's most entrenched
divides implying crucially that former oppressive and hostile relations need to
be transformed into equal and cooperative ones. A key focus of reconciliation
studies, therefore—both before and since South Africa's transition—has been
on the quality of relations that reconciliation promises to produce, as opposed
to those that it actually produces.

In Chapter 1, I challenged the claim that South Africa's political leaders
Nelson Mandela, F. W. de Klerk, and others, acted primarily from a paradigm
of *forgiveness*. In Chapters 2 and 3, I sought inter alia to counter elements of *liberal critiques* that have decried South Africa's TRC as a restorative-justice exercise that fell short in terms of democratic and liberal principles. In this chapter,
I address some of the criticisms from a third political framework against which
South African reconciliation is routinely evaluated, namely that of *distributive
justice*.

The brunt of this framework's critique of reconciliation in South Africa
centers on the idea of broken promises. The claim is that black South Africans
were persuaded to relinquish economic power in favor of political power, and
that the TRC consolidated this exchange by defining social justice in terms of
abstract notions of personal dignity rather than in terms of concrete social and
economic gains. The implication is that South Africa's present constitutional dispensation (including the TRC) is little more than an elaborate ruse for white

South Africans and big corporations to hold on to their ill-gotten gains. The critique is that reconciliation was an empty promise made to black South Africans, and that, along the way, this promise has been allowed quietly to die.[2] Critics on the left argue that whereas reconciliation promised inclusivity and justice, not only as elements of the process but *as features of a new society*, it was unable to deliver on either. According to this reading, black South Africans are now politically included, but remain socially and economically excluded, and the whole social system remains fundamentally unfair.

In this chapter, I examine the critique that the architects of South Africa's reconciliation process were unable or unwilling to deliver on its justice promise— at least as far as the design of the new dispensation was concerned. Leaving the question of whether reconciliation has delivered "better lives for all" for later, I begin by considering the challenge posed by Mandela in the epigraph to this chapter and ask whether reconciliation created "a basis to better the lives of all South Africans." To assess South Africa's reconciliation process in these terms, I first elaborate on some of the arguments that criticize South Africa's transition from a social justice point of view, then I focus again on CODESA and the TRC but, this time, in relation to whether they helped to establish the basis for post-apartheid social justice. This opens the door for a brief retrospective account of change in South Africa as measured against reconciliation's justice promise.

Difficult Questions from the Left

In the mid-1980s, just a couple of years before Nelson Mandela began quietly talking to his captors, a group of South African theologians developed an important argument against forms of reconciliation that masked ongoing power relations. In a statement known as *The Kairos Document*,[3] the theologians argued that calls for reconciliation with an unrepentant apartheid government at that particular time (or "kairos") would amount to nothing less than heresy. Drawing strongly on the experience of Latin American countries at the time, the theologians argued that reconciliation with the apartheid regime would not lead to a significant shift toward justice, but would remain illegitimate until conditions changed sufficiently to make justice a realistic prospect. "No reconciliation is possible in South Africa without justice," they argued, making it clear that justice would entail nothing less than the total dismantling of apartheid. Instead, they called for a radical association with the poor and disenfranchised, and for a commitment to social justice. Only then, they argued, could reconciliation be considered.[4]

Barely two years after the publication of the *Kairos Document*, Mandela's prescient judgment that conditions had changed, and that a fundamental shift toward a more just and interdependent society was becoming politically possible, motivated him to reconsider reconciliation as a transitional framework. Certainly as far as recorded statements go, justice was always a nonnegotiable condition for Mandela when he was considering reconciliation as political option. In a letter to F. W. de Klerk in December 1989, written from prison, Mandela asked how one works for reconciliation "under a state of emergency, with black areas under military occupation, when people's organisations are banned, leaders are either in exile, prison or restricted, when the policy of apartheid with its violence is still being enforced, and when no conditions for free political expression exist?"[5] He continued that "the very first step on the way to reconciliation is obviously the dismantling of apartheid, and all measures used to enforce it. To talk of reconciliation before this major step is taken, is totally unrealistic."[6]

Mandela feared that certain kinds of reconciliation processes would allow apartheid and colonial power relations to remain intact, and not deliver justice at all. He therefore spelled out his rejection of the apartheid government's efforts toward reconciliation on the basis that this would not deliver adequate political justice, pointing out that

> the five-year plan of the NP … is yet another example of the Government's attempt "to modernise apartheid without abandoning it" … What this plan means, in effect, is that after resisting racial oppression for so many years, and after making such heavy sacrifices during which countless lives were lost, we should at the height of that heroic struggle, yield to a disguised form of minority rule. In this one, whites will go on preaching reconciliation and peace, but continue to hold firmly and defiantly to power.[7]

It is clear from statements like these that Mandela was keenly aware of the dangers of a superficial reconciliation process that would allow apartheid and colonial power relations to remain intact. For this reason, he declined P. W. Botha's earlier offer to release him on condition that he renounce violence. In the famous response, smuggled out of prison and movingly read at a rally in Soweto by his young daughter Zindzi, Mandela said in 1985:

> I cannot and will not give any undertaking at a time when I and you, the people, are not free. Your freedom and mine cannot be separated. I will return.[8]

After securing the release of all political prisoners, and the unbanning of all political organizations, Mandela helped to ensure that reconciliation became accepted as a framework for nonviolent engagement between sworn enemies on the basis that their futures were interdependent, and with the absolute, non-negotiable aim of achieving "justice for all." Articulated as an embrace of racial interdependence (as both a political reality and a social norm), Mandela's reconciliation project insisted that *reconciliation's key outcome and justification must be the concrete redress of apartheid injustice.*

Mandela's speech to the South African parliament after his first hundred days in office took as its central theme the relationship between reconciliation and reconstruction. Consequently, Mandela went on to discuss both the principles on which the TRC would be based, and the establishment of the Reconstruction and Development Programme. On this, and numerous other occasions, Mandela confirmed that

> From the outset, the government of National Unity set itself two interrelated tasks: reconciliation and reconstruction, nation-building and development. This is South Africa's challenge today. It will remain our challenge for many years to come.

Although at its inception, reconciliation may have been a tactical means of furthering a political agenda, in combination with the Reconstruction and Development Programme, it promised more than political reform: it promised social transformation. It was against the construction of a more just and inclusive society, more than any other measure, that reconciliation was set up for judgment. This was clear, not only from Mandela's tough stance on efforts by the apartheid regime to secure a white veto on political or any other form of power, but also from many of his public statements.

The sense that reconciliation would have to deliver on social justice or fail was a constant theme of the transitional period. Mandela often articulated reconciliation's key outcome as comprehensive and socially orientated justice, rather than as a primarily legal matter. His assumption was that society would need to change radically for reconciliation to deliver on its promise, and that bettering the lives of all South Africans involved more than material redress; it included the nonmaterial restoration of the "human and civic dignity" of all South Africans.

However, not all South Africans accept this version of history. Some doubt whether social justice was indeed foremost in the minds of politicians who promoted reconciliation as a means of moving beyond apartheid. For example, economist Sampie Terreblanche has alleged that "the whole transition process was orchestrated by what he has called the 'minerals–energy complex' with [mining magnate] Harry Oppenheimer and, to a lesser extent, [industrialist] Anton Rupert. They organised everything."[9] For those who adhere to this somewhat conspiratorial perspective, the adoption of reconciliation as political paradigm meant that radical socioeconomic transformation was deliberately and cynically abandoned with a view to safeguarding vested economic interests with dire consequences for the poor. The result, Terreblanche has argued, was an entrenching of inequality, disempowerment, and poverty. Thus, despite gaining the formal right to exercise a democratic vote, black South Africans were, in fact, made worse off because they were now deprived not only of their rightful claims for material redress but also of the rationale to revolt by virtue of the fact that they now lived in a democracy.

Wole Soyinka, the celebrated Nigerian author and Nobel laureate, expressed a similar sentiment about the South African experience in somewhat different terms. Referring to the TRC, he asked if "the Truth shall set you free?" He answered his own question with: "Maybe. . . . But first the Truth must be set free."[10] Soyinka went on to argue that the TRC would have been better able to fulfill its promises had it been constituted as a Truth and *Restitution* Commission, noting that[11]

> where there has been inequity, especially of a singularly brutalizing kind, of a kind that robs one side of its most fundamental attribute—its humanity—it seems only appropriate that some form of atonement be made, in order to exorcise that past. Reparations, we repeat, serve as a cogent critique of history and thus a potent restraint on its repetition.[12]

Soyinka argued that without reparations, the resentment and hatred engendered by South Africa's racist and economically exploitative past would remain intact, and the "truth" would remain trapped. He asked, "What really would be preposterous or ethically inadmissible in imposing a general levy on South Africa's white population?"[13] Someone of the "non-establishment stature" of Desmond Tutu, Soyinka mused, could mount his pulpit one day and address his compatriots:

> White brothers and sisters in the Lord, you have sinned, but we are willing to forgive. The scripture warns us that the wages of sin are death but, in your case, they seem to be wealth. If therefore you chose to shed a little of that sinful wealth as first step toward atonement . . . etcetera.[14]

Instead, Soyinka continued, the adopted formula for the harmonization of South Africa "erodes, in some way, one of the pillars on which a durable society must be founded—responsibility. And ultimately—justice."[15] Soyinka's sobering assessment of South Africa's reconciliation process was based on what he saw as a key missing outcome—that reparations had been promised but not made. Reparations, Soyinka argued, was the missing link between truth and reconciliation. The structuring is secondary, the principle essential—that some measure of restitution is crucial after dispossession. For this reason, he concluded, the South African example is "not one that we dare recommend, untouched, for the travails of this continent."[16]

Arguing along similar lines, Mahmood Mamdani first criticized South Africa's transition in 1996 in an essay titled "Reconciliation without Justice," in which he offered a conception of justice as the transformation of historical and political power relations. To Mamdani, justice is not derived primarily from jurisprudential dictates, but from a historical analysis of concrete sociocultural and political conditions, and from the transformation of these. His analysis offers a compelling picture of how colonial power, via its bifurcated state systems, subjugated African people through the legal language of rights and civility. By applying civil rights to settlers only, he explained, colonial states relegated "natives" to second-class citizens who answered to "customary law," and which did not entitle them to the same privileges as settlers.[17]

Contrasting the human rights paradigm (which he associates with the reconciliation agenda in South Africa) with the paradigm of justice that inspired earlier African liberation movements, Mamdani went on to argue that whenever power relations are unaccounted for and history is ignored, transitional processes will go wrong, no matter how much lip service is paid to reconstructing the rule of law. Citing the 1962 Rwandan transition, he described how the quest for justice degenerated into a quest for revenge because it failed to acknowledge and reorganize the power relations inherited from colonialism; it merely replaced one oppressor group with another.

In South Africa, despite commendable innovation, Mamdani claimed, the transition failed to transform power relations between white and black citizens beyond the limits of the political elite. He argued that this occurred as the result of a failure to shift the focus from the perpetrators of apartheid crimes to the beneficiaries of apartheid policies, and from victims of gross human rights violations to victims of day-to-day dehumanization under apartheid. Noting that South Africa differs from many other transitional societies—in that victims and perpetrators continue to live together in a context in which perpetrators still wield considerable power—Mamdani argued that this makes the transformation of historical power relations even more important.

For Mamdani, political reconciliation will be durable only if it broadens into social reconciliation, and this is achievable only in relation to a historically developed notion of social justice. "Limiting justice to criminal justice, to punishment, is not necessarily to benefit victims," he argued—implying that the notion of justice as the punishment of violations of individual human rights is too narrow. Durable peace, he said, requires a move from the delivery of justice as an individualized, ahistorical right to "a need to right historical wrongs, and thus to provide a measure of justice to previously excluded groups."[18]

In 2013, Mamdani delivered a lecture looking back on the significance of the post-apartheid transition in which he concluded that "the downside of the South African transition was silence as regards to the social question."[19] He went on to explain that at CODESA, political justice was achieved, but at the expense of social and criminal justice. While it would have been naïve to expect social justice to be on CODESA's formal agenda, it could at least have been on the "discursive agenda." He argued that the responsibility for removing social justice from the country's reconciliation agenda lay with actions taken largely by the TRC. For Mamdani, the TRC individualized victims by defining human rights violations as actions that violated the bodily integrity of an individual, thus ignoring the structural violence inherent in the apartheid regime, such as forced removals, pass laws, and job reservation. Further, the TRC individualized perpetrators instead of holding the state itself accountable in any way. Defining victims and perpetrators so narrowly, Mamdani concluded, was the key to silencing the discourse on social justice.

Mamdani built on Soyinka's views in two interesting ways. First, he acknowledged the importance of CODESA as a model for achieving political justice. In so doing, he avoided the common mistake of equating South Africa's entire reconciliation process with the TRC. Second, like Soyinka, he was critical of the TRC as an instrument, although his criticism was not of the TRC's failure to make adequate restitution per se, but rather of the TRC's mandate as such, formulated as it was within the paradigm of individualized human rights. Instead, he proposed that the TRC should have built on the momentum of CODESA's relative success, and aimed to expand political justice into the realm of the social, rather than personalizing and individualizing apartheid violations in ways that, in his view, took social justice off the negotiating table.

Viewed through a social justice lens, it is true that apartheid's crimes related more significantly to social and economic injustice than to physical violence. Social justice advocates consequently view the redistribution of ill-gotten gains as central to the restoration of post-conflict relationships. Without such justice, and a more equal and equitable sharing of resources across historical divides, reconciliation cannot restore relations in any real sense. To this end, social justice advocates argue that the focus of reconciliation ought to be primarily on patterns of social injustice and economic exclusion rather than exclusively on instances of gross human rights abuse. This is especially the case in situations like South Africa's, where the effects of structural violence have been disastrous for millions of people, and where relatively few suffered direct physical abuse. Consequently, the responsibility of beneficiaries of injustice ought to match the need for the radical redistribution of material and other resources to those they had systematically excluded before.

Such critics remind us that, even with good intentions, reconciled relationships may retain some of the qualities that caused conflict in the first place. If relations

rebuilt in a reconciliation process turn out to be unreconstructed, coercive, violent, or exclusionary, they arguably leave the conflict in a worse place than before.
The worsening of relations as a result of half-hearted reconciliation processes is
obvious in areas of entrenched conflict when, despite the hopes generated by
peace talks, adversaries discover that abusive power relations remain intact, and
violence flares up again. Abusive relations may be reflected in political systems
that favor one group over another, economic systems that rely on exploitation,
or social and cultural stigmas that deny the dignity of one group or another.

To address these criticisms, and to assess South Africa's reconciliation process in terms of its promise to deliver justice, I revisit two important transitional
outcomes: first, a selection of important documents and agreements associated
with, and contributing to, the adoption of the country's final Constitution in
1996; and, second, the TRC's impact on social justice. My focus is on whether
these processes kept the issue of social justice on the negotiating table or not.
I attempt to answer the question of whether they were part of creating "the basis
for a better life for all," or acted as obstacles to that cause.

Constitutional Design and the Justice Promise

Mamdani claimed that social justice was sacrificed on the altar of political reconciliation during the CODESA process. To establish whether this is true or not,
it is perhaps useful to distinguish between the *design* of the constitutional edifice (that is, its laws and institutions) and its *implementation* in terms of policies
and processes.[20] On the one hand, the South African transition's justice dividend
can be judged in terms of its constitutional design and the institutions it has
created. On the other hand, the process can obviously also be judged in terms of
its social outcomes—what Mamdani called the concrete "transformation of historical and political power relations"[21] as a result of political leadership and the
collective will to implement the constitutional framework. First, I focus primarily on South Africa's constitutional design, asking whether it is correct to claim
that the settlement reached in the name of reconciliation was anti-poor from the
outset, and whether poverty and ongoing inequality were indeed embedded in
the new dispensation's constitutional DNA.[22]

As early as January 1986, the ANC established a constitutional committee
that was tasked with translating the principles of the Freedom Charter into
constitutional language. In the same year, South Africa's Federated Chamber
of Industries proposed and published a charter of economic, social, and political rights.[23] A few months later the then minister of justice instructed the Law
Commission, which was responsible for advising the state on legal reform, to investigate and make recommendations on the definition and protection of group

rights in South Africa, and on the possible extension of apartheid laws to protect individual rights.

These initiatives set in motion a decade-long process of negotiating a Bill of Rights for South Africa. Several conferences on constitutional reform took place in the ensuing years, including one organized by the Organisation of African Unity in Harare in 1989, at which the ANC was present and where conditions for negotiations toward a nonracial, united, and democratic state were determined and publicly adopted by participating countries. Also in 1989, the South African government's Law Commission released a working paper in which it proposed a Bill of Rights establishing universal franchise and political rights (as opposed to cultural and religious and linguistic rights), which would be protected *as* individual rights and implemented with judicial oversight. Although property rights would be protected, affirmative action and economic redress were both recommended in the wake of the many apartheid-era measures, which the commission conceded had been deeply destructive.

In October 1990, after Mandela's release, the ANC's own Legal and Constitutional Committee circulated a draft Bill of Rights for public discussion. It stated that social justice could be achieved only through enforceable obligations.[24] The draft bill sought a balance between the right to hold property without fear of arbitrary confiscation on the one hand, and the just claims of the people who lost property through apartheid policies on the other. The architects of the draft bill argued that compensation for such losses should be "just," and should take into account the interests of current as well as previous owners. Ultimately, the Bill of Rights was designed to promote a more equitable distribution of land and resources. Included, too, were minimum and enforceable rights to food, shelter, and education, and the notion that the state would have a duty to establish institutions to promote and to expand on these rights.

Importantly, at the time, law professor and ANC member Kader Asmal argued strongly that "if the Bill is not to become a bill for whites, it must help us thrash out a reconstruction accord to deal with one of the most unequal societies in the world, the result of deliberate policies based on racial discrimination."[25] In 1991, the ANC released its "Constitutional Principles for a Democratic South Africa,"[26] in which the organization acknowledged the importance of "guarantees of opportunity for a Dignified Life for All," stating that

> A new South Africa can never evolve if the white part of the population lives in relative luxury, while the great majority of South Africans live in conditions of want, squalor and deprivation. Appropriate constitutional expression must therefore be found to guarantee basic human rights in relation to nutrition, shelter, education, health, employment and welfare. Government should be under a constitutional duty to

work towards the establishment of a guaranteed and expanding floor of social, economic and educational rights for everybody. It is particularly important that the Constitution facilitate access to education, employment and land, so that people have real and effective opportunities for improving their situation and pursuing happiness.

To enforce these principles, the ANC proposed a permanent human rights commission, an ombuds office, a public protector, and various other institutions, including a constitutional court, to ensure the appropriate checks and balances on the powers of both the legislative and executive branches of government.

In 1991, the South African Law Commission released its final report, together with comments made on the first draft, and concluded that the majority of South Africans accepted that apartheid was over. The Law Commission also indicated that strong support existed for a Bill of Rights to protect individual rights, overseen by an independent judiciary. Importantly, however, the commission differed from the ANC in arguing that socioeconomic rights should not be enforceable by a court of law, but should rather remain a matter of consensus and debate—a position later adopted and promoted by the NP during formal talks.

At the very least, therefore, the social justice question was very much on the table, both formally and discursively, in the buildup to the CODESA talks. How did this important ideological battle develop over the next months and years? Did the ANC's firm stance in favor of social justice change during the formal talks, or was the NP forced to compromise? Did the process eventually deliver a constitutional dispensation true to its justiciable promise of social justice, or was the ANC outmuscled by demands for minority rights and the (implicit) protection of privilege, as Mamdani implied?

During the second CODESA process that commenced in March 1993, seven technical committees developed thirty-four constitutional principles on which the new Constitution was eventually based. A Bill of Rights was also drafted to govern the transitional period. Leon Wessels, who represented the NP in this process, remembers that there was profound disagreement about which rights to include and exclude from this draft Bill of Rights.[27] Whereas the ANC wanted to limit the number of rights included so that an elected assembly could compile a full list, the NP wanted to include as many individual guarantees and safeguards as possible to reassure the anxious and insecure white community.

Representing a delicately balanced trade-off between various conflicting sets of rights (including particularly the right to property and the right to redress), the Interim Constitution was signed on November 17, 1993. This provided the legal and constitutional basis for the first democratic elections and the establishment of a government of national unity, but it was also deliberately limited and deferential to a future final Constitution.[28] Thus, it can be argued that the Interim Constitution sought to provide basic guarantees of individual rights, including property rights, but still aspired to make social justice a central concern.

To illustrate this latter point, it is useful to revisit the section on equality in the Interim Constitution that made provision for the right to the restitution of property lost under apartheid. Vitally, the right to economic activity was limited so as *not* to preclude

> measures designed to promote the protection or the improvement of the quality of life, economic growth, human development, social justice, basic conditions of employment, fair labour practices or equal opportunity for all, provided such measures are justifiable in an open and democratic society based on freedom and equality.[29]

However, it is also true that although present in embryonic form, the social justice provisions in the Interim Constitution were not spelled out in as much detail as they had been in earlier ANC documents, including the African Claims document and the Freedom Charter.[30] The fact that, at this crucial moment in the transition, the ANC settled for these more muted references to social justice— as opposed to the far more forthright demands they had made earlier—is what appears to have motivated commentators such as Mamdani to conclude that the ANC lost its battle for social justice during the CODESA process.

What Mamdani's analysis fails to appreciate, however, is the deliberately limited, but vitally important role assigned to the Interim Constitution by its drafters. Its purpose was to form *a political bridge* to the final Constitution—no more and no less. The Interim Constitution thus never claimed to be the final word, most importantly because it had not been drawn up by elected representatives; it prepared the ground for those representatives to be elected and then to draft the final Constitution. With this in mind, the goal was to provide broad guidelines for those who would draft the final constitution. In this light, it is perhaps understandable that social justice concerns were less expansive, albeit decidedly present, in several of the principles to which the final constitution had to adhere.

After the 1994 election, and the establishment of the constitutional assembly, the process of drafting the final Constitution got underway. Zac Yacoob, who was deeply involved in drafting both the Interim and the final Constitution, and who later became a Constitutional Court judge, remembers many debates about the right to equality in the constitutional assembly. Whereas several minority parties thought that a formal acknowledgment of equality would be enough, he recalls that the ANC insisted on enshrining redress measures—including land reform and affirmative action—as constitutional principles.

Then, while elected representatives debated the contents of the new Constitution, the process was opened up for public participation. The constituent assembly determined that a comprehensive program of public participation would include publication of debates, consultations at village level, and public education radio broadcasts. Submissions by members of the public were encouraged, and citizens were called upon to participate with the slogan: "You've made your mark, now have your say." Approximately 73 percent of South Africans were reached by the campaign and 2 million submissions were made,[31] making the process one of the most democratic constitution-making exercises to date anywhere in the world.

As a result, it is safe to assert that the dignity, equality, and freedom of all were firmly enshrined as fundamental values in the South African Constitution, which was adopted on February 4, 1997. The Constitution is widely recognized as "progressive" to the extent that it guarantees as justiciable, not only political rights but also the social and economic rights of all citizens. Yacoob wrote in 2004 that the South African Bill of Rights, which in an integral part of the Constitution, is the only rights instrument in the world that includes socioeconomic rights as justiciable.[32] The Bill of Rights contains an extensive set of fundamental, inalienable rights that can be limited only in ways that are "reasonable and justifiable in an open and democratic society based on human dignity, equality and freedom."[33]

By building significantly on the limited provisions made for social justice in the Interim Constitution, and reacting to the massive public engagement, the final Constitution actually recovered the original list of principles put forward by the ANC in 1991; namely, the right to adequate housing, health care services, sufficient food and water, and social security—thereby opening the door for the Constitutional Court to develop case law in areas previously not within the purview of the courts.

The Constitution further protects each of these rights separately, and obliges the state to ensure that these rights are expanded to ever more South Africans over time. Article 10 of the Bill of Rights speaks about the equal dignity of everyone, and of their right to have their dignity respected and protected. Vulnerable groups in the South African context—women, children, individuals with disabilities, and the aged—are mentioned by name. Article 8 indicates the state's responsibilities, not only to avoid discrimination, but also to ensure equality. And while acknowledging a need for redress, Article 25, which deals with property rights, states that

> no one may be deprived of property except in terms of law of general application, and no law may permit arbitrary deprivation of property. Property may be expropriated only in terms of law of general

application for a public purpose or in the public interest; and subject to compensation, the amount of which and the time and manner of payment of which have either been agreed to by those affected or decided or approved by a court.[34]

Furthermore, Article 25 provides that "the amount of the compensation and the time and manner of payment must be just and equitable, reflecting an equitable balance between the public interest and the interests of those affected, having regard to all relevant circumstances."[35] The context in which these provisions may be of relevance include "the nation's commitment to land reform," and "reforms to bring about equitable access to all South Africa's natural resources." Furthermore, "property is not limited to land." As the Constitution states:

> The state must take reasonable legislative and other measures, within its available resources, to foster conditions which enable citizens to gain access to land on an equitable basis. Moreover, a person or community whose tenure of land is legally insecure as a result of past racially discriminatory laws or practices is entitled, to the extent provided by an Act of Parliament, either to tenure which is legally secure or to comparable redress. A person or community dispossessed of property after 19 June 1913, as a result of past racially discriminatory laws or practices is entitled, to the extent provided by an Act of Parliament, either to restitution of that property or to equitable redress.[36]

These provisions, and the document as a whole, certainly appear to make a strong and unambiguous case for social justice. This emphasis is further evident in the range of so-called Chapter 9 institutions brought to life by the Constitution, of which the Land and Gender Commissions are but two examples.[37]

Arguably the most important institution created by the Interim Constitution was the Constitutional Court, which superseded the previous apex judicial institution, the Supreme Court of Appeal in Bloemfontein. This new court, situated symbolically on Constitutional Hill in Johannesburg, has been served by a set of brilliant and broadly credible justices, and has fast become the principal symbol of the new Constitutional order. With eleven justices representing the country's diversity, headed by a chief justice, the Court commenced hearing cases in February 1995, and has managed a case load of about twenty-five cases per year ever since. Its foundational task was to certify the new Constitution as being in agreement with the list of principles set out in the Interim Constitution. As part of this process, a first draft was actually rejected and sent back for revision.

Overturning apartheid-era legislation has become one of the Court's other main tasks, including the notorious death penalty. It has also issued several landmark judgments on, for example, the right to shelter, to health, and to social services—in each case compelling the government to align its policies with the country's constitutional aspirations of social justice.[38]

It is therefore difficult to agree with Mamdani's assertion that CODESA was marked by a "silence regarding the social question."[39] If anything, the social question played a fundamental role in shaping the constitutional framework. Thus, at least in its design, South Africa's reconciliation process delivered on its promise to place a spotlight on social justice at the inception of political rapprochement.

But Mamdani and Soyinka's criticisms also concern the TRC. Were the TRC's mandate and operations in line with the constitutional vision of social justice, or did the commission detract from social justice by personalizing crime and shifting the focus away from structural violence? Was Soyinka correct to argue that unpaid reparations were the missing link between truth and reconciliation?[40]

The TRC: A Setback for Social Justice?

Mamdani is correct that structural violence was not an overt focus of TRC. Its mandate—to focus on gross human rights violations—was limited primarily by perceptions of what a truth commission could conceivably and realistically achieve at the time. The TRC's mandate, correctly in my view, insisted on individualizing both victims and perpetrators, partly to bring home the personal responsibility of perpetrators, and to restore the personal dignity of victims, but also to discourage the notion of collective punishment. Extending the TRC's mandate into the realm of structural justice would have escalated the number of participants from several thousand to several million, and this, it was felt, would result in a mandate that would be impossible to fulfill within what a TRC could realistically achieve. At the same time, structural redress was made the remit of sister bodies to the TRC, such as the Land Commission and the Commission for Gender Equality.

However, this whole edifice, together with the TRC's limited mandate, has been challenged on principled grounds by Mamdani and Soyinka.[41] And it could also be challenged on more practical grounds in light of the fact that the TRC did find ways to deal with the larger than expected numbers of individual victims who came forward to submit testimonies. That is, to cope with the twenty-one thousand victims of gross human rights violations who came forward, written testimonies had to be submitted, and only a few of these were selected to speak at public hearings. By adopting a similar mechanism, the argument goes, the TRC could potentially have accepted submissions from victims of structural violence as well. Of course, the jump from several thousand to several million would have been enormous, and possibly unmanageable, but perhaps merited some consideration at least.

Yet given all these considerations, and with the benefit of hindsight and the lessons learned from close to forty other truth commissions established since the South African one (including some that have had structural violence included in their mandates), there are prominent TRC analysts who argue that truth commissions function best with more limited mandates. For example, UN Special Rapporteur Pablo de Greiff has stated that "there is a tendency by some to view TRCs as a solution for all the problems of a nation with a difficult past . . . but this approach is questionable. TRCs need to focus on what they are good at, namely truth-telling about gross human rights violations."[42]

Despite its limited mandate, the TRC's work did in fact influence the prospects for social justice in three ways, and for me, they mean that Mamdani's argument falls short in important ways. First, structural violence was formally acknowledged in the TRC's *Final Report*, and the struggle against apartheid was, as result, declared a "just war"; the TRC was the first statutory body in South Africa ever to formally declare this.[43] Second, the TRC recommended that various kinds of reparations be offered to victims to make some practical and symbolic amends for damages they suffered under apartheid. Third, structural violence was arguably also countered by the TRC's strong emphasis on restoring the personal dignity of victims. Each of these three issues is discussed in more detail below.

Acknowledging Structural Violence in Its Report

After overcoming numerous legal challenges, including from F. W. de Klerk, the IFP, and the ANC, the first five volumes of the TRC's *Final Report* were submitted to President Mandela in 1998.[44] The report contained a double message: one acknowledged that apartheid was a crime against humanity, and the other condemned all the human rights violations that had occurred regardless of who committed them. According to evidence from a survey of public opinion conducted by Gibson and McDonald (2001), the majority of South Africans from all race groups consequently claimed the TRC to be an essential component of the reconciliation process.[45] Gibson wrote, in another landmark study, that if "reconciliation means nothing more than accepting the Truth and Reconciliation Commission's truth about the past, then at least some degree of reconciliation in South Africa has indeed taken place."[46] Such a positive rating, despite many well-documented shortcomings, may point to the fact that the TRC successfully furthered both inclusion and a sense of even-handedness and fairness in how citizens were treated.

By affirming that apartheid was a crime against humanity (as the UN had proclaimed two decades earlier), the struggle against apartheid was designated a "just war." The TRC argued that there can be no moral equivocation between the struggle for and against apartheid, and made it clear that it sided unambiguously with the liberation movement in its fight against apartheid and for justice:

> the Commission followed the internationally accepted position that apartheid was a crime against humanity. Accordingly, it upheld and endorsed the liberation movement's argument that they were engaged in a just war ... (but) a just cause does not exempt an organisation from pursuing its goals through just means.[47]

The TRC went further, though, and held F. W. de Klerk morally responsible (as discussed in Chapter 2).[48] Although not mandated to investigate structural violence, the TRC's explicit reiteration of the UN's position amounted to an official acknowledgment of the levels of structural violence present during apartheid. In a six-page history lesson, the report stated that

> Apartheid redrew the map of South Africa. The wealth, the cities, the mines, parks and the best beaches became part of white South Africa. A meagre 13% of largely barren land was parcelled out in a series of homelands in which African people were forced to live, while the able-bodied were driven to seek a living as migrant workers in the cities.[49]

In interpreting its mandate, the TRC acknowledged that a strong argument could be made that the consequences of

> the violations of human rights caused by "separate development"— for example by migrant labour, forced removals Bantustans, Bantu education and so on ... cannot be measured only in human lives lost through deaths, detentions, dirty tricks and disappearances, but in human lives withered away through enforced poverty and other kinds of deprivation.[50]

Accordingly, the TRC (albeit in a limited way) held what it called institutional hearings on various structural aspects of apartheid, including on the judiciary, faith communities, businesses, political parties, and so on. It also systematically probed the ways in which the security sector enforced apartheid (both legally and illegally under apartheid law) using violent suppression.

Thus, contrary to Mamdani's charge that the commission ignored structural violence, and despite its limiting mandate, it can be argued that the TRC used its powers to interpret its mandate widely enough to record the context, antecedents, and structures in which gross human rights violations were embedded during apartheid, and this involved developing an analytical focus on structural violence.

Emphasizing the structural context of gross human rights violations added impetus to arguments in favor of social justice. If apartheid as a political system was a crime against humanity, then the post-apartheid state had a moral duty to correct these systematic wrongs. Admittedly, the TRC could have done more with this, by making the implications of its findings more explicit for other institutions and for other areas of policymaking and reform. Thus, while some of its recommendations included proposals for institutional reform, the TRC might have been able to harness its own momentum more effectively by, for example, addressing the Gender or Land Commissions, or by making proposals on economic policy. Arguably, the *Final Report* could also have paid more attention to recording the many ways in which structural violence was systematically meted out beyond well-known instances such as the forced removals from District Six and Sophiatown.

The Issue of Reparations

A second feature of the TRC's work that promoted social justice was its focus on reparations. Its mandate charged the TRC with the responsibility to restore the "human and civil dignity of victims."[51] This was to be done by establishing "as complete a picture as possible of the nature, causes and extent of violations of human rights committed"; by determining "the fate or whereabouts of the victims of such violations"; by affording victims "an opportunity to relate the violations they suffered"; and by "recommending reparation measures in respect of" those who suffered from these violations.[52]

In a nationwide survey conducted in 2001, 74 percent of black South Africans (against only 30 percent of white respondents) agreed that the TRC had done a good or excellent job in "awarding compensation to those who suffered abuses under the apartheid regime."[53] This high rating—despite the government's failure to pay adequate reparations—may have been due to the fact that compensation was understood, at least partly, in symbolic terms, as the restoration of personal dignity, but possibly also that most South Africans still expected the government to respond convincingly to the TRC's recommendations—an expectation that has since largely been dashed.

The first five volumes of the TRC's *Final Report*, published in 1998, included proposals that the government implement a reparations policy with six broad categories: urgent interim reparations, individual grants, symbolic reparations (which included legal and administrative measures), social benefits, community rehabilitation, and institutional reform. After this, however, public attention quickly shifted away from reparations, focusing instead on the deeply contested perpetrator findings and the amnesty hearings. These two processes dragged on for five years after the TRC had officially closed its doors. Reparations were delayed and some remain unpaid to this day—a disappointing end to the TRC, and an issue that has undermined much of the progress made earlier towards restoring victims' dignity. To some degree, this delay remains a mystery. Officially, the government offered the ongoing amnesty court cases as a reason. It promised to respond to the whole TRC report once the amnesty hearings were concluded, a process that dragged on for five years. But this did not really convince victim groups, especially since there was no compelling reason not to begin the reparation process earlier, even if the amnesty process were still on-going. Rather, as has become clear in more recent statements such as that of the erstwhile chief of the National Prosecuting Authority, Vusi Pikoli, it seems there was a decided lack of political will, or perhaps even active resistance against the implementation of the TRC's recommendations from the Mbeki administration. In a supporting affidavit in a groundbreaking court case that would reopen possibilities for prosecuting apartheid-era criminals in late 2015, he said: "I confirm that there was political interference that effectively barred or delayed the investigation and possible prosecution of the cases recommended for prosecution by the TRC."[54] Reasons for this political meddling, which went beyond barring prosecution to include reparation processes too, remain unclear. It may, in part at least, have included considerations on the fiscal implications of an extended reparations program on South Africa's larger development project. But there was also a more subtle, but powerfully present, antipathy from government toward the TRC because of the well-publicised Mbeki/Tutu standoff over the content of the TRC report.

President Mbeki received two further volumes of the TRC's *Final Report* in 2003, and, in response, promised victims individual payments of approximately US$3,000 per person. This was just a sixth of what the TRC had recommended. Not surprisingly, victims who had been waiting for payments since 1998 were thoroughly disenchanted. Not only was the amount unacceptably small to most, but scores of victims who had not participated in the formal TRC process (for whatever reason) were left in the cold. A limited, and under-capacitated TRC Unit belatedly set up in the Ministry of Justice has since done little to remedy this "unfinished business." The President's Fund that was set up to finance reparations, and is administered by the TRC Unit, has been used mainly for exhumations, and for the transport and accommodation of families at reburial ceremonies.

There can be little disagreement that reparations as a whole have fallen well short of expectations. Importantly, though, this failure cannot fairly be laid at the TRC's door in terms of either the design or implementation of its mandate. Arguably, it is more about a lack of political will and institutional capacity, as well as about competing priorities in government, than about the work of the TRC as such.

Moreover, the TRC's recommendations included proposals for wide-ranging institutional reform, and in the last two volumes of its *Final Report*, the TRC made strong claims about the role of big business in supporting and benefiting from apartheid. Calling for the establishment of a Business Reconciliation Fund, the TRC recommended a wealth tax, a once-off levy on corporate and private income, a once-off donation of 1 per cent of the market capitalization of each company listed on the Johannesburg Stock Exchange, as well as a retrospective surcharge on corporate benefits and on all golden handshakes given to senior public servants since 1990. Arguing that such a fund "could provide non-repayable grants, loans, and/or guarantees to business-related funding for black small entrepreneurs in need of either . . . skill or capital for the launching of a business," the TRC concluded that, at the very least, business had a "moral obligation to assist in the reconstruction and development of post-apartheid South Africa through active reparative measures."[55]

Restoring Human Dignity

The TRC's most important contribution to eradicating structural violence was arguably through the many ways in which its work undermined all the cultural justifications that supported structural violence, understood as systematic and systemic discrimination, under apartheid. Unmasking apartheid's cruelty through truth-telling was not only an important building block in national reconciliation, as argued earlier, but it also helped to expose the "cultural violence" of the apartheid system. As Johan Galtung writes:

> cultural violence refers to any aspect of culture that can be used to justify violence, either directly or structurally. . . . Cultural violence makes direct and structural violence look, even feel, right—or at least not wrong. . . . Cultural violence [involves] those aspects of culture, the symbolic sphere of our existence . . . that can be used to justify or legitimise direct or structural violence.[56]

Galtung also explains that "direct violence is an event; structural violence is a process with ups and downs; cultural violence is an invariant, a 'permanence,' remaining essentially the same for long periods, given the slow transformations of basic culture."[57] That is, direct violence can be understood "as direct cruelty perpetrated by human beings against each other and against other forms of life and nature in general," whereas cultural violence is a "substratum" from which direct and structural violence "derive their nutrients."[58]

If Galtung's basic thesis is accepted—specifically that cultural violence can act as a justification for structural violence—the TRC can be said to have played an important role in helping to erode the justifications for apartheid's structural violence. Arguably, the TRC was set up to challenge the cultural violence of apartheid: its racism, the systematic and comprehensive indignity it bestowed on black South Africans, and its assumptions that racial segregation was the only workable dispensation for southern Africa. Through truth-telling, the TRC helped to unmask the apartheid regime as inhuman and exceptionally cruel, without criminalizing all white South Africans or Afrikaners. Yet, crucially, all pretence that apartheid was the last bastion of the European mission to "civilize" Africa fell away as apartheid's human rights abuses became public knowledge, and were openly and overwhelmingly broadcast across South Africa, during eighteen months of public human rights and amnesty hearings. There was literally no way to escape the reality that the apartheid regime had been cruel in a myriad of vindictive, petulant, and dehumanizing ways.

In his foreword to the 1998 *TRC Report*, Tutu wrote, "we believe we have provided enough of the truth about our past for there to be a consensus about it."[59] The TRC's aim was to establish a national memory, a national truth framework to assess the causes, motives, and extent of human rights violations during apartheid, and then to create a consensus that South African society should move decisively away from mass violence, in the form of apartheid, ethnic cleansing, or even genocide.[60]

But it was also arguably in the area of addressing "cultural violence" in its gendered dimensions, that the TRC received strong criticism. Louise du Toit has argued that "that the TRC's failure to do justice to victims of rape is not a simple oversight but rather is *constitutive* of the patriarchal political and symbolic order dominating our political landscape."[61] Too often seen as an "add-on" to reconciliation, gender justice cuts to the heart of what is understood here as political reconciliation. Rebuilding inclusive and fair societies after war and oppression require a specific, systematic, and systemic emphasis on gender, not least because of gender violence's well-documented, and often central, role in fostering conflict supported by a patriarchal "symbolic order" that not only supported the conflict, but may well continue to undergird efforts to make peace as well. Mainstreaming gender within transitional justice now forms a prominent part of the field's innovative thrust, precisely because feminists believe that without upending patriarchy, gender violence, particularly against women, will continue to mark the new dispensation even if the formal war ends—begging the question of those articulating the case for reconciliation, whose peace are you talking about?

The South African TRC has therefore rightly been criticized for its lack of systematic focus on gender violence.[62] At the same time, gender violence in contemporary South Africa remains at epidemic levels. Thus, despite having politico-legal frameworks that formally safeguard gender equality, South Africans are far from realizing gender equality on the streets and in communities, bedrooms, and boardrooms. Conversations about gender redress, and what justly interdependent gender relations should entail, are long overdue. Leila Emdon argues

> that in post apartheid SA society addresses gender-based violence symptomatically—focussing only on gender equity (having more women represented in positions of power) and addressing women as "victims" of gender-based violence. However very little has been done to look at the root causes of gender-based violence, and to locate it within a society that privileges violent masculinities which have a negative effect on both men and women.[63]

Current gender violence has at least some of its roots in apartheid chauvinism. That the TRC did not more to help the country understand this dimension of its past may go some way toward explaining the country's ongoing challenges in this regard.

Nonwithstanding these weaknesses and failures, in contemporary South Africa, the TRC process as a whole also symbolizes a series of lost opportunities—perhaps less in the way that Mamdani described, and closer to what Soyinka hinted in relation to the neglect meted out to the TRC's recommendations, specifically on reparations. In terms of the social momentum it created and the moral legitimacy it gained, Soyinka may well have a point that the TRC could have done more to effectively direct restitution from those who benefited from apartheid to those who suffered all manner of psychological, physical, and structural violence because of it. This is a point to which I return later. Even so, I believe it is incorrect to argue that the TRC had no bearing on structural injustice or worse that it helped to strengthen it; on the contrary, it highlighted structural injustice in startling and compelling ways. At the very least, the TRC did nothing to undermine social justice, although responses to it from the state, the corporate sector, and even civil society may well have done.

The Rainbow Nation at Twenty-Four

It was indeed tempting to believe that most of the hard work of reconciliation had been done when the TRC closed its doors, and that henceforth, life could continue, and society would somehow become more "normal." Certainly, it did not take long for those who accompanied and oversaw the political transition to begin enjoying the spoils of democracy. Political contestation descended to the level of the tit-for-tat squabbles that is typical of democracies mostly everywhere. And some within the governing party quickly built a formidable edifice linking black interests across the corporate and governance sectors in both legitimate and illegitimate ways. As all this happened, the brave new and rapidly integrating political elite inevitably lost some of the urgency that carried it across the political threshold from apartheid to democracy.

The TRC delivered truth-telling in ways that rendered public discourse fundamentally more inclusive, at least of victim perspectives. Thus, if the TRC left South Africans and others disappointed, it was less because of its mandate or even its operational history, and more because of the sustained disinterest so far shown by government and big business alike in following up on the TRC's recommendations, whether in terms of prosecutions of the approximately three hundred names that the TRC handed to the National Prosecuting Authority or indeed of reparations in its various forms. There can be little dispute that the new government's failure to act convincingly has created widespread disappointment about the extent to which reconciliation's promises will be honored. As noted earlier, David Backer provided concrete evidence for this conclusion, showing that approval for the TRC declined dramatically in South Africa between 2003 and 2008.[64] According to Backer, this shift is mainly due to government inaction in response to the TRC's recommendations.

In response to the void left by the government's inaction on this issue, some community-driven processes have begun to open new possibilities for interracial reconciliation, built patiently where individual citizens took the initiative. For example, on Christmas Eve 1996, Olga Macingwane was just another South African doing last-minute shopping in Worcester, a small South African town about an hour or so east of Cape Town. That night, two bomb blasts shook the little town, and indeed the country. One of the bombs went off in the shop Olga was in, and she became one of the sixty-seven direct victims of this racially motivated attack, with injuries so severe that she will never again be able to resume regular employment.

The bombers were four Afrikaner men, among them eighteen-year-old Stefaans Coetzee. Some thirteen years into his imprisonment, Stefaans contacted Khulumani, which is a support group for victims of political violence, and asked if it would be possible for him to meet the victims of his attack. In 2011, four affected members of the Worcester community, including Olga, made the more than thousand-kilometer journey by car to Pretoria Central Correctional Facility to meet Stefaans. An extraordinary process of reconciliation followed that has the potential to make a significant impact, not only on relations between the victims and perpetrators of this specific and atrocious attack, but also on the way that all the townspeople of Worcester go about their everyday lives. A movement called the Worcester Hope and Reconciliation Process has been formed, which is steered by Olga, and she has been campaigning for Stefaans to be brought to Worcester to serve out the remainder of his service in the community that he once sought to destroy.

Although such stories remain relatively isolated, they do act as a reminder to the broader society that reconciliation remains a real possibility for those who are willing to do the work. And should they become a more regular feature in communities across South Africa, such local reconciliation processes could help fill the void created by the disappointment in how the TRC process ended.

Contesting Assessments

If post-TRC South Africa has seen isolated cases of reconciliation at the local-community level, how should its broader nation-building process be assessed? In this context, political analyses tend to fall into one of two dominant narratives, both centered on the country's most obviously unfinished business in terms of post-apartheid reconstruction, namely, the vast poverty and shocking inequality that continues to bisect society, mostly but no longer precisely, along racial lines.[65]

As often happens with political analyses, the opposing narratives choose one incontrovertible fact as the systematic lens through which they evaluate progress as a whole, and by implication too, reconciliation's success or failure. The one narrative, promoted by the ANC government, could be called "A Good Story to Tell,"[66] while the counter-narrative, which is widely present in critiques of the new dispensation, might be "Things Have Gone Terribly Wrong." A book by erstwhile TRC deputy-chairperson Alex Boraine is one example: its subtitle, *On the Brink of a Failed State,* has drawn much attention.[67]

Accordingly, the ANC built its campaign for the 2014 general election around "The Good Story," proclaiming that most South Africans are demonstrably better off under ANC rule than they have ever been before. Meanwhile, like Boraine, the opposition parties focused on the facts that South Africa remains the world's most unequal society, that poverty has not been reduced anywhere near as much as had been hoped in 1994, and that at least to some degree, elite collusion and corruption are to blame for this. Simply but starkly, these critics allege that the plight of poor no longer really matters—that the sense of doing things together, of discovering and affirming interdependence between white and black during the transition, was not extended to a similar sense of interdependence between rich and poor, between the combined new and old elite on the one hand, and the still-excluded black poor majority on the other hand.

Many critics allege that economic inequality would have looked different today were it not for gross mismanagement by government, indifference from the private sector, and a civil society that has been systematically undermined, excluded, and depleted by lack of funding and support. Thus pride and disappointment face off, with opposing camps both deeply angry over what they believe to be the other side's deliberate obfuscation of undeniable realities. For the ANC, critics like Boraine deny the depth of apartheid's social legacies, which they argue are being systematically addressed and gradually overcome. For critics of the government, the ANC, led until 2018 by the controversial Jacob Zuma, is characterized by farcical leadership, disastrous mismanagement, and endemic corruption, all contributing to a culture of impunity in the public service and the private sector, and to the spread of increasingly violent protests, as well as outbreaks of xenophobia, in poorer communities across the country.

To both sides, the picture may in fact be considerably more nuanced than they are willing to admit, but the stories remain startlingly opposed. Moving beyond this politicized and polemical debate requires a careful conceptualization of social justice, not in abstract terms, but as an outcome of political reconciliation within the concrete post-apartheid context. This implies an understanding of social justice that is closely linked to redress and inclusion, rather than simply to the provision of infrastructural improvements while communities, for all intents and purposes, continue to live in isolation, with no sense of redress or even acknowledgment of how economically and socially excluded they are. Also necessary is an analysis that is flexible and comprehensive enough to recognize that these opposing narratives are built on two sets of incontrovertible facts and thus facts that both need to be acknowledged in a more nuanced view. Aspects of the lives of most South Africans *have* improved over the last twenty years. However, the lack of credible political and civic leadership means that rising factionalism, increased corruption, mismanagement, and gross accumulation in the face of rising poverty are also true. All this is feeding South Africans' discontentment with the levels of inequality and insecurity they experience.

Inter-Racial Trust Limited by Inequality

So what do ordinary South Africans think about how reconciliation has delivered on its early promise of reconstituted relations marked by greater levels of inclusion and fairness? Since 2003, the IJR has conducted annual surveys to measure South African attitudes to reconciliation and has published the findings as annual *South African Reconciliation Barometer Reports*.[68] In 2014, the IJR decided to analyze all the survey data collected over the previous decade to try to discern trends and changes over time. Their 2014 report thus examines how South

Africans have evaluated levels of inclusion and fairness over the years since apartheid ended.

In terms of social inclusion, while levels of interracial contact and socialization have improved over the past eleven years, and thereby levels of interracial trust, the poor remain largely excluded from such contact.[69]

> The percentage of South Africans who report often or always talking to someone from another race in a social setting increased from 10.4% in 2003 to 23.5% in 2013. However, when we disaggregate this figure by class, we see that South Africans in the higher living-standards measure (LSM) groups are much more likely to socialise across race than the middle LSMs, and the lowest LSMs are the least likely to socialise across race.[70]

From 2003 to 2013, the difference between interracial socializing by the poorest and richest South Africans widened considerably from 17.6 percent to 27.2 percent. The IJR therefore concluded that

> not only are the poorest South Africans excluded from interracial socialisation relative to the middle class and wealthier South Africans, but the degree of this exclusion also seems to have increased between 2003 and 2013, as the percentage of South Africans socialising across race has increased by a greater amount than those socialising in the lowest LSMs.[71]

Since the first survey was conducted in 2003, the survey findings have increasingly pointed to income difference as the most important source of social division in South Africa. Although this important finding should not be taken to imply that race is no longer salient (poverty is still highly racialized) or that the poorest are necessarily among the most prejudiced.

James Gibson, who worked closely with the IJR in the early years of the survey's development, draws on the survey data from 2013 to argue that while racial isolation remains considerable, the problem of race in South Africa has become somewhat less of a problem over the course of the twenty years of democracy.[72] Gibson notes that despite the fact that considerable racial prejudice, together with high levels of isolation, persists, and even though this will not be eradicated through casual contact between race groups alone, there is evidence that seems to indicate that South Africans themselves believe that race relations are improving. Interracial contact is becoming more common, he says, and for white people at least this is reducing prejudice. Gibson thus concludes that

South Africa "is on a path to becoming a society that would have been virtually unimaginable 20 years ago."[73]

At the same time, a large section of the black population remains significantly isolated from the rest of society in what can only be described as a social justice deficit. South Africans do therefore agree that reconciliation is not possible to proceed much further than it has already come without a serious change in current levels of socioeconomic inequality.

Growing inequality therefore points to one possible aspect of disappointment with the justice promised as outcome when Mandela and De Klerk sought to justify reconciliation over ongoing armed conflict, and when South Africans "practiced reconciliation" during the National Peace Accord, the Multiparty negotiations, and the TRC hearings. Articulated clearly and enacted in compelling ways as a foreshadowing of the society that was to come, South Africa's reconciliation process promised justice as inclusivity *as well as* justice as fairness.

The South African government today claims that it has upheld the justice promise. As evidence, it points to the important steps the country has taken to fight the abject poverty in which apartheid forced blacks. As evidence for this claim, in April 2014, Statistics South Africa's statistician-general, Pali Lehohla, announced that poverty levels had indeed decreased from 2006 to 2011. This somewhat counterintuitive claim was based on metric data collected through income and expenditure surveys run in 2006 and 2011 plus a survey of living conditions conducted from 2008 to 2009.[74]

However, while poverty had decreased, Lehohla also noted that inequality (as measured by the Gini-coefficient) remained largely unchanged at 0.69, marginally better than the score of 0.72 measured in 2006, but still one of the highest levels of inequality anywhere in the world. And I would contend that it is precisely such levels of inequality, rather than marginal—or in some cases more marked—successes in overcoming poverty, that stokes discontent and disappointment, and the sense too that reconciliation politics enabled the white elite to "get away with their ill-gotten gains" while enriching only a coterie of politically connected black leaders. Such perceptions undermine directly reconciliation's early promise of justice as inclusion contained both in its political justifications and subsequent practices.

The perception that whites are indifferent, or even hostile to, social justice is further strengthened not only by current levels of (largely racialized) inequality, but also by findings such as those of the Reconciliation Barometer's 2014 report,[75] which points to a radical difference between races in relation to supporting social justice when this is understood to include some form of concrete, material redress. Perhaps linked to increasing levels of denial, white South Africans seem to be significantly less willing to support material forms of redress, and the already low percentage of those who supported this in the past seems to be on a steady decline.[76] The same trajectory is true of white respondents' agreement with the statement that "apartheid resulted in the poverty of many black South Africans today." This lack of acknowledgment among apartheid's primary beneficiaries remains one of the major outstanding issues on the reconciliation agenda. In the early 2000s, following the work of the TRC, levels of denial about the extent of apartheid criminality were significantly lower in the white community; by 2014, denial among whites had risen significantly.

Coupled with what appears to be a steady decline in poverty levels, changing attitudes toward race relations might suggest that critics of the government have it wrong. Certainly these indications seem to belie Boraine's assessment that South Africa is on the brink of becoming a failed state. Nevertheless, the glibness of the ANC's 2014 election manifesto appeared to be terribly out of touch with the sentiments of citizens. It is significant that, although a majority of voters returned the ANC to power, the number of registered and unregistered citizens who did not vote in 2014 constitute more than half of all the eligible voters in South Africa. Thus, the ANC is losing millions of supporters, but this does not mean that opposition parties are winning them over. Disaffected voters seem to be choosing to stay home on election days.

National Unity Eroded by Corruption

A second important cluster of trends relevant to how South Africans evaluate reconciliation relates to a growing perception that South Africa is not led in ways that are fair and transparent, and that its political leaders care more about amassing private wealth than about representing the interests of their constituencies. This finding, reflected in increasing disillusionment with the notion of a united South African identity, I would argue militates directly against reconciliation's promise—both articulated and enacted—of justice as fairness. This is reflected in increasing disillusionment with the notion of a united South African identity.

Support for a united South Africa decreased from a 72.9 percent in the years after Mandela's retirement in 1997 to 55 percent in 2014. This diminished enthusiasm for the "rainbow nation" mirrors, almost exactly, a dramatic decline in trust for the political leadership. In 2003, more than 70 percent of black South Africans trusted parliament and 62.5 percent trusted national political leaders. By 2013, these figures had fallen dramatically to 52.9 percent and 53.8 percent, respectively. For other racial groups, these figures were not high to begin with and stayed at more or less stable low levels.[77]

This finding points to dramatically reduced trust in public officials, and the trend has been strong even if (given Mandela's popularity) the new government started on an unusually high base in this regard. Of course, growing awareness of corruption among the elite is a factor. The ANC was able to install Jacob Zuma as president because the country's National Prosecuting Authority decided to drop approximately seven hundred corruption charges against him on grounds that there was suspicion of executive meddling in the case. Zuma's controversial presidency has since been dogged by scandal, including the widely publicized charge that he unlawfully benefited from "security upgrades" at his personal residence to the tune of more than US$20 million. His deputy, Cyril Ramaphosa, was also implicated in ordering a crackdown on striking miners that led to the shooting of thirty-four employees at a mine owned by Lonmin in the Marikana area near Johannesburg; Ramaphosa was a non-executive director of Lonmin at the time. However, since his election in December 2017 as president of the ANC, and subsequently as President of the Republic in February 2018 a sense of cautious optimism has returned. At the very least, Ramaphosa's ascendency to the South African presidency, has for the time being, ignited the hope that the days of the Zuma-centered cleptocracy that immobilized South Africa for so long, may well be numbered. Although, for now, it is too early to tell exactly to predict how this will play out, but South Africans are hoping that more inclusivity and fairness will mark the Ramaphosa era than did the calamitous Zuma years.

In a study published in 2014, Hennie van Vuuren, an expert on corruption in South Africa, identified two emerging trends. First, that government corruption is approaching levels that were last seen in the final years of apartheid. Second, that elite networks within government and business are deeply compromised, and that this is shaping and destabilizing anti-corruption efforts. He claims that South Africa is

> a functioning democracy but with elements of the political elite that have anti-democratic tendencies. These elements do not launch a direct attack on democratic institutions, but rather seek to undermine them by ensuring that the rule of law is applied inconsistently, and [that] a climate of uncertainty exists within management of public institutions.[78]

South Africa's fiercely independent and vocal media have ensured that the pervasiveness of corruption is firmly lodged in the public mind. Not a week goes by without stories of corruption in the corridors of power. Of course, rampant corruption, and the consequent loss of trust in the country's political leadership, strengthens public perceptions of a fairness deficit.

In 2014, for the first time since 1994, clear signs of rising racial tension emerged. On the one hand, there was a spike in highly publicized racist attacks by whites on blacks. On the other hand, relatively young black activists, such as Julius Malema, made increasingly militant demands for the repossession of land and wealth, so much of which is still in white hands. Although 2014 was initially touted as one for reflection after Mandela's passing in late 2013 and for celebrating the milestone of twenty years of democracy, social fragmentation seemed to intensify. For example, in a highly charged move, COSATU, South Africa's largest labor federation and traditionally part of an alliance with the ANC and the South African Communist Party, expelled its largest affiliate, the National Union of Mineworkers in South Africa (NUMSA). NUMSA has been working to create a new labor federation outside the ANC-led alliance, thus signifying a significant loss of support for the ANC. Within the governing elite, evidence of factionalism increased. Dramatic stand-offs occurred in parliament, prompting the Speaker to call in security police to remove opposition MPs. At the same time, the president was the subject of another inquiry regarding corruption charges against him. Some observers began to speculate that South Africa was finally facing its "Zimbabwe moment."

These trends intensified during 2015 and into 2016 and produced a new form of social protest, a mass student movement that swept the length and breadth of the country. Emanating from #RhodesMustFall, students attending South Africa's most prestigious universities succeeded in forcing President Zuma to announce a zero percent increase for fees in 2016. Significantly, the students extended their struggle to include "outsourced" workers, causing, in some cases at least, the universities to take reverse "outsourcing" in favor of full employment. For most part, these protests were restrained and disciplined, and interestingly, marked by intense debate and dialogue among students across all sorts of social divides that plague the post-apartheid society. Clearly, structural exclusion was a major theme, but conversations went deeper. In many cases, a new generation began to deliberate on what can (and has) been called "cultural violence," the abiding deep-seated prejudices, biases, and assumptions that implied and enforced racial and gender hierarchies for centuries, and that, so the students claim, continue to bedevil reconciliation in South Africa.

Social unrest culminated in late 2015 and early 2016 with a renewed focus on Parliament, and its relationship with the Executive, specifically, President Zuma, who had earlier been fingered in a Public Protector report as having unduly benefited from grossly inflated security upgrades at his private residence, Nkandla.[79] While opposition chants of "Pay back the money" immobilized the most important Parliamentary moment of the year, the Presidential State of the Nation Address, and reduced it to a farce, many of the more violent protests later in the year ended at Parliament too. On several occasions, security forces had to intervene forcefully to keep protesters from entering the chambers. Coming against the backdrop of the Nkandla scandal and the resulting Parliamentary crisis of legitimacy as it struggled to hold the President to account, the IJR reported through the Afrobarometer survey on a radical drop of public trust in South Africa's political leadership. Indeed, President Zuma's approval rating dropped from 64 percent in 2011 to a meager 36 percent in 2015, lower than his predecessor at any moment of his own controversial presidency.[80]

It stands to reason that neither corruption nor inequality could adequately be analyzed without reference to the private and civic sectors. Determining more precisely what the contours of these failures and measure of collusion between government, the private sector, and civil society are that have given rise to a justified sense of disappointment in reconciliation in South Africa is therefore crucial.

Increasingly central in the distrust of President Zuma has precisely been his relationship with a controversial Indian family, the Guptas, who run a business empire in South Africa and stand accused of buying political favors through their close connection with the president. Symptomatic of this allegedly collusional relationship was the permission granted to a Gupta private plane to land at a national air force base. The outcry that followed again raised the president's proximity to various friends and connections obtained during the struggle years, after several hundred charges against him were controversially dropped in the run-up to his presidency, charges that have been reinstated once Zuma left office.[81] Clearly, corruption will remain a central concern for years to come.

With its "youth bulge," its disaffected middle class, its drop in political trust, its apartheid history and commodities-based economy, and the on-going fight for accountability, South Africa continues be a candidate for renewed political conflict down the line. What stands between it and such a scenario is arguably a credible and widely accepted political system, ongoing social service delivery (imperfect as it may be), and a relatively organized security apparatus compared to peer countries elsewhere. But in all these areas there have been setbacks rather than gains during recent years. And so, while justice retains a fighting chance in South Africa, and while the political transition brought important and stable gains to a majority of citizens, the country has its work cut out if it is realize the ideals with which it embarked on reconciliation in 1994.

Conclusion

South Africa has achieved much since Nelson Mandela first walked free on February 11, 1990. Nevertheless, a prominent discourse of disappointment has emerged among South Africans and many seem to feel let down by the country's reconciliation process in particular. Capturing this discourse, well-known journalist Sisonke Msimang, for example, lamented the "end of the myth of the rainbow nation" as one of those "who are tired of the empty politics of reconciliation—which assumes that whites have paid for their sins and blacks have forgiven them."[82]

In this chapter I considered whether South Africans are justified in feeling disappointed by reconciliation, an idea that played such a central role in framing the country's transition from apartheid to democracy. Critics who claim that the transition has been a complete failure with regard to social justice are misguided. The transition delivered a constitution with social justice as its central concern, a range of initiatives to monitor progress toward transformation, and a TRC, which despite its limited mandate recommended some specific measures for material redress. The facts of declining poverty levels, improved race relations, and vastly improving services for the poor must count as significant gains.

I disagree that in South Africa's case reconciliation originally offered opaque and utopian goals, such as those linked to emotional closure or forgiveness, as implied by Sisonke Msimang's characterization of reconciliation quoted above. Instead, reconciliation as articulated by Mandela and De Klerk, and as enacted in the NPA, the MPNP, and eventually the TRC, promised decisive steps towards justice—but deliberately refrained from promising full justice, complete forgiveness or total emotional closure. Instead, the promise was for justice, not understood primarily as judicial justice, but as comprehensive sociopolitical justice achieved in a phased approach that would prioritize political justice as a basis for a wider social and economic justice.

Despite achieving sustained democratic rule, somewhat improved race relations, and declining poverty rates since 2003, many South Africans are disappointed at the measure to which reconciliation has delivered on its justice promise. High levels of inequality and corruption mean that citizens question their leaders' commitment to reconciliation's promise of justice as increasing fairness and inclusion. This explains the growing sense of disappointment that South Africans express about the country's reconciliation process.

This finding should not be read as a denunciation of South Africa's political transition or indeed a rejection of reconciliation as a framing concept for political transition elsewhere. To the contrary, reconciliation has produced significant gains in conflict resolution, constitutional development, and transition management. It has, however, not made good sufficiently on its justice promise as far as social inclusion and fairness are concerned—or, at least, this is South Africans' view today.

In my view, inclusivity and fairness had not been sacrificed at the time when reconciliation shaped the political transition. Instead, they were compromised more recently, to the extent that inclusion across social divides failed to materialize and to the extent that political leaders deviated from serving the common good. At the same time, too many civic leaders and ordinary citizens have tolerated (or colluded in) growing corruption and inequality.

This begs the question as to why inequality (accompanied by persistent racial acrimony) and corruption (accompanied by a failure to build national identity) have increased to the extent that they have. Where does responsibility lie for these failures of a democratic state that militates against the very terms of its founding? Is it due to a fundamental design fault in the peace process and thus by implication in the characterization of reconciliation that drove developments during this period, or is it a failure of political, civic, and private sector leadership subsequently? I have argued for the latter. After all, while operating within significant constraints not least to appease a nervous white military and an equally nervous white capital base, the former nonetheless delivered a manifestly fair and inclusive political dispensation with a Constitution that explicitly advocated for, and legally sanctioned, radical social transformation.

It is largely what happened subsequently—the failure to act on the TRC recommendations, the dropping of key economic commitments linked to the constitutional promise of equality for all, the subsequent rise in levels of inequality and thus persistent levels of racial isolation, but also the growing levels of corruption undermining a sense of national unity—that is foremost in South Africans' mind when they articulate their disappointment with reconciliation.

So if South Africa had to undergo its political transition again, what would be done differently, and what would be repeated? In my opinion, a sense of fundamental and comprehensive interdependence would still be the most relevant, useful, and ethically sound insight around which political leaders and citizens at all levels and on both sides could be persuaded that violence offered no viable solutions to the conflict. Straddling peacemaking, transitional justice as well as social transformation, the notion of interdependence derived its potency from the de facto reality that apartheid tried so hard to deny, and also from its power, once articulated by the political leadership, to open up ethical options for a shared future.

If given the option to relive their transition, South Africans may very well once again opt to begin by expressing their interdependence, and follow this with a series of transitional mechanisms and platforms that would gradually become more inclusive and fair, eventually culminating in an agreement as to what an inclusive and fair future would involve. Also included in the broad design would be a public process of accounting for the past and a drive toward social transformation that aims to overcome not only the trauma of political violence but also the injustice of structural violence. In short, South Africa underwent a political transition that worked, and for this reason, it is hard to imagine equally or more successful alternatives.

Yet, in the years following 1994 there is plenty that the country would wish to do differently a second time around. Social justice for victims of apartheid's structural violence would have been pursued with far more concerted national focus and urgency—possibly driven by a specialized transitional mechanism focused only on social justice that could broker agreements between public and private sectors on the scope and modalities of redistribution of wealth. This body would be composed of a combination of political and civic leaders, and be empowered to hold both government and the private sector accountable against the justice promises they made. Called something like the Social Justice Commission, it would have needed at least a ten-year mandate, and would have advanced the work of the TRC in two ways.

First, as discussed earlier, such a commission would have allowed the TRC to narrow its focus to political rather than structural violence, but with a much more overt focus on gender violence. That is, gender violence should have been acknowledged as a stand-alone category of political violence (as opposed to being subsumed under the category of "severe ill treatment"). In addition, a far more concerted effort should have been made to understand the impact of structural violence on the dignity of victims of gross human rights violations. That is, although structural redress, as a political and technical process, would have fallen outside the remit of the TRC, it could have made the dehumanizing effects of both structural and political violence explicit, showing how one form of violence feeds off, enables, and justifies the other, and has a negatively cumulative effect on the dignity of victims.

Second, such a commission would have monitored the delivery of reparations, effectively curtailing the government's unilateral control over the implementation of reparations packages. Governments all over the world have generally proven ineffective and reluctant when it comes to following through on reparations. Germany, Chile, and Morocco are positive exceptions but, in Africa, where TRCs in Kenya, Liberia, Sierra Leone, and beyond have followed South Africa's example, governments have simply failed in this regard.

In addition, if given a second chance, the social justice commission would have issued a very clear instruction to government not to attempt to implement reparations as development projects through its existing line functions. Blurring the distinction between reparations (as a special form of symbolic and material redress for wrongs suffered) and development (government's core task in any context) robs victims of the acknowledgment and apology that is crucial to restoring human and civic dignity.

As far as accountability is concerned, the overall design of a limited, conditional amnesty process, with its delicate balance between restorative and retributive justice, ought to be retained. In my view, it was also correct not to try to force perpetrators to show remorse, but a fourth criterion for amnesty could be added.

Thus, over and above full disclosure, proof of political affiliation and motive, and the proportionality of the crime in relation to the political objective, some form of personalized redress directly from the perpetrator to the families of victims—similar to the community rehabilitation process instituted in Rwanda through the Gacaca courts—would lessen the sense that perpetrators "got away with it" and also provide some basic sense of direct redress that had been largely absent as the process in fact played out.

In addition, knowing what we know now about the extent to which the police service has struggled to overcome their heavy-handed habits associated with apartheid policing,[83] a very strong argument can be made for a more thorough lustration process that would prevent any perpetrators from staying on in the police or defense forces after coming clean at the TRC.

Finally, to bolster accountability still further, more consideration should have been given to ways in which politicians could account for their role in furthering political violence. The case of F. W. de Klerk was instructive in this regard. Had the ICC been in existence at the time, it might have provided added leverage in forcing such politicians to play a more constructive role at the TRC. It may also be important to emphasize that top leaders should issue personal apologies, and not just collective ones on behalf of the regime. Leon Wessels's apology that he "did not know because he did not want to know" proved far more meaningful to victims than De Klerk's generalized, collective statement.

SECTION TWO

THEORETICAL LANDSCAPES

5

The Forgiving Embrace

Moving beyond the South African case, I now consider how reconciliation has been thought about and enacted more broadly.[1] At face value, reconciliation theories, definitions, and processes have multiplied beyond the point of being categorized easily.

My lawyer friends in the transitional justice arena often complain about this "fuzziness." Some feel that this rules out reconciliation's utility as a policy framework—precisely because of the lack of consensus and clarity on what is meant by the term. My somewhat jocular retort is that reconciliation may indeed be a confusing concept, but then justice is arguably even more contested; that it has generated even more debate, disagreement, and confusion; and yet remains central to policymaking. The more serious point is that conceptual differences about its meaning, should not disqualify reconciliation as a meaningful policy contributor. If handled correctly, the debates generated by what reconciliation does or should mean, may in fact become one of the concept's most meaningful contributions to stimulating progress during political transition. This is precisely where differences become clear but also where common ground may emerge.

For some of the theorists discussed in the pages that follow, it is precisely this diversity in approach and conceptualization to reconciliation that prompts the ongoing search for common themes that could make some sense of the need to compare, inform, warn and evaluate reconciliation processes not only within given contexts, but also across them. It is therefore important, even as differences and contestations are acknowledged, not to give up on pursuing theoretical clarity that at least attempt to account for what can be expected, offered, and hoped for when societies seek to reconcile. But clearly humility is a good place to start with this enquiry. In this section, I use the notion of ideal types or typologies[2] as a means of making the large variety of reconciliation discourses in circulation at least *somewhat* more comprehensible.[3] Max Weber, the pivotal

German sociologist, explained that an ideal type, "in its purely fictional nature, is a methodological utopia [that] cannot be found empirically anywhere in reality."[4] It is therefore possible, indeed probable, that no individual theorist discussed in the next three chapters would identify wholly or completely with the reconciliation typologies I associate them with. However, I am of the view that it is possible to discern certain "family traits" among existing theories, so as to identify with sufficient accuracy at least the following three "ideal types" of reconciliation (summarized in table format in an appendix on pages 237–239).

The first typology or "ideal type", and which forms the focus in this chapter, is typically associated with the notion of political forgiveness, and developed within a framework which I call "social restoration." The following two chapters focus on two other typologies respectively: reconciliation as "liberal peace" and reconciliation as "agonist deliberation." In each chapter, and in keeping with the structure I developed in the first section, I first examine how that particular framework thinks about the ways in which reconciliation makes a start in hostile, violent contexts, its beginnings.[5] Then I discuss some of the concrete milestones typically associated with this "type" of reconciliation once it broadens into institutional arrangements and processes. Finally, I focus on the promise of, and (therefore also the) justifications for, each "type" of reconciliation. A brief discussion of the first type of reconciliation theory, developed within the framework of social restoration, now follows.

A Call to Communities of Reconciliation

Reporting on South Africa's TRC as a journalist, the author and poet Antjie Krog made the point that reconciliation may have been a misleading term to apply to South Africa's transition in the first place, because there was no bygone era in which racial harmony had ever prevailed and to which society could return as is seemingly implied by the prefix "re-" in reconciliation.[6] Apartheid, Krog explained did not fracture a once-positive relationship between whites and blacks. Instead, it doggedly solidified, in law, politics, and social structure, the exploitative relations that had existed under colonialism. In fact, since Europeans first set foot in the Cape, and possibly even before, South African history had been one of separation, subjugation, and division. This is as true of the genocide against the original inhabitants of the Cape, the Khoi, as it is of Cecil Rhodes's "purchasing" the area known today as Zimbabwe from the bemused Ndebele chief, Lobengula, for a thousand rifles.[7] And it is as true of the 1913 Land Act that rendered black South Africa landless in the country of their birth, as it is of apartheid's outlawing of sexual relations across the color line and refusing black South Africans a decent education, and of countless other examples besides. From trading post to imperial possession to apartheid state,

South Africa proceeded consistently along lines that ensured the exploitation of the black population by white settlers. Perhaps, therefore Krog's proposed, "conciliation" would have been a better term to use, and it might have captured more accurately the radical changes proposed by Mandela's project.

Historically, Krog's observation is largely accurate. In fact, it holds for most post-colonial societies. Yet, history also testifies to the fact, as I showed in an earlier chapter, that South Africans generally had little difficulty in accepting reconciliation as a national project after Mandela was released and the ANC and other liberation organizations were unbanned in 1990. And this was true despite the obvious fact that no one was able to invoke a golden age to which South Africans could return via the path of reconciliation. South Africans' popular, almost intuitive, acceptance of the notion of reconciliation was true of communities of most, if not all, backgrounds and persuasions and were evident in a succession of opinion polls and even election results.

It is not easy to explain this phenomenon, if as Krog implies, reconciliation may have been a misnomer in the first place. Yet, by adjusting Krog's idea somewhat, reconciliation's popularity post-1990 may become more comprehensible. Is it possible, to think of the call "to reconcile" as a moral rather than a historical call? And that South Africans understood this, namely that Mandela, and other leaders' were issuing a moral rather than historical challenge? Was it perhaps meant, and duly received, as a call to return to a moral community that South Africans could all agree *ought* to have been, instead of one that had in fact existed?

If we pursue this line of thinking, we can postulate that reconciliation processes can be thought of, in principle at least, to begin with a call to "something new" rather than as a return to "something old"; that it is essentially a progressive, forward-reaching call towards a moral ideal rather than a reclamatory, backward-looking call to return to a golden era?

South African political analyst T. O. Molefe seems to think so. Referring to reconciliation's original emergence as an accounting term, Molefe has argued that political reconciliation could be explained as a "reconciling" of the current state of affairs in a country with an ideal one—much as reconciling one's books at the end of a month implies both harmonizing the way that transactions are reflected on paper with the ways in which events actually occurred, as well as structuring transactions in ways that meet auditing requirements. Molefe notes that this process implies a delicate give and take between that which is and that which ought to be.[8]

Similarly, the reconciliation theorists I focus on in this chapter argue that reconciliation begins when visionary leaders call their peers (and, by implication, society at large) to help create a form of community that is morally desirable, whether or not in fact such a community ever existed before. Leaders typically use imaginative verbal and symbolic gestures, metaphors and imagery to issue such calls—for apologies, for forgiveness, for expressions of solidarity—but the message amounts to the same thing: reconciliation for these leaders, and the theorists that seek to interpret their actions, is about the restoration of an ideal, a moral community yet to emerge.

Drawing on firsthand experiences during the war in the former Yugoslavia, the Croatian theologian Miroslav Volf produced a study of reconciliation that is often cited as representative of this framework which sees reconciliation as a call to a new moral community—the kind of reconciliation theory I call "reconciliation as social restoration." Appearing just as the South African TRC commenced its work, but describing a distinctly Balkan context, Volf's book *Exclusion and Embrace*[9] made a significant impact in reconciliation studies. Volf's conception of reconciliation invokes the metaphor of the "drama of an embrace, in four acts," mirroring the physical action of two human beings who enter an embrace by opening their arms, waiting, closing their arms around one another, and then opening their arms again. Volf emphasized the importance of the embrace being set in motion by an opening of arms—a signaling of "desire for the other" that is borne of a discontentment with a self-enclosed identity. Opening our arms signals that we have created space for the other, and made the boundary between ourselves and others permeable. The gesture invites the other to enter and, at the same time, it is a "soft knock" on the other's door. Not a storming down of the door, the gesture is a request that respectfully invites another into communion.

This beautiful metaphor paints a vivid picture of reconciliation as entering into community with one's enemy, and yet, evidently harbors real risks at the same time. History illustrates that, all too often, oppression and violence, rather than peace and justice, return in the name of "moral politics" that advocate one form of social restoration or another. Vladimir Lenin in post-Bolshevik Russia was but one example of a political leader who called for unity under a single, moral vision. But to realize his communist "restoration" of society, Lenin also built brutal concentration camps, punished political opponents by engineering famine in their communities, and prevented the emergence of democratic governance, thus ultimately helping to create one of the most oppressive and violent states the world has ever known. Indeed, without Lenin's moral idealism, Stalin would have been unable to reign with the unprecedented levels of terror that he did.[10] As Andrew Schaap put it, "there is good reason to be suspicious of the ideal of community as it is in the name of this ideal that oppression is legitimised."[11] This is anything but an idle, abstract discussion. It is often a critical question facing citizens emerging from terrible periods in their countries as they are trying to evaluate whether or not to follow one or another leader into the kind of community his or she is advocating to restore.

The realization that idealism and totalitarianism are often barely a breath apart has prompted reconciliation theorists such as Volf and others, to carefully track some of the implications and conditions attached to calls for the restoration of community in the name of reconciliation. Put simply, they have pointed out that not everyone calling for social restoration is to be trusted or followed, however compelling their arguments and imagery. Social restorationists have been particularly careful to determine how to avoid a return to violence under reconciliation's guise, particularly in contexts of ongoing violence and oppression. Whether they have been successful in producing a theoretical approach that achieves this, will be discussed again in the concluding section of this chapter. Volf emphasizes pointedly that the aim is to enter into an embrace "that is not a bear hug," but rather a gentler, less-threatening touch.[12] Clearly, important implications and assumptions, not only about the nature of society but also about individuals and the link between the two, are embedded in this call to embrace.

Social restoration as a "type of reconciliation" implies a worldview with features that, its adherents claim, does in fact set it apart from oppressive and totalitarian calls for community. To support this claim, it is necessary to unpack carefully certain basic assumptions within the social restoration framework, about the nature of the world and how it all fits together—what philosophers call ontological assumptions. For theorists like Volf, these basic assumptions are precisely the safeguards which protect reconciliation as social restoration from excesses such as those experienced under Leninism, for example.

The basic articles of faith belonging to reconciliation understood as social restoration are found across a wide range of disciplines and thinkers. These include communitarian and multicultural political scientists, social psychologists and narrative philosophers, restorative justice theorists, traditional-culture practitioners, advocates of political forgiveness, peacemakers, and theologians across the religious spectrum, to name just a few. All these traditions have contributed ideas about what the call to reconciliation as social restoration might imply for the fundamental ways in which we understand society or "the world", and vice versa.[13]

So far my argument has been that for social restoration, reconciliation is initiated with a call to restore a moral (not historical) community—a community based on reconciliation as a set of practices of relational restoration.

A *first* key feature that theorists in this line of thinking highlight, that sets communities of reconciliation apart from oppressive, exclusionary and unjust communities, is the key belief or assumption that all relationships are firstly human relationships, including crucially also political relationships, and therefore that political reconciliation happens in broadly the same way as "normal" interpersonal processes of relational healing. Political relations should therefore first and foremost be acknowledged as "thick relations"; that is, the diversity, individuality, and cultural specificity of identities, and specifically of political relationships, need to be taken into account when countries seek to build a new political community out of the ashes of war and/or oppression. It is when these identities are ignored or buried under calls "for a common humanity," or "universal brotherhood," that things often go wrong, and that totalitarianism raises its ugly head, these theorists claim.

This assumption does enjoy obvious appeal in many post-conflict situations, given the fact that issues of identity often play a crucial role in conflicts. For example, the importance of social identity in Canada's struggles to politically reconcile its French and English-speaking communities, has prompted Canadian Charles Taylor's important work on the concept of *recognition*, which, in turn, builds on the work of Friedrich Hegel. It has become hugely influential in shaping reconciliation theory and political theory more generally.[14]

Famously, the struggle for recognition in Hegel's thought begins with the master recognizing his dependence on his slaves. Prior to this, the master believes himself independent of his slaves and views and treats them as personal property. To confirm his power over them, the master sets out to annihilate his slaves. But in planning this, he comes to realize that he is, in fact, dependent on the slaves for his own identity. After all, he cannot be a master if there are no slaves. In a moment of what Hegel calls "proto-recognition," the master is forced to acknowledge that he cannot do away with the slaves, because his sense of self and self-certainty depends on their existence.[15] The slaves, in turn, also come to understand their power over the master, and this forms the basis for a struggle in which the slaves risk death in order to establish their own sense of self-recognition—as subjects who can shape their own destinies, not objects of the master's supreme will. This process, which Hegel uses to illustrate the reconciliation dynamic, sets in motion a series of events that eventually results in restored, more reciprocal relationships.

Building on these ideas, Taylor argued that recognition consists of an acknowledgment of identity and of the different ways in which identity manifests in society and the restoration of society after conflict. Thus, for Taylor, social identity plays a fundamentally important role in community cohesion. Consequently, Taylor argued, a failure to recognize identity has the potential to harm communities just as much as physical violence does.[16] It is not coincidental that so many dictators, from the former Yugoslavia's Tito, to Spain's Franco, Lenin, Saddam Hussein and many others justified their brutality in terms of calls to some notion of universal identity, whilst denying any acknowledgment of those social and political identities which happened to be viewed as threatening to their regime.

Martinique-born Algerian writer, psychiatrist, and political philosopher Frantz Fanon applied similar ideas to colonial and post-colonial Africa. Taylor credits Fanon with illustrating better than anyone how the colonial ploy to convince Africans to accept their role as the colonized not only lent credibility to colonial mastery, but wreaked psychological havoc among the colonized on a par with any level of material exploitation and physical violence Africans may have endured. However, despite appearances to the contrary (including the apparent acquiescence of the colonized), for Fanon, a lack of recognition of the colonized eventually results in counter-violence, as the "native" rebels against the imposition of identity. In typical fashion, Fanon wrote, for example, that

> as soon as the native begins to pull on his moorings, and to cause anxiety to the settler, he is handed over to the well-meaning souls who in cultural congresses point out to him the specificity and wealth of Western values. . . . But it so happens that when the native hears a speech about Western culture he pulls out his knife.[17]

The politics of recognition implies therefore that the unique identity of an individual or group—their distinctiveness from everyone else—is acknowledged. Ignoring, glossing over, or assimilating this distinctiveness into a dominant or majority identity is seen as a kind of violence that militates against the possibility of moral community, even if (as in Leninist Russia) assimilation happens in the name of moral politics. Thus, within the social restoration framework, identity assimilation is a cardinal sin against the ideal of authentic reconciliation,[18] whereas an acceptance of the need to recognize diverse identities produces a sense of multicultural awareness premised on political tolerance, and ultimately gives rise to a moral community. As Fanon so vividly pointed out, the violence of failing to recognize identity often produces counter-violence. To overcome both violence and counter-violence, and establish a reconciled society, the recognition of identity within politics, also the politics of reconciliation, must always have a central role.

A *second* assumption widely shared by proponents of reconciliation as social restoration is that human beings are essentially dialogical and relational; that we live in "webs of interlocution," are "dependent on inter-subjective relations with others," and consequently can be called upon to put ourselves in others' shoes.[19] Others' opinions of us also therefore matter fundamentally, for better and for worse, because these opinions, in the forms of ascribed identity, help to shape our sense of self negatively (as explained above) but potentially also positively; that is, the opinions of others shape us in ways that are foundational to our understanding of ourselves and the world.[20] For this reason, thinkers such as Taylor agree that identity needs to be recognized, not in abstract terms, but as a phenomenon that is shaped by the specificities of particular settings. This idea has often been explained by Desmond Tutu and others as inherent in the African philosophy of ubuntu, where it is understood that people are fully human only through their engagement with other people. Humanity is thus both a given and a moral call; one can in fact "lose" one's humanity if one treats the other in inhumane ways. As Tutu remarked to black compatriots, with bitter irony at the height of the struggle against apartheid: "Be nice to the whites, they need you to help them rediscover their own humanity."[21]

Ultimately, therefore, even as reconciliation as social reconstruction insists on recognition of identity, it also acknowledges that human beings live in "overlapping social territories" and that identities are fluid.[22] Reciprocity is therefore established, not simply through mutual recognition (as Hegel and Taylor claim), but as the fruit of self-giving that presupposes a recognition of the other. Hierarchies cannot simply be leveled or *inverted* through struggle, they must be *subverted* in more radical ways, by allowing identities to interact in mutually enriching ways. This is why, in addition to recognition, self-sacrifice is seen as essential. Volf argues that, although an embrace has an undetermined outcome and carries the risk of being misunderstood, despised, or even violated, without this "gamble on the account of grace," a truly human life is impossible.[23]

Implicit here is a *third* assumption: that how individuals reconcile holds important insights for how groups reconcile. In other words, the relationship between the realms of the interpersonal and the social is understood as being characterized by continuity not discontinuity. Because human beings are essentially relational, and because our relationships are fundamentally determined by who we are (in our own eyes as well as in those of others), larger social realities are acknowledged as being ever-present in interpersonal relationships. As an individual white Afrikaner male, for example, I cannot reconcile with my fellow South African (who may be a black female) without acknowledging that historically determined issues of gender and color are real and present, structurally, culturally, and also personally, in how we relate to one another, even though we might have long rejected these as decisive elements of our own individual identities.

For proponents of social restoration, recognizing the inverse dynamic, from the social towards the individual, is equally important: social healing between individuals is believed to be possible only when communities, at a group level, follow the dictates of the forgiving embrace, and abide by time-honored, culturally embedded sequences of interpersonal relational healing and reconciliation. Taylor argued that liberals are mistaken when they describe individual identity as a secondary aspect of political life that is relevant only after rights are established between "rational subjects." Instead, he says, identity makes human rights possible, because it is not possible to understand human rights without reference to the concrete needs, aspirations and ideals of individual and social identities. Furthermore, since language contains the shared life of a community and produces identity and culture, he argues that language is irreducibly a "social good." As many of us express our identities mainly through language, identity can also be said to be essentially narrative.[24]

Thus, within the social restoration paradigm, reconciliation begins when a call is uttered with cross-cutting moral appeal, a call to individuals to embrace those they have seen as enemies and to restore ethical moral community based on recognition. But this is not any kind of moral community: individuals' embraces should aim to restore ever-more reciprocal relations between erstwhile enemies, between masters and slaves. The implication is that such a call, backed up by appropriate action, has the potential to precipitate a return to a moral society, and help communities to move away from the ruins of war and oppression.[25] The call to reconciliation is thus essentially not backward looking, but forward looking. Looking ahead, the call challenges, provokes, and nudges people to reconcile what *is* with what *ought to become*, rather than with what *has been*.

Moreover, the call to reconciliation acknowledges the fundamentally relational character of society. This relational focus is premised on a respect for differences, in whatever mode such differences may manifest—often between cultural and religious groups. War and oppression often destroy respect for difference, thus harming the appreciation of relationships on which community ought to be based. Reconciliation is initiated when such destructiveness is recognized, and a moral call is made to adversaries and others to return to a community based on respectful relations that are shaped by an acknowledgment of differences. These respectful relations then set the reconciled community apart from oppressive ones.

The Unfolding of the Forgiving Embrace

A second set of shared features of reconciliation theories within the social restoration framework, regards the question of, how once a call for a return to moral community is heeded, the process in fact unfolds and develops. Which traits and processes characterize reconciliation as social restoration, and how is this type of reconciliation understood to bring about the radical political change that is foreshadowed in the call to a moral community based on a recognition of identity? Put simply, how concretely does the call to return to moral community usher in change?

As indicated earlier, Volf developed the metaphor of an embrace to track the renewal of relationships that, when multiplied across society, constitutes reconciliation. At the same time, his moving account acknowledges the difficulties of embracing those who have caused untold misery (in his case, as a Croatian to Serbs and vice versa). Yet, despite the acknowledgment of how difficult it is to embrace the enemy, Volf did not balk at setting the moral bar very high for himself and other victims. For him, reconciliation as embrace demands an extraordinarily high degree of self-sacrifice if citizens are to emerge fundamentally altered by an encounter with "the other." An important question that follows from this, and to which I return later, is if such a moral standard is realistically achievable when prescribed to individuals across an entire society, not least in the context of profound political and social change.

Volf warned, as noted, that it is important to prevent the embrace from becoming an intrusive "grasping." Waiting patiently for reciprocity is important. Coming out of the self and toward the other, the self "postpones desire" and halts at the boundary of the other. "If the embrace does take place, it will always be because the other has desired the self just as the self has desired the other."[26] When the time is right, two pairs of arms enter one embrace—signifying significant commitment—and yet, for such an embrace of mutual giving and receiving, a soft touch is necessary. "At no point may the 'self' deny either the 'other' or itself."[27] For this it is important to develop the capacity, not only to understand the other, but to preserve the "otherness" of the other. Finally, an embrace always ends. Bodies do not become "welded together" in an embrace; the "I" does not dissolve into "we," as often occurs in totalitarian regimes. Rather, the "I" must let go of the other, acknowledging that the embrace can never produce a final settlement, but requires repeated gestures to have a lasting effect.

Political scientist Daniel Philpott draws on the "overlapping consensus" that he sees as emerging from Islamic, Christian, and Judaic theology, as well as from restorative justice theory, to postulate his own description of the grammar or movement of reconciliation as social restoration. His *Just and Unjust Peace* is an ambitious attempt to graft liberal political outcomes onto restorative justice and theological roots. His compromise endorses liberal approaches to peacemaking, insofar as these involve human rights, democracy, the rule of law, and so forth, but he does not endorse classic liberal philosophical values such as Isaiah Berlin's much vaunted "value pluralism."[28] Despite his nod to the importance of liberal consensus, Philpott's main point of departure is in line with the general assumptions underlying the social restoration model, and concerns the nature and extent of the damage that war typically causes in society. War's fractures create a need for holistic and comprehensive approaches that include restoring a society's wholeness (beyond simply imposing judicial and political rules abstracted from the concrete conditions of the society it seeks to serve). Reversing the logic of classic liberalism, which sees reconciliation primarily as "doing justice," Philpott defines the ethic underlying political reconciliation as

A concept of justice that aims to restore victims, perpetrators, citizens, and the governments of states that have been involved in political injustices to a condition of right relationship within a political order or between political orders—a condition characterised by human rights, democracy, the rule of law, and respect for international law; by widespread recognition of the legitimacy of these values; and by the virtues that accompany these values.[29]

Philpott's reconciliation theory, similarly to Volf's, also reflects to some degree he classic approach to the grammar of the embrace within Christian theology—acknowledgment is followed by apology, forgiveness, and reparations, or as Volf put it, the opening of arms, the waiting, the embrace, and the release. This sequence is premised on the model of a divine-human relationship that involves sinners realizing their sins, confessing and repenting of them, and receiving forgiveness, for which they, in turn, dedicate their lives to putting right that which they have done wrong.

Philpott's theory finds its epicenter in the practice of *forgiveness*. For him, this amounts to reconciliation's key contribution within society and the politics of transition. The moment of forgiveness, more than any other, enables and completes reconciliation. This is where reconciliation manifests itself; it is what makes profound renewal possible. Significantly, Philpott argues that forgiveness can be enacted at a political level—be writ large, as it were, across society through symbolic actions such as those often associated with Nelson Mandela and Desmond Tutu.

Along these lines, other scholars too have investigated the role of forgiveness in overcoming broken relationships.[30] For example, Pumla Gobodo-Madikizela is a former South African TRC commissioner and psychology professor who interviewed apartheid-era mass killer Eugene de Kock (nicknamed "Prime Evil"), who was released on parole in 2015 after serving nearly twenty years of his sentence of two life sentences and 212 years in a maximum-security prison. In her writings, Gobodo-Madikizela describes in moving detail how she wrestled with the notion of engaging with De Kock's "human-ness," of what caused him to descend to the level of a mass killer, and subsequently what would constitute a possible restoration to society and of his lost "human-ness." She explores in depth what it means to try to "end the trauma caused by apartheid" when this trauma is constantly revisited as victims and perpetrators try to live together in a post-apartheid society.[31] In a later essay, she argues, contrary to the adage that to "forgive is divine," that to forgive is firstly deeply human. Disputing Hannah Arendt's notion of the unforgiveable, Gobodo-Madikizela develops a case for forgiveness being the most appropriate response to the perpetrators, beneficiaries, and bystanders of serious international crimes in situations where victims have to learn to live together with their violators in the same society.[32]

For Philpott, forgiveness involves neither forgetting nor condoning evil deeds; nor is it an absence of punishment. He states that radical evil may even provide grounds *not* to forgive. He argues, however, that forgiveness is essential to reconciliation, both individually and politically, because it enables a "letting go" of the hurt of the past. This entails both a kind of liberation for the victims, as well as restoring the "good standing" of the perpetrators—thus forgiveness offers a kind of liberation for perpetrators too. He argues further that forgiveness ultimately serves justice by being uniquely able to facilitate the restoration of "right relationships." Without forgiveness, he says, the healing of broken relationships and the forging of "right relationships" is impossible.

"Right" relationships in post-war situations involve creating respect for human rights and addressing those wounds typically caused by war. Philpott identifies six such "primary wounds of war," which include the destruction of trust, national loyalty, state legitimacy, and other forms of social capital. The primary wounds cause a range of secondary, subtler but no less serious, wounds through a cause-and-effect chain involving memory, emotion, judgment, and action. As a remedy, Philpott proposes a political/transitional-justice agenda comprising six reconciliation practices meant to address the six primary wounds, namely: institutional reform, punishment, acknowledgment, reparations, forgiveness, and apology. In short, for Philpott, liberal peace as traditionally conceived is not "wide enough" to address the whole range of wounds caused by war, and in shunning humanity's cultural and religious traditions, it cannot be "deep enough" either to make the requisite difference in postwar situations.[33] For this, the restorative power of reconciliation as forgiveness is needed.

Restorative Reconciliation's Healing Promise

From the ideas of theorists such as Taylor, Volf, Gobodo-Madikizela, Philpott, and others, a template emerges for reconciliation theories within the social restoration paradigm. The four areas of commonality between these theories discussed above also help to clarify what this template offers in relation to the *outcomes or promise* of reconciliation processes as social restoration.

First, these theories view the restoration of moral community after war or oppression as a key promise. They tend to draw heavily on theological, philosophical, psycho-cultural, and other normative constructs to offer inspirational images of how a community ought to be: to avoid renewed oppression and ensure a level of tolerance of difference, relations within the healing community are characterized by a recognition of diverse social identities. Furthermore, a distinct ontology is at play within this type of reconciliation theory. Human society is not viewed primarily as an arena of danger and violent competition, but rather as a delicate web of cooperation, through which sufficient levels of trust exist, or can be generated, to fulfill shared ambitions.

This view of reconciliation appears to challenge a basic referent of liberal thought—the free and independent individual. Instead, it views human beings as essentially relational rather than atomistic. War is therefore seen as what happens when things go fundamentally wrong in this community of human relations. Unlike liberalism, where violence is often seen as an inevitable consequence of competition between atomistic entities, whether nations or individuals, for social restorationists, violence is primarily understood as a disastrous denial of how the world does and should work. As explained earlier, three assumptions form the backbone of this ontology: first, that human beings are intrinsically relational; second, that interpersonal reconciliation works in a way similar to, and holds important insights for, intergroup reconciliation; and, third, that political and social relations are continuous, implying that political reconciliation has to take into account the "thickness" of cultural and other factors that are particular to a specific conflict.

A second promise involves the "forgiving embrace" as the seminal moment in a restorative sequence of events—acknowledgment, apology, forgiveness, restitution, and/or reparations. These "turning points," although essentially descriptive of individual human (or human-divine) relationships, can affect dramatic *social* and *political* change when their logic is allowed to develop across society. Captured in political practices, declarations, and actions, they can trigger profound and powerful social change. For individuals and groups, everything changes in the event of forgiveness. At the group level, especially, "turning points" may include more outward, ritualistic events or "practices," whether cultural or religious, or indeed a combination of inward and outward events. From the moment or start of a process of forgiveness and its acceptance, relational restoration follows. A core assumption is that reconciliation requires a profound commitment, and that forgiveness is the moment on which this process turns. A review of the literature on forgiveness reveals ongoing debates about whether to conceive of it as conditional or unconditional, and how to tell whether political relations have been restored or not. But can forgiveness really be predicted, programmed, and adapted to function in political contexts? Some say yes, others no. I return to these points later in this chapter, and again in the final section of the book.

The third promise of reconciliation as social reconstruction relates to their fundamental optimism about possibilities for the healing of relations, including political relations, and about achieving justice. This optimism not only stands in stark contrast to the measured pessimism inherent in theories of both justice and reconciliation framed from a liberal perspective, but also turns basic concepts within the liberal paradigm on their heads: instead of classical *retributive* justice, forgiveness leads to a healing restoration of relationships conceptualized as *restorative* justice. Thus, for advocates of social restoration, justice is achieved not when abstract judicial principles are implemented with no regard for context, but when damaged relations are restored in ways that enable society to overcome historical injustices. Thus, healing is expected to follow reconciliation, and justice is expected to follow healing in an almost linear way. Howard Zehr writes that working within a restorative justice paradigm offers a lens that reveals injustice to be "the violation of people and relationships. It creates obligations to make things right. Justice involves the victim, the offender, and the community in a search for solutions which promote repair, reconciliation, and reassurance." By contrast, retributive justice views crime as a violation of the state, "defined by lawbreaking and guilt. . . . Justice determines blame and administers pain (just deserts) in a contest between offender and the state directed by systematic rules."[34]

A fourth promise within the social restoration paradigm—and indeed an essential outcome of all restorative justice processes—is the deep healing of victims as a primary goal. "Forgiveness is a power held by the victimised, not a right to be claimed," writes Martha Minow in her important work on this theme.[35] For this and other reasons, restorative justice has developed significant support as an alternative form of justice, even in societies traditionally organized along liberal lines.[36] In Minow's view, restorative justice depends on the restorative power of truth-telling, the presence of sympathetic witnesses, on the placing of suffering in a larger context to help individuals to make sense of their experiences, and, finally, on the acknowledgment and recognition of identity (as described, for example, by Charles Taylor). When one or more of these elements are absent, the whole process suffers. From within this framework, the key question that faces post-conflict societies is not how law and order can be established, but how a moral community can be restored and form the basis of a more just and law-abiding society. The rule of law then becomes an outcome of, not a prerequisite for, reconciliation, and justice is not dependent primarily on the establishment of impartial rules, but on restored relationships. In short, justice is redefined as reconciliation; that is, as the restoring of relationships. Reconciliation as social restoration also promises healing, not only at an individual and interpersonal level but also at intergroup, social, and political levels, following the profound experience of a forgiving embrace, and it can occur at an individual or at the social and/or political levels.

Questions about Social Restoration

As powerful as this vision is, it has also been criticized, not least by liberal theorists. Commenting on the South African case, Gutmann and Thompson agree, arguing that if "healing of the nation" is taken to mean forgiveness by the victims and repentance by the perpetrators of apartheid crimes, this is a utopian aim, and not even a positive one.[37] For such critics, the aim of conflict resolution should not be to seek in comprehensive social harmony but to deliver on its promise of mitigating and managing hostilities. Another such critic, Harvey Weinstein, a US-based academic, writes that, whereas the concept of closure is murky, that of reconciliation is even more questionable, and should be carefully reassessed if not dropped from the post-conflict lexicon. He argues that the notion of reconciliation offers opaque, imprecise, and ultimately utopian ideals that may be generations away, and which no political leadership should pretend to be able to deliver.[38]

These criticisms raise three important open-ended questions in relation to the typology that frames reconciliation as social restoration and forgiveness, to which I turn in conclusion. First, to what degree is the restoration of community an appropriate political aim for transitional societies? Second, who gets to define the new moral community and the processes that will take society there? Third, can forgiveness really be translated into political practice in the ways suggested above?

Restorative Reconciliation as a framework for Political Transition

Is it not asking too much to expect erstwhile enemies during times of vast political transition, to engage in socially restorative processes with one another with the aim to heal relationships, historic grievances and deep-seated trauma? Given the realities of perpetrator recalcitrance and denial in any given number of contexts, such an expectation appears, at least to some, as unrealistic, if not also undesired. Even in rare moments where genuine perpetrator remorse is forthcoming, it is also important to reflect on the profound pressure felt by victims when perpetrators request forgiveness from them, especially in public settings. Sometime they are simply not ready; on other occasions they may be wholly unimpressed with the moral sincerity of the perpetrator, or they may simply reserve their right to privacy. In South Africa, the example of apartheid Minister of Police Adrian Vlok comes to mind. Vlok has, since appearing before the TRC and subsequently striking a plea bargain in court related to undisclosed crimes for which he had not received a TRC amnesty, developed extensive relationships with victims of apartheid atrocities, including the former director of President Mbeki's office and prominent cleric Reverend Frank Chikane, who was nearly killed in an attempt by Vlok and others to poison him during the struggle years. In meeting victims, Vlok insisted on washing their feet as a symbol of his repentance. This ritual impressed some victims, Chikane included, but angered others immensely. There is simply no guarantee of how victims will react when confronted with someone who had destroyed significant parts of their lives. Nor indeed, one could argue, should there be such a guarantee, for to pre-scribe forgiveness is arguably to violate victims' dignity afresh by robbing them of their individual moral agency.

I recall a personal encounter with a former Liberian warlord, now evangelical preacher, who was known as "Colonel Butt Naked," in reference to his habit, be-fore combat, to strip down naked in the belief that this would make him invin-cible. He eventually received amnesty from the Liberian TRC and subsequently attended a conference in Kenya which I also attended. On first meeting him, he struck me as an exceedingly jovial fellow. At a reception one evening, he was in a particularly good mood and insisted on being the resident photographer, moving around the table and chatting with everyone. As we were socializing, I noticed another colleague from Liberia next to me not participating. I struck up a con-versation, and asked her how she was and why she had been so quiet. "To be honest," she said, "I have a headache. I have had a headache ever since I arrived here. I guess I am not coping that well with the colonel's presence here. You see, one of the groups associated with him killed my father back during the civil war."

It is one thing to succeed to convince former mass murderers to confess. Often they simply do not. But if and when they do, sometimes in a haze of religious escapism, it can leave survivors and victims even more confused, upset and traumatized than before. Without necessarily passing judgment on whether the perpetrator's transformation had been genuine, victims may feel, as did my colleague at the Nairobi conference dinner, that they are not ready even to face the perpetrator, let alone engage in a process of restorative justice, not least when the perpetrator now seems so utterly convinced of his own redemption and is seemingly getting on with his life with a joy thoroughly unmatched by that of the victim herself.

If these kinds of facilitated engagements face such tremendous difficulties, then, on a large scale, it would seem that this model taken to its extreme, sets transitional societies up for failure. I would suggest that, at the very least, the reality of moral failure ought to be factored into reconciliation processes from the start. Key to this would be to find ways to "move on" with political and social redress even if victims are not prepared or able to forgive, or perpetrators are unable or unwilling to rise to genuine remorse. They should never be allowed to hold the healing of a nation hostage. And what is social restoration's "Plan B"? It seems that when "Plan A" falters—and it very often does—social restoration in its classic form does not seem to offer an alternative.

Others, such as Charles Villa-Vicencio and Ernesto Vedeja, have responded by redefining the outcome or promise of reconciliation within the social restoration paradigm in more "modest" ways.[39] Instead of speaking of healed relations as the outcome of reconciliation, they use terms such as "respect" or "trust." Ernesto Verdeja, for example, developed his theory of political reconciliation largely on the premise of social restoration, but his account is less outcome-driven, more process-oriented, and less dependent on whether or not forgiveness actually takes place, than some of the examples discussed earlier.[40] Verdeja also provides a distinctly secular justification for reconciliation.

Drawing on Latin American post-dictatorship experiences of the 1980s and 1990s, Verdeja entitled his study of reconciliation *Unchopping a Tree*, borrowing a phrase from poet William Merwin to describe the impossibly delicate nature of reconciliation. "Which pieces go where? Will they grow together or collapse with the first soft wind?" asks Verdeja. His theory is a good example of political reconciliation that has social restoration as its point of departure but does not demand forgiveness, or posit the high social ideals of restorative justice as nonnegotiable prerequisites for reconciliation. Rather, it seeks to shape these ideals to accommodate what is politically realistic.[41] There is good reason, as discussed, for such modesty. Verdeja argues that reconciliation cannot wait for the day that all differences have been resolved before it can begin or indeed progress. Reconciliation has to be a process that is based on the commitment of former enemies to work together nonviolently, despite historic differences and the unfinished business of the past, on the understanding that issues will be resolved over time. He accepts that forgiveness, as a prerequisite for reconciliation, can put unfair pressure on victims to put the past behind them in the name of the greater good, and that confessions and remorse from perpetrators may not always be realistic. However, if neither victims nor perpetrators can find the moral courage to confess or forgive, national reconciliation processes can be designed in such a way that society can move on with the majority of its citizens.

For Verdeja, reconciliation as normative goal therefore involves restoring a "condition of mutual respect among former enemies, and it requires a reciprocal recognition of the moral worth and dignity of others. It is achieved when previous, conflict-era identities no longer operate as the primary cleavages in politics, and when citizens acquire new identities that cut across those earlier fault lines."[42] He also accepts that reconciliation is an "uneven, disjunctured, and multi-levelled" process, which includes political and institutional reform, civil society activism and individual change.[43] He emphasizes too that although his theory is normative, it is essential to be context-sensitive when embarking on political reconciliation, not least in situations (to which Verdeja limits his account) in which extreme violence has occurred between sides occupying the same territory. Thus, as an inter-subjective, reciprocal norm, respect is the proper goal of political reconciliation. Respect as a normative goal, for Verdeja, includes truth-telling and truth seeking, the recognition of victims, accountability, and the rule of law; it is more than resigned acceptance but less than Volf's notion of embrace.

Reconciliation On Whose Terms?

Another concern with culturally and theologically driven reconciliation processes, for all its talk of reconciliation's non-coercive "soft embrace" as opposed to oppression's straight jacket-type, remains the extent to which such processes can produce truly participative, inclusive communities. Traditional restorative justice processes in Africa for example have sometimes been accused of reinforcing gender injustice or other forms of chauvinism, even as they seek to restore communal relations after conflict under the watchful eye of the (male) Chief. Thus, the second critique concerns the question on whose terms reconciliation ought to be advanced—whose morality should determine the shape of the restored community and identify the steps that will take society there? Who issues the call to moral community, who decides about its implementation and who are required to follow? If one accepts that reconciliation should be a moment for profound moral renewal, for wider and deeper participation than ever before, and for shaping a radically more inclusive and fair future, it can then be profoundly counter-productive when the processes and goals for reconciliation are too closely predetermined, especially from within the moral universe of one of the participating identity groupings or traditions. There is a danger (at least in principle therefore) that carefully circumscribed restorative justice processes, despite the very best of intentions, stall the very change they wish for.[44]

An associated danger is that the recognition of identity, so fundamental to reconciliation as social reconstruction, may in some cases be dependent on what can be described as an essentialist view of "culture" where identities of the other and the self are presupposed (by the self) and ascribed unilaterally. This act, ostensibly an act of recognition, often in the name of multiculturalism, in fact may simple promote the self at the cost of the other, in so far as it imposes an identity on the other that it pretends to "recognize." This kind of oppressive "recognition" was of course part and parcel of colonialism and apartheid, which both in their own ways professed respect for the "difference" of the natives they encountered and sought to rule. Andy Schaap, for one, agrees, and makes the point that initiating reconciliation via a politics of recognition often depends on those very identities according to which past wrongs have been committed and which it seeks to overcome: "In order to overcome our perception of the other as enemy—the transgressor of our values—we are called upon to "understand him [sic] as he really is."[45] Yet this very act of imposing the understanding of one side on the other risks renewed violation of the other's dignity, even if the imposition consists of refusing to see a perpetrator for the intolerant, violent, and bigoted individual he or she in fact is. The most extreme version of such an ascription of identity is found in genocide and crimes such as ethnic cleansing or apartheid, where identity is used as the basis for wholesale subjugation or even annihilation.

The question remains, not whether individuals are essentially relational, but whether and how, when identity is understood in essentialist terms, reconciliation can become an oppressive or even violent imposition that is enforced by powerful actors.[46] In this respect, Fanon's warning against ascribed identity rings out as loud as ever.

Reconciliation as Political Practice

The danger therefore persists that a moral vision becomes a form of violence and that the requirements of a forgiving embrace lose the "soft touch" that Volf describes, solidifying into a moral code that has to be followed, as if the steps from enmity to reconciliation were simply formulaic. If this occurs, forgiveness can be instrumentalized in deeply damaging ways—specifically on the political terrain, which raises the third area of concern.

Interestingly, in the Abrahamic traditions, "two contradictory logics are in dispute" about how forgiveness functions.[47] The one makes forgiveness conditional on apology and restitution, whereas the other views forgiveness as unconditional, regardless of the attitude or reactions of the guilty party.[48] A central claim in theories of reconciliation within the social restoration paradigm is that forgiveness is facilitated by specific political practices that can be replicated when the will exists to do so. Jacques Derrida famously questioned this "grammar" of forgiveness, arguing that both traditions of forgiveness—the unconditional and the conditional—should be retained, but with due understanding of each and their subtle interdependence. For Derrida, while forgiveness has to find concrete form in political contexts, it must always also remain something wholly "other"— from beyond, unexpected—"the madness of the impossible."[49] Perhaps this is the real source of the forgiving embrace's potential to influence society and help it overcome self-defeating violence.

For Derrida, the restoration of interpersonal relations foreshadows the mending of intergroup relations, yet forgiveness is not predictable or replicable; it cannot be forced, and is, more often than not, not forthcoming. In its worst incarnation, during public forgiveness processes one set of political dictates simply replaces another. To avoid this, it is vital that those who attempt to implement theories of reconciliation based on social restoration keep Derrida's distinction between conditional and unconditional forgiveness in mind. If forgiveness has an unconditional, "other" character, at least to some extent, any moral codes associated with reconciliation seem unlikely ever to become fixed, unalterable sets of principles that preempt the spaces and processes that reconciliation seeks to create and set in motion. Morality ought to develop incrementally and iteratively as we occupy spaces with those who are radically different from ourselves, and as we find respectful ways of engaging with one another to carve out space for a moral community.

6

Restoring the Rule of Law

> In this new age of accountability, those who commit the worst of human crimes—be they rank-and-file foot soldiers or top political leaders—will be held responsible.
> —Ban Ki-moon, ICC Review Conference, Kampala, October 2010

As shown in Chapters 3 and 4, South Africa's TRC tried to achieve a careful balance between restorative and retributive justice. But this nuance was often lost on observers, and the South African reconciliation process came to be viewed as largely synonymous with an attempt at political forgiveness, not least because of the inexcusable lack of political will, subsequently, to pursue those prosecutions recommended by the TRC.

The drive to establish truth commissions internationally following South Africa's experience has given rise to further debates about social restoration, political forgiveness, and restorative justice—all of which tend to be associated with political reconciliation "the South African way." Such developments did not sit well with many liberal observers, however. Reed Brody, an American human rights lawyer and spokesperson for Human Rights Watch, argued in 2001 that the human rights movement was facing a "South Africa problem":

> It seems that because of South Africa, the international community has become blindly besotted with truth commissions, regardless of how they are established and whether they are seen as precursors or complements to justice or, very often now, as substitutes for justice.[1]

Consequently, those who accept liberalism as a theoretical framework were left with a choice either to reject the South African model or to reframe reconciliation in terms acceptable to key tenets of liberal thought. In 2000, Amy Gutmann and Dennis Thompson developed a strong argument for why reconciliation "the South African way" is potentially illiberal. They expressed concern about Desmond Tutu's references to "healing the nation" as a goal of reconciliation, contending that this was both utopian and misleading. Since healing is not, in their view, a legitimate aim of political reconciliation, they argued that the TRC's "trading criminal justice for general social benefits such as social reconciliation requires a[nother] moral defence if it is to be acceptable."[2] Although left unsaid, Gutmann and Thompson clearly meant that reconciliation's alternative moral justification would have to be acceptable to a liberal framework.

Taking up the challenge of developing a moral justification for reconciliation that does not depend on Tutu's promise of healing, liberal thinkers began seeking alternatives. A decade-long conversation ensued, resulting in a range of studies broadly outlining what I identify as a second "type" or theory of reconciliation, namely reconciliation as liberal peace, which is achieved primarily through the establishment of the rule of law.

At the outset I would like to acknowledge the limits to my discussion of liberal reconciliation in its various theoretical guises. The first is that my focus is on liberal ideals as *they function in reconciliation frameworks*, not on liberalism as such. Thus my criticism of liberal reconciliation does not imply a rejection of the liberal paradigm or of particular values popularly associated with it—including human rights, the right to privacy, the rule of law, gender equality, etc. These, in my view, ought to remain key outcomes of peace processes, regardless of what theories of reconciliation might prevail at any given time.[3] I am more interested in the intersection between theories, policies, and practice, and how liberal goals are pursued in the wake of post-authoritarian and post–civil war societies, who stands to benefit from these processes, and how they relate to ongoing power struggles in society. The discussion is therefore crucially informed by the urgency that the need for practical conflict resolution brings to political theory and policy formation.

This chapter is furthermore structured along lines similar to the previous one. First I focus on the beginnings of liberal reconciliation, then I focus on the concrete processes that are seen as typical of how this kind of reconciliation unfolds, and finally I examine what it promises as outcomes, and how its proponents therefore justify its use.

A Call to the Community of Liberal Democracies

Liberal theories of reconciliation enjoy significant traction internationally. They form a key constituent of the international transitional justice frameworks that are driven by international organizations, NGOs, and governments that subscribe, at least formally, to the tenets of liberal democracy.

Philpott developed a useful working conception of liberalism for the purposes of investigating its influence on the ways in which reconciliation, and more specifically the inception of reconciliation, is conceptualized. First, he argues that liberalism implies a concept of justice that is closely associated with human rights, equality, and the rule of law. Second, he notes that reconciliation within a liberal framework is promoted by the international system of institutions and actors who have internalized this concept of justice. Most notable here is the UN, which "is arguably the most prominent promoter and espouser of liberal peace," together with other international agencies and professionals that constitute the international transitional justice community.[4] Third, political engagement by these actors tends to be characterized by distinctive activities—often called "best practices," "principles," "benchmarks," or "pillars." These include establishing and securing ceasefires; facilitating the development of political dispensations premised on human rights, free markets, and a free press; and finally, creating specialized mechanisms to find the truth about, and hold accountable, those guilty of mass atrocities.[5]

It is almost trite to remind ourselves that, seen from a liberal perspective, reconciliation can have no other goal than the establishment of liberalism. Liberal reconciliation politics is always a prelude to the spread of liberal ideals. Reconciliation is the tune to which those who seek to leave mass violence behind must march, ending supposedly in a triumphant crescendo of a fully "liberated" (read liberal) society. For advocates of this process, it does not really matter who plays the instrument as long as the correct tune is played, and the grand finale takes the form of a liberal state.

Liberalism as the preferred outcome of political transition clearly enjoys unmatched influence among the more powerful players in the international community. As Kora Andrieu, a human rights officer employed at the time by the UN in Tunisia, remarked, the international outcry when the Libyan National Transitional Council announced its desire to anchor the first post-Gaddafi constitution in Islamic law, and the reluctant acceptance of the results of Tunisia and Egypt's first elections (which were won by Islamic parties), were powerful indicators of the normalization of liberal democracy.[6] "In the thought and practise of the international community," she argued, "liberalism is indeed the only criteria of political acceptability, the *telos* of any 'normal' political progress."[7]

Liberal peace, that is, peace premised on the entrenching of "human rights, democracy and the rule of law" is therefore the unquestioned goal of liberal reconciliation.[8] As Bashir and Will Kymlicka wrote:

> On this view, reconciliation should be understood as a juridical and legal approach that is primarily concerned with the prosecution of perpetrators of crimes, restitution (where possible) to the victims of

these crimes, and the establishment of the rule of law. . . . This is an influential approach particularly among international organisations, who find it easier to accept politics of reconciliation when it is cast primarily as the upholding of universal human rights.[9]

Within this framework, reconciliation's *inception*, the way it makes a start in conditions hostile to its enactment, is therefore understood to be the act of political persuasion that brings errant leaders in line with international liberalism, and that is thought to provide the basis for a more just and peaceful society. More generally, we can assume that liberal reconciliation is born when local adversaries agree to use international benchmarks and standards for political best practice, and accept the assumption that liberal democracy, marked chiefly by adherence to the rule of law, is the principle outcome of political transition.[10]

But the call to comply with international benchmarks may not be as simple as it sounds. To begin with, there is no single example of "pure" liberalism. Thus, while liberalism in its more classic political form is found in the writings of John Locke, John Stuart Mill, Immanuel Kant, and in some respects John Rawls, these authors all differ on key points. The conclusions of any one of these thinkers might not apply to others in the group, and making general comments about the group as a whole is difficult.[11]

The writings of John Rawls offer an example of how complex liberalism is. Many take his *Theory of Justice* (published in 1971) to be an authoritative statement of liberal political theory. Yet, as is well known, Rawls developed the notion of justice as inclusive of both freedom and redistributive equality, and his inclusion of fairness and equality brought him into conflict with classic libertarians such as the American philosopher Robert Nozick. Thus various criticisms of "classic liberalism" may not even apply to Rawls.[12]

While contemporary liberalism may have further complicated efforts to define liberalism precisely, this has never been a simple exercise. As Hannah Arendt pointedly observed, private rights had their origins in efforts to enable social and political life, not, as Hobbes and Locke would have us believe, the other way around.[13] In other words, politics did not develop solely for the purpose of protecting private property. Locke viewed political society as existing for "no other end but to secure every man's possession of things of this life."[14] Arendt however, turned this logic on its head by demonstrating that, in classical Greece, private property operated *as means to a public life*. The domestic scene, Arendt reminds us, was one of survival and necessity, whereas it was in the social sphere that relative freedom existed:

> Without owning a house a man [*sic*] could not participate in the affairs of the world because he had no location in it which was properly his own.[15]

Private property was therefore not always, Arendt contended, understood as the means to relentless material acquisition, as it has become. Her analysis implies that social and political institutions in ancient Greece did not exist to guarantee private possessions. To the contrary, the right to private wealth existed to enable a more inclusive and fairer social and political life.

These and other conceptual ambiguities and complexities within the liberal tradition are mirrored in its political role across the world. Under some regimes, to be liberal is to be regarded as progressive or "leftist." In socialist environments, the same principles are deemed to be sure signs of conservatism. To get a feel for the latter perspective, one need look no further than a comment by liberation theologian Miguez Bonino, who wrote that "the ideological appropriation of the Christian doctrine of reconciliation by the liberal capitalist system, in order to conceal the brutal fact of class and imperialist exploitation and conflict, is one—if not the—major heresy of our time."[16] And in South Africa, where liberalism was once considered progressive, liberalism is now routinely branded as the embodiment of conservatism and angrily dismissed. Much to their dismay, many erstwhile anti-apartheid liberals are now finding themselves accused of preserving white privilege under the guise of individual rights.

Internationally, too, powerful nations are often accused of manipulating the discourse of human rights and the rule of law for the purpose of maintaining international power relations. This is especially true when crimes committed by the powerful against the less powerful are overlooked by the international community, while less powerful nations are sometimes held accountable—or at least those over which the fledgling International Criminal Court (ICC) has some leverage. Of course, there are instances when such accusations function simply as pretexts for "big fish in small ponds"—the developing world's rich assortment of dictators and war criminals—to try to claim the moral high ground as victims of imperialism so that they can escape accountability for the injustice and abuse they have inflicted on their compatriots. Nevertheless, liberalism is clearly a deeply complex and contested paradigm on the international stage, as indeed in many national contexts.

As in the case with approaches to reconciliation as social restoration, a distinct ontology (or world view) lies at the heart of the kinds of liberalism that inform reconciliation discourses and initiatives in many contexts across the world. These assumptions are often overlooked when local leaders are called upon to reconcile, and because some of these assumptions appear antithetical to local values, reconciliation can find itself dismissed as a "Western import" alongside transitional justice and other values associated with international liberalism. There are, therefore, compelling reasons to examine what these often unspoken assumptions are all about.

And so, as in the previous chapter, our focus shifts to the nature of the kind of community into which one is invited in the name of liberal reconciliation. If reconciliation begins when the call to international liberalism is heeded, what kind of society is presupposed?

A *first* assumption is revealed in Andrew Schaap's treatise on political reconciliation. Schaap observes that Locke saw human beings as "driven into political society by insecurity."[17] This observation points to one of liberal reconciliation's most prominent assumptions, namely its inherent pessimism about the kind of societal change that is possible, or even desirable, through national reconciliation processes. Locke's fundamental mistrust of the public realm—as a sphere of intrinsic hostility, rather than shared morality—stands in stark contrast to social restoration's pronounced optimism.

Judith Shklar identified this as "the liberalism of fear," and has argued that its deepest grounding is also "the conviction of the earliest defenders of toleration, born in horror, that cruelty is an absolute evil, an offense against God or humanity."[18] For many, this has made liberalism the de facto (and almost unquestionable) conceptual framework for transitional justice, as well as for efforts to establish accountability and respect for human rights after mass violence. After all, human rights were originally designed primarily to protect individuals and groups from violence, and few would deny that the 1948 Universal Declaration of Human Rights was a watershed moment in establishing a safer world.

Locke's sober world view results in theories that draw a sharp distinction between political and social relations, with the latter requiring strong protection from the former. Discontinuity, rather than continuity, marks the relationship, with strong limits being placed on what political relations may legitimately seek to accomplish. As we have seen, social restoration theories by contrast focus instead on the cultural contexts within which political relationships occur and the continuities, rather than discontinuities, between culture and politics.

Locke formulated his views when trying to separate the realms of church and state amid the excessive violence of the Reformation and the Counter-Reformation in seventeenth-century Europe. His aim was to contribute to the evolution of a more peaceful society, based on containing and managing irresolvable religious differences. Church and state are "absolutely separate and distinct," he declared, and he went on to argue that much discord would be avoided if the church stuck to the salvation of souls and the state to the welfare of the commonwealth.[19] Consequently, liberal notions of reconciliation, if not quite as stark and absolute as Locke's, still tend to hold that political relations and affairs of state, not cultural or social relations, ought to be the sole focus of political reconciliation.

US-based academic Colleen Murphy argues that political reconciliation "is fundamentally a question of how to transition towards the realization of normatively desirable political relations," which includes centrally the rule of law.[20] Murphy then describes reconciliation as the cultivation of reciprocal agency. In a similar vein, UN Special Rapporteur Pablo de Greiff developed a theory of reconciliation as civic trust, also based largely on a liberal premise. De Greiff identified a number of "limitations" that a (liberally) acceptable notion of reconciliation has to respect, to ensure that reconciliation operates within a strictly political realm, and does not transgress in undesirable ways into the cultural, social, or religious spheres. These limitations run, to some degree, counter to religious and cultural notions of reconciliation, including moral ideals such as forgiveness or apology. They also ensure that, for De Greiff, reconciliation is confined to the sphere of the civic rather than the personal; complements rather than replaces or transforms formal justice processes (into restorative justice initiatives, for example), does not transfer responsibility from perpetrators to victims (by expecting victims to forgive); does not pretend to "wipe the slate clean"; does not demand extraordinary moral behavior from citizens (that would be "akin to sainthood" in his view); and does not depend exclusively on any particular set of religious beliefs.[21]

A *second* assumption inherent in liberalism's more proscribed, or as De Greiff put it, "deflationary" notion of reconciliation is that the focus shifts away from repairing personal relationships to building institutions that uphold the rule of law, thereby producing fair and democratic political relationships. The implication is that genuine reconciliation does not arise first as a result of attitudinal rapprochement between adversarial groups (although attitudinal change may of course result from reconciliation), but from a call for thorough institutional reform heeded by leaders who are committed to liberal democracy, *thereby* changing attitudes and relationships.

For theorists such as Murphy and De Greiff, democratic institutions— that is, institutions capable of guaranteeing the rule of law—form the basis of what reconciliation demands from post-conflict societies and their leaders. Reconciliation commences when leaders commit themselves to building such institutions. Attitudinal change is seen as a secondary outcome that will come about as long as the "right" institutions are built. That is, national reconciliation processes should aim to correct political systems, and personal reconciliation, as a desirable but inessential outcome, might then follow. Thus, even if victims and perpetrators never reconcile personally, political reconciliation based on developing liberal institutions that, in turn, enhance civic trust ought to be able to prevent a relapse into mass violence.

Thirdly, in addition to their inherent pessimism about the measure of social change one can expect from reconciliation, their separation of the political and the socio-cultural relations, and their focus on institutional transformation rather than attitudinal rapprochement, liberal reconciliation theories assume a particular sense of self or identity. Reams have been written on this, but essentially this theory tends to assume what has become known in the literature as the "liberal subject."[22] That is, for liberals, human beings harbor a sense of self that exists in some ways prior to entering into relationships with others. The implication is that human beings do not need community at any existential level, and that we are human because of our own, internal core identities, not because of our relationships. Of course, this refutes another basic premise of reconciliation as social restoration—that human beings are *essentially nonessential*, that we are both dialogical and relational.

This individual "core," which many pre-Enlightenment and Enlightenment thinkers identified as the "image of God" in us, and which secular twentieth-century activists then claimed as the "rights-bearing subject," makes the liberal project both possible and necessary. As the cornerstone and ultimate guarantor of the liberal peace, "right-bearing subjects" deserve unqualified respect. Among other things, the right to respect includes the right to protection from abuse. This is especially relevant, of course, where groups are targeted for systematic exclusion, violence, or discrimination.

Finally, reconciliation theories conceptualized within a liberal framework, not surprisingly given the previous assumptions, place a high premium on individual accountability and reparation after mass violence. The core assumption is that human beings who inflict violence on others must be called to account, not as agents of a system or members of a group, but first as individuals who can and must take responsibility for their actions. Within this paradigm, justice is less about repairing damaged relationships or social restoration than it is an effort to rehabilitate damaged individuals on both sides of a violation—perpetrator and victim. Perpetrators can be rehabilitated only through a process that establishes and punishes their personal failure to live up to their own inner sense of responsibility; victims are rehabilitated through efforts to repair the damage done to their personal dignity by abuse they have suffered, and through a process that involve the restoration of damaged relations.

Put simply, reconciliation as a dimension of liberal peace is restrained in the personal realm. Instead it focuses on truth-seeking and establishing perpetrator accountability for human rights violations, on redress for victims, and on institutional guarantees of non-recurrence. Through such processes, its proponents hope, this type of reconciliation will help institute the principles of legal justice, regulate political power, and forge or strengthen democratic institutions—all key indicators of a liberal society.

Peace and Justice as Markers of Liberal Reconciliation's Unfolding

In what follows, I draw attention of the some of the primary political and institutional milestones identified for reconciliation framed as liberal peace. The question is, what do liberal theorists look for when they seek to determine whether a particular political transition qualifies as reconciliation?

Since this model of reconciliation is so closely associated with establishing liberal democracy, the early signs of a genuine reconciliation process would be the efforts to establish accountability for mass atrocities and crimes through criminal trials, truth-telling, and formal apologies, as well as reparations and institutional reforms. The International Centre for Transitional Justice (ICTJ) provides a good standard definition of this kind of theory that links liberal notions of reconciliation to transitional justice:

> ICTJ works to help societies in transition address legacies of massive human rights violations and build civic trust in state institutions as protectors of human rights. In the aftermath of mass atrocity and re-pression, we assist institutions and civil society groups—the people who are driving and shaping change in their societies—in considering measures to provide truth, accountability, and redress for past abuses.[23]

According to this theory of reconciliation, increasing levels of civic trust result from instituting accountability measures for past atrocities. Since the transitional justice movement's advent during the early 1990s, much debate has taken place about how to balance and sequence the institutionalization of these key milestones, rather than about the constituent parts themselves—truth, account-ability, and redress have remained fairly uncontroversial. These largely uncon-troversial goals correspond closely to the mandate of the UN' special rapporteur for transitional justice, which includes encouraging "truth, justice, reparations and guarantees of non-recurrence." If accounting for and redressing past abuse are the key goals, then the key reconciliation activities are truth commissions, criminal trials, and reparations, as well as institutional reforms designed to foster liberal democracy, and all these activities should be marked by growing levels of civic engagement and trust as the primary outcome.

However, if liberalism is concerned with establishing *both* security and ac-countability, the tensions in the classic transitional justice agenda become clearer. Indeed, the need for stability or security is a quintessential liberal concern. Yet, this concern is not so easily married to accountability, another of liberalism's key commitments. As became clear earlier when discussing the South African negotiations, there are often profound tensions between establishing account-ability and establishing stability, not least early on in reconciliation processes. The ways in which this particular tension is conceptualized and resolved have implications for the actual processes leading to civic trust. And so, within the typology or family of reconciliation theories shaped by a liberal framework, there has been a debate about the more precise relationship between these two key milestones of reconciliation, security and accountability—a debate largely driven by the many concrete situations where these milestones appear in direct opposition to one another as a country seek to find its way during a protracted political transition from conflict or oppression towards liberal democracy.

As to the more precise relationship between stability and accountability as core liberal markers at least three alternative combinations have been hotly debated within the transitional justice field, all of which use peace as a proxy for stability in the classic liberal sense. These are: *peace versus justice, peace and justice*, and *peace as justice*. To outline the current thinking in liberal circles about what concrete reconciliation processes look like, I briefly describe the evolution of the debate.

While it is tempting to associate these approaches with distinct periods in the evolution of transitional justice over the past two decades, and to see one approach as following from and building on a previous one, the reality is that the debate did not occur in a neat linear way. Even if a measure of temporality is evident in the progression, and if, conceptually, there appears to be a level of evolution from one to the next, in fact the three approaches often overlapped or circled back on themselves.

The *peace versus justice* approach can be traced far back into historical political debates. In recent years, heated exchanges followed widespread perceptions that, as noted earlier, the South African TRC embraced restorative justice as its primary modus operandi and had thus been "soft" on prosecutorial justice. Interestingly, this perception spread, despite the fact that the TRC's mandate was actually quite muted in its embrace of restorative justice and had in fact demanded retributive justice for those who failed the test of conditional amnesty. In no small way, this perception was the result of the way that the process had played out, rather than a fault in its design—but in many commentaries this distinction was lost. An overriding sense that the perpetrators "got away with it" pervades this critique.

Typically, peace-builders and mediators sympathetic to liberal democracy took a more defensive stance toward the South African approach, and faced off against human rights activists and lawyers with similar overriding biases towards liberalism in this debate.[24] The peace-builders accused the human rights activists of being high-handed idealists, and of not being attuned to the actual dynamics of peace-building, arguing that when negotiating between parties who both have blood on their hands, some measure of clemency or amnesty has to be accepted before talks can even begin. Often the underlying charge was that human rights activists were unwittingly promoting a crude form of neoliberal imperialism by demanding that prosecutorial justice (the "Western way") be a nonnegotiable constituent of reconciliation.

In turn, human rights activists accused peace-builders of being "soft on justice," of turning a blind eye to human rights violations in their efforts to bring adversaries to the negotiating table, and thereby offering victims an inferior form of peace. The "peaceniks" were also alleged to be proffering "cheap" reconciliation when, for example, victims were requested to forsake retributive justice in favor of perpetrators' accepting their crimes and seeking forgiveness.

Over time, these debates became increasingly acrimonious. Participants were almost forced to "take sides" and "show their credentials" one way or another as debates became intensely polarized, not least within international human rights circles. More seriously, processes on the ground began to be impacted by this impasse too, with lobby groups staking their claims and rushing to outdo one another in offering advice to parties implementing transitional justice.

The consequences of this stand-off have been felt not only in academic circles and "on the ground," but also in the newly created international institutions established to implement global justice. The genesis of the ICC, in the signing of the Rome Statute in 1998, represented, in some ways, the zenith of international liberalism—the idea of an international legal and political regime governed by the rule of law, human rights, collective responsibility for security, and the principle of social equality and economic justice. Soon, thereafter, however, liberalism's main international sponsor, the United States, and its key ally, Israel, withdrew their commitment to ratifying the Rome Statute. Following the events of 9/11, realpolitik hit back at what was perceived by conservatives as "liberal idealism" in the form of the ICC and other human rights instruments and agreements, with unexpected ferocity. This backlash took the form of an adherence to a largely unbridled Cold War–era style of national interest positions justified by recourse to political "realism" that seemed increasingly to justify regular, even systematic, use of violence and coercion to ensure security, and the flouting of international law. The United States has, for example, variously over the last decade defended its use of torture and detention without trial, of killing enemies extra-judicially, "collateral" damage as a result of targeted drone killings, and its nonparticipation in the ICC—reaching new heights under the Trump administration's blatantly anti-internationalist, anti-liberal stance. This ongoing defiance from important international players such as the United States, but also Israel, Russia, China, and increasingly the African Union, has left the ICC, and indeed the entire project of liberal internationalism, searching for support.

It has also left the ICC with a near-impossible mission. As a court based in Europe yet with a mandate that has involved almost exclusively African countries, and with no means to enforce arrests and limited means, it now has to "do justice" in an environment where power relations remain fundamentally skewed. While speaking the language of principled human rights, it operates in an international system very much dominated by the powerful, ruthless, and well-resourced.[25] No wonder, then, that after more than a decade of existence, the

ICC has managed to round up forty-two indictees and nine convictions, with all defendants coming from relatively weak African countries.

This situation engenders deep concern in those who would like to see the ICC become a universally relevant and capacitated institution, not only as a last resort for holding to account the world's most heinous and powerful criminals, but also as a crucial source of pressure toward ensuring that peace-building processes take accountability and justice seriously as a key component of guaranteeing the non-recurrence of violence, even where this is not the ICC's direct mandate. At the very least, it is felt that the ICC should not be reinforcing established power relations that keeps the world such an unequal place. Thus, ever more prominent international figures are calling for a serious overhaul of the ICC system, whereas African states have at times argued in favor of a whole-sale withdrawal from the Rome Statute.[26] This would, of course, be a devastating blow for efforts to build global justice, but it is also, arguably at least, partly an outcome of the polarization and propaganda that has dominated the transitional justice field.

The simplistic handling of the peace-justice debate as a zero-sum trade-off between justice and reconciliation, happily, is not the only way the topic has been discussed. In some circles, the conversation has morphed into a more complementary mode, with collaboration between peace-builders and human rights advocates seen as a non-negotiable starting point. Here it is possible to talk of peace *and* justice as mutually enhancing goals without one party being accused of being soft on justice, and the other careless about peace.

Advocates of this rapprochement between *peace and justice* promote the idea that organizations and processes can "have it all," that is, both peace and justice can be simultaneously present from the onset in (liberal) reconciliation processes. The inference is, "we have heard one another and accepted the validity of both justice and peace aspirations, and we should promote both goals." In this spirit of mutuality this approach favors inductive methodologies—observing closely what people were doing "on the ground" instead of imposing normative hierarchies from above.[27] To give concrete expression to this complementarity, the peace and justice discourse further typically produces lists of three, four, five, or more "constituent elements" or "pillars" of both reconciliation and transitional justice, which cover a diverse range of goals and outcomes straddling both peace and justice.

Thus transitional justice or reconciliation "experts" are expected to subscribe to a list of "building blocks," "principles," or "practices." It seems that marrying peace and a justice agenda primarily takes the form of listing them next to one another as parallel processes that would theoretically work together to produce both justice and reconciliation for societies in political transition. Often-cited examples of such "pillars of transitional justice" include prosecutions, reparations, truth-telling, and institutional reform. By working inductively, studies along these lines seem to identify inventories of transitional justice practices, and then declare the transitional justice agenda as inclusive of all these practices—*but crucially* without producing convincing theoretical positions or indeed developmental pathways that link these often-opposing initiatives with one another or indeed with a larger, more comprehensive political transition.

In 2008, the *Nuremberg Declaration on Peace and Justice* emerged from an international meeting sponsored by the governments of Finland, Germany, and Jordan. The conference that gave birth to this declaration sought to highlight this more complementary, collaborationist stance between peace and justice. The declaration listed the "complementarity of peace and justice" as its first principle, and then listed four further principles, namely "ending impunity," "a victim-centred approach," "legitimacy," and "reconciliation."[28]

In fact, a commitment to complementarity was already visible in embryonic form, in the UN's 2004 *Report of the Secretary-General on the Rule of Law and Transitional Justice in Conflict and Post-conflict Societies*, which sought to establish a "common basis in international norms and standards" for the UN's approach to this issue, while avoiding "one-size-fits-all formulas and the importation of foreign models."[29] The report stated that "justice, peace and democracy are not mutually exclusive objectives, but rather mutually reinforcing imperatives." Consequently, the document conceded that advancing all three imperatives in fragile post-conflict settings requires strategic planning, careful integration, and a sensible sequencing of activities. Importantly, however, the report did not provide more concrete direction about how such an agenda ought to be realized.

Sierra Leone bought into this dual peace and justice approach in 2002, when it established both an international criminal tribunal (the Special Court of Sierra Leone, which was set up jointly by the government and the UN) and a Truth and Reconciliation Commission. These were expected to work in a complementary way. Unfortunately, reality did not quite match up to expectations. The often-vexed relationship, and the contradictory claims and counter-claims, between the court and the commission in Sierra Leone have been well documented, and arguably pointed, then already, to the need for a more integrated, systematic methodology, rather than the simple "both justice and peace" approach. Ozonnia Ojielo, who was Officer-in-Charge for the TRC in Sierra Leone, wrote that the TRC had been subjected to "haphazard funding" while for many supporters in the international community the Special Court was "the more important mechanism."[30] The Sierra Leone case made clear that, instead of loose building blocks or pillars placed next to one another, there is a need for a more concise idea of how these notions should hang together, lest complementarity becomes a guise for hidden hierarchies and biases within the international system.

Aside from expressing a formal commitment to the ideal of complementarity, most of the debates and discussion documents, and even various official policy documents, have provided scant practical guidance on ways of integrating the mutually competing interests of peace and justice in a complementary way. It gradually became clear that this new inclusive agenda merely imported the conceptual and practical tensions of the peace versus justice debate into one framework, without resolving the contradictions between them, and without integrating the kinds of practices associated with peace on the one hand and justice on the other into a single complementary process. Put differently, although acknowledging the need for prosecutorial justice and political negotiations, the peace and justice approach failed to provide sufficient guidance on how to sequence these processes in ways that strengthen reconciliation.

Key theoretical questions re-emerged, including what kind of societies transitional justice was aiming to establish, and for which atrocities it would demand accountability. Should transitional justice investigations include socioeconomic discrimination and exclusion? Should all those guilty of human rights violations be prosecuted, and if not, which perpetrators should be excused, and on what basis? How were diverse practices (such as judicial prosecutions, community reparations, and truth-seeking commissions) best integrated to benefit communities and societies at various stages of recovery from harrowing violence?

These larger questions of how to integrate processes meant to further peace and justice, both conceptually and operationally, became increasingly difficult to ignore. A presidential task team commissioned to set up a TRC for Burundi, for example, posed precisely these kinds of questions to me as one of a advisers present at an intensive planning session near Bujumbura. For these officials, integrating peace and justice into a coherent reconciliation process was not an academic exercise. To this small, impoverished, and landlocked republic in the heart of Africa, it meant the difference between a more peaceful and just future or returning to a dreadfully violent past. Their forthright questions tore through some of the glib "both and" doctrines about peace and justice which claimed that one could have both peace and justice by simply instituting parallel processes and institutions. Yes, they said, we support an end to impunity, and we recognize that no international crimes can go unpunished, but tell us how? How is this done in a context of extreme fragility, with one rebel group still in the bush, a government that consists largely of leaders from a rival group, and with abject poverty all around?

What became clear was the need for grounded, experience-based theory, for a thorough and systematic integration of the two seemingly contradictory goals of peace and justice into one coherent and locally driven transitional-justice agenda. There was, and remains, a clear need to think through how post-conflict interventions can not only reflect the best of various different political traditions, in self-aware, internally consistent and inclusive ways, but also, and most important, how such initiatives can benefit those who stand to lose the most if they fail.

A third paradigm therefore emerged, which can be called the *peace as justice* approach. As the name suggests, this approach acknowledges the tensions inherent in the peace and justice framework, and, in attempting to resolve this, it conflates reconciliation with justice, but crucially as understood in liberal terms and not in a restorative framework. Simply put, the dictum is: "if in doubt, do justice and reconciliation will follow." In some ways, therefore, the debate about peace and justice has come full circle, with a more hard-line emphasis on justice gaining the upper hand, if not in the practice of international diplomacy, then at least in the official rhetoric within some international agencies. Finally it seems, the "South African problem," as perceived by Reed Brody, has been overcome, at least as far as transitional justice discourses within the international community are concerned.[31] Instead of pursuing *justice as peace*, as the South African was erroneously portrayed as having done, the notion of *peace as justice* has become a dominant approach.

The overt privileging of justice as accountability for past abuses over peace or stability includes, not surprisingly, a renewed emphasis on theory. The shallow mutuality of the second approach was becoming evident as theorists and practitioners alike were prioritizing their chosen "pillars," paradigms, and models on the transitional justice landscape. It became a game of co-option by stealth, as classic political theories and frameworks reasserted themselves against the unsettling novelty of transitional justice. Frustratingly for some but reassuringly for others, familiar schisms opened up—including the classic communitarian-liberalism debate—and discussions retreated back into enclaves where only the like-minded talked to one another.

A shift to a stronger insistence on justice, is also evident in the UN Secretary-General's 2011 report *The Rule of Law and Transitional Justice in Conflict and Post-Conflict Societies.* Assessing progress made in the implementation of the 2004 report cited earlier, the 2011 report states that the UN's "rule of law initiatives are indispensable to international peace and security."[32] The focus of the report is almost exclusively on establishing the rule of law as the goal of transitional justice. Little attention is paid to reparations, reconciliation, or more informal truth-seeking mechanisms, or to the raft of other practices that are associated with transitional justice.

The negative impact risked by this second wave of theorizing is twofold. First, new transitional justice theories are in danger of forfeiting the innovation that the notion of transitional justice promised precisely because of its original hybridity, and tend to reproduce simply that which had been said before in other disciplines, whether that be development, gender, or rule of law work. The catchphrase has become: "transitional justice is full justice"—which could be taken to mean: "transitional justice is full (liberal) justice," or indeed, full prosecutorial justice. While it is undoubtedly true that transitional justice ought never to offer second-hand or watered-down justice to victims, it is equally important to in-terrogate what we mean by "full justice," and what the contextual demands are specifically within transitions that may require adjusting methods and expec-tations to achieve realizable outcomes. For this very reason, transitional justice practitioners have always sought to bring together the concerns of justice and peace in on-the-ground processes and mechanisms, and to really think through how concerns for peace and justice can best be balanced.

Second, and closely related, transitional justice theories simply cutting and pasting from the liberal handbook may appear internally consistent but run the risk of being unfit for purpose. Post-conflict societies are complex and multifac-eted, as are the demands they make in relation to transitional justice. To some degree, expectations of what reconciliation and transitional justice might deliver seem to be falling in the context of what the more traditional disciplines such as international law, peace-building, and various disciplines in political science seem to promise. Increasingly, a kind of schizophrenia is emerging between what the international community professes and what it does when it comes to tricky post-conflict questions, such as whether or not to grant amnesty.

Meanwhile, initiatives to pursue individual accountability and justice, and, above all, *prosecutions*, have become the primary markers of reconciliation processes within the liberal paradigm. Nowadays, if one wants to know whether international agencies consider a country to be engaged in a fully fledged reconciliation process or not, one need only ascertain whether the country is involved in efforts to: learn the truth about past violations; prosecute war criminals; develop reparations packages related to individual violations; and institute institutional reforms that try to "guar-antee" non-recurrence. Concerns for relational rapprochement, beyond that which is required (or perceived to be required) as part of the processes thought to lead to liberalism, remain strikingly absent from this list.

In this prosecution-focused context, Pablo de Greiff, the UN Special Rapporteur for Truth, Justice, Reparation, and Guarantees of Non-Recurrence, has played an important role to recapture some of the important considerations within the United Nations at least, on how a balance between justice and peace is best achieved. In what can be seen as representing an important develop-ment in this regard, De Greiff has presented a thoughtful series of reports to the General Assembly on the four different aspects of his mandate.[33] Arguing for a comprehensive *and more integrated* approach to transitional justice, the Special Rapporteur, especially in his report on "Guarantees of Non-Recurrence," makes mention of societal, cultural, and individual interventions in addition to in-stitutional interventions as part of a comprehensive set of measures designed to prevent the recurrence of violent conflict.[34] Although not explicitly linked to the concept of reconciliation, this is clearly an attempt to overcome the peace versus justice debate in a more theoretically integrated way than has been the case in previous similardocuments.[35]

Despite these positive developments, much work remains in theorizing more precisely and with reference to concrete developments in given political contexts the complementarity, sequencing and mandates of key reconciliation institutions to have become associated with political transitions towards liberal democracy, such as international and hybrid tribunals, truth-seeking and truth-telling processes, reparations programmes and various kinds of institutional reform. In keeping with previous chapters, I now turn from these institutional milestones and arrangements to outline the specific promises made in the name of liberal reconciliation.

Liberal Reconciliation's Promise of Civic Trust and Reciprocity

De Greiff's (earlier) notion of reconciliation projects civic trust as its major outcome. More than mere reliability, civic trust "involves an expectation of shared normative commitment that can develop at different levels of intensity."[36] As such, it is a "scalar concept," argues De Greiff, and can be less "thick" than interpersonal trust.[37] At the same time, it involves the trust that citizens have for one another as part of a single political community that subscribes to roughly the same basic values.

Trust then unfolds horizontally between groups of citizens, as well as vertically between citizens and their state institutions. Reconciliation, for De Greiff, amounts to the conditions under which citizens can trust one another as citizens again (or anew). That is, they are sufficiently committed to the norms and values that motivate their ruling institutions, sufficiently confident that those running the institutions do so on the basis of those same norms and values, and sufficiently sure that their fellow citizens will abide by the rules laid down by their institutions.[38] An unreconciled society, he proposes, is filled with resentment and anger because norm-based expectations between citizens or between citizens and their institutions have been threatened or defeated. Transitional justice initiatives such as prosecutions, truth-telling, reparations, and institutional reform work together to foster civic trust and thus reconciliation.[39]

As with De Greiff, Colleen Murphy's theory of political reconciliation as reciprocity and respect for moral agency is not dependent upon forgiveness.[40] She claims that the strength of her theory is its eye for what is distinctively political (as opposed to interpersonal or psychological). Yet, taking a line of argument in some ways different from that of De Greiff, for Murphy, "to evaluate whether policies will facilitate desired change, one needs to know what such change would look like."[41] Politics therefore requires a normative framework that makes clear where and how things have gone wrong in society, not just in political institutions, and thus what kinds of goals ought to be valued in rebuilding society, and how these goals could best be achieved.

Murphy thus addresses institutional *and* interpersonal or social dimensions of *political* transition. In keeping with liberal sentiments, however, Murphy understands political relations in minimal terms, and claims that civil war and/or oppression systematically erode these relations by undermining reciprocity and respect for moral agency. Drawing on three existing moral frameworks— rule-of-law theory, political-trust theory, and capabilities theory—Murphy's notion of reconciliation is deeply complex and multifaceted, a process that simultaneously restores respect for the rule of law, builds political trust, and creates capabilities for change on the ground.

Reconciliation's first goal is to restore the rule of law, thereby "maintaining a framework for interaction premised on reliable and stable mutual expectations of how others will behave."[42] Murphy argues that reconciliation then has to involve the rebuilding of civic trust between citizens and officials.[43] Finally, owing to the fact that conflict undermines ordinary people's opportunities to achieve central "relational goods"—such as being respected, joining the political party of their choice, and participating in the social, economic and political life of a society—reconciliation has to entail restoring these capabilities. In each area, the restoration of reciprocal agency forms "the theoretical core" of Murphy's argument, leading her to claim that her theory is internally consistent. Cultivating citizens' agency and ability to act reciprocally arguably also provides criteria for measuring the success of a reconciliation program and the advancement of democracy. For Murphy, TRCs and international tribunals both have a contribution to make, and prosecutions can advance but do not depend on political reconciliation.

To varying degrees, theories like Murphy's, which build on, but then move beyond the classic liberal constraint with regard to societal change, tend to accept that reconciliation offers something new to politics, and often seek to align this new element with liberalism as its extension into the developmental realm. Along these lines, reconciliation theories now range from the full liberalization of reconciliation (as in the work of Timothy Garton Ash, for example)[44] to the grafting of a fully fledged communitarian agenda onto liberal roots (as in the work of Philpott, for example).[45] Philpott also refers to this range of views as "variances" in the internal arguments within the liberal peace tradition.[46]

Liberally inclined reconciliation processes thus project values such as civic trust and political (and increasingly developmental) agency as their main outcomes. Beginning with a clear sense of where it is headed, liberal reconciliation assumes a formal equality among citizens, and sets out to ensure an equal exchange of views, perspectives, and contributions in order to create a more inclusive political dispensation.

Questions about Liberal Reconciliation

Intent upon the importance of achieving its desired outcomes, liberal reconciliation displays a penchant for *outcome-orientated thinking*. My claim, though, is that an adequately developed *process-based orientation* that probes the ethos and means through which measures are established and outcomes are achieved, is too often absent from liberal theories of reconciliation. This brings into view an inherent inconsistency often present in liberal notions of reconciliation. On the one hand, liberalism builds a strong case for refraining from moral or normative overreach. That is, by remaining firmly within the political ambit, and leaving room for democratic deliberation between different viewpoints, irresolvable moral and religious differences are managed but not arbitrated. On the other hand, an analysis of Murphy and De Greiff's theories reveals that liberal reconciliation processes are in fact also strongly normative and outcomes orientated. Thus, while remaining skeptical of moral overreach, supporters of this approach show little hesitation about suggesting normative choices of their own, albeit secular ones, for post-conflict societies. However, there is nothing in principle to suggest that secular norms are necessarily imposed less hegemonically, or preached with less dogmatism, than religious ones.

At face value, private/public discontinuity is liberal reconciliation's main defense against accusations of inconsistency. It acts normatively on the political terrain by prescribing the values of civic trust, and reciprocity or agency after conflict or political oppression, but refrains from engaging with the domain of private morality, thus declining to tackle issues such as deep-seated attitudinal change or indeed systemic exploitation. The key rationale for maintaining this private/public split is the protection of individual freedom. Thus, advocates of liberal reconciliation seek the restoration of trust and reciprocity because they claim that these values enable, assert, and defend the individual freedoms that become all the more important when freedom has been abused through oppression or war.[47]

The problem is that while we might all be able to agree that a transitional society ought to establish some measure of individual freedom to safeguard citizens from the ongoing impact of a conflict (such as identity-based victimization, ideological hegemony, material looting, etc.), liberal reconciliation theories, thus far, have offered little by way of *theories of change* that challenge or transform root causes of a particular conflict (other than, of course, political abuse). Focusing on inherent power relations at the root of a conflict would fundamentally challenge liberalism's cherished private/public split. Presumably, the individual freedom that liberal reconciliation pursues can follow only *after* full political and socioeconomic empowerment has taken place, and only to the extent that more private issues, such as patterns of belonging or wealth accumulation, have been challenged by an essentially *public* politics—but this leads us back to what the nature of a responsible politics of reconciliation ought to be about.

If restoring relationships, including political relationships, is to mean anything at all, a careful balance of political and economic power has to be worked out, not only between political adversaries, but also between those who have inherited power (by virtue of simply who they are, or through having benefited materially from the past) and those who have inherited powerlessness.

It can therefore be counterproductive to limit political change to traditional (liberal) boundaries, during or after a political transition. Apartheid was a political system with intensely private and personal implications that cut deep into, and radically shaped, individual but also social and cultural identities. It promoted not only systemic racism but also systematic impoverishment, and both factors remain crucial in determining the identities of millions of South Africans. But as we saw in Chapter 4, perhaps in their eagerness to answer the call to join the family of "mature" nations subscribing to the strict tenets of international liberalism, South Africans did not remain in the "transitional moment" for long enough to deal with economic restructuring effectively, thereby squandering a possibly unique opportunity to harness the momentum of political change toward more radical social transformation.

This illustrates furthermore the problem that the "liberal subject," whom liberal reconciliation seeks to restore, cannot be taken for granted as a basis for change in transitional contexts. Reconciliation comes under great strain when a political dispensation is created in which identity becomes invisible in the name of human rights, or is rendered visible only as an incidental trait of a liberal subject. To address such issues, reconciliation politics has to reach deep into what is usually considered the private sphere of attitudes, perspectives, motives, and even personal wealth accumulation. For this very reason, reconciliation's elasticity—its ability to stretch its meaning across multiple layers of society, from the political to the personal and into issues concerned with social transformation itself—is an asset, not an embarrassment, even if processes like these take generations to complete. After all, conceptually, reconciliation's continuum from the personal to the political and into the social implies both difference and continuity and follows the double injunction of inclusivity and fairness.

On one level, of course, Murphy and De Greiff are correct that the depth, texture, and profound personal commitment associated with personal reconciliation is not appropriately determined from within the public realm. They are also correct, as I stated in my critique of social restoration, in claiming that too strong a focus on the personal may set the bar too high for ordinary citizens, not to mention war-crime perpetrators, warlords, and other political criminals, who are not exactly renowned for their moral standards. Thus, the failure of political criminals to live up to reconciliation's purported standards of genuine remorse could stall reconciliation, and a strong case can be made that such individuals should never be allowed to obstruct peace. Expecting victims to forgive also brings a whole set of well-debated moral problems into play that need not be repeated here, but suffice to say that the importation of personal reconciliation into the public realm can, and indeed sometimes does, constitute exactly the kinds of moral overreach that liberals fear.

At the same time, though, a strictly public notion of reconciliation does not seem to offer nearly enough to societies making the transition from a terrible past to (hopefully) a better future, because it does not retain enough continuity between reconciliation as both political *as well as* economic and socio-cultural transformation. The strict demarcation that Murphy erects between personal and political forms of reconciliation ultimately renders her theory of reciprocity somewhat impotent given the kinds of changes—of heart as well as politics—that are essential in post-conflict situations, even considering her important inclusion of developmental outcomes as part of reconciliation.

While the various outcomes identified by De Greiff and by Murphy (trust, rule of law, capabilities) are crucial to the success of political reconciliation, it is my view that reconciliation theories based on a strictly liberal framework *crucially underestimate what it takes to achieve real reconciliation.* That is, liberal reconciliation is big on ideals and outcomes, but falls short when it comes to providing context-specific and process-oriented guidance to help individuals and societies move away from the devastation of mass atrocities and toward the values of liberal democracy. In other words, liberal theories present clear goals but tend to suggest hazy processes based on uncertain and untested chains of causality.

As I explain in the final section of the book, my counter-claim is that a special kind of politics, *a politics of reconciliation*, is needed to help steer divided and traumatized societies through the processes of initial peacemaking, negotiating a shared normative framework, instituting radical yet progressively realized institutional reform, and, ultimately, facilitating social transformation toward a mutually agreed, manifestly inclusive, and fair society.

Given the dominance of the liberal paradigm, reconciliation initiatives increasingly focus on prosecutorial justice, and law courts seem to be the preferred instruments of reconciliation. Although other measures may be included, it is widely assumed that judiciaries should take precedence as arbiters and architects of new dispensations. The failure to fully appreciate the difficulties that transitional societies face is inadvertently magnified by its ambition to limit political power. As the legal specialist Bert van Roermund has commented, "law . . . can only be enacted and enforced between parties whose identity is mutually related to their respective roles in the past. For all of them, to live under the rule of law is to engage in the daily effort to find good reasons to do so."[48]

Van Roermund points to the need to take into account, and make explicit, identities that have played a negative role in the past. However, if politics is limited from the outset, reconciliation can stand powerless against other forms of deeply destructive power that challenge societies in transition, and that may count among the root causes of the conflict. Referring to John Locke's call for reasonableness in the context of sixteenth-century religious conflict in Europe, Andrew Schaap points to the need for reconciliation to include substantive conversations about morality, values, the worth of things, and so forth. Failing to bring these issues into the conversation (as strictly liberal practitioners would propose) leaves too much unsaid and can undermine the justifications that tend to help former enemies to live together.

As acknowledged above, Murphy's emphasis on restoring capabilities as part of a reconciliatory agenda goes some way toward acknowledging the need for such "substantive" conversations. Her focus is always on restoring reciprocity and the capacity to engage; basic living conditions form an important part of this. However, the abiding contribution of liberal theory is to remind us to respect the limits of what is possible when developing public ideals. Yet if we acknowledge the need for deep social transformation that both exposes and transforms the patterns of "belonging" and "having" that are shaped by, and in turn influence, conflict situations, political reconciliation has to offer more than reciprocity or trust.[49] It needs to include substantive discussions about the future, and about normative frameworks that can guide the shared realization of this quest, including the deepest memories, assumptions, and aspirations of groups and individuals seeking to reconcile.

Liberal preoccupations at the onset of reconciliation processes might, in fact, produce a kind of "benign indifference," as Schaap put it,[50] rendering reconciliation largely impotent in the face of existing power configurations in conflicted societies. If reconciliation is to be truly transformative, it has to be both essentially public and deeply private at the same time. Perhaps the gross violence associated with war and political oppression scrambles the personal and the political to such a degree that simply restoring these boundaries cannot provide sufficient transformation. Reconciliation politics provides an opportunity for specific continuities between the private and public to be asserted in order to create or recreate a fairer and more inclusive society, and making time for communities to draw on existing moral resources to help them move toward commonly held values and ideals.

As Schaap writes, the point is not "to debunk security, impartiality and limited government as important values of public life but to show the limits of toleration as an ethic that might animate political reconciliation."[51] When confronted with Schaap's idea of reconciliation as a process of founding a political community prior to the formulation of a shared morality, Murphy responded that providing no norms at the onset of a reconciliation process carries bigger risks than providing some norms, as she proposed. This raises two final questions.

The first is whether it is correct to view the considerable consensus on liberalism (supported as it is by many democratic states, international agencies, media houses, and influential intellectuals) as evidence that the liberal paradigm should be the unshakeable normative framework for political transitions globally. Can the framework itself not be questioned, adapted, or improved upon? And are existing liberal democratic models the only, or even the best, way to guarantee human rights in post-conflict societies? To my mind, the liberal paradigm as it functions in major international agencies especially, in fact tends to obscure liberalism as a *political tradition*, as a school of political thought with different trends and histories, legacies, and possible applications and the ability to evolve and self-correct, thus stultifying a rich legacy within overly fixed and prescribed categories. In so doing, some of reconciliation's most creative possibilities are foreclosed—as was evident at various stages of the evolution of the *peace-versus-justice* debate cited earlier.

So much creative potential exists within the liberal paradigm that its transformation, beyond what the fragmented, consumer-driven, "Western" democratic model currently offers, must be possible. This is especially so when secular liberalism meets societies characterized by different cultural assumptions and ideals, some of which might be more communitarian. For example, Locke's "state of nature" argument forms an important element of liberal thought, but it is often forgotten that Locke *also* presented a picture of society living "together according to reason, without a common Superior on Earth," and advocated social connectivity and interdependence.[52] Locke's sense of interconnectedness is often lost in modern versions of liberalism.

The second question is whether contemporary liberalism closes down not only deliberation about liberal values and their evolution but indeed *all* debate between liberals and other schools of thought. At present, open, non-coercive debates with hardline liberals can be very difficult, like any conversations between fundamentalists and nonbelievers tend to be. Hard-line liberalism runs the danger of producing a deeply ironic form of intolerance (albeit offered in the name of tolerance) to societies trying to break with oppression or war. The tendency seems to be to either try to "solve" dilemmas by closing down difficult questions and silencing dissenting voices in favor of predetermined international orthodoxy or best practice, or to sink into silent indifference and despair when overwhelmed by the magnitude of what is involved in political transitions.

Deliberative democracy and liberalism may not always have a straightforward relationship. It is one thing to allow for as much participation as possible in creating a new society from the ruins of war; its quite another to afford all contributions equal importance. So who gets to decide which contribution is more equal than another, and how are such decisions taken? Gutmann and Thompson, in the article referred to earlier, recognized that deliberation has to sit uncomfortably next to decision-making, but they do not help us understand how decisions are actually taken. Somewhere, somehow a first draft of a new constitution has to be drafted, others need to comment on and amend it, and someone has to sign the document into law. A line has to be drawn somewhere, decisions have to be made and laws drafted.

If moral pluralism is to be genuinely facilitated, on what basis should a post-conflict society make choices? On this point, too, liberal notions of reconciliation have been critiqued. Communitarians, for example, ask whether all visions for a post-conflict society can be equated normatively, and on what basis moral pluralism allows for consensual decision-making that holds normative value. Does the practice of moral pluralism not undermine the possibility of making moral decisions on behalf of society, not least when a society emerges from war or political oppression?[53] Such questions seem to point to a fundamental inconsistency within liberal politics, namely, that its formal commitments to human rights stand in unresolved tension with its commitment to moral pluralism.

Deliberative democracy allows for participation, but under conditions shaped exclusively within the liberal crucible. Agonists too are critical of this approach, and accuse liberals of double standards. On the one hand, liberals are unwilling to allow religious claims on the public domain on the pretext that this is morally prescriptive, yet they also try to prescribe the ground rules that determine the morality of a new society. Should liberalism not simply submit its assertions and values into the public domain as one possible way forward, rather than as the self-evidently correct way? In one sense, Murphy's and De Greiff's theories of reconciliation are excellent examples of the kind of hybridity that follows when concerns for peace and justice are equally pressing, as they tend to be in times of political transition following large-scale violence. In another sense, it appears that they do not go far enough in addressing the root structural and cultural causes of a conflict. In the next chapter I offer an analysis of theories of reconciliation that prioritize the goal of political community building in radically diverse contexts over seeking consensus on (liberal forms of) justice.

7

Valuing Political Difference

The largely opposing views of the social restoration and liberal theorists (reflected in the last two chapters) are rooted in long-standing debates that exceed the boundaries of any one academic discipline. Each position has been shown to harbor important weaknesses as well as obvious strengths. What they share, however, is a desire for certainty amid radical change, consolidation amid transition. Both sides seek to mitigate the risks associated with uncertain, volatile, and challenging circumstances, and to deal with a volatile past once and for all in order to usher in more secure, more predictable times.

Frustratingly, however, reconciliation is often slow to yield certitude. It tends to emerge slowly, unevenly, and messily. It often fails to produce the hoped-for outcomes against agreed timelines, and remains unfinished decades after it began. This raises a question: shouldn't reconciliation processes rather engage the uncertainties associated with political transition more openly, in which risk and ambiguity, rather than closure and certainty, are prominent features?

Taking this position, a third typology of reconciliation theorists are gaining prominence. Called agonists, they emphasize that reconciliation is fundamentally open-ended and deliberative and has to strive consciously to include "conflict through other means."[1] Seen through this lens, reconciliation is more a process-oriented activity than an outcomes-driven one. It draws a line against violence, not through recruiting opposing sides into a shared moral vision facilitated by forgiveness, or by converting them to international liberal norms and standards in the first place, but primarily through asking them to commit to sustained, nonviolent, and deliberative engagement that makes uncertainty a virtue rather than a vice.

Agonists seek ways of ensuring that political transitions can accommodate irreducible differences and uncertainties, and sustain adversarial debate on those agreements that bind a body politic together after conflict. For agonists, it is misguided to attempt to eliminate social divisions, no matter whether these are based on class, culture, gender, or ideology. Instead, they propose a mode of political engagement that enables people to contain their differences, while relating to one another in new and less violent ways, and highlights the conditions on which their differences can coexist as central to their ongoing debates.

Erik Doxtader has written that

> when distanced from the divine, released from the notion that it is strictly a gift and action of God, the faith of reconciliation appears poetic. Reconciliation promises a beginning, the creation of that which we can neither hold nor control. It is something that goads our imagination and extends our knowledge. We quantify reconciliation at the risk of rendering it banal.[2]

It is precisely because attempts at political reconciliation so often extend no deeper than the superficial and banal, fed by the quest for control and quantification over what is to be expected at the expense of imaginative beginnings which may surprise us with their creative potential, that agonists question the usefulness of social restoration and liberal theories of reconciliation. For agonists, respect and understanding for the nature of history and politics, and for what constitutes genuine change, must be central to any theory of reconciliation.[3]

The following section draws together the main points in the standoff between social restoration and liberalism to explain why agonists see the resulting stasis as a sign of opportunity, rather than defeat; in line with previous chapters, this illustrates how agonists conceptualize reconciliation's beginning—born as a constructive response to the moment of stasis when radical opposites meet. A subsequent paragraph then look more closely at agonists' sense of how reconciliation unfolds concretely over time, including those indicators that would reassure agonists that a productive form of reconciliation may be in progress. And finally, as before, the spotlight falls on reconciliation's promise—its outcomes and goals—also from an agonist perspective.

When Approaches Clash: An Opening for a Different Type of Reconciliation?

As discussed, social restoration theorists tend to view human society as an intricate web of interaction and interdependence, and see human beings as inherently dialogical. From this perspective, political relations are first and foremost *human* relations. Accordingly, the public/private split is especially difficult to maintain in the wake of conflicts that typically scramble such divides—and groups can be expected to reconcile much as individuals do.

Advocates of liberal models of reconciliation, by contrast, view insecurity and hostility as "natural" tendencies in any society. The liberal "subject" is seen as primarily self-contained rather than dialogical. Political and public relationships are viewed as distinctly different from social or private relationships; hence the public/private split is marked by a fundamental discontinuity. Liberals thus conclude that groups and individuals do not reconcile in similar ways, and assume that private and public reconciliation processes are fundamentally different. They argue, therefore, that political reconciliation processes should focus primarily on institutional reform rather than prioritize attitudinal rapprochement.

When adherents of these two schools of thought face one another across conference halls, policy workshops, or "in the field," their approaches, are often so different that a kind of stasis, marked by procedural confusion, policy impasse, and recrimination, often follows. Concretely, this impasse may give rise to opposing and unconnected reconciliation initiatives that operate in isolation or at cross purposes of one another.

In Chapter 6, I discussed the peace versus justice standoff, and showed how disagreements within the formal policy discourses of UN agencies that deal with transitional justice evolved into a peace-as-justice position. This position largely reflects the tenets of liberal reconciliation and, in my view, was developed at the cost of not taking social restoration theories sufficiently seriously. Essentially, in the absence of an elegant and widely acceptable philosophical compromise, practitioners went with the framework they knew best, and behind which they could rally the most supporters, namely liberal reconciliation. Even though truth commissions (with the incorporation of some restorative justice features) remain firmly part of the UN "toolkit" for postwar reconstruction, such mechanisms are now required to work within the ambit of, and in deference to, tenets of justice understood the liberal way.

This option for liberalism has not resolved matters, however. For example, at international level, the checkered operational record of the ICC and the controversies around its activities in Africa bear testimony to the lingering and somewhat debilitating presence of the debate. The main protagonists— the advocates of liberal internationalism, on the one side, and various African leaders, on the other—have engaged in lengthy debates, much mutual recrimination, and very little constructive discussion. Africans claim that the ICC is targeting their leaders because they are "easier to get to" than the superpowers, which they claim tend to operate with impunity. And it cannot be denied that Russia, China, and the United States (that is, at least three of the "P5" in the UN Security Council) are unlikely to sign the Rome Statute any time soon—while at the same time not hesitating to invoke the ICC to impose sanctions on leaders of countries they have quarrels with.

Implicit in the dispute about the ICC is an accusation of inherent racism in the attitudes of international bodies toward Africa, but liberals point out that if African leaders improve their domestic records on accountability, it would be unnecessary for the ICC to intervene. They argue that thirty-three African countries signed the Rome Statute and should therefore cooperate with the ICC, and point out that the ICC took up some of its cases at the invitation of Africans themselves.

Despite the evident, if selective, truths behind both sets of arguments, the ICC's ongoing silence about conflicts in which the world's major powers have strong, vested interests and military histories—Iraq, Gaza, Chechnya, Sri Lanka, and Syria—speaks loudly indeed. Meanwhile, the ICC's vulnerability to criticisms of geopolitical favoritism has become a significant drawback in its mission to serve the cause of justice. For all these reasons, the relationship between the African Union and the ICC remains "embattled," and the stasis between social restoration and liberalism remains solid.[4]

This stasis is evident in national contexts too. As mentioned, in Sierra Leone, a truth commission and a criminal tribunal famously operated alongside one another, with no integrated political or legal framework to guide meaningful cooperation between them. The result was not only an obvious lack of cooperation, but, at times, a mutual undermining. As one commentator observed:

> the different mandates of the TRC, intended to render restorative justice as a substitute for criminal proceedings in the light of the amnesty granted by the Lomé Agreement, and the Special Court whose mandate swept away the amnesty bore a potential for conflict: although the establishment of the TRC and the Court had different objectives, the jurisdiction of the latter overlaps with the competence of the former.[5]

Despite the real potential for overlap and conflict in jurisdiction, no integrated framework, legal or political, was created to ensure that the goals of social restoration and liberalism could complement one another in an integrated effort to realize both reconciliation and justice. The result was confusion, impasse, and stasis. In its final report, Sierra Leone's TRC remarked that some perpetrators had refrained from testifying before the TRC for fear of prosecution.[6] In other cases, those implicated by the courts, but nonetheless willing to testify at the TRC, were prevented from doing so. For example, in 2003, Chief Samuel Hinga Norman, a prominent political leader in Sierra Leone and indictee of the Special Court, requested permission from the court to appear before the TRC. Ultimately the Special Court rejected Hinga Norman's request, arguing that TRC hearings conducted in public before the conclusion of trial would "severely weaken the position of an accused pleading not guilty and end up in a 'spectacle' detrimental to the proper administration of justice."[7] Sierra Leone's TRC, one could argue, operated largely in a vacuum alongside the criminal tribunal. The

TRC worked from within a social restoration paradigm, whereas the tribunal ascribed to a notion of reconciliation based on liberal values.

Another startling illustration of the stasis between social restoration and liberalism, as it manifests this time at the community level, occurred in Northern Uganda. In one of the world's most vicious conflicts, communities in Northern Uganda suffered enormously as a result of a brutal insurrection led by the Lord's Resistance Army [LRA] and the counter-insurgency measures adopted by the Ugandan army. Untold thousands lost their lives, and approximately 1.8 million people were internally displaced, many of whom were tortured, raped, and left destitute. Close to 30,000 children are estimated to have been abducted and forced into serving as soldiers and sex slaves to the LRA. Meanwhile, at one stage, it was reported that 1,500 people were dying per week in government camps for displaced persons.[8]

In 2004, the ICC's chief prosecutor Luis Moreno Ocampo announced that, at the government's invitation, the ICC would investigate crimes committed in Uganda. The announcement was made at a public news briefing held jointly with the Ugandan president, Yoweri Museveni, who thus publicly endorsed the ICC indictments of his enemies, as of course he would. Yet because many Ugandans believed that, as commander-in-chief of the Ugandan defense force, Museveni was also responsible for serious human rights violations, they found the ICC's appearance alongside him at the media briefing as absolving the one side of the conflict while indicting the other—and this before a proper investigation into government conduct had even been launched.

In addition, the indictments came at a time when there were signs that the conflict was beginning to unwind. Amnesty was already being granted to child soldiers returning to their communities—many of whom were indisputably both perpetrators and victims of gross human rights violations. In addition, an important mediator between the LRA and the Ugandan government, Betty Bigombe, was preparing the ground for high-level peace talks between the adversaries, which when it finally began became known as the "Juba Talks."

Yet in what is now widely acknowledged as a failure to integrate formal justice with ongoing peace efforts, the ICC arrest warrants issued by the ICC for five LRA leaders put the peace talks under severe pressure. Speaking from Bujumbura, Burundi, where she was based at the time, Bigombe said:

> [Y]ou can no longer talk to the LRA as before, the dynamics have changed. The situation is different and I would not like to talk to the LRA now because the ICC has not yet given me details of the warrant.[9]

It was no surprise, therefore, when it emerged that community leaders were beginning to voice their outright opposition to the ICC across much of the region,

calling instead for amnesty, forgiveness, and a ritualistic form of cultural reinte-
gration of all former combatants into their communities of origin. Not only did
the indictments seem to jeopardize the regions' best chance at peace for decades,
but on the ground it became abundantly clear that that the ICC's presence was
markedly slowing down the rate at which former LRA soldiers were willing to
come forward to reintegrate into their communities. Ultimately, the Juba Talks,
which lasted for two years from 2006 to 2008, failed—at least partly as a result
of the warrants of arrest issued by the ICC against the leadership of the LRA.
This unresolved tension between two competing visions of reconciliation, social
restoration and liberalism, so painfully felt in Northern Uganda's communities,
prompted Lino Owor Ogora, who has worked extensively with victims of this
conflict, to ask pointedly, "if the arrest warrants issued by the ICC for the LRA
commanders played a role in denying victims the right to a lasting peace, can we
conclude that the ICC is in fact promoting the rights of victims?"[10]

Current efforts of Ugandan civil society to promote and systematize traditional reconciliation practices, combined with government efforts to develop
a national capacity to prosecute war crimes, are some of the more innovative
attempts yet to move beyond the impasse between social restoration and liberalism.[11] By 2014, a fifth draft of a National Transitional Justice Policy was being
debated in Uganda. Ultimately, this legislation seeks to provide guidelines, in
ways not dissimilar to those adopted in South Africa, to combine both retributive and restorative justice elements within a single integrated framework.

What should we make of this stasis between social restoration and liberal
approaches to reconciliation, so keenly felt in places like the AU headquarters in
Addis Ababa, or in Sierra Leone and Uganda, and many other places besides? At
a continental level, the promise of justice, equality, and fairness for Africa after
centuries of racism, slavery, colonialism, and economic exploitation appears to
clash head-on with the "rule of law" as embodied by the ICC—at least for those
who claim that the ICC is unfairly targeting Africans. At national level, the culture of the forgiving embrace, which Sierra Leone's TRC sought to foster as a national metaphor for reconciliation, contradicted the efforts of other mechanisms
to establish a sense of accountability and liberal order after the chaos of the civil
war in that country. In Northern Ugandan communities, the call to restore a
moral community encompassing both victims and perpetrators in the battered
communities of Acholiland seemed to contradict the call to isolate, charge, and
punish offenders while embracing international liberalism as represented by
the ICC.

For those who seek certainty after the chaos of war and political oppression,
the stasis between different interest groups and their theories of reconciliation
becomes a crisis when reconciliation is promoted as the road to certitude, predictability, and control. In their efforts to manufacture this predictability, international

support agencies understandably try to impose fairly fixed frameworks as well as core practices or "pillars" that are meant to guarantee progress toward the desired goal. What is missing in this approach, however, is a sense of how these practices ought to be sequenced and coordinated so that they work together rather than in isolation or in opposition to one another. Regularly absent, too, are channels through which local communities can integrate peace initiatives into their own transitional "stories" and support these processes with their own tried and tested community resources, rather than having primarily national or international processes imposed on them.

In many respects, this stasis has created uncertainty and volatility. For advocates of forgiveness and liberalism alike, the deadlock symbolizes reconciliation's absence. All too often, this contestation about reconciliation becomes politicized, as adversaries view one another across ideological lines as being as guilty of prolonging the postwar status quo and undermining concerted moves toward the "ideal reconciliation process" as those who perpetrated violence in the first place. The intensity of the ideological battles between liberals and social restorationists is perhaps exceeded only by their desire to bring some certainty and predictability into post-conflict situations, and this may go some way toward explaining why their exchanges have been, at times, so fierce and so bitter.

Cognizant of this standoff, we earlier discussed the way by which Dan Philpott attempted a synthesis between the two schools of thought. The restoring of "right relationships," which is central to Philpott's socially restorative approach, is, he claims, also compatible with liberalism—in that it grafts redress, and the healing of the multiple "wounds of war," onto the restoration of human rights typically associated with liberal peace. As noted, Philpott argued that "one can converge with liberal peace insofar as it endorses human rights, democracy, the rule of law, punishment, etc., but without sanctioning philosophical values such as autonomy or Berlin's value pluralism."[12] However, Philpott did not work out in sufficient detail how this convergence is possible without endorsing the liberal view of individual autonomy. Indeed, a certain tension runs through, and remains present in, Philpott's argument—a tension he appears to acknowledge when he writes (with reference to religion's public role within liberalism) that, as noted earlier, it appears impossible to find a balance between excluding what is allegedly inimical to liberal democracy, but including enough to allow what is essential to it.[13]

By contrast, and instead of attempting an overarching synthesis as Philpott sought to do, agonists' reaction to the stasis and the conflict it has created has been to embrace the differences between the two positions as a sign of the opening of precisely the kind of space for engagement in which, what they regard as a more genuine form of reconciliation has a chance of being born. For agonist thinkers, reconciliation is first and foremost a *verb*. Unfinished and open-ended, reconciliation, for them, sets in motion a kind of politics that is concerned with the founding conditions of societies, thus raising fundamental questions about both the liberal and restorative paradigms. In answering these questions, the only unacceptable outcome is the cessation of debate. No holy cows are tolerated, uncertainty is embraced, and what is important is robust engagement between erstwhile enemies as they search for a shared peace. In this sense, a certain level of political reconciliation is not an outcome of justice, but an essential prerequisite to it.

A Call to Political Community

While liberal and social restoration theories are premised on the eventual overcoming of difference, agonists offer an alternative. Sarah Maddison explains that "a central task of reconciliation is the (re) constitution of deeply divided societies through the creation and expansion of political spaces in which the full range of views and perspectives can be heard,"[14] so that, as Erin Daly and Jeremy Sarkin warned, this kind of coexistence never amount to assimilation, integration, absorption, or forced unification.[15]

Together, the agonist charge goes, liberals and social restorationists fail to respond usefully to the messiness of political transition, because they set fixed goals, and have no "Plan B" should their best options fail. The agonist critique is not that the ideals of forgiveness and the rule of law are undesirable, as such; rather, it is that by preemptively positing these as "the ideals worth pursuing," their achievement is actually jeopardized. Agonists argue that encouraging the open-endedness of true political engagement can help guide a society away from mass violence and toward more peaceable modes of coexistence, while simultaneously developing a robust ability within that society to prevent a return to mass violence.

In the wake of the Holocaust, Hannah Arendt developed a theory of politics in which the *prevention* rather than the *punishment* of mass violence stands central. In fact, politics, for Arendt, is nothing other than the refutation and sustained prevention of genocide.[16] She argued that genocide has as its goal the disappearance of people from public life into the black hole of oblivion. Politics, by contrast, enables people to appear (or reappear) in the public space through political engagement. Politics is thus a space for public *appearance*, for talking to one another in refutation of the mute violence characterized by the forced "*dis-appearance*" of the other. Crimes against humanity are therefore crimes against human diversity, whereas politics, properly understood, affirms diversity.[17]

These Arendtian views have played an important role in shaping what is increasingly recognized as an agonist "type" of reconciliation theory. Drawing on Arendt, Andrew Schaap argues that "our sense of reality depends on the disclosure of the world as an object held in common but perceived from a multitude of perspectives."[18] Politics is, therefore, not only the act through which we appear publicly, but also the activity through which a common, inter-subjective sense of reality is created. To achieve inter-subjective insight into how the world works, reconciliation depends on a particular kind of civic friendship that consists of "an openness to others" and "pleasure in the other person."[19] This civic friendship requires more than (liberal) tolerance, Schaap observed, "it entails a passionate and potentially agonistic encounter with the other . . . [and] a willingness to engage in *incessant discourse* in which difference and lack of consensus is understood not as an obstacle to communication but as a precondition for it."[20] In other words, agonists see reconciliation as a passionate endeavor, indicating a sustained willingness to step into direct, confrontational debate with those whom one once fought, in order to work out not only how it might be possible to live together but also how to construct a common understanding of the world.

Arendt argued that the disappearance of anyone from political life—whether through self-censure or violent imposition—entails "an almost demonstrable loss to the world."[21] Each person prevented from contributing their insights represents a setback in terms of efforts to construct a common understanding of the world. What Arendt famously called "dark times" ensue when withdrawal from the world (and from politics) is widespread, as is often the case during mass violence, genocide, or political oppression. By contrast, reconciliation makes politics possible (again), "by framing a potentially agonistic clash of worldviews within the context of a community that is 'not yet.'"[22]

This means that reconciliation is not ushered in by calls for restored community or liberal peace, but by the willingness of enemies to "appear" before one another in the name of a community that is yet to be born. This is obviously risky; we are called to determine how it might be possible for us to live with others, with no concrete guarantees. Not anchored in the surety of moral vision or liberal consensus, the call to reconcile agonistically is conditioned by *plurality, intersubjectivity, frailty,* and *contingency,* each of which I now explore in a little more depth.

Agonist reconciliation calls on enemies to recognize the fundamental and irreducible *plurality* of the political sphere, and this acknowledgment lies at the heart of the call towards agonist reconciliation. However, this is not what sets agonists apart from liberals. After all, John Locke's idea of tolerance also emphasizes moral plurality. The distinction is that, for liberals, deeply held moral differences should be restricted to the private domain and tolerated as a guarantee against sectarian violence.

For agonists, however, the private sphere is a means of enriching and sustaining public life. Thus, agonists maintain that a desire for peace and security is not all that enemies have, or ought to have, in common. Out of care for the world and for one another, they ought also to bring their deeper, existential differences into the public sphere (and into reconciliation processes) in an effort to contribute to a more informed common public life. Maddison agree that agonist reconciliation entails

> a very cautious approach to developing a unified national identity . . . (i)nstead, agonistic reconciliation suggests a transformative view of citizen identification, implying vibrant contestation over belonging and identity, but acknowledging that these contests may only lead to democratic outcomes if there is some limited consensus that binds the diversity of citizens.[23]

In an agonist framework, differences are not only tolerated for the sake of security, but faced head-on in the name of what agonists call civic friendship, in the interests of creating a shared world for citizens who agree on the need to engage one another in continuous debate about how to live together. For these reasons, agonists claim that the liberal view of tolerance, largely concerned with cooperation for the sake of security, "conceives of human interdependence too narrowly," because it does not take into account the profound creativity that resides in political engagement conceived of along agonist lines:

> [P]olitical interdependence is based not only on the need for mutual protection but on the desire for meaning, for a sense of the reality and worth of things. The possibility of reconciliation depends on this world-disclosing potential of politics.[24]

For social restoration theorists, the clash of moral views is acknowledged, but their aim is to overcome this in favor of an existential harmony ushered in by the forgiving embrace. As Maddison explains, agonism "takes a decisive step away from community harmony as a goal, instead prioritising the pursuit of just enough respect to allow democratic contestation without violence."[25] For liberals in turn, moral clashes ought to be largely private affairs, and as such, should be, in principle, irrelevant to politics. Agonists claim that both of these views underestimate and unduly limit the creative potential of political engagement in the aftermath of serious conflict:

> [B]y limiting politics to the end of security, toleration forecloses a politics that would enable citizens to call into question (and so potentially

discover reasons) why they should want collectively to secure the conditions that make society possible between them in the first place.[26]

Agonists maintain that the "world in common" appears differently to parties that engage in political discourse via a reconciliation process, and that the aim ought not to be to overcome or harmonize such differences. They argue that human commonality is not revealed in shared or consensual insights, but in reaching consensus via the kinds of politics that allow for contestation between radically different perspectives. Maddison drew on William Connolly's work to put forward the position that "an agonistic view of this type of coexistence insists on relations of 'adversarial respect' between 'interlocking and contending constituencies'[27] rather than pursuit of communitarian ideas of consensus."[28] In Schaap's elegant description, "plurality is not a condition of politics, but its achievement."[29]

An acknowledgment of the inherently plural character of the political sphere invites enemies to consider and formulate *intersubjective* insights—that is, conclusions that draw on different, often-opposing views to make plain how the world appears from varying perspectives and how, collectively, it might be possible to shape the world in more peaceable ways.

As Arendt noted, the inherent *frailty* of reconciliation processes is accepted as the result of being dependent upon "unrealiable and only temporary agreement of many wills and intentions."[30] She also pointed out that totalitarianism, by contrast, displays a profound lack of concern for sustaining the web of human relations, trying to remake the world not as a product of frail agreements but as the product of an idea. In so doing, totalitarianism destroys the fragile web of human relations, and with it, one assumes, society.

Contingency acknowledges that things can go wrong, but also entails the freedom to do the unprecedented and unnecessary, or that which could have been left undone, because "things could always have been otherwise."[31] The contingent nature of reconciliation is inseparable from the gift of freedom, which is the main concern of so many societies emerging from conflict.

For agonists, reconciliation's outcomes are contingent, open, and uncertain, and it is precisely this uncertainty and openness that is radically novel, that creates fresh possibilities, and that helps society draw a line under past violence—not least in situations where public participation has been violently stifled. Enemies engaged in violent conflict, in Uganda or Sudan, for example, have the option of becoming political adversaries instead, thereby investing in the creative potential of their future together, while understanding the risks involved in outcomes that are fundamentally uncertain, fragile, and risk-prone. After periods of hardened and violent opposition, even such uncertainty can signal that reconciliation is possible.

Importantly, therefore, this paradigm can work not only for political antagonists on a battlefield, but also for ideological adversaries squaring off over what form reconciliation should take—whether these are community elders or international agencies. The point is that in an agonist process, all groups understand the relativity of their own positions. They do not impose solutions, but commit to developing intersubjective insights, drawing on the perspectives of all sides to design self-consciously *provisional* solutions for how a post-conflict environment ought to look.

Agonists see their take on reconciliation as transformative, creative, constructive, and able to create new risky and adversarial *political* relationships, where only violence existed before. These relationships presume no preexisting moral values, nor are they forced to submit to the powerful international consensus that sees liberal democracy as the "best way to go." Instead, the protagonists acknowledge that the finely threaded and fragile web of human relations is a resource that can be used to help them weave a more plural society.

Agonistic Reconciliation's Unfolding

So if it is inaugurated as a call to civic friendship in taking care of a common world, of joining a fragile pre-moral political community, how does agonist reconciliation manifest itself over time? In his book *Sympathising with the Enemy*, published in 2010, Nir Eisikovits set out to "provide some concrete guidance for designing" a process of agonist reconciliation.[32] Differentiating "reconciliation as sympathy" from forgiving, forgetting, and recognition, he argued that "reconciliation must be understood neither in legalistic terms nor through the metaphorical language of healing and restoration."[33] Instead, agonistic reconciliation manifests in self-consciously open-ended dialogue. As an institutionalized form of political humility, this approach to reconciliation appears via processes of dialogue that have undetermined and even indeterminable outcomes. Thus, agonism offers a possible response to the liberal accusation of the normative overreach of social restoration, but also to those who criticize reconciliation as an uncritical extension of liberalism, and as such, normatively hegemonic. Schaap outlined four traits that can be considered characteristic of agonist reconciliation's unfolding through concrete processes of political transition.

The first mechanism that marks a milestone for agonist reconciliation is the adoption of constitutional politics, meaning processes that encourage all sides to reflect on what it would take to constitute an acceptable, shared political life after war. This occurs by *constituting* or constructing a space for politics (as described by Arendt and others), by bringing to life the *legal institutions* that guarantee this space for politics going forward, and by constituting the "we" in an *ethical* sense—"we" being the postwar society that is to occupy the political space.[34] This is fundamentally a future-focused effort to create a political and social covenant, wrote Audrey Chapman, on the basis of which a shared existence becomes possible.[35] However, within this triad of politics, law, and ethics, politics takes precedence over the law because ultimately a "we" can emerge only on the basis of politics, and not through legal decree. Furthermore, a community cannot precede the engagements that shape its existence; a community emerges from political interaction. The existence of a "we" thus fundamentally depends on the continued political will of a group of people to live together. Therefore, "the ethical constitution of a 'we' . . . depends on forsaking the certainty of law for the risks of politics."[36] "The challenge," wrote Maddison,

> as with the making of agreements, is to ensure that the process of (re) making a constitution creates enough stability to allow new political spaces to open up, while resisting the sense of closure or completion that such an endeavour may engender, which would effectively close such spaces down.[37]

This point helps to clarify how liberal frameworks often underestimate what it takes to make peace. War destroys not only the rule of law but also the social fabric of society—the sense of a world held in common—as citizens withdraw from common space. To revitalize society takes considerably more than re-establishing a legal regime. It requires meetings of citizens in public spaces at a time when such meetings feel risky or even impossible. This is where politics proper has to begin afresh, where institutional arrangements can be agreed upon (always provisionally). Then, gradually a "we" becomes a reality, and one can talk of reconciliation having begun. This constitutional dimension of reconciliation—of establishing a space for politics, legal institutions, and a sense of "we"—entails both "beginning and promising."[38] More akin to revolution than restoration, reconciliation makes a radically new beginning possible by drawing a line under a violent past, proclaiming that such violence should never recur, and promising that ways of living together that were previously thought impossible or even unthinkable are achievable.[39] This promise is not based on a prior golden age, or even on any visible sign that a new community is emerging. The promise itself becomes the primary symbol of reconciliation, an assumption that the present denotes the beginning of a community that is not yet visible or concrete. Reconciliation implies the faith to begin speaking of a "we" before this is a political or social reality. The faith to make such a promise is found in boldly declaring "never again" and beginning anew.[40]

Forgiveness, which can be defined as relinquishing a just claim and setting aside resentment, is the second trait of agonist dialogue. As reconciliation unfolds between the memory of a bad past and a future that is not yet realized, forgiveness is essential. The agonist defines forgiveness as a willingness to stop judging others as enemies, and to release them from the consequences of their actions in order to enable them to act (politically) differently in future. This clears the way for citizens to resume political responsibility—that is, to act freely in a political space—which is essential to reconciliation. Forgiveness involves acknowledging the obligation to repair harm wrongfully inflicted, and a willingness to explore ways of living with "the other."

Experiences in contexts of political transition indeed seem to suggest that there is a need "to reverse the order of our moral thinking."[41] Forgiveness does not signal a closure of contestation or disagreement, but instead opens new possibilities for political disagreement and nonviolent discussion. Instead of ushering in closure and social harmony, Schaap thus suggested, and Maddison concurs, that forgiveness facilitates and opens up possibilities for people to resume political responsibility.[42] Forgiveness also brings to light the world that victims and perpetrators hold in common, and that needs to be rebuilt through political engagement. Political reconciliation is thus sustained by a willingness to forgive, again and again. It then also opens the way for those implicated in state wrongs to assume (political) responsibility. Forgiveness is not based on just reasons to release wrongdoers from the consequences of their actions (the liberal rationale), nor on necessity as an irreplaceable social good (the social restoration rationale), but rather acts as an offer to the other to assume responsibility for past wrongs and enter into remaking the world held in common.

The third marker of agonist reconciliation is the assuming of *political responsibility* by citizens. This feature of the risky encounter between enemies in pursuit of a common society concerns the ways in which ordinary citizens may be collectively held responsible for tacitly supporting or benefiting from an unjust regime. Karl Jaspers and Hannah Arendt, who wrote mainly with reference to Germans during the Second World War, argued for a distinction between moral blame and collective responsibility. For them, collective responsibility relates to political failings, whereas personal responsibility operates at the legal and moral levels. Claiming collective responsibility for the kinds of crimes committed during war and oppression amounts to a plea of irresponsibility, and, from the perspective of future generations, this failure to take responsibility can seem like an ongoing injustice.

Reparations, if executed correctly, demonstrate precisely the illegitimacy of past acts, and for this if no other reason, they constitute an important symbolic benefit, argued Jaco Barnard-Naudé.[43] Given that we cannot bring back the dead or undo the suffering of victims, reparations have value in acknowledging wrongdoing, but no amount of reparations can ever presume to repay or settle such debts.[44] In other words, assuming political responsibility is not about purifying a tainted identity through demonstrating one's good intentions, it is about acknowledging that one is implicated in past wrongs as a "consequence of one's entanglement in history."

The fourth and closely related trait of agonist reconciliation occurs via the *collective remembrance* of past wrongs. The "never again" dimension of constitutional politics depends on the revelation of the facts of what went wrong. Verdeja suggests that in this context, official apologies can help to promote the restoration of victims' sense of moral and civic value, generate debate about new social norms, and reframe the past by undermining apologist historical accounts.[45] At the same time, the power of redemptive narratives, which reveal how isolated acts formed part of a larger whole, opens new possibilities for debating the past, for discovering new ways of living together, and for affirming the possibility of achieving freedom in the present. But for Schaap, remembrance creates a regard for the past that emphasizes moments of greatness, and this attests to the possibility of greatness in the present. Revealing our roles in history as part of a larger narrative redeems the past, and demonstrates how the past continually re-emerges from actions in the present.

Reconciliation's Agonist Promise: To Remain Forever "Not Yet"

Having outlined its inception and concrete manifestation over time, we turn to what agonist reconciliation promises, and (therefore) the outcomes against which it ought to be judged. Agonists maintain that embarking on a reconciliation process means being willing to be confronted with the utter fragility of political processes every step of the way. As soon as fragility gives way to too much certainty, alarm bells should ring. Agonist reconciliation resists closure at every turn. Provocatively, Schaap wrote that political reconciliation is only a "good" as long as it is not realized; it is not sustained by striving for a desired, premeditated end or goal, but by the "will to live together" and by "incessant and continual discourse."[46]

As a fragile politics of plurality, agonist reconciliation ceases to operate the moment it appears to have been realized. To be present, it must, by definition, not be present *yet*. It requires accepting the risk of encounters in which differences are not harmonized, and in which adversarial (but nonviolent) political relations can be fostered. This is not only an invitation to courageously embrace political humility, but a reprimand to anyone who thinks that the public sphere can belong to them or be dominated by their ideas.

A major contribution of agonist theories of reconciliation is their focus on the nature of political transition, and their insistence that reconciliation is a process of transition that must be locally owned, and should be expected to unfold in un-expected and challenging ways. This rings true to those embedded in transitions the world over. Hardly ever does a political transition usher in expected results in good time; profound disappointments, positive surprises, and completely un-expected outcomes are almost inevitable.

Social restoration theories tend to reduce politics to a moral agenda. Liberal theories of reconciliation tend to underplay the need for politics in favor of criminal justice. Neither view is able to fully account for transition in the sense of moving from one political system to another. Agonists, mean-while, point out that what takes a society through such a transition, and into a better (more inclusive and less violent) dispensation, is the cultivation of a particular kind of politics. Such politics are more likely to encourage the emergence of communities that can accommodate radical differences, ac-knowledge their agency, and develop radically new solutions.

Interestingly, Schaap suggested that forgiveness is what provides sustenance for such a political community. Conceding that forgiveness is more often asso-ciated with the moral ideals of social restoration than with agonistic politics, he nevertheless argued that forgiveness lies at the heart of reconciliation—that it renews political relations and makes it possible for former enemies to work to-gether, not as victims or perpetrators but as political opponents engaged in a ro-bust exchange of ideas. In other words, forgiveness is portrayed not as the basis for the restoration of *moral* community but of *political* community and, more-over, not as helping to reclaim a historical community that once existed but of helping to shape a community that has yet to be born. Forgiveness, he argued, ushers in the unexpected in ways that create possibilities for renewed political relations.

Questions about Agonist Reconciliation

Agonists seem to presume that politics is always an arena of robust and forth-right engagement between confident adversaries, but in reality post-conflict societies are much more often dominated by fear and insecurity. One needs only to visit the Kitgum district of Northern Uganda, or the small city of Yei across the border in neighboring South Sudan, or any number of villages in rural Burundi, to realize how devastating and destructive of human agency civil conflict can be. If this rules them out of agonist reconciliation processes, and if agonist reconciliation is relevant only in situations where an agency-deficit is not a problem, then it raises serious questions about agonism's relevance to post-conflict societies.

That mass violence silences and traumatizes has been well documented; often it is not a cacophony of well-articulated political perspectives that dominates a post-conflict landscape but an eerie silence. Into this void, advocates of reconciliation try to invite, nurture, and facilitate a reclaiming of political voice. Schaap does admit that "so long as people's lives are dominated by fear or struggle for sheer survival, they are not free to engage agnostic politics."[47] This is underscored by Daly and Sarkin: "desperately poor people have neither the time, the energy, nor the hope to participate in programmes designed to foster democracy, reconciliation or justice."[48]

And this is precisely the problem. The lives of most people who have lived in areas of intense conflict are dominated by fear and struggle. A lack of agency is radically exacerbated where mass violence is linked to crimes against humanity or genocide. In such cases, social devastation is related not only to concrete conditions, such as the loss of home, family, and livelihood, but also cuts to the heart of people's social and cultural identities. Dealing with the violence suffered as a result of genocide or crimes against humanity, and engaging in a transition process, calls into question the very identities on which such societies, for better or worse, have been built.

At a practical level, therefore, agonist reconciliation faces a problem of inception: how can this kind of politics be introduced in arenas that are radically devoid of agency at so many different levels? Colleen Murphy placed this question at the center of her theory of reconciliation, and, as noted in Chapter 6, she concluded that reciprocity is best invoked through establishing the rule of law, creating political trust, and enhancing certain basic capabilities. But here, too, the question of inception remains: who decides what the "rule of law" should look like, and how will it be implemented? Political trust and reciprocity are fine goals, but they are also notoriously elusive in post-conflict settings. How are such ideals best cultivated?

The question deepens when one considers that, to develop agonist reconciliation processes takes time and farsighted leadership skills, two commodities that are often scarce in post-conflict settings. Ideally, political leaders need to consistently and truthfully reflect (and reflect on) their constituencies' interests, but also understand that the security and prospects of both sides depend on the security and prospects of the other. Such leaders have to be prescient enough to step back or step up, and to contest elections fairly when the time comes. Thus, it is necessary not only to empower ordinary citizens to enter the political arena, but also to persuade military leaders to make the shift from strategizing militarily to organizing politically. Schaap's answer seems to be that leaders need courage to embrace the risks of agonism. But what if such courage is lacking?

Again, Murphy's answer, creating political trust, seems sensible but offers too little sustenance for what is essentially such a fragile process. Reconciliation processes have to be able to proceed when trust is at a breaking point, such as when the ANC broke off talks with the government in South Africa over ongoing police brutality, and the state denied having anything to do with the attacks. What motivates former enemies to overcome setbacks and forge a way back to the negotiating table against all odds? Perhaps it does take a level of faith, as Schaap observed, but I suspect that more has to be at play, for even the most faithful doubt the outcomes of political transitions from time to time. In this context, an open invitation to continuing a risky encounter is unlikely to be enough: a more compelling and less fragile set of reasons have to be available to validate and justify ongoing political engagment with the enemy. In fragile post-conflict situations, the overwhelming need is not for risk and fragility, but for security, certainty, and consolidation. In situations where political, economic, and social frameworks have been destroyed, an invitation to embrace a deliberate (and indefinite) suspension of certainty seems unlikely to win much support.

In this regard, Eisikovits developed agonist theory in important ways, explaining that, in protracted negotiation processes, the notion of political generosity plays a key role. His view is that generosity, born of a sympathy with those you once fought against, and of the ability to place yourself in their shoes, is contingent on detailed exposure to the enemy. And yet there is a problem with this too: Eisikovits seems to confuse outcomes with requirements. Some form of prior engagement seems necessary for the development of compassion and generosity. So the question of inception remains: when security and trust are radically absent, how can enemies be persuaded to engage with one another for long enough to develop any measure of mutual compassion? If institutional arguments in favor of establishing a liberal peace, and moral arguments in favor of social restoration, cannot impress hardened political foes, how likely is it that an invitation to participate in a risky agonistic process will succeed?

My second major concern with agonist reconciliation is its emphasis on process at the expense of any or all stated outcomes. Certainly, given the goal-orientation of liberal peace and social restoration, agonism's emphasis on process is a welcome innovation. However, agonists appear to emphasize process at the cost of identifying any goals, or making any promises at all. Reconciliation is posited as a regulative ideal—that is, an ideal "whose realisation would undercut the conditions that constitutes its possibility."[49] This seems to come extremely close to admitting that reconciliation is little more than an empty promise. And even if agonist politics does become institutionalized, what does this mean for those outside the privileged circles of top leadership, and what does reconciliation promise for them?

Liberal peace and social restoration both make concrete, albeit radically different, promises. But what does agonism undertake to deliver? It appears to promise sustained debate about the terms of political association, thereby forging new political relations. Schaap's theory does not, to the best of my understanding, assure the establishment of concrete outcomes up front. Yet, the promise of some outcomes are crucial to whether reconciliation will be accepted popularly, or not. Furthermore, the longer-term credibility of any reconciliation process (as opposed to the violent overthrow of an oppressive regime or reaching the kinds of accommodation with such regimes that involve a blanket denial of atrocities) is crucially dependent on the degrees of institutional and social transformation achieved in its name.

Eisikovits added the idea of fair coexistence to his notion of sympathy as minimum requirements for reconciliation. His view is that attitudinal shifts have to be accompanied by structural fairness. This echoes Murphy's threefold requirement for reconciliation. Yet socioeconomic justice seems to be something of an afterthought in both Eisikovitz's notion of sympathy and in Murphy's idea of reciprocity. That is, its importance is recognized but it is not systematically integrated into either theorist's primary arguments. Murphy comes closest to saying that political reciprocity is, to some degree, premised on socioeconomic capacity, but apart from this, I fail to detect a coherent picture in her theory of how political and socioeconomic outcomes are related.

Does agonism take sufficient account of justice? Or does this approach lean too far toward the kinds of transitional politics that are unable to deliver on the expectations vested in them: expectations such as a just, credible, and inclusive political dispensation or indeed a transformed society? Can the agonist approach accommodate criticisms such as those leveled by Mahmood Mamdani and Robert Meister that reconciliation is essentially a tactic used by those in power to distract the "chattering classes" from the revolutionary approach demanded if they are to achieve social justice, redress, and equality?[50] Agonism does not approach conflicting parties with narrowly conceived arguments about achieving security through institutional reform or introducing human rights. It does not appeal to cultural or religious values, or to any form of morality. It also does not enjoy the kind of diplomatic clout that could match the liberals' so-called overlapping consensus. It simply seeks to persuade with the promise of a new political community, one that can accommodate radical differences without seeking to integrate these into one moral code that can acknowledge and encourage the agency of all parties in the production of radically new, home-grown solutions. Importantly, this promise carries no guarantees, and this is a point that agonists belabor. The outcomes cannot be certain. Essentially it is an invitation to risk displaying vulnerability toward former enemies in the conviction that this has the potential to produce a better dispensation characterized by a different kind politics.

I have argued that this approach runs a major risk with reference to the inception of reconciliation. Much can go wrong when enemies make a promise such as this. The challenge here is twofold: first, the process needs to provide more guarantees for adversaries to be willing to make themselves so vulnerable. "Trust me, this is for your own good" may not be a strong enough argument. Second, the agonist assumption that political community ensues when agency is exercised across lines of division has to be addressed in light of the patent lack of agency prevalent in so many conflict zones. It is tempting to conclude that reconciliation is simply not possible where groups are not strong and organized enough to enter into meaningful political relations. Yet, peace remains elusive, and violence remains present in so many contexts precisely because agency is either severely diminished or subverted.

Agonists argue that reconciliation exists only as long as it cannot be reached, and so refuse to name concrete goals at the start of a reconciliation process. This departure from normativity is a double-edged sword. On the one hand, it avoids the pitfalls of potential moral overreach and intolerance discussed with reference to liberalism and social restoration. On the other, it weakens its own case, especially when trying to gain the support of aggrieved and previously disadvantaged groups.

SECTION THREE

TOWARD INTERDEPENDENCE

8

Reconciliation as Interdependence

In this final section, having first revisited South Africa's transition in some detail, and then traced the conceptual contours of current theorizing on reconciliation, I now set about the task of developing a coherent framework for political transition— *as reconciliation*. It should be evident by now that, at heart, the idea of reconciliation implies an improvement of broken relationships between enemies under the watchful guise of its justice promise. My argument has been that this central focus, if allowed to frame political transition, can help to integrate peacemaking, political dialogue, transitional justice, and social transformation into a comprehensive framework able to guide political transition toward a more just, and thus stable, society.

A further claim has been that reconciliation achieves this by providing important direction at three crucial junctures: first, when political relationships are first sought and established amid ongoing conflict; second, when these relationships begin to provide the basis for negotiating institutional and political change, thus gradually broadening the movement beyond the political elite; and third, when social relations at large become more inclusive and fair. Cast specifically as interdependence, this theoretical approach to reconciliation explains how relationships emerge in unfavorable conditions; how once a modest beginning is achieved, cooperation can grow, trust can be built, and understanding deepened; and how eventually a fundamentally more just society is built—all as part of a comprehensive, integrated agenda for political transition.

Passing through the varied moments that make up political transition, relationships at the heart of reconciliation have to weather many challenges and cycles: of trust and mistrust, respect and disdain, consensus and disagreement, cooperation and stalling. A key question (and aim) therefore is how *sufficient* levels of trust, respect, and consensus can be generated and maintained to sustain reconciliation as it is *progressively realized* through good times and bad.

While maintaining the relations at its core, reconciliation further ought to remain resolutely *future-oriented*. Otherwise, when dominated by conditions created by past violence, it risks circling back on itself and degenerating into renewed violence. Achieving a shared and just future, and not settling old scores, therefore fundamentally informs and sustains reconciliation. Yet at the same time, it will become clear in what follows that a resolute focus on the future never excludes dealing with the past. Indeed, dealing with the past is an essential component of moving forward—but there should be grave caution about dealing with the past as an end in itself, as revenge, and at the cost of imagining and realizing a radically new future. Turning back to face the past ought to be thought of as a way of moving forward toward overcoming that very past.

In what follows, the aim is to highlight the key lessons and insights from the book's first section on South Africa, and to build on the strengths of the three typologies outlined in the second section (while hopefully avoiding their weaknesses) to develop a workable framework for political transition. Before addressing the respective tasks of initiating reconciliation, facilitating its progressive realization, and fostering just societies, it is important to make a few general remarks regarding reconciliation as a framework for political transition.

An Overview of the Argument

As discussed in the previous section, a range of theorists have attempted to identify a core idea at the heart of political reconciliation. They have done so by assigning to reconciliation specific descriptors that might differentiate "real" or "true" reconciliation from "false" or "superficial" reconciliation. In this way, Villa-Vicencio argues that real reconciliation is characterized by authentic, free, and fearless speech. For Verdeja, reconciliation is marked by respect, while De Greiff prefers trust. Philpott emphasizes the restoration of "right relationships," whereas Murphy identifies the establishing of reciprocity through various means as reconciliation's key descriptor. Eisikovits links reconciliation to sympathy; and so on. In the preceding section, I organized some of these theories in three major typologies, outlining what I believe to be some of the major contours in the theoretical landscape within which reconciliation is thought about today.

A key insight to emerge when comparing sections 1 and 2, is that South Africa's reconciliation story does not fit very well into any of Section 2's typologies, somewhat abstract as they may be. Reconciliation in South Africa first gained momentum when leaders dared to articulate its possibility, at a time when the very idea of reaching out seemed dangerously utopian or even immoral. It came to include the establishment of robust negotiation platforms as well as transitional justice mechanisms that, together, gave rise to a progressively realized sense of inclusion and fairness. Finally, it morphed into what was hoped would be a sustained attempt to create a more just society (even if efforts thus far have largely disappointed citizens). Across these different phases, the notion of reconciliation remained central.

Yet, even as reconciliation remained a central theme, the same cannot be said for forgiveness, the rule of law, or indeed political (agonist) contestation premised on irresolvable difference. None of these paradigms accompanied South Africa's reconciliation journey throughout. As became clear when examining Mandela and De Klerk's relationship, forgiveness was not a prominent force during the early political stages. Establishing the rule of law, in the liberal sense, was not the sole or even primary concern, either. Rather, the goal was reaching a political settlement acceptable to all and thus ending the political violence threatening to engulf the country. And although valuing political difference featured prominently as a feature of the constitutional negotiations, this sentiment was replaced post-1994 by a drive for consensus-seeking on the need to address the social ills inherited from apartheid. Therefore, even if South Africa's reconciliation agenda overlapped at times with one or more of these paradigms, none of them functioned as the central guiding framework throughout. I argue on this basis that therefore these frameworks do not assist sufficiently to theorize South Africa's transition, and possibly, those of other countries and regions. South Africa does affirm some of the assumptions inherent in these approaches, but no single one seems to capture its crux. By and large, something *different* therefore seems to have been at the heart of South Africa's reconciliation process.

To develop a theoretical framework for political transition closer aligned to the South African experience, I therefore propose "interdependence" as a key designator for reconciliation. Earlier, we saw the extent to which it had been this idea, that had given South Africa's reconciliation process coherence, direction, and versatility. Unsurprisingly, it was precisely the opposite of the central idea that drove apartheid, namely, that racial groups are better off apart than together. By contrast, reconciliation politics propagated the idea that South Africa's racial groups were (and remain) fundamentally (unchangeably) and comprehensively (politically, economically, socially, and morally) *inter*dependent—not only as a matter of normative ideal, but first as a matter of unavoidable socio-political reality. This provided a compelling rationale for taking reconciliation seriously— and twenty-four years on, it still does.

Early on, Mandela and De Klerk acknowledged the reality of interdependence as the centerpiece of their respective political agendas. Captured in the phrase "we have no choice," this reality drove the negotiating partners together time and again, pushing them toward a political settlement based on an interdependent future, and helping them forge agreements on how to deal with the past. And the undeniable reality of interdependence continues to shape social transformation in the post-apartheid era, too, crossing the lines of race, gender, nationalism, ethnicity, class, and all the other fault lines that divide South Africans. It is my view that a similar kind of interdependence features in relations between communities in many other conflict zones, hinting at one reason for South Africa's ongoing relevance in terms of the study and management of political transition.

In light of the South African case and existing theory, my argument here is that *political reconciliation is best understood as a complex and evolving form of interdependence.* This is to say that reconciliation takes form in relationships in which deeply entrenched antagonists articulate, negotiate, and embrace a shared future on the basis that this is not only desirable but (eventually) unavoidable. *Working toward fairness and inclusivity, reconciliation entails the mutual acknowledgment, the progressive institutionalization, and the long-term socialization of a comprehensive and fundamental interdependence.* This working definition implies that reconciliation politics applies equally to different stages of political transition by consistently and coherently promoting the idea of restoring fair and inclusive relationships.

It also suggests that reconciliation operates both "vertically," by seeking to restore relations between citizens and the state (encapsulated in the "social contract"), as well as "horizontally," by improving social cohesion marked by fairness and inclusivity. Furthermore, it implies that reconciliation often begins, not with a clear-cut, well-articulated moral commitment shared across enemy lines, but rather with acknowledgment by all sides of the reality that envelops all of them, namely, that no segment or class of the society can exist easily, and certainly cannot thrive, in the absence of the security and prosperity of the others. From that acknowledgment comes a gradual move toward shared norms and values in terms of which to build a more just future. This shared acknowledgment involves a conception of justice that is fundamentally future-oriented, though not to the exclusion of dealing with a troubled past to the extent that it prevents the realization of a desired future.

Recognizing the progressive nature of reconciliation is of fundamental importance. Starting from a deliberately narrow set of moral assumptions (we have to make it work for the sake of our people) rooted in a strong sense of realpolitik (we are in this together whether we like it or not), reconciliation does not assume an a priori agreement on where society is headed, or indeed how, exactly, to apportion and punish blame for the wrongs of the past. The bare but essential basis for initiating the process of reconciliation is a principled agreement that a future society ought to be just, inclusive, and fair for all. Nir Eisikovits warned that insisting too early on *absolute justice* might well lead to *absolute injustice.* He explains, correctly in my view, that rigid, unwavering demands by one party, for example, can lead to catastrophic counter-claims and a resumption of violence.

By contrast, a carefully crafted compromise about the weighing of past injustices within a contested political terrain has the potential to yield more, if not (yet) "full," justice.[1] A progressively realized reconciliation process therefore allows for decidedly less-than-perfect institutions and arrangements as long as they take society forward to ever-widening and deepening forms of justice.

This is not to imply that justice is always relative or limited to how it appears "in the eyes of the beholder." How can there ever be ambiguity about the evils of apartheid, or who enforced it? Yes, of course, there are many qualifications of who was responsible within that system, for what forms of agency applied, and so forth. But nothing said so far should be taken to deny the fundamental injustice of the apartheid regime, or for that matter of war and political oppression elsewhere in the world. Some events transcend politics, and are simply morally wrong. At the same time, my argument is that redressing the wounds caused by such mass violations of human rights effectively does require taking into account the reality of ongoing interdependence between erstwhile enemies, and turning this reality from being an oppressive one, to a liberating force, first for victims, but ultimately for all citizens.

Although reconciliation therefore has to retain some measure of normative open-endedness (that is, the ability to forge a shared ethics *together* as the process develops), opting for reconciliation nonetheless requires choice, and therefore a strong normative and ethical commitment to "justice for all." It is, after all, only one of various possible conflict-resolution scenarios. And it is one that demands the nerve to face interdependence as a fact, and the resolve to learn how to work and live with one's former enemy (given this interdependence), while seeking mutual understanding in the absence of full agreement—all in pursuit of fundamentally more just relations. Such respect for difference, however, does not exclude working toward shared agreements so that a measure of consensus and predictability is gradually accomplished. Predictability premised on sufficient consensus, in turn, is crucial for the requisite trust to develop.

Alternative frameworks for political transition, that in my view cannot be described as reconciliation, include: segregation or secession, where acknowledging interdependence does not lead to integration but to separation and, arguably, to the official recognition and permanent institutionalization of conflict lines (as arguably has been the case in the Balkans after the dissolution of Yugoslavia); outright military victory, in which one group defeats another and then unilaterally sets the agenda and determines the ground rules for post-conflict societies (as in post-Hussein Iraq under American occupation, for example); majoritarian rule that excludes minorities from meaningful participation in shaping a common future (as in Myanmar and perhaps Sri Lanka at present); tenuous peace treaties that rely on external peacekeeping forces and fail to secure buy-in from locals and thus lack a sense of restoring damaged relations in society (arguably the case in the Eastern Democratic Republic of the Congo); or, indeed, ongoing conflict where interdependence continues to be denied (as in Israel/Palestine). None of these alternatives, in my view, qualifies for the description of reconciliation as interdependence.

Reconciliation is normatively committed to realizing just relations within the context of an interdependent society. But promising justice is not the same as promising healing, closure, or, indeed, forgiveness. Whereas reconciliation without justice implies outright failure, the same is not true of reconciliation's relationship with forgiveness, healing, or closure.

Given all this, it becomes clear why, although forgiveness is a desired outcome, it is unrealistic and politically unproductive to posit forgiveness as reconciliation's non-negotiable precondition. I was first made aware, many years ago, that there may be a distinction between reconciliation and forgiveness by Charles Villa-Vicencio. For him, forgiveness concerns what Paul Ricoeur called the "poetics of existence," that is, "a political ideal to lure nations toward achievements not yet realised." By contrast, reconciliation describes a somewhat "lower level of encounter" within which "the enemies of yesterday need to explore what it means to cooperate in resolving the issues that initiated and sustained the conflict."[2]

Given the reflections in the preceding pages, I would not describe reconciliation as "lower" than forgiveness, but perhaps rather as logically "prior" to it. Therefore, in my view, reconciliation-as-interdependence cannot, and therefore *should not*, promise forgiveness either, even if it remains a desired goal. A more "modest notion of reconciliation," to borrow a phrase from Villa-Vicencio, will have delivered sufficiently against its promise if justice (understood as a progressively inclusive and fair society) is achieved, *even* if forgiveness, healing, and complete closure remain elusive.

Forgiveness might occur as a consequence of reconciliation, but it might not. The relationship between forgiveness and reconciliation is therefore best described as one where reconciliation enhances the conditions for forgiveness, but does not imply or prescribe it. If and when forgiveness does happen, it necessarily implies the prior achievement of a significant measure of reconciliation. However, the inverse causality does not apply. That said, the forgiveness paradigm is important for making plain the fundamentally relational world in which we live, and on which reconciliation-as-interdependence too draws to make its arguments.

Similarly, there is some overlap between interdependence and agonist politics. As explained in the previous chapter, for agonists, reconciliation begins when opposing groups are willing to risk engaging politically rather than militarily, on the basis that it is in their mutual interest to do so. The idea that "the world is an object held in common,"[3] as agonists claim, powerfully supports the notion of fundamental and comprehensive interdependence. Understanding and addressing the challenges related to this "world held in common" presumably depends on being able to share its political spaces with one's enemy. It also implies a theoretical interdependence in seeking to understand not only the common challenges, but also the nature of reconciliation itself.

The idea of interdependence also overlaps to some degree with the cultural construct of ubuntu, widely accepted in southern Africa. Ubuntu complements the social restoration paradigm, which sees society as relational and refuses to adopt uncritically the political/social split affirmed by classic liberalism. Ubuntu is a cultural ideal, which affirms that people become fully human only through their interactions with other people, and that disregarding the human dignity of others fatally wounds one's own humanity. South African archbishop emeritus Desmond Tutu has written that

> ubuntu speaks of the very essence of being human. When we want to give high praise to someone we say, "*Yu u nobuntu*", "Hey so-and-so has ubuntu." Then you are generous, you are hospitable, you are friendly and caring and compassionate. You share what you have. It is to say, "My humanity is caught up, is inextricably bound up, in yours. We belong in a bundle of life."[4]

Although initially articulated in southern Africa, ubuntu clearly portends to have universal relevance. Tutu sees it as "Africa's gift to the world." The idea certainly has powerful cultural and religious resonance across many African societies.[5] Across the continent the restoration of community after massive violence has been a major emphasis of reconciliation, and has often occurred in the name of ubuntu: the work of religious leaders in post–civil war Northern Uganda is one example; Mozambique with its emphasis on localized community reconciliation is another; then there are the Gacaca community courts in Rwanda, and so on.[6]

However, as noted, cultural and religious arguments for reconciliation are not based only or perhaps even primarily on moral arguments. They carry fundamental ontological assumptions about how the world "works," how it has evolved (as a result of the conflict), and how it could, and *therefore*, should be in future. Ubuntu, too, functions as much more than a moral injunction to behave *as if* human beings are essentially social. It includes an implicit ontology, a worldview, that claims that whether we acknowledge it or not, we are in fact already intertwined and interdependent. If accepted, this claim has powerful implications that operate quite apart from any moral considerations—and I believe that many of those who criticized Desmond Tutu for moral overreach during his leadership of the TRC failed to understand this point that is central to his thinking.

It is for this reason that cultural and religious arguments in favor of reconciliation can develop significant traction in conflict zones. Such arguments can also provide an assessment, culturally determined though this may be, of where things went wrong, how they ought to have been, and how they could be improved. Central to ubuntu's ontology of interdependence is the insight that human interests are interdependent in all relations and identities. This kind of culturally determined realism, in my view, has a much better chance of providing leverage when seeking to convince enemies to reconcile than moral injunctions, which tend to appeal, often in vain, to individuals to act according to their highest moral values.

Despite these similarities, I refrained from using ubuntu as reconciliation's key descriptor because, even if the idea has universal application, as Tutu claims, its cultural and historical roots do not. Less culturally specific and historically loaded, the term "interdependence" hopefully carries a similar appreciation for the relational nature of human society, including those societies that are trapped in conflict.[7]

As noted earlier, the relationship between interdependence and reconciliation entails more than a description of the nature of entwined realities, and emergent norms, important as these are. It also has an important bearing on the thinking and theorizing about reconciliation itself. I hope I have illustrated the theoretical interdependence that characterizes reconciliation studies, much as political and economic interdependence marks its practice.

Instead, therefore, of rejecting any of the different types of theory described in Section II, one needs to draw on them in various ways to create the framework for reconciliation as interdependence. In a very real sense, the various theories currently in circulation need one another in order to come to an adequate framework of political transition that is able to guide and inform a process that begins with peacemaking, passes through a phase of negotiating the future and the past, and eventually issues into longer-term processes of social transformation.

I also choose to use the term interdependence over more neutral terms such as "interconnectedness" or "networking" because these terms do not go far enough in describing the given-ness of the relationships between most groups that are in conflict with one another. Presumably, if one is connected, one can break a connection and walk away, much like ending a telephone call. Yet, if one is interdependent, and walks away, one is harming oneself, because interdependence remains at the heart of the situation whether it is acknowledged or not; it cannot be unmade by either side walking away. It is simply there—always present and real, whether it is accepted or not. I have argued that once acknowledged after periods of denial, this fundamental reality provides leaders in conflict with strong arguments in favor of choosing the path of reconciliation.

Admittedly, interdependence does impose some limits on notions of freedom and self-determination. The implication is that one is free and independent, but only to the degree that one can maintain just relations of interdependence with others. For those engaged in liberation struggles against oppressive regimes, this holds a sobering reality: one can throw off the yoke of unjust rule but never escape from relating to one's former oppressor. Equally sobering, oppressors have to learn that the existence of their "safe" enclaves fundamentally depends on those they have excluded, and that the fulfillment of their aspirations depends ultimately on the aspirations of those they previously regarded with contempt being met. Even if a dominant group can maintain power by force for a while, they can never be safe and free, no matter how loudly they might claim the opposite, as long as they contribute to keeping their neighbors unfree and unsafe. The challenge is thus to build relations between conflicting groups on fundamentally more just bases than before.

Having provided an overview of the concept of reconciliation as interdependence, I now turn to work out in more detail what this means for each of the three dimensions that constitute this framework—beginning, institutionalization, and socialization.

Fragile Beginnings

As discussed before, the politics of reconciliation almost always requires making a start in conditions that militate against its inception. I am suggesting that the conditions for reconciliation are created amid adversity when both sides acknowledge that the realization of their own hopes and dreams are impossible without the cooperation of the other side. Key to my argument *for* interdependence as reconciliation's key designator, has been that its acknowledgment does *not* require fully restored trust, political forgiveness, or indeed any form of intimacy. It does, however, imply a break with the politics of violent hostility and the willingness to embrace seeking to work with and understand the enemy. Consequently, often the first signal that a reconciliation process is underway is when leaders acknowledge that realizing the interests and aspirations of their own constituency both includes and depends on accommodating their enemies' demands, fears, and hopes.

What motivates such leadership, and by implication reconciliation's inception, in the face of extreme hostility and historical injustice? What pushes leaders beyond their freedom struggles and into a radical new agenda of seeking to reconcile with one another? Individual motivations, geopolitical conditions, and local dynamics all play a role. However, when pushed, Mandela and De Klerk articulated and defended their decision to reconcile in terms of a given mutuality, an interdependence that up to that point had been denied. That is, they conceded to themselves, to their respective constituencies, and, eventually, to one another, that their own historical struggles (for Afrikaner as well as African self-determination, for economic security, for justice, and for human rights) were self-defeating when conducted in opposition to, and to the exclusion of, the other. And in reaching out to affirm a relationship they knew existed already, *a beginning was made to transform that relationship* even if at that moment they would not have agreed on much, especially not on how a shared future would look.

The act of acknowledgment does more therefore than reflect a given reality. It is an expression of the inherent *value* of interdependence premised on equality. To the extent that it is indeed mutual, the counterintuitive *acknowledgement* of interdependence during periods of hostility in and of itself becomes a *performance* of interdependence, affirming and transforming relationships in precisely a context where it is virtually impossible to imagine anything other than violent relations. Reconciliation's creative spark originates exactly in this interplay between acknowledgment and interdependence. But it is not that acknowledgment creates relationships from nowhere. Rather, it makes an already existing interdependence explicit and hints at new possibilities for this relationship.

It is an act that demonstrates both the reality and potential of this given interdependence, and therefore also has the ability to create and sustain a mutual interest in transforming historically frozen relationships, precisely because the positive potential of what may at first be experienced as a deeply negative imposition of the presence of an enemy is made explicit. That is, when opposing political leaders acknowledge their fundamental and comprehensive interdependence on the enemy they have been fighting in the name of self-realization and freedom, the question of how to view and where to take relationships that are given but that at the same time have gone badly wrong immediately and necessarily arises, often expressed as a longing for reconciliation.

Consider Central and East Africa's patchwork of battlefields as a series of interrelated conflicts that display a fundamental and comprehensive interdependence between fighting groups. In a belt stretching from Kinshasa in the DRC across Bujumbura, Gulu, and Khartoum to Asmara and Djibouti on the Red Sea, conflict lines zigzag and criss-cross through villages and towns, playgrounds, churchyards, and vegetable gardens. Throughout these settlements, supporters of opposing groups live cheek by jowl. Nothing like the trench warfare associated with twentieth-century Europe, battles are fought across intimate, uncertain, and meandering front lines that can be here today, and elsewhere tomorrow. When combatants are cornered, they often disperse into communities, scattering like quicksilver, and resuming life as ordinary citizens until the next opportunity to mobilize occurs.

Northern Ireland's conflict, in turn, runs along carefully demarcated, but also intimately interlinked lines, designated by walls, wires, and lookout posts that bifurcate neighborhoods and suburbs. Opposing murals glare at one another across pedestrian crossings, walls, pubs, and parks. These symbols, shaped as much by the battle *against* the other as *for* the self, remind residents daily—lest they dare forget—which group they belong to. Perhaps the murals' primary function is to help maintain lines of conflict in the face of all that binds the two sides together.

These "intimate conflicts" also occur in Myanmar, Sri Lanka, Syria, Iraq, Colombia, and Ukraine. Here too, enemy groups share a fundamentally and comprehensively interdependent fate, not because of any moral ideal, but simply as a matter of fact. Their histories intersect, and are captured in memories stretching back generations. Moreover, their current fortunes are entwined, and for better or worse, they face a shared future. People often travel, trade, love, and live across enemy lines in ways that let slip the fact that their interdependence is at least as fundamental to their realities as is the conflict that divides them.

Despite radical differences across enemy lines, in perspective, aspiration, and outlook, often these relationships display a remarkable, if unacknowledged proximity. The hostile intimacy that results from sharing such proximity, however, falls dramatically short of the kind of interdependence that reconciliation seeks to establish. It may in fact be its opposite. It produces the denial, contestation, and eventual destruction of the rights of others to an equal say in the relationship. Containing the intimate enemy, rather than reconciling with him, necessitates, for example, structural violence, often sustained by prejudiced cultural beliefs about the other. Often it also leads to physical violence as well when containment turns to the thirst for genocide. Until not so long, traveling on the ever-narrowing and increasingly potholed road from Kampala to Kitgum in Northern Uganda was a visceral reminder of how a refusal to acknowledge interdependence between neighboring tribes had resulted in civil war, deliberate neglect, and deeply entrenched bias across tribal lines.

The task is therefore to have enemies recognize that they are in fact interdependent; and to create conditions for the kind of deep, normative interdependence that reconciliation promises. Until the playing field is level, enemies cannot turn away from false intimacy. Apartheid was not a state of interdependence but the denial of interdependence, because one side had such a strong upper hand (as Israel does over Palestine) that the powerful party really did not acknowledge in any meaningful way or to any serious extent its fundamental dependence on the weaker adversary. Do the Israelis really need to acknowledge their interdependence on the Palestinians? Did the Afrikaners really face their long-term interdependence on the blacks and coloreds? Only in a limited way, nothing like a mutual the conscious embrace of interdependence that could only follow the courage of a cold, hard look at reality.

Conversely, acknowledging the extent to which others co-determine our worlds can help to motivate leaders of groups that are locked in conflict to find alternative modes of expressing the reality of their codependence and transform it into genuine interdependence. That shift occurs only when the reality of mutual dependence is redeemed from conditions of gross power inequalities separating the powerful from the weak. Unhealthy forms of dependence, or "co-dependence" becomes interdependence only through the establishment of conditions of justice—conditions that respect and redress the historical reality of past human rights violations. As Rwanda, Sierra Leone, Liberia, and Burundi, among other countries, have taught us, part of embracing the prospect of reconciliation is to develop a finely tuned system of establishing levels of accountability that would allow the conflicted communities and the majority of those who fought one another to develop modes of coexistence that transcend the simple binary of victim/perpetrator. This, of course, is not to draw a blanket of impunity over humanity's worst excesses, but much rather to allow a fragile post-conflict society to define itself for the future in ways that transcend, and *thereby* begin dealing with the violations of the past in ways that take society closer to a just future instead of further away from it.

This approach avoids the potential moral overdetermination associated with some forms of reconciliation. Overdetermination occurs when the shape and content of a restored relationship is predetermined, with no input from those involved and prior to the restoring of their relationships: for example, when forgiveness is expected to be an inevitable outcome or even a precondition for reconciliation, or when political liberalism is held up as the inevitable outcome of all legitimate forms of social transition. Rather, it requires accepting that aspirations and dreams for the self is unlikely to materialize without some measure of accommodation of, and collaboration with, the other, to ensure the realization of their aspirations and dreams, and that in this sense, reconciliation's promise is "justice for all" as the ultimate criterion against which it is to be held accountable.

The Promise of Justice at Reconciliation's Inception

Although open-ended, reconciliation-as-interdependence carries within a promise that the ways in which unequal interdependence as a reality militates against interdependence as a normative ideal will be addressed, and that once acknowledged, a truly and deeply interdependent society can be imagined as a more just society. Just forms of interdependence tend to be characterized by the values of equality and reciprocity, and by forms of governance that work to benefit the majority of citizens, rather than oppress or exploit them. Before enemies can agree on what a future just society will look like, they need to agree to a process of generating this agreement—with an express commitment to realize a common vision. In this limited but very real way therefore, the hope for the promise of justice is present at reconciliation's inception, even if its articulation, its institutional enactment, and its eventual realization in society may be decades away.

If Emmanuel Levinas is to be believed, at a fundamental level encountering the other is to be *simultaneously and necessarily* confronted with the demand for justice—and one could add, with the demand for reconciliation too. One cannot look the other in the eye without looking justice in the eye—and one cannot look the other in the eye without being confronted with the need for reconciliation. Levinas was a Lithuanian Jew who survived the Second World War, and became one of the most respected voices in European political and philosophical debate during the latter half of the twentieth century. Outlining his dense arguments is risky, yet holds significance for reconciliation: for Levinas, the moment when the gaze of the other is met is the moment when the world beyond my world (the world I cannot ever fully know) enters my world, upsets it, turns it upside down, and calls everything I knew before into question. In some ways, meeting the other signals the end of my world as I knew it, and perhaps as my ancestors too knew and articulated it for generations. Such moments, he argues, represent at once the price and possibility of freedom, but also hold within them possibilities for true ethics and justice.[8] Reconciliation is one possible outcome of such an encounter with an unavoidable other and, at the first meeting of the eyes, the question of justice inevitably arises. Both the demand and possibility for reconciliation and justice emerge when once first faces the other.

Although an inevitable consequence, justice is therefore distinctly not an afterthought of reconciliation. Rather, it is structurally embedded *from the beginning* in the promise of new relationships offered in reconciliation's name. The notion of justice challenges the structural asymmetries, the power relations and inequalities, that are at play at the onset of any engagement, while at the same time accepting the reality that for the time being, these asymmetries would be present. This double-play creates opportunities for widening inclusion and deepening fairness—opportunities that can be embraced or denied. If a relationship subsequently develops in violent or oppressive ways, it means that the potential for justice inherent in that first encounter is actively denied.

The idea of a promise of justice in the moment where enemies seeking to reconcile first meet challenges the notion of justice as *primarily* a backward-looking, forensic discipline, concerned with retributive redress, important as this is, especially in the liberal paradigm. At play here, rather, is a notion of justice concerned with acknowledging that which had gone wrong, not in the first place as a sin against an abstract moral or legal rule, but as a sin against my sister or brother on whom I depend for my own existential fulfillment, and as such a sin also against myself, my humanity, and my future. The concrete appearance of the other motivates me, then, not to consider the past, but the future, by realizing and acknowledging the irrevocable interdependence in which her and my existence had been cast—an interdependence however that exists beyond our volition, but the nature of which lies well within our ability to shape.

Thus, justice is reconciliation's primary promise—and *not* forgiveness, *or* the rule of law, *or* indeed that an abiding space for political contestation. Important though these outcomes might be, an acknowledgment of interdependence primarily involves a promise of qualitatively more equal and reciprocal relationships, and these, I suggest, reside in the very DNA of reconciliation-as-interdependence as a concept.

On the one hand, acknowledging interdependence *as a fact* requires societies to understand and make the most of our reliance on others in order to realize our own aspirations. On the other hand, acknowledging interdependence *as a norm* requires us to imagine what constitutes a just interdependence, as *interdependence*, as opposed to allowing violence or oppression to shape false norms within skewed power relations. Once interdependence becomes a shared political insight, it not only *demands* but *enables* deeper forms of engagement, including the possibility, though not the inevitability, of forgiveness. In this way, the road to justice depends largely on sustaining the credibility of the process in the eyes of those directly involved, through accumulating levels of inclusivity and fairness.

In summary, then, political leaders who acknowledge and articulate the comprehensive and fundamental if unequal interdependence that exists across enemy lines—first as an unjust reality and over time as a normatively articulated one—*create* the possibility for reconciliation and for justice to occur, even when prevailing conditions seem to militate against both these ideals.

Transitions that Work

What enables reconciliation to develop in more inclusive and fair ways, ultimately aimed at making good on the justice promise that lies at the heart of genuine reconciliation? It necessarily requires, I have argued, reconciliation's embodiment within a wide range of initiatives, mechanisms, processes, platforms, and transitional arrangements which all help to create the conditions to set in motion the transformation, not only of a set of elite political relationships, but of an entire political system—and ultimately of society.

The answer, of course, about what such processes would look like concretely, is not straightforward. John Paul Lederach first developed the notion of "infrastructures for peace," in which he sought to capture various key principles, processes, and mechanisms of peacemaking, largely based on his experiences as a mediator in Latin America (especially Nicaragua) and Africa.[9] In line with the argument I develop here, Lederach's notion of reconciliation spanned pre- and post-agreement stages of peacemaking, but also the various levels in society that need to be involved in a comprehensive approach to transforming conflict into sustainable peace. Lederach argued for a creative and systematic integration of the interdependent "multiple levels of society, from grassroots to high-level political processes" involved in comprehensive peacemaking. Such "vertical integration" was the single most significant weakness of peace processes and required "strategic infrastructures and creative, sustained engagement."[10]

Because the notion of "infrastructure" may denote a certain inflexibility, Lederach over time shifted from an emphasis on "institutions" to "platforms" to emphasize the danger of bureacratizing peace processes, something institutions are often predisposed to. Although institutions emphasize the important turn away from "project"-focused, externally driven and ad-hoc approaches, they tend to fall victim to "self-perpetuation." And so to be responsive, flexible, and adaptable remains crucial. Lederach likens peace processes therefore to complex-adaptive systems more akin to dynamic, generative, and responsive music such as jazz, rather than "merely" complex systems, reflected in musical terms by a marching band combining successfully a variety of instruments but with a predetermined pace and rhythm that is not adaptable or open to change. By contrast, jazz musicians, Lederach reflects, can "play the same tune in five different ways on five different nights."[11]

A truly transformative process, I would agree with Lederach, requires more than technocratic competence and foresight. Over and above these smart techniques and innovative platforms, political transitions seem therefore to require a certain *alchemy*. Reflecting on the South African case but also others, it is evident that, in time, reconciliation comes to resemble something of the miraculous, the magical, the unquantifiable. As it unfolds, deeply hostile political and social relations are somehow transformed, albeit gradually and unevenly, into more productive ones. This attitudinal change, impossible to predict, prescribe, or determine, happens through the work of the decidedly less-than-perfect initiatives typically associated with political transition: peace talks, political negotiations, and constitutional assemblies, governments of national unity, criminal trials, and truth commissions. But how?

To get closer to an understanding of how the alchemy of political transition unfolds, I analyzed the South African case in some detail (in Chapters 2–4 in particular), and then outlined how three major types of reconciliation theory have since attempted to conceptualize the process reconciliation aims to set in motion. In these differing theoretical landscapes, the alchemy required to transform hostile relations into productive ones was sought respectively in the grammar of forgiveness, in invoking the rule of law through preemptive performances in political trials and so forth, or in embracing risky political spaces that preserve irreducible difference. For me, none of these mechanisms adequately captured key elements of the South African case, and, by implication, I suspect they would fail to fully account for, or help to facilitate, other cases of political transition as well.

It is my view that in various ways, reconciliation's alchemy is partly observable (where transitions work out) in the shift from denying any relations with enemies, to coming to acknowledge such relationships eventually as a reality that merits (grudging) acceptance, and finally as a future potentiality, an avenue toward possibilities for the greater well-being for all. Through the discussion in Sections 1 and 2, two observations emerged. The first is that initiatives tasked with ushering in transition—in South Africa at least—displayed a set of twin traits or values, namely: *widening inclusivity* and *deepening fairness*. Through seeking progressively to embody and express these values, the initiatives gradually came to foreshadow the society they sought to establish, thereby building momentum toward that society. The second observation is that the manner in which these initiatives are integrated into the larger and more comprehensive political transition is of crucial importance. This includes questions of timing, sequencing, and complementarity between different kinds of initiatives, including peace forums, political negotiations, election commissions, and constitution-making bodies, as well as between the courts and the TRC.

Often expressed as local ownership, inclusivity required a sense that "we have no choice" since "we are in this together."

As such reconciliation in South Africa became the diametric opposite to what is referred to as "regime change," that is, externally driven change in government as a result of (often nefarious) foreign interest and intervention. Frequently, it is not the failures of local leadership that cause peacemaking to fail but foreign influence protecting vested interests. Ahmad Mouath Al-Khatib Al-Hasani, the former president of the National Coalition for Syrian Revolutionary and Opposition Forces, told me that it had not been the disparity of the Syrian rebels in the first place that had made his job so difficult; it had been the dozen or so foreign states seeking to further their agendas and securing their interest, all converging on, and claiming a stake of the "Syrian pie."[12]

Ebrahim Rasool, former South African Ambassador to the United States, writes compellingly about the alarming record of coups, and associated regime change, in the developing world that can be contributed directly or indirectly to the influence of powerful external actors, the most recent being Egypt:

> "Whatever its unique narrative and mythology, the overthrow of Morsi is a twenty-first-century imitation of the coups that took place in Iran in 1953, the Congo in 1960, Chile in 1973, Haiti in 1991, Turkey in 1997 and Haiti again in 2004. Egypt has elements of each one. . . . In most of the coups there is a lingering suspicion of the hidden hand of the United States or British intelligence."[13]

Political reconciliation includes citizens of all backgrounds, interests and political persuasions in a series of explorations, failures, renewals, and cessations, yet always with frequent returns to inclusive and fair spaces held open by credible (preferably local) custodians. Repeated cycles of opening and closing are evident as attempts are made to address the most pressing and difficult questions a conflicted society faces. Raising the historic questions, putting them on the table, disagreeing openly, and engaging in robust discussion becomes an early exercise in democratic inclusion. From these engagements, however open they are to different views, a degree of provisional closure has to be reached—that is, a "sufficient consensus" needs to be generated from time to time to move another step further. This is critical for maintaining a sense of momentum. In seeking provisional closure on crucial matters, the ability to work out productive compromises seems equally essential. This involves yielding to legitimate demands without compromising on issues of legitimate self-interest, thus ultimately ensuring that all stakeholders emerge somewhat better off. These processes are often longer and more taxing than anticipated, not least when ongoing violence undermines them; the ability to discern when and how to suspend talks, without breaking off the process entirely, is thus also important.

Once aspirations for a fair and interdependent future have been captured in a mutually accepted agreement or progressive agreements, a credible national process for dealing with the past can be developed. For reasons that have emerged throughout the book, dealing with the past seems significantly more likely to succeed in such a context than when a society remains divided about where it is heading. Crucially, this process ought to take its cue from those who, arguably, paid the highest price for the new dispensation, and who were previously the most systematically excluded from society, namely, victims of human rights violations. This is their time to take center stage. The process needs to offer symbolic and material reparations, not only to these individuals but also to the collective, in acknowledgment of their full and unqualified inclusion in the new dispensation. Their sense of inclusion can be strengthened through the publication of historical records about the conflict, including their own accounts of crimes committed against them. These accounts can also act as reminder to the nation to never repeat the past, as well as form a basis for developing understandings of the past that take both sides of the story into account. At the same time, the exercise of dealing with the past ought to be as fair and even-handed as is humanly possible. In this context, arguments in favor of prosecuting only those "most responsible" has obvious and serious flaws. Nevertheless, however it is conceived, the system for establishing accountability ought to be demonstrably fair. The South African approach was, as we saw, both innovative and defective in this regard, the latter not least for failing to hold to account senior decision makers who ordered members of the security forces to commit gross human rights violations but were shrewd enough to cover their tracks.

Rwanda's Gacaca courts broke interesting new ground in this area. Much of the critique about these community-based courts to which Rwanda looked to handle the more than 1 million genocide-related cases that had piled up after 1994, has focused on shortcomings in due process rather than on what could be argued was a politically biased mandate. Had their mandate been less one-sided—that is, had it included war crimes and crimes against humanity rather than focusing on genocide alone (the latter mandate ensured that virtually all victims would be Tutsis and all perpetrators Hutus according to a careful political framing of what counted as "genocide")—the mechanism might have made a stronger contribution to reconciliation in Rwanda. In my view, limited procedural shortcomings within a largely fair process would have been a relatively small price to pay for an initiative that had the capacity to process over a million cases, thereby potentially creating a sense of even-handedness in dealing with genocide and related violence that would have been largely unparalleled elsewhere, and at the same time freeing up the nascent post-genocide legal system to continue its day-to-day efforts to rebuild a society based on the rule of law.[14]

However, fairness is more than even-handedness; it implies that victims obtain a measure of satisfaction that justice has been done. How such accountability mechanisms should be arranged is, again, not written in the stars. This is a matter for national deliberation in the wake of agreements about how a nation will operate in future, with victims themselves having a critical say in determining the nature of such mechanisms. In these consultations and deliberations, civic leaders also have a critical role to play in bolstering inclusivity and fairness, thus gradually enabling leaders to convert their awareness of interdependence from an acknowledgment of reality into a desired ideal, and eventually into a lived reality.

An important contribution of liberalism is the insistence on the rule of law as a form of justice to be expected as a result of reconciliation processes. I agree that in some way or another, the law as agreed between conflicting parties ought to rule over the subsequent dispensation, standing in judgment of both the actions of the legislative and the executive. But how does one arrive at a consensus on what the rule of law looks like? Perhaps the first step is to accept that it can appear quite markedly different depending on where you stand.

Transitions and the Rule of Law

Few groups or leaders would ever openly argue against human rights or the rule of law as guiding principles for these processes. Yet political realities dictate that opposing groups almost always understand these concepts differently—and therefore need time to evolve a mutual understanding. A UN summit on the rule of law in 2012 illustrated just how controversial a concept like the rule of law can be. The then-president of Iran, Mahmoud Ahmadinejad, said at the meeting:

> [T]he belief in the oneness of the Almighty God . . . is an outlook that respects all human beings, nations, and valuable cultures in defiance of all types of discrimination in the world, and commits itself into a constant fight to promote equality for all before the law on the basis of justice and fraternity.[15]

Ahmadinejad went on to refer to the "inhuman policies in Palestine" as an example of not upholding the rule of law. Official representatives from the United States and Israel boycotted the presentation but the Israeli ambassador to the United Nations, Ron Prosor, commented that "the leader of an outlaw country that systematically violates the fundamental principles of the rule of law has no place here." He added that "allowing Ahmadinejad to give a speech to the UN on an issue like the rule of law is like appointing a pyromaniac as a fire commissioner."[16]

Clearly, very different notions of the rule of law were at play in this exchange, and yet both parties appeared firmly committed to the principle. So whose version is to be believed? Imagine for a moment that Prosor and Ahmadinejad would be facing off over a negotiation table, and would be told that they needed to pursue the rule of law together, as citizens of the same country. A considerable process of dialogue would be needed to create sufficient consensus and trust to even *begin* to debate, in productive terms, what the rule of law in "their country" would look like. What would sustain such a difficult conversation? My answer has been: when they realize they have no choice but to work out a local solution that would work for both of them and, more important, for both their constituencies.

I argued earlier that instead of mitigating the uncertainties associated with transition, liberal reconciliation programs can compound the risk of a return to violence by trying to prescribe to those emerging from oppression or war how the rule of law ought to be applied, just when the need for local ownership of political processes is often at a peak. This kind of liberal overdetermination has to do with a failure to integrate transitional justice mechanisms into a much larger political transition, so that related considerations, such as institutional complementarity, timing, and sequencing are well managed. Instead, often rule-of-law "exercises" such as political trials can become one-off (often internationally sponsored) events that are largely disconnected from the efforts to build a domestic system to uphold the rule of law.

Another example is that of Burundi. Both before and after its historic peace agreement reached in Arusha in 2000, the international community spent several years insisting that Burundi conduct criminal trials for acts of genocide and war crimes. Burundians resisted this in part at least because they were acutely aware of the country's political fragility, and that if some of its political leaders were implicated in such trials, they might opt out of the process and resort to violence again. This fear was based on solid historical evidence: between 1962 and 2014, Burundi experienced no fewer than four presidential assassinations, six coups (or attempted coups, depending on one's definition of a coup), and no fewer than four nationwide insurrections and killing sprees, resulting in nearly a million deaths. Apart from its own fragilities, turbulence in neighboring countries has also frequently affected Burundian politics, with refugees or militias crossing its porous borders, and there by heightening domestic political tensions.[17]

In August 1995, the UN Security Council attempted to provide some momentum to Burundi's fledgling peace process by adopting Resolution 1012. The resolution called for an international commission of inquiry to establish the circumstances surrounding the assassination of the Burundian president in 1993, as well as the massacres and other serious acts of violence that followed. The commission was also asked to recommend measures that would bring to justice those responsible, prevent the repetition of such acts, eradicate impunity, and promote national reconciliation. The resolution prescribed that the commission should be composed of five internationally respected experienced jurists selected by the UN secretary-general.[18] Significantly, the resolution described the 1993 violence as "genocide."

Operating for two distinct periods, the commission subsequently heard 661 testimonies, including sixty-one from military officers; its report also names ten military officers who failed to appear.[19] Astonishingly, after all this effort, a lack of security, combined with inadequate resources, prevented the commission from making any formal findings whatsoever.[20] Instead, it opted to submit evidence to the UN secretary-general with a view to building future cases against perpetrators for crimes that the commission confirmed could indeed be considered "genocide." Importantly, the commission's main recommendation was that the time for justice had not yet arrived:

> Impunity has, without any doubt, been an important contributing factor in the aggravation of the ongoing crisis. But while at the outset it was one of the causes of the present situation, it has now become an effect. To make suppression of impunity a precondition for the solution of the crisis is completely unrealistic and can serve only to give excuses to those who are unwilling to take the necessary actions. Impunity can only be suppressed through a fair and effective administration of justice. The Commission can find no way in which such administration of justice can be established while the present situation of the country has not been brought under a minimum of control.[21]

Several years of public consultation (and international contestation) followed, in which various mechanisms and combinations of mechanisms were considered, before Burundians decided that a truth and reconciliation commission would be the most appropriate vehicle for dealing with its vexed past. The initiative has been heavily criticized for shunning international criminal-justice processes, and just as the commission was about to start its work, widespread instability and violence erupted in Burundi once more when the country's president announced his intention to run for a (constitutionally questionable) third term. This was followed by an attempted coup, and a presidential counterattack that sent thousands of citizens fleeing to neighboring countries and underscored in chilling fashion that, in the absence of political inclusivity embedded in an increasingly inclusive and fair dispensation, no transitional arrangements, however well intended or cleverly designed, can have the desired effect.

Burundi's difficulties and dilemmas emphasize the importance of local relationships and their impact on the consequences and opportunities for both conflict and peace. This is a key element of reconciliation as interdependence. Undoubtedly, respect for the rule of law is as crucial an outcome of reconciliation-as-interdependence as it is for liberal reconciliation. Importantly, though, the interdependence approach is perhaps better able to make allowances for a gradual move toward justice than is its liberal counterpart. In this regard, truth commissions, public apologies, court cases, reparation schemes, acknowledgments of wrongdoing, and so on may or may not be useful, and may (but hopefully not) resemble what has gone before. What is important is that they find their proper place alongside a range of other measures with a view to realize a desired, mutually articulated future. It is equally important to maintain momentum toward agreement on what an inclusive and fair future would entail, and to take concrete steps to overcome obstacles that are bound to spring up along the way. This may require the process to start with a relatively low threshold for accountability in order to include as many potential spoilers around the table as possible, gradually both building this inclusivity to include civic actors in addition to political ones, but also deepening fairness and accountability as determined by the increasingly inclusive process.

This virtuous cycle—where greater inclusivity feeds deeper fairness that, in turn, draw more actors to the table—may account for at least some of reconciliation's mysterious alchemy that is able to turn hostile relations gradually into more productive ones. In this process, over time, the unpredictability of random violence and willful oppression is replaced by ground rules that all can abide by, thus laying the foundation for a society based on the rule of law. This dynamic was in evidence in South Africa, but is also displayed in countries such as Tunisia and Sri Lanka, both of which are at various stages of their political transitions from civil war and military rule toward democracy and the rule of law.

I propose, therefore, that credible levels of fairness and inclusivity are crucial for reconciliation to progress beyond political articulation and into the processes that usher in the civic and state institutions that have the capacity for the alchemy required to bring about the kind of social transformation in line with reconciliation's inherent justice promise. On accepting interdependence as the basis for establishing a new dispensation, the basic legal and institutional arrangements for an inclusive and fair society ought to be debated and provisionally established in increasingly inclusive and fair forums, including both political groupings and civic alliances whenever possible. For this reason, despite major limitations and constraints, Burundi may still be able to establish a credible truth commission. Burundi, after all, despite its ongoing fragility, has already been through a protracted process of negotiating a shared future; Hutus and Tutsis have acknowledged their interdependence, and ethnic interdependence is now acknowledged in a constitutional agreement that provides the basis for Burundians to revisit their deeply troubling past together.

If inclusivity and credible fairness are twin criteria for the success of reconciliation-as-interdependence, what do they entail, more precisely? I contend that a process that has acquired *credibility* across lines of conflict requires, at a minimum, a basic fairness in form and outcome that is acceptable to all major sides. "Credibility for whom" is an important consideration. As mentioned with reference to the voices of victims, credibility implies more (and sometimes less) than an "objective fairness"; it requires fairness that is recognized and accepted as such by adversaries.[22] That is, when a process is sufficiently fair for adversaries to embrace, it can be said to enjoy credibility. Many post-conflict processes that go by the name of reconciliation regularly fail this test, especially in the context of violent conflict or its immediate aftermath. What is credible to one party is often totally unacceptable to the other and, indeed, to international onlookers or stakeholders. In any case, international solutions seldom have real credibility for those involved in conflict.[23] The question that remains is how to distinguish between genuine objections about unfairness, and objections made in bad faith with the intention of prolonging violence.

Processes that I define as *inclusive* are broadly democratic and inclusive of all significant parties, serving the greater good of all citizens, as opposed to being elitist, exclusionary, or parochial.[24] Important here is the possibility that certain processes might, at times, have to accommodate arrangements that are less than "fully just," as long as these remain broadly acceptable to all parties on the understanding that justice is underway, even if it is not fully possible immediately. Both Myanmar and Colombia have recently made strides amidst challenging setbacks toward reconciliation in different ways and to different degrees but both cases illustrate the power of a progressive, incremental approach toward justice for all but also the failures often associated when processes do not include significant (minority or majority) groups in such a process.

The extended argument is that reconciliation based on interdependence is made sustainable through future-oriented processes that are broadly inclusive of political and civic actors, and also broadly credible to all involved. The alchemical reaction that it likely to follow such an approach transforms relations marked by an unhealthy, ignored and resented forms of *co*-dependence (as under apartheid) gradually into more productive, fair and inclusive relations marked by *inter*-dependence. An acknowledgment of the fundamental interdependence between enemies thus has far-reaching consequences for reconciliation processes seeking to transform hostile, co-dependent and unjust relations. First, they need to become more inclusive, to ensure that the interests of all groups are duly taken into account. Second, they have to be credible, in the sense of being perceived as fair by those involved. This means that the promise of justice has to be present at reconciliation's inception, it has to feature as a process element throughout, and ultimately it has to form the basis for sustainably transformed relationships. The promise is made both rhetorically by political leaders, but also enacted in the various institutions tasked to guide transition. Eventually, too, both the political leadership and the new country's democratic institutions should be held accountable for its realization. If reconciliation is to be successful, interdependence transforms itself along the way from a fact into norm, from an acknowledgment of a given, historical reality (often experienced as oppressive, unjust, or violent) into a more ethical basis for engagement across enemy lines.

It is important to note, too, that inclusivity and credibility are themselves interdependent. Thus, for a reconciliation process to be credible, it has to be inclusive, and for a process to be inclusive of all parties, it has to display a certain

level of credibility. However, while it is difficult to conceive of a credible reconciliation process that is not inclusive, nominally inclusive processes that are less
than credible are certainly possible, notably when one or more of the stronger
parties maintains unfair power relations over another, and is able to force the
weaker party to accept unfavorable and possibly unfair terms. Thus, it is possible
for credibility and inclusivity to become competing values, with the one making
the achievement of the other more difficult.[25]

It is almost inevitable, at times during political transition, that a proper
balance between inclusivity and credible fairness will be skewed. At such times,
the key to sustaining reconciliation, and keeping it true to its justice promise,
is the re-realization that the fundamental and comprehensive interdependence
between the negotiating partners also opens possibilities for new, more inclusive, and fairer modes of coexistence based on interdependence rather than co-
dependence. When negotiating parties are driven back to negotiations time and
again, to ponder afresh how to balance inclusivity and credibility, the potential
is there for them to create precisely the alchemy needed to transform relations
between them from hostility to cooperation, and ultimately to peace.

The "toolbox" that tends to be used in contemporary transitional justice
and peace-building—truth commissions, court trials, reparations, mediated
talks, and so on—should be seen as merely containing examples of what has
been useful in previous experiences, in similar fashion to how I treated the
South African case in this book, but no more than that. No structure, mechanism, or process can ever really be a stand-alone solution when it comes to
resolving conflict. And if attempted in isolation or imposed on a situation,
rather than emerging organically, any of the tools can potentially do more
harm than good.

Daniel Philpott, as noted in Chapter 5, identified a concrete polit-
ical/transitional-justice agenda comprising six "reconciliation practices,"
namely: institutional reform, punishment, acknowledgment, reparations,
forgiveness, and apology, in response to what he identified as the six "primary wounds of war." Associated with both the liberal and restorative justice
paradigms, Philpott's list of practices should in my view be regarded as an in-
ventory of *possible* options and previous experiences, but should not be elevated to the level of principle. In my view, by demanding that the same set
of pre-determined practices are implemented under all conditions, Philpott's
approach runs the risk of predetermining (and thus overdetermining) reconciliation processes. Overdetermined reconciliation processes typically set the
moral bar too high in the early stages of a process, thereby disturbing the delicate balance between inclusivity and credible fairness—as well as threatening
to diminish local ownership of reconciliation processes with plans not of their
making.

At the same time, turning practices into principles also risks *underdetermining* reconciliation. That is, this approach fails to indicate adequately how these practices relate to one another in terms of balancing inclusivity with credible fairness. Although the reconciliation-as-interdependence approach is compatible with social restoration theories' embrace of a relational ontology—including the various implications this has for analyzing both conflict and peacemaking— it is much less prescriptive about *how* to restore relations, or what a restored relationship or, as Philpott calls it, a "right relationship" ought to be. Moreover, setting the bar for genuine reconciliation as high as forgiveness, as Philpott tends to do, would disqualify or exclude many key stakeholders who would need to be present at the table. Demanding prosecution in typical liberal fashion up front can have the same effect.

Those who look for signs of forgiveness as evidence that reconciliation is present during a political transition will tend, more often than not, to be discouraged by what they see. The routine failure of opponents to show adequate remorse or offer genuine forgiveness can be profoundly discouraging if these are seen as crucial indicators of genuine reconciliation. As shown in Chapter 1, in the South African case, forgiveness was not a crucial aspect of the early parts of the transition, and it certainly did not feature strongly in the processes that led to reconciliation becoming a national process. As explained, the forgiving embrace may expect too much from adversaries by way of intimacy, inclusion, and the restoration of personal relations during a political transition. Social restoration theory seems to lack a "Plan B" to apply when key protagonists fail to honor the grammar of forgiveness and relinquish its embrace.

Reconciliation-as-interdependence corresponds with Volf's moving account of the forgiving embrace preventing itself from becoming an intrusive "grasping." Waiting for reciprocity is indeed important. Coming out of the self and toward the other, the self "halts at the boundary of the other." This ability to wait for reciprocity movingly captures the patience needed during reconciliation's initial moves during the fledgling years of trying to find one another, at the same time as political power is allowed to shift hands peacefully. At the same time, I noted earlier that a key element in reaching "sufficient consensus" in South Africa was the notion that disappointment would inevitably form part of the process. The acknowledgment that disappointment would be the long and inevitable shadow of reconciliation seems to have paved the way for progress beyond seemingly intractable dilemmas and contestations. Adrian Little has written interestingly about the importance of accepting disappointment as an inevitable aspect of reconciliation, and that it can spawn fresh bouts of creativity when political processes run out of steam.[26]

Similarly, liberal peace tends to demand an unrealistic commitment to liberal principles from political leaders who are often expected to offer themselves up for scrutiny and accountability in the name of contributing to a rule of law that may or may not take hold sometime in the future. To be sustainable in the aftermath of civil war or religious violence, reconciliation has to cross many hurdles and achieve much before genuine accountability or even forgiveness becomes an option. Liberal theory simply has no answer as to what drives reconciliation processes *before* accountability is even thinkable. It also lacks a coherent "theory of change" to explain how enforcing the rule of law in relation to certain crimes encourages an entire society to embrace the rule of law. In response to these weaknesses, I propose reconciliation-as-interdependence as an alternative. This approach overcomes such challenges by allowing social values including basic ideas about the rule of law to emerge gradually, as the result of engagement between adversaries, rather than as part of a prescribed moral code or political system.

Living in South Africa twenty-four years after apartheid ended, one must ask, how then, does one judge whether or not reconciliation—the consistent drive for fair and inclusive relations amid a vast process of political and social change—is a justified approach? How does one even begin to make sense of both the accolades and the criticism that come reconciliation's way? To know how to judge or evaluate reconciliation, one needs to be sure about what it promises. To this promise, and ways to remain true to it, we now turn.

Social Change

In an earlier chapter I made the point that reconciliation theories within the social restoration framework run the risk not only of overdetermining reconciliation processes, but also of overpromising their outcomes, not least when reconciliation is required to act as the guiding metaphor and framework for political transition. Indeed, the promise of healed relations *and* forgiveness may prove a bridge too far for many in a society caught in the throes of vast socioeconomic change or indeed its excruciating absence. This is not to say that genuine remorse, forgiveness, and redress may not be present at all in ushering in new dispensations, or that they do not potentially have an important role to play—but they do tend to be exceptions to the rule and can therefore not feature as reconciliation's promise to an entire population.[27]

On the other hand, a promise postponed (indefinitely), the approach I associated earlier with agonism, risks becoming a promise denied. Agonist theories make a point of not (over-)promising concrete outcomes beyond the risky, fragile undertaking of political engagement based on civic friendship. Yet when we acknowledge that our future well-being is fundamentally and comprehensively dependent on those we are in conflict with, the articulation and enactment of reconciliation cannot but include a promise of justice, not to be endlessly deferred, but to be issued as soon as interdependence is first acknowledged, and then progressively realized with each new step in the process.

Nevertheless—as agonists remind us—reconciliation processes do need to be free and open-ended enough to produce new and genuinely shared outcomes, and they must be robust enough to accommodate the tensions and fallouts associated with political transitions. Reconciliation manifests, above all, in urgent, directed, and transformative exchanges and engagements, within which difficult and long-term conversations are begun, and in which interim solutions, combined with a sense of concrete progress and outcomes, are vitally important. It should never be allowed to descend into a carnivalesque exploration of the new without constraint or direction, nor a debating forum in which conflict is reified for its own sake.

As we have noted, in some liberal theories of reconciliation, civic trust is seen as the most appropriate outcome of reconciliation, but this too provides little or no remedy for addressing or redressing entrenched power relations based on historically unequal and unfair configurations of race, religion, ethnicity, gender, or class.

Is it possible therefore, if one wants to avoid either overpromising or underpromising, to be more precise about what as reconciliation's justice promise entails? What kind of justice ought reconciliation to promise? Colleen Murphy proposes that three outcomes—the rule of law, trust, and enhanced capabilities—combine to ensure genuine reciprocity within restored relationships. Although operating mainly within the liberal framework, as I mentioned before, Murphy's reliance on capabilities takes her reconciliation agenda beyond the usual liberal scope and strengthens her theory of reconciliation as reciprocity.[28]

My argument has been that reconciliation, which respects its own limits with respect to what it can achieve, nevertheless does not shy away from making, and pursuing, a *justice promise as a relational good*—realized over time and in all spheres of society as both widening inclusion and deepening fairness—and ultimately transforming oppressive and hostile relations of co-dependence (understood, as explained earlier, as imposed togetherness where one party dominates and violence is prevalent) into more liberating and productive ones characterized by interdependence. Reconciliation at heart therefore promises processes which are able to realize more inclusive and fair relationships at all levels of society. Conversely, any process that fosters relationship-building in the absence of progressive justice undermines genuine transformation, and cannot really be considered reconciliation at all. Traditional formulations of the "right to reparation" for victims— reparations, compensation, rehabilitation, and restitution—all ought to be understood as efforts to rebuild more just relations between those who previously lived in exploitative and violent expressions of interdependence.

In this way, the promise of justice provides normative direction to political processes in wake of war and oppression. It also and importantly adds urgency and drive, not only to the reaching of a political settlement but also to the socially transformative processes that have to be instituted in its wake.

Political reconciliation only becomes truly sustainable when the transforming society delivers on the promise of justice; that is, when society becomes evidently and obviously fairer and more inclusive. In this way, interdependence between erstwhile foes becomes apparent to all, not only as a fundamental aspect of how society has always maintained unjust power relations, but now primarily as the source of a comprehensive and just peace, and therefore of new and unrealized potential for how society can function in the future. To paraphrase Hannah Arendt, interdependence challenges the dark times when political opponents "disappear" from public life, and instead favors encouraging their presence as equals.[29]

Along these lines, the conception of reconciliation as interdependence proposed here promises more than liberal theories of reconciliation—for substantially more inclusive and fair relations require more than civic trust. It demands substantive as well as procedural justice. Of course, the process of achieving a shared articulation of such a "just society" as mutual ideal is often a messy one, and requires single-minded determination on all sides.

On the one hand, a crucial part of this conversation relates to accountability for past crimes. I have argued that imposing accountability measures before a shared agreement has been reached can have the opposite effect to what is intended. That is, in the drive toward the future, it might well be best to deal with the past relatively late in the process, when society is stable enough to face the difficult questions and ponder its most pronounced failures.

On the other hand, to populations whose dignity has been systematically undermined by structural and other forms of violence, justice means the restoration of the human and civic respect due to them as human beings and as citizens *as well as* some kind of material reparation. Justice (at least in transitional contexts) is therefore best understood comprehensively, not only as the basis for political security and economic prosperity, but also as the basis for socially and morally acceptable behavior in relation to the individual and collective self, as well as to the wider world. Most human beings have a fundamental need not only to be included in groups, but also to be recognized as *human beings* within the groups they belong to; that is, we need to have our dignity and moral standing affirmed in relationships that do not operate through co-dependence premised on oppression or violence, but interdependently.

In this context, restitution relates to both material redress as well as the redress of power, voice, agency, and the restoration of human dignity; it is about reciprocity and equality, and about challenging historical injustices and inequities. If political reconciliation is about acknowledging and restoring relationships so that they express their fundamental interdependence, how then are relationships restored so that they become more reciprocal and equal, and so that all parties enjoy the freedom of their own agency in society?

Such deep change renders the aims of real reconciliation nothing short of radical,[30] something Mandela already foresaw all those years ago when negotiating from prison. Whereas reconciliation may commence with carefully crafted political compromises, it proceeds via the radical transformation of systems and relations that once allowed inequality, exclusion, and marginalization to flourish. To this end, even as the identities of the past begin to dissolve in favor of new, more bipartisan, and less hostile ones, it is important to recognize the ongoing impact of past violence—ideally in ways that enable a movement forward rather than return to the past. The assumption here is of course that identity is a social construction—a performance that can be both learned and unlearned.

If understood in this comprehensive way, the redress agenda—including reparations, empowerment plans, and ultimately the transformation of the entire society toward a fairer and more inclusive dispensation—seeks to respond to the effects of violence as described by Galtung's threefold distinction between direct, structural, and cultural dimensions of violence, mentioned earlier. With this in mind, I will briefly explain the contours of institutional and structural reform and, thereafter, cultural transformation. Together this constitutes a comprehensive agenda that aims to restore human dignity after such dignity had been systematically undermined. Redress acts as both the basis for, and outcome of, reconciliation understood as the restoration of just relations based on the acknowledgment of a fundamental and comprehensive interdependence between those in conflict. It is borne of a courageous political realism willing to carve out a common future with the enemy.

In 1994, South Africa achieved a manifestly more just political dispensation as a result of its reconciliation process and, on this basis, was able to conduct a process of public acknowledgment of past wrongs—albeit one that had obvious shortcomings. The TRC, together with all the processes that led up to the first democratic elections, helped to lay the foundation for a promising new era of racial interdependence based on the core values of the widely canvassed new constitution, namely: non-racism, non-sexism, equality, and the right to difference. Today, however, the country is caught in an uncomfortable period of struggling to realize a concrete, structural, and cultural equality between all its peoples. On the one hand, some progress has been made, and compared to many peer countries elsewhere these gains have been impressive. On the other hand, a range of realizable goals have been left unfulfilled, due to largely avoidable conditions that have exacerbated both inequality and corruption, radically limiting both trust and unity within the new South Africa.

The South African case seems to be illustrative of a wider trend in Africa. Writing for the IJR's Afrobarometer in 2013, Jan Hofmeyr reported that, despite widely held perceptions that "Africa is rising," backed by a decade of steady economic growth (averaging 4.8% from 2002 to 2011), African citizens remain deeply dissatisfied with the ways in which their governments manage their economies, and consequently their levels of human and material security.[31] "Economic growth appears to benefit only a few," wrote Hofmeyr, because Africa's growing economies are not creating enough jobs nor making life significantly better for the poor. He went on to report that, in thirty-four countries, a majority of Africans rated the condition of their national economy as either "fairly bad" or "very bad," compared to 29 percent that rated them positively. Among the five countries rated lowest by citizens, Egypt and Tunisia experienced a change of government as part of the so-called Arab Spring. The other three—Tanzania, Kenya, and Uganda—had experienced high levels of growth over the decade. Nevertheless, more than 80 percent of Kenya's population agreed that the condition of the national economy was "very" or "fairly" bad. For a country that has experienced sustained economic growth of close to 5 percent for a decade, this is a staggering finding. Add to this that fully 71 percent of Kenyans describe their personal living conditions as either "very bad" or "fairly bad," as opposed to the 14 percent who rate them as "fairly good" or "very good," and a picture emerges of the deep-seated discontentment among the large majority about the material conditions they face. Hofmeyr concluded that glowing GDP figures tend to offer little solace to the poor, and that "if the proceeds of growth are not shared equitably through society, the impact of rapid economic expansion may ultimately become more destructive than good for society."[32]

Those who have benefited from the oppression of others therefore have a special responsibility to demonstrate their solidarity with their erstwhile opponents, who might well continue to suffer material deprivation under the new dispensation and therefore continue to experience a form of unhealthy co-dependence rather than the liberating interdependence marked by inclusion and fairness which properly conceived reconciliation processes ought to promise. This project is necessarily intergenerational and open-ended, but it still ought to be judged against commonly accepted interim outcomes or milestones. It needs to be approached with the same urgency, inclusivity, and fairness as political negotiations, and ought to involve credible efforts to extend voice, access, and opportunities to the most marginalized and disempowered. As a major line of division separating citizens from one another, social inequality ought to be a focal point for reconciliation efforts that involve everyone.

And again, as with peacemaking at the onset of reconciliation, the motivation for this radical social transformation is not firstly a form of abstract moral idealism; it is a simple reality check that will seek to transform co-dependence between the rich and poor into interdependence. Fostering such realism, however, requires exceptional strength of character and courage, and thus it is, in itself, a moral exercise. Moral leadership in the lead-up to, during, and beyond political transition has as much to do with incisive, clear thinking and a willingness to act on a given reality, than it has with propagating moral ideals—indeed, it may well be that the former is more important, and more difficult, and ultimately yields more morally desirable outcomes.

Just how difficult it is to face up to reality "as it is" has been well documented in the critique of South Africa's handling of the demands for gender justice subsequent to apartheid as discussed in Chapter 4.

In my view, the focus on interdependence as reconciliation's key designator implies *a gendered approach* to reconciliation to which gender is not incidental or optional, but indeed central. If reconciliation is the restoration of just relations and if gender relations are typically a primary site of violence during war or oppression, it remains a primary target for social transformation toward a more equal society. In short, reconciliation is not possible without gender justice.

Given that gender constructions determine how women and men are supposed to engage with post-conflict and post-authoritarian contexts, it is vitally important to ensure that reconciliation interventions are gender-inclusive (including not just the traditional "male" and "female" genders but everyone on the gender continuum), gender-focused, and gender-transformative. Within this larger agenda, a more specific challenge remains in how to ensure that reconciliation processes respond to the needs and experiences of women and girls, but presumably working with all groups, including males, in this endeavor. It is at the same time important not to reinforce gender stereotypes or suggest that women's participation and leadership on reconciliation issues *as such* are enough to address gender justice.

In framing reconciliation as the transformation of relationships, it is absolutely necessary to focus on the existing power relations between men and women in war-affected and authoritarian contexts—and, indeed, also in postwar and post-authoritarian contexts. This requires a sharp focus on masculinity and how it has traditionally "performed" in the context of war or following war. There is a need therefore to articulate a gendered approach to reconciliation that engages with men and masculinity too, writes Tim Murithi.[33] Inclusive reconciliation processes would need to strive to reconfigure the asymmetrical power relationships between men and women, and open spaces in which masculinity, in particular, can be performed differently. This would include confronting the challenge of redefining masculine and feminine roles in the aftermath of conflict and during reconciliation processes.

A gendered approach to reconciliation would need also to address "the tensions between cultural sensitivities and the rights and involvement of women in reconciliation processes."[34] This is likely to be a common challenge facing future reconciliation initiatives, given the prevalence of patriarchy around the world, not least in more traditional societies. In order to confront this challenge, sustained dialogue with political and cultural leaders can counter potential reluctance to include women as equal stakeholders in the transformation of society. Ultimately, a comprehensive treatment of these issues is beyond the scope of this book, which suggests that additional research and analysis is required to further articulate how a gendered approach to societal transformation can be advanced by stakeholders in the interests of achieving and sustaining inclusive reconciliation.

At an individual level, this kind of redress requires a focus on, among other things, the psychosocial and comprehensive well-being of traumatized individuals who have borne the brunt of political violence. In transitional societies, these individuals are everywhere, including in high office. In South Sudan, for example, which is emerging from the world's longest-running succession of civil wars, generations of citizens have suffered untold misery, and trauma is palpably present at all levels. Without programs to deal with this, trauma can overwhelm individuals' abilities to cope, making it possible that the changes associated with political transition simply add a further layer of damage.

How humans heal from trauma has, of course, long been a subject of psycho-analysis. By 1914, Freud had already identified a tendency to "repeat" instead of "remember" as one of the main obstacles to psychoanalytical progress after trauma. This means that, in some cases, traumatized individuals can develop a psychological need to return to, or hold on to, the "safety" of past worldviews, even though these might have been steeped in struggle and bloodshed. "Working through" (*durcharbeiten*) this tendency to repeat past evil requires the courage to focus on the past's morbid manifestation and acknowledge it both as "an opponent worthy of respect" and as an intrinsic part of oneself.[35]

Approaching this dilemma from a narrative philosophers' perspective, Paul Ricoeur wrote an essay in 2000 entitled "Can Forgiveness Heal?" He followed this up with a book titled *Memory, History, Forgetting*, in which he ponders the ways in which stories can be retold so as to overcome traumatic experiences, and to cast perpetrators in a light that enables victims to heal.[36] "Unconditional forgiveness is an act of justice to oneself as the victim," writes Allan Boesak, former UDF leader and theologian.[37] And yet so few are able to rise to these heights. Ricoeur rightly asks therefore how it is that so many people seem unable to embrace forgiveness after experiencing suffering caused by another. Preoccupied with the past, he observes, they seem to suffer from "too much memory," as if they are "haunted by the recollection of the humiliations they suffered in a distant past as well as that of glory past."[38] By contrast, others seem to cope by denying the past, and consequently suffer from "too little memory" as if "they were fleeing from an obsession with their own past."[39] Donald Shriver, who has also written powerfully about political forgiveness, explains:

> The mind that insulates the traumatic past from the conscious memory plants a live bomb in the depths of the psyche—it takes no great grasp of psychiatry to know that. But the mind that fixes on pain risks getting trapped in it. Too horrible to remember, too horrible to forget: down that path lies little health for the human sufferers of great evil.[40]

For Ricoeur, the answer to moving on lies at least in part in a "critical use of memory" that aids the process of working through, advocated by Freud. In this, he suggests, narrative can play a crucial role in this. It is in "the story [the art of narration] that memory is carried to language."[41] Susan Dwyer writes about such a narrative strategy for reconciliation that may or may not involve forgiveness:

> Coherent incorporation of an unpleasant fact, or a new belief about an enemy, into the story of one's life might involve the issuance of an apology and an offer of forgiveness. But it need not. Reconciliation, as I have presented it, is conceptually independent of forgiveness. This is a good thing. For it means that reconciliation might be psychologically possible where forgiveness is not.[42]

I agree. Equally clear, though, is that embracing peace, and finding a way to live reasonably productively and peacefully with trauma, requires more than individual change at whatever level: it requires society itself, its basic belief and narratives, to be reframed so that it no longer supports division, inequality, and conflict. Instead, social narratives must begin to articulate and affirm interdependence as both fact and norm. This takes social redress beyond the individual and into the realm of social and cultural identity, including areas such as education and memorialization.

An incident at a South African university in 2015 reveals that South Africans still have much to accomplish in this regard, not only at the level of material redress, but also in relation to symbolic and cultural reconciliation. In March 2015, more than twenty years after democratization in South Africa, students at the University of Cape Town were galvanized into action when one of their number approached a statue of Cecil John Rhodes, university benefactor, arch-imperialist, erstwhile prime minister of the Cape Province, and one of the wealthiest men of his generation, and covered it with human feces. The provocative act immediately resonated on the otherwise tranquil campus, and led to black students forming the Rhodes Must Fall movement to sustain public protests and sit-ins in the main administration building on campus. Initially met with a degree of bemusement from some quarters, the protests led to the dramatic removal of the statue from the campus just a month later. In the process, the movement drew support from across South Africa, mobilizing groups on several other university campuses to demand the implementation of transformation measures aimed at creating greater equity and access for black students and academics alike. One interesting response was a project headed by white students to think through more carefully what the legacy of white privilege entails and what possible responses to this may be.[43] The movement also elicited vehement criticism, some of it vulgar and racist, others more thoughtful reminders that reconciliation should not be about forgetting the past, but should remain open to add new layers to existing stories.

Rwanda adopted a somewhat different approach to the symbols of its past. There, a concerted government campaign to create a new "Rwandan" identity led to the creation of a set of radically new symbols, concepts, and narratives, and the near-total banning of any symbolism related to the previous regime. Rwanda's current government blames the previous regime entirely for the ethnic genocide that claimed nearly a million lives in 1994, and their "official narrative" has been of central significance in Rwanda's approach to transitional justice. Yet, high levels of cultural violence (including exclusionary historical myths such as the so-called Hamitic hypothesis) were also a hallmark of Rwanda's colonial and post-colonial eras. These myths served to justify deeply ingrained levels of structural violence (first against Hutus and later against Tutsis), and ultimately provided the ideological framework for the ideology of Hutu Power that drove the genocide's extraordinarily high levels of direct violence.

In my view, by silencing credible alternative historical perspectives (such as those of moderate Hutu historians, for example), and closing down spaces for public participation in producing a genuinely shared view of Rwanda's past, Rwanda's official post-genocide narrative is not helping its own stated cause, namely to memorialize the genocide as a basis for ethnic solidarity. By forcibly silencing its critics, it is in fact bolstering various forms of crude revisionism and "genocide-laundering," which seeks to deny or downplay the magnitude of the genocide.[44] The ongoing prevalence of these two opposing historical frameworks, one that favors Hutus and the other Tutsis, underscores the need for Rwandans to develop the means to counter invocations of history that might serve to justify renewed cycles of cultural or other forms of violent exclusion.[45]

Reconciliation in post-conflict societies such as South Africa and Rwanda requires at a minimum the building of some common ground between conflicting historical accounts of the past. As Mahmood Mamdani argues, "the identification of both perpetrator and survivor is differently constructed in conflicting historical narratives. This is why it is not possible to think of reconciliation between Hutu and Tutsi in Rwanda without a prior reconciliation with history."[46] "Reconciliation with history" requires, but is not limited to, the creation of opportunities for engagement with historical difference as part of the quest for national unity, together with space for individual narratives to be voiced, recorded, and formally acknowledged. Thus, for a transitional justice process to contribute to reconciliation in the sense of eradicating cultural violence, it has to foster open debate about the past, as well as the recording and acknowledgment of "little narratives," that is, the stories of individual witnesses to past violations.

Ultimately, redress at the societal level raises the question of remembering and forgiveness once again. True reconciliation must include a transparent accounting for why and how violence, exclusion, and injustice came to subvert relations of positive or constructive interdependence between different groups in society. While transitional justice approaches tend to insist on the need for remembering past atrocities, and stress the dangers of "denial," Nietzsche observed that overcoming the past requires the ability to forget in order to move on, but forgetting in a way that is different from simply denying the past. He warned against "an excess of history," in the sense of being dominated by a past that cannot be forgotten—a condition that can become life threatening—which he elsewhere called "a malady of history."[47]

This paradoxical notion of overcoming the past by "forgetting but not denying" may help to explain what is meant by "moving on." Denial, or what Ricoeur calls "oblivion," is characterized by a refusal to engage with the past at all.[48] However, denial does not necessarily imply simply *not* talking about the past. In fact, denial often coincides with obsessive and oppressive remembering and fervent documenting of history in ways that are designed to exclude and subjugate opposing groups. This form of denial is, indeed, one way in which history can become a form of cultural violence, as it tends to justify the use of direct violence against those portrayed as perpetrators, or as outsiders who pose a danger to society. By contrast, *to forget without denial, one first has to remember.* Reconciliatory forgetting engages with the past, not for its own sake, but in order to move beyond it. Forgetting without denial lays the past to rest after a thorough confrontation with what happened. This kind of forgetting presupposes a vigorous engagement with the past, whereas denial shuns such engagement in favor of silence or glib and inaccurate histories.[49]

Forgetting without denial entails moving beyond a preoccupation with one's own traumatic experiences, difficult though this is, toward a wider understanding of the past, and developing the ability to interpret one's own experience in a broader context. Forgetting but not denying is akin to psychological closure: one finds a way to "forget" the singular horror of personal exposure to human rights violations in favor of a more historical and comprehensive view of events. For Ricoeur, to develop a critical memory is to remember essentially through storytelling. He recommends that care be taken to tell stories about the past differently, and from the point of view of the other, acknowledging that "it is at this level that the work of recollection is the most difficult."[50]

Forgetting but not denying thus involves democratizing the debate about the past to some extent, and allowing others to engage with the history of one's own suffering (for victims) or one's own crimes (in the case of perpetrators). Forms of remembering that take diverging views into account form the basis of desirable forms of post-conflict memorialization—of remembering collectively, inclusively, and with a view to future stability. In this way, *forgetting eventually enables deeper and fuller remembering.* As Ricoeur remarked: "This modifying of the past, consisting in telling it differently and from the point of view of the other, becomes crucially important when it concerns the foundations of the common history and memory."[51]

However, reconciliatory forgetting cannot occur in the abstract; it requires specific and concrete preconditions. For "victims" and "perpetrators" to be willing to forget past atrocities, and to be reconciled as citizens, a number of basic conditions have to be met. For example, a representative political dispensation must be in place, and citizens must have a reasonable chance of attaining better living conditions. In the absence of political and economic justice, the patterns of exclusion that marked the previous dispensation are bound to be perpetuated, and any willingness to "forget" is likely to be severely compromised. Forgetting but not denying can therefore be described as useful or desirable when survivors of violent intra-state conflict declare themselves willing to relinquish their identities as victims or enemies in favor of a common citizenship that allows them to share political rights, as well as pursue post-conflict reconstruction, across social fault-lines, and within a single political and economic community. A willingness to "forget" past suffering is decidedly *not* the same as denial. After deliberate remembering has taken place, survivors embrace their identities as "citizens," thereby escaping futures dominated by "too much memory." However, where voices representing opposing perspectives are systematically excluded via hegemonic and coercive portrayals of the past, and where such exclusion is experienced as ongoing cultural violence, it becomes difficult or impossible for those who are excluded to "move on." Denial through excessive remembering becomes the opposite of forgetting.

Whatever we conclude about how public memory functions, or ought to function, and whether or not the South African students were justified in what they did and demanded and managed to change on their campus, it seems remarkable that this event drew such fervent support from so many students, many of whom were born after 1994 and thus, technically at least, never lived under apartheid. I would suggest that the students put their finger on a crucial aspect of redress that has been largely neglected in South Africa, namely, the lingering presence of "cultural violence." Earlier I mentioned John Galtung's definition of cultural violence as the cultural prejudices and stereotypes that operate across generations to subtly justify structural and even interpersonal violence. Apartheid's structural violence was obviously supported by extensive cultural prejudice and racism—and some of the more tangible reminders of these views are still present. To South Africa's new generation, the statue of Rhodes casting his proprietary gaze across the landscape embodied this kind of cultural violence and helped, in their view, to sustain their ongoing exclusion from various aspects of university life. Thus, while some apartheid symbols and statues were dismantled in the mid-1990s and early 2000s, this example makes it clear that not nearly enough has been done.

Ricoeur's narrative approach counters the misperception that the future is open-ended and undetermined, whereas the past is fixed. In fact, Ricoeur asserts, the meaning of what has happened in the past always remains open to new interpretations. It is therefore always possible to change the moral load of the past, and shift its burden on the present. This, Ricoeur argues, is how the work of recollection, "of narrating differently and from the perspective of the other, puts us on the track of forgiveness."[52] What forgiveness adds to remembrance and mourning is generosity; it is a gift, to be granted, not applied for or taken for granted. To beg for forgiveness is to be ready to be met with refusal, says Ricoeur. It can never be owed, only pleaded for.[53]

Conclusion

Reading South African history through the lens of interdependence helps explain the disappointment that many South Africans feel in relation to reconciliation, despite the newly democratic state's many impressive achievements. Rising inequality, deepening social exclusion, and levels of civic trust that are declining in inverse proportion to rising levels of corruption imply that the justice promised by political reconciliation seems somehow to have been lost.

While South Africans are justified in feeling let down by reconciliation, I have argued that it is wrong to view Mandela's approach to reconciliation as the root of the problem. In my view, Mandela's concept of reconciliation (with its emphasis on just interdependence) was abandoned too early, allowing former and new elites to maintain and develop various new forms of exclusion and unfairness in the post-apartheid era. It is not *because of too much reconciliation that justice was not realized, but because of too little.* More reconciliation will lead to deeper justice, less reconciliation, to resurgent forms of injustice.

The growing solidarity across political schisms that marked the transitional era should have led to increased cohesion across class and other social fault lines, but this failed to materialize. As a result, South Africans are seeing racism and xenophobia flourish alongside persistent economic inequality and worrying levels of corruption. They urgently need to recapture lost momentum in their nation-building project. Thus, the South African example provides not only positive lessons but also several negative ones for those following its progress.

Visionary leaders who can articulate both existing co-depencies and their potential to be transformed into interdependencies now will be crucial to the country regaining some momentum toward deeper levels of reconciliation. We need spaces in which citizens can learn to trust and respect one another, and to debate and develop ways of overcoming the social, structural, and cultural legacies of apartheid and colonialism in favor of increasing inclusivity and fairness. Such conversations might well be more difficult than the political negotiations of the early 1990s, and will have to include articulating and acknowledging the deep traumas that linger on and contribute to present-day levels of crime and violence.

Historic injustices and the present-day privileges they spawned must be honestly engaged. Race, racism, and racial identities must be sharply dissected—precisely because apartheid made this its organizing principle—and in ways that give the notion of race less and less power; we cannot afford, in the name of reconciliation, to further apartheid's agenda by reifying race in perpetuity. Notions of gender, nationality, class, and ethnicity urgently require similar treatment.

Under Desmond Tutu's strong leadership, the TRC report remained largely immune to political interference. Re-reading the recommendations contained in Volume Five within the context of South Africa at the time of writing this (2018) reveals both some farsighted predictions and important blind spots, both of which have affected the country's ongoing reconciliation efforts. Inexplicably, the report was never popularized, translated, or distributed to the wider public, despite early attempts by some private NGOs to produce a popular version.

Thus, although the full reports are available online, precious few educational tools exist today that could assist educational institutions to make constructive use of the material in schools or universities. Civil society organizations and the artistic community have produced some materials, but, as yet, these remain inadequate.[1] Perhaps its absence from the public terrain made it easier for political powers subsequently to ignore crucial recommendations and for civil society structures and organisations to fail to critically interrogate the report sufficiently to determine both those recommendations worth following, as well as those that had been forgotten, those in need of revision, and those that needed to appear in the report but never did.[2]

In my view, inclusivity and fairness had not been sacrificed at the time when reconciliation shaped the political transition. They were compromised more recently, to the extent that inclusion across social divides failed to materialize and political leaders deviated from serving the common good. At the same time, too many civic leaders and ordinary citizens have tolerated (or colluded in) increasing levels of corruption and inequality.

This raises the question of why both inequality (accompanied by persistent racial acrimony) and corruption (accompanied by a failure to build public trust) have increased to the extent that they have. Where does responsibility lie for these failures of a democratic state that militates against the very terms of its founding? Is it due to a fundamental design fault in the peace process, and thus by implication in the characterization of reconciliation that drove developments during this period, or is it a failure of political, civic, and private sector leadership subsequently? I have argued for the latter. After all, while operating within significant constraints—not least, those designed to appease a nervous white military and an equally nervous white capital base—the peace process nonetheless delivered a manifestly fair and inclusive political dispensation with a Constitution that explicitly advocated, and legally sanctioned, radical social transformation.

It is largely what subsequently happened—the failure to act on the TRC recommendations, the abandonment of the Reconstruction and Development plan promised by President Mandela as a necessary complement to the TRC, the growing inequality and thus persistent levels of racial isolation, and the growing levels of corruption undermining a sense of national unity—that is foremost in South Africans' minds when they articulate their disappointment with reconciliation.

An important caveat of my argument has been that although I have only presented explicit evidence of South Africans' disappointment in the failure of political leadership, it stands to reason that neither corruption nor inequality could be analyzed adequately without reference to the private and civic sectors. Determining more precisely the contours of these failures and the extent of collusion between government, the private sector, and civil society that have given rise to a justified sense of disappointment in reconciliation in South Africa, falls outside the scope of what is possible in this book, but deserves more sustained scrutiny elsewhere.

In countries with sustained but inequitable growth patterns, it is hardly surprising that the poor feel left out, forgotten, and dispensable. If the poor are the same group who were previously excluded and oppressed, inequality clearly represents a very significant fault line, and one that reconciliation processes ought to address. The social justice deficit in South Africa is often cited as resulting from compromises made by those lobbying for reconciliation at the dawn of democracy. The kind of reconciliation I propose would, in addition to advancing political reform, have made explicit both the reality and potentiality of *economic, social, and indeed moral interdependence* between the (mainly but no longer exclusively white) rich and the (predominantly black) poor. In South Africa, this is reconciliation's unfinished business. The question is whether, having pushed reconciliation aside too early in the rush to "normalize" and return to "business as usual," South Africa's increasingly disappointed and sceptical citizens will be willing to give reconciliation a second chance.

Reflecting on a hundred years of "the betrayal of being discriminated against on the grounds of race or colour," then–deputy chief justice of South Africa Pius Langa noted that he hoped we had learned something from this as we cannot afford another hundred years "of waste and costly mistakes."[3] Justice and reconciliation are interdependent, Langa asserted, and justice means more than adhering to the basic minima of the Constitution or simply holding public authorities accountable. At heart, justice is about restoring the equilibrium— leveling the playing fields—between the historically disadvantaged and those who systemically benefited from the past. Langa warned that urgent attention should be given to correcting the wrongs of the past, adding that not doing so would undoubtedly bedevil the future. He referred to the Constitution as a "*now* document"—a document that should be implemented without delay.

So what needs to be done? Business as usual, marked by basic levels of stability and economic growth, does not seem to be sufficient to sustain progress toward social cohesion and equity in countries such as Kenya and South Africa. A renewed sense of urgency about tackling material redress has to be coupled with deliberate efforts to create a sufficient national consensus on how material exclusion ought to be handled. In this context, the South African TRC's call for the establishment of a Business Reconciliation Fund, supported by a once-off wealth tax for those who benefited from apartheid, is worthy of further reflection.

In South Africa specifically, the argument made more recently by Steven Friedman that reconciliation has not failed but, in fact, simply hasn't been attempted for much of the past two decades, also deserves to be considered. Friedman argues that the post-apartheid reconciliation process should have been characterized by initiatives to encourage people to talk about race and racial identity in ways that would reduce their impact; and, to "recognise that, if one group has dominated another, more is needed to change this than conversation—economic and social changes are essential. And so a serious strategy would have found ways to encourage bargaining on how to reduce the inequalities the new democracy inherited while retaining the capital we need to grow. Yet this is still to happen."[4]

Such initiatives also need to be supported by effective and fair land reform; an urgent improvement in the delivery of public education, health, and basic services; as well as aggressive job creation. Arguably, the government has been focusing on precisely this agenda since 1994. Perhaps what has been missing is credible leadership, coupled with political will and urgency, as well as the sense of being in this "together," which South Africans had during the political transition. A more overt commitment to material redress from all South Africans, arrived at via some kind of public consensus, would go some way toward establishing this.

White South Africans have a special responsibility in this regard. As mentioned, there is a growing perception that whites "got away with their ill-gotten gains." This perception is fueled by another: that whites are not really remorseful for the pain they caused. Whether this is true or false for individuals makes little difference, given the fact that important elements in the political choreography have supported this perception: De Klerk's unconvincing apology at the TRC; the relatively weak participation of whites at TRC hearings; the failure of the majority of white business and political leaders to endorse, let alone implement, meaningful redress measures; and economic statistics that continue to show white people's disregard for material redress in apartheid's wake.[5]

In this context, I believe that white leaders, specifically in the private sector, have a responsibility to hear pleas for material redress from their black counterparts, and, together with government and others, to develop a shared framework for implementing a far more directed and effective redress package than has been implemented thus far.

In addition, high levels of inequality and corruption continue to keep social unity out of reach, even though reconciliation promised forms of justice that were supposed to widen inclusivity and deepen levels of fairness within South African society. It can be argued that, in 1994, few South Africans understood the urgency with which the Constitutional vision needed to be realized. Perhaps some measure of post-transition euphoria was inevitable; after all, the country had accomplished the near impossible.

Nevertheless, as little as six years later, leaders such as Langa were already warning that the job was only half done—that a vital task lay ahead, and that true reconciliation could only be actualized through social justice. There would be no freedom without justice, Langa warned, arguing that South Africa would never be able to sustain a vibrant government without addressing issues of inclusiveness in a common nationhood, and justice for all. He implored South Africans to address the fact that although Johannesburg's suburbs of Sandton and Alexandra are geographically within shouting distance, they remain worlds apart. Unfortunately, for the most part, his words seem to have fallen on deaf ears.[6]

As a political precursor, all such conversations about social transformation will need to meet at least three criteria: inclusivity in relation to who participates, fairness in terms of all participants having equal opportunities to be heard, and a commitment to concrete outcomes that advance the promise of justice for all. This requires challenging the violence and injustices of the past as they linger on in the individual, structural, and cultural relationships between citizens at all levels. I would argue that these conversations should be pursued in tandem with the historic quest for reconciliation, as long as they can be based on an acknowledgment of humanity's profound interdependence.

South Africa's story, with all its glories and its bitter disappointments, needs to be told and retold, not as a romantic tale of forgiveness, a vindication of liberal internationalism, or indeed as an example of reified political contestation. It needs to be told for what it was and still is: the story of a deeply divided society coming to terms with, and learning to appreciate, the fact that peace and prosperity depend on *acknowledging and transforming* the deeply interdependent relations that sustain it from the co-dependent relationships imposed on it during colonialism and apartheid. For the reasons set out in this book, South Africa's story retains relevance for many different conflict situations where peace remains elusive.

Imagine that Marwan Bishara's wish, as recounted in the introduction, comes true: Israel elects its own "De Klerk." At the same time, a Palestinian "Mandela" emerges who enjoys the respect of a majority of Palestinians. Imagine further that these two leaders begin to articulate the manifold interdependences that characterize the Israeli/Palestinian reality. They speak about shared towns and villages, acknowledging the deeply interwoven histories and present realities. In the process, each side searches to make sense of the other's beliefs, motives, and perspectives. Imagine, further, that they are able to agree that continuing to deny this reality undermines their own security and prosperity, as well that that of others. Imagine that by acknowledging their need for one another, they could begin talking about how to work together to further everyone's interests.

Imagine still further that, when confronted with the inevitable "backlash" from hardliners, these leaders are to make plain the constantly escalating costs (in terms of security, international isolation, human loss, suffering, lack of development, and so on) involved in denying the need for reconciliation, as well as the time, energy, and resources that would be available if both sides focused instead on developing a productive and peaceful region. Imagine such political realism taking hold (we cannot achieve this without them), the likes of which would generate a compelling rationale for reconciliation, despite the misgivings there would be.

Imagine these arguments being communicated to key constituencies inside both the Palestinian and Israeli establishments so that, despite the resistance of isolated hardliners, the support of the majority is secured on both sides. Imagine further, that as the process gets underway, it breaks off intermittently as spoilers seek to scupper the fledgling negotiations. Many people, after all, are deeply vested in ongoing conflict. More acts of senseless violence follow. A suicide bomber may wreak devastation at a bus stop in an Israeli neighborhood. Some Israeli soldiers may shoot a protester at one of the checkpoints. Each time, this escalates further unrest and damages trust around the table

Yet see the negotiators refusing to give up because they understand they have no choice but to reach a settlement. Imagine the international community, not least the United States, Russia and Iran, being content to play a background role, supporting this development from a distance and giving it room to grow, so that instead of facilitating talks or trying to broker backroom deals, they allow the Israelis and Palestinians to work things out for themselves. Imagine a process that is resolutely future-focused; that dealing with past injustice is postponed, but within the framework of an unshakable promise of justice, progressively realized; that "dealing with the past" would commence within a context of political stability where social institutions can be established to manage it.

Alternatively, imagine the status quo persists. Israel continues to maintain strict control over Palestinian areas where basic rights such as the freedom of movement, political freedom, and the right to a decent life remain in jeopardy. It continues to rely on military strength to maintain some modicum of domestic normalcy while Palestinians continue to attack the Jewish state through any means at their disposal. The appalling conditions in which Palestinians live in Gaza, stateless and impoverished, remains and the Israeli state remains locked down under a cloud of international condemnation and with a constant fear of being attacked from outside or inside its own borders. Imagine too that the Jewish and Palestinian diasporas, in cahoots with various international forces, continue to radicalize the conflict from afar (without having to live with the immediate consequences of these decisions), rather than accepting the need for peaceful coexistence on the ground.

My aim has been to ponder ways to move beyond the kind of dead-end situations sketched above through processes framed by the central concern of improving relations across enemy lines. The argument has been that acknowledging interdependence holds the promise of reconciliation and, eventually, of comprehensive, if not complete, justice. In the process, a relevant, recognizable, and justifiable concept of reconciliation has been developed in terms of which the political transitions of societies in conflict can be promoted, pursued, and ultimately accounted for. Political relevance, inclusivity, and credibility, as well as social justice, formed the crucial building blocks of this approach.

Reconciliation politics are morally committed to the restoration of fair and inclusive relationships. This non-negotiable normative commitment ought to guide and inform reconciliation's pragmatic realpolitik through all the various phases of a radical transformation of society. As such, it is one of various possible post-conflict scenarios. Rival options include segregation or secession, military victory, strict majoritarian rule, externally kept peace, or indeed ongoing conflict.

Because reconciliation involves relationships between groups and countries, as well as individuals, the simple grammar of interpersonal forgiveness is inadequate to explain reconciliation's dynamics on the political stage. Forgiveness remains a desired, if often elusive outcome, but it is unrealistic and politically unproductive as a precondition for reconciliation's start.

Instead, first, a politics of reconciliation ought to be realistic and relevant to real-life decision-making processes in conflicted and post-conflict societies. Such political realism is found in the simple acknowledgment of leaders, in the midst of war or its aftermath, of a *fundamental, de facto, and comprehensive interdependence* of the conflicting sets of aspirations that may have caused the war in the first place. The acknowledgement of interdependence signals that a reconciliation process is underway emerging in statements by top leaders, often to the consternation of their own followers and indeed their enemies, that they acknowledge and understand that there is another group with its own demands, fears, and hopes, and that it might be a good idea to listen to them and to what these demands may be.

Second, reconciliation ought to extend beyond the top leadership to include representative engagement among all legitimate political groupings, as to all the root causes of the conflict. Ultimately, this should lead to a shared framework for future aspirations on the basis of which a shared strategy to deal with the legacies of a troubled past can be developed. Much less a strict linear process, and much more a frequent return to inclusive, fair, and democratic spaces held open by credible custodians, political reconciliation becomes a movement of opening and closing (albeit temporarily) the most pressing and difficult questions a conflicted society or societies face. The willingness to return multiple times to the negotiation table will be tested. Fundamentally, it is the realization of the *fundamental, de facto, and comprehensive* interdependence—that we have no choice since we are in this boat together for better and worse—that will prove the most compelling reason to sustain negotiations, just as this idea was the most compelling basis for leaders to begin to entertain reconciliation as political option.

Third, reconciliation requires the actual realization of equal relationships, within the framework of a commonly accepted future. To this end, even as the identities of the past begin to dissolve in favor of new, more bipartisan, and less hostile patterns of identification, it is important to recognize the ongoing impact of past violations and violence on sections of the population. There rests a special responsibility on those who may have benefited from the conflict to act in concerted fashion to demonstrate their solidarity with erstwhile opponents who continue to suffer material deprivation in the new dispensation.

In my view, reconciliation-as-interdependence as set out in this theoretical frame has the ability to explain reasonably coherently how reconciliation can be initiated amid ongoing conflict. Rendering interdependencies visible can transform them into engines for change that can help to further negotiation processes. Propelled forward in this way, transitional arrangements can both broaden and deepen reconciliation's reach, and ultimately contribute to the realization of manifestly and increasingly inclusive, fair, and ethical societies.

The value of reconciliation as a potential framework for large-scale societal transition—in addition to its core focus on restoring just relations—is precisely that, in my view, it provides an important link between processes designed on the one hand to settle conflict, and those designed on the other hand to create a new, inclusive, and prosperous future. Reconciliation provides this link by emphasizing the fundamental importance, across the various processes, of restoring just relationships as a basis for an inclusive and fair peace. For this reason, too, reconciliation provides guidance on how to sequence and integrate various elements of political transition, including mechanisms, processes, and institutional arrangements commonly associated with transitional justice (truth-seeking exercises, criminal trials, reparations, institutional reform, memorialization, education, lustration, and vetting) into a larger, more comprehensive political and societal agenda that seeks to address both vertical state/citizen and horizontal, social relations.

Focused on building just relationships between erstwhile enemies, the concept of reconciliation developed here is fundamentally future-oriented (although not to the exclusion of dealing with crimes of the past), justice-oriented (though not to the exclusion of providing for accommodation, negotiation, and compromise between enemies), gendered (though not to the exclusion of other identities), locally owned (though not to exclusion of international engagement), and progressively realized through a combination of initiatives and processes ranging from peacemaking to transitional justice and social development (though not to the exclusion of a clear, focused understanding of reconciliation across these areas of engagement).

In seeking to overcome oppression or violent conflict, reconciliation is *forward-looking* and predicated on rebuilding relationships in deeply divided societies as part of building a new society that overcomes the violence of a previous dispensation in sustainable ways. Addressing and dealing with a violent past is therefore not an exercise embarked on for its own sake. It is taken up because of the value dealing with the past has for reaching a desired, more comprehensively just future. A violent past is often the most important obstacle to reaching the future, and must therefore be dealt with. Otherwise resentment, revenge, and renewed hostilities often prevent sustainable peace. At the same time, without a shared agreement on where society is headed, exercises meant to lay a difficult past to rest often derail.

Processes such as truth-telling and reparations are therefore most successfully pursued in the wake of comprehensive peace and constitutional agreements that provide a clear vision of a desired, shared future. Moreover, establishing accountability and/or punishment for the wrongs of the past also promotes an inclusive future insofar as they prevent reoccurrence and a sense of satisfaction among victims, and are therefore seen as building blocks for a new future. Yet, these two are best pursued once society has some measure of agreement on what a more just and inclusive future will look like.

Reconciliation also fosters *just, inclusive and fair societies*. It does not paper over the injustices of the past, but instead fundamentally challenges unjust, violent, and oppressive relationships. As Desmond Tutu remarked at the conclusion of South Africa's TRC, "reconciliation is never cosy." It can be no other, for if enemies are to learn to live together peacefully, that peace has to be just. Justice is written into reconciliation's DNA, so to speak. I have argued that the standoff between those advocating for transitional justice and those who prioritises reconciliation is both artificial and misconceived. This false distinction is overcome in the concept of reconciliation proposed here—a concept that builds on experiences and insights generated mainly on the African continent over the past two decades since the post-genocide reconstruction of Rwanda and the post-apartheid transformation of South Africa began.

Moreover, reconciliation as understood here is *locally owned and driven*. It is primarily and most effectively managed by those who have to live with its consequences. Although no reconciliation process plays out in a vacuum, and even as the international community often supports and encourages reconciliation processes to meet national human rights standards and requirements, such processes ought to be led and managed by those directly involved in the conflict and who have a direct stake in its peaceful resolution. This, in my view, greatly enhances the chances of reconciliation to make a lasting and transformative impact.

Reconciliation reminds those in charge of political transition that if the process is not owned by those who have to live with its consequences, it is unlikely to succeed. After all, if reconciliation is about restoring relationships, it is only those within these relationships who can achieve the desired change. Reconciliation therefore assumes higher levels of ownership and commitment than enforced peace or segregation, by drawing erstwhile enemies into a process that acknowledges their agency and leadership in shaping a new dispensation, not only among the elite, but indeed across all levels of society. In this regard, within a genuine reconciliation agenda, political power ought to reside alongside with, and accommodate, civic influence. Reconciliation, with its inherent promise of more just relations, therefore does not rest with a political or institutional reform, but insists on societal transformation shaped by the ideals of inclusivity and fairness.

A further objective here is to make explicit the need for a *progressive approach* to reconciliation, one in which its realization across many events, processes, and initiatives includes a broadening range of stakeholders and deepening fairness. Reconciliation recognizes the inherent interdependence and interconnection between citizens themselves, and between citizens and the state. These relationships are progressively re-established in more just ways. In so doing, it helps to create conditions in which social goods such as forgiveness, the rule of law, or democracy become possible. This means that reconciliation requires the progressive realization of these goods but cannot require them as preconditions.

Reconciliation foreshadows healing, forgiveness, and closure, in short a future no longer dominated or determined by a violent past, in the way enemies are able to bracket self-interest for the sake of mutual interest. At the same time, reconciliation cannot *promise* forgiveness or healing. Instead, more reservedly, by foreshadowing forgiveness it makes an important contribution toward creating the conditions for it to occur in the future.

Similarly, reconciliation initiatives foreshadow the rule of law in the ways it requires a basic sense of inclusion and fairness (in the eyes of the participants) from all initiatives conducted in its name. It does so by creating space—even where law and order have broken down or where deep differences exist about what the rule of law should look like—where enemies can debate and articulate the ground rules of a new, fair, and inclusive society, and in the process conditions for the rule of law to take hold are created.

Reconciliation also foreshadows democratic participation, especially with reference to articulating and endorsing what a shared vision of an inclusive and fair society would look like. It provides spaces for political participation, democratic contestation, and difficult dialogues about the root causes of the conflict. It prepares a society divided and accustomed to exclusion at different levels for participative democracy. As such, it helps to create conditions favorable to democracy.

APPENDIX

This table contains a summary of the comparisons drawn in Section II between three types of reconciliation theory

Key Questions	Key Groupings			
	Liberal Peace	*Social Restoration*	*Agonist Deliberation*	*Interdependence*
How are enemies persuaded to reconcile?	A Call to join the Community of Liberal Democracies	A Call to Moral Community	A Call to Political Community	A call to acknowledge a fundamental and comprehensive interdependence with the enemy
How is reconciliation (or its absence) recognized in post-conflict settings?	Acknowledging the wrongs of the past as the result of intolerance Punishing perpetrators Paying damages to victims	Theological and/or secular sequences of embrace, i.e. acknowledgement, repentance, forgiveness, reparation and non-repetition.	The presence of a risky and fragile political conversation holding together the twin promises of "never again" and starting afresh without seeking closure	Increasingly inclusive and fair institutional arrangements to settle the future and deal with the past
Against which promise are reconciliation's outcomes to be evaluated?	Respect for human rights Restoring the rule of law	The "right relationship" or "restored community," variously conceptualized as justice, respect, trust, or healing	Former antagonists recognize each other as adversaries	A progressively inclusive and fair society

	Key Groupings			
Key Questions	Liberal Peace	Social Restoration	Agonist Deliberation	Interdependence
How is interdependence between enemy groups conceived?	Interdependence is rooted in a common concern for security	The human beings are socially interdependent	Security, but also meaning, reality, and worth of things are interdependently realized within a fragile political community	As a fundamental (unavoidable) and comprehensive (cross-cutting) reality that ties the mutual well-being of enemy groups together
What does this typology say about identity?	Identity prefigures as the liberal subject	Identity is recognized as diverse and constitutive of social engagement	Identity is fluid and shapes the posturing within political engagements	Identity is constituted through ever-widening circles of social solidarity, including but not limited to, traditional enemies.
What is the central idea about reconciliation?	Reconciliation is the establishment of mutual security and the rule of law both of which breeds civic trust founded on the predictability of citizen and institutional behaviour.	Reconciliation is the restoration of a moral community out of ruins of war and oppression.	Reconciliation is a regulative ideal that exists as a good only as long as it is not thought to have been reached. It requires sustained political engagement that accepts the risk associated with agonism in the hope that it may initiate new relations whilst constantly debating the terms of togetherness across difficult divides.	Reconciliation is the political, institutional and social change that follows the acknowledgement of interdependence as a fundamental reality of groups in conflict and turning this (often negatively perceived) reality into an opportunity for mutual well-being.

| What are potential weaknesses? | It fails to challenge social and political identities sufficiently which may lie at the root of the conflict. It does not offer a convincing "theory of change", namely how to move from political settlement, to institutional reform and from there towards social transformation. | It does not have a "Plan B" for moral failure by key participants in the reconciliation process. It does not answer sufficiently the question about who would be dominant in the restored community. | It presupposes unrealistic levels of willingness, trust and agency within post-conflict settings, especially for victims. It is possible that forever-postponed promises would result in promises denied. It therefore does not offer sufficient or concrete enough guarantees of justice especially to victims and other vulnerable groups but also citizens in general. |

NOTES

Introducing the Argument

1. Bishara, "Sobering Up after Israeli Elections." Bishara is of course not the first to seek to extract lessons from the South African transition for the Israeli-Palestinian conflict. See, for example, Adam and Moodley, *Seeking Mandela*, in which they compare the two conflicts in relation to economic interdependence, religious divisions, third-party interventions, leadership, political culture, and violence, and conclude that the two contexts have more differences than similarities. Nevertheless, they argue that the South African transition has valuable lessons for the Israeli-Palestinian conflict, of which "preparing an indoctrinated public on both sides for a painful transition by means of a truth commission remains perhaps the most important one", 241; see also Adam and Moodley, *Imagined Liberation*.
2. Thompson, *A History of South Africa*, 241.
3. See IJR, *South African Reconciliation Barometer Survey 2014 Report*, 16.
4. I have worked for the IJR since its inception in 2000, first as a program manager and, from 2008 to 2016, as executive director.
5. See Arthur, "How 'Transitions' Reshaped Human Rights"; and Bell, "Transitional Justice."
6. Transitional justice differs from the more routine ways in which stable societies deal with the past by being particularly concerned with past political atrocities and the challenges these pose for peace and justice in times of political transition or in the aftermath of major civil conflicts. The scope, intensity, and legacies of past political atrocities tend to combine with the fragility of transitional and post-conflict societies, to shape the characteristics of transitional justice processes and mechanisms.
7. See Rigby's discussion of the Spanish case in his book *Justice and Reconciliation*, 1, 2.
8. In the context of transitional justice, the phrase "dealing with the past" has come to serve as accepted shorthand for dealing with "past atrocities," "crimes against humanity," or "gross human rights abuses."
9. See Huyse, "Justice after Transition"; and *Traditional Justice and Reconciliation*; see also Kritz, *Transitional Justice*; and Offe, "Disqualification, Retribution, Restitution."
10. For important additional considerations of this question, see: N. Dimitrijević, "Justice beyond Blame: Moral Justification of the (Idea) of a Truth Commission," *Journal of Conflict Resolution* 50, no. 3 (2006): 368–82; L. Fletcher, H. Weinstein, and J. Rowen, "Context, Timing, and the Dynamics of Transitional Justice: A Historical Perspective," *Human Rights Quarterly* 31 (2008): 165–220.
11. C. Bell and C. O'Rourke, "Does Feminism Need a Theory of Transitional Justice? An Introductory Essay," *The International Journal of Transitional Justice* 1 (2007): 23–44.
12. Kritz, "Where We Are and How We Got Here," 21–45.
13. Arthur, "How 'Transitions' Reshaped Human Rights."
14. Doxtader, "A Critique of Law's Violence."

15. See Alexander et al., "Truth Commissions and Transitional Justice," 20; see also Witwatersrand University and South African History Archive, *Traces of Truth*.
16. For example, while it is often claimed that making perpetrators accountable for their past atrocities will prevent a recurrence of political violence and atrocities in future (as against counter-normative claims for the superior virtues of forgiveness and reconciliation), empirical investigation aims to determine the actual (possibly unintended) consequences of both scenarios.
17. See Gibson, "The Evolution of Race and Politics"; IJR, *South African Reconciliation Barometer Survey 2014 Report*; Elster, *Closing the Books*; Mamdani, *When Victims Become Killers*; Nino, *Radical Evil on Trial*; Stover and Weinstein, *My Neighbor, My Enemy*; Van der Merwe et al., *Assessing the Impact of Transitional Justice*; and Wilson, *Politics of Truth and Reconciliation*. Another significant development was the launch of the *International Journal of Transitional Justice* in 2007.
18. The comparative study of transitions from authoritarian rule, known as "transitology," includes much material and discussion relevant to transitional justice, but this is not my main concern. Seminal works include Huntington, *The Third Wave*; and O'Donnell and Schmitter, *Transitions from Authoritarian Rule*.
19. Volf, *Exclusion and Embrace*.

Chapter 1

1. See, for example, Adam and Moodley, *The Negotiated Revolution*; Callinicos, *The World That Made Mandela*; Max du Preez, *Pale Native*; Esterhuyse, *Endgame*; Friedman and Atkinson, *The Small Miracle*; Graybill, *Truth and Reconciliation in South Africa*; Lodge, *Mandela*; Lodge, *South African Politics since 1994*; Mandela, *Long Walk to Freedom*; O'Malley, *Shades of Difference*; Saunders, "Of Treks, Transitions, and Transitology"; Sparks, *Beyond the Miracle*; Sparks, *The Mind of South Africa*; Sparks, *Tomorrow Is Another Country*; and Leonard Thompson, *A History of South Africa*.
2. Harold Wilson's much maligned policy of appeasement toward Hitler during 1938 and 1939 comes to mind as an example of a leader who sought reconciliation with an opponent who had no intention of meeting him halfway. Wilson's actions thus carried considerable risk for the United Kingdom.
3. John Paul Lederach's notion of "moral imagination" describes this type of visionary thinking compellingly. See Lederach, *Moral Imagination*.
4. Mandela, *Long Walk to Freedom*, 624. The word "mealies" is derived from the Afrikaans word for corn—"mielie."
5. Mandela, *Long Walk to Freedom*, 624.
6. The fact that some beneficiaries of the apartheid regime have remained silent, distrustful, and cocooned in middle-class comfort in the face of such magnanimity, and that the legacy of apartheid inequality is still destroying lives, cannot detract from the obvious grace in this kind of politics. Mandela is rightly honored as one the twentieth century's greatest leaders.
7. Freud, *Civilization, Society, and Religion*. In this regard the phrase "narcissism of petty differences" was coined by Freud (and draws on the work of British anthropologist Ernest Crawley) to describe the oversensitivity to "details of differentiation" (a "taboo of isolation") that often arises between communities that occupy adjoining territories. The more general point about valuing the universal in the local was made by Scott Appleby in personal correspondence with the author.
8. Mandela, *Long Walk to Freedom*, 525.
9. Ibid., 526.
10. Mandela, "I Am Not Prepared to Sell the Birthright of the People."
11. Mandela, "Notes for His Meeting with P. W. Botha."
12. See, for example, O'Malley, *Shades of Difference*, 501ff.
13. Mandela, "I Am Not Prepared to Sell the Birthright of the People."
14. OAU, "Harare Declaration."
15. Alexander, *An Ordinary Country*, 22ff.
16. See Asmal et al., *Legacy of Freedom*, 1.

17. Du Toit and Doxtader, *In the Balance.*
18. See Doxtader, *With Faith in the Work of Words*, 35–126; and Doxtader, "The Potential of Reconciliation's Beginning."
19. The Anglo-Boer War was fought between British and Boer forces from 1899 to 1902. The conflict was essentially a battle for control of South Africa's lucrative gold fields, which were inside Boer territory. Some 28,000 British soldiers and 4,000 Boer guerrillas died in the war. Many Afrikaners still deeply resent the Scorched Earth Policy used by the British, which included the systematic destruction of crops, the slaughtering of livestock, the burning down of homesteads, and the poisoning of wells. In addition, tens of thousands of women and children were forcibly moved into concentration camps, where they were terribly mistreated, and where an estimated 26,000 women and children died.
20. By the same token, it is important to remember that many apartheid hardliners never really needed such philosophical justifications in terms of reconciliation, however flawed, to affirm their belief that black and white people were inherently unequal, and accepted that the material interests and systemic advantages secured by the white minority through centuries of colonialism and decades of apartheid should be legally and militarily entrenched.
21. Esterhuyse, *Endgame*, 20.
22. Soko and Villa-Vicencio, *Conversations in Transition*, 42.
23. Botha, *The Afrikaner's Emancipation*, 175.
24. Waldmeir, *Anatomy of a Miracle*, 63–83.
25. Giliomee, *The Afrikaners*, 621.
26. Ibid.
27. Sparks, *Tomorrow is Another Country*, 21–36.
28. The mandate for building a strong "middle ground" between De Klerk's and Mandela's teams was constructed on painstaking political argumentation within each group that gradually extended into spaces where real rapprochement became possible.
29. Brody, "Justice." Brody's view is discussed in more detail in Chapter 6.
30. Philpott, *Just and Unjust Peace*, 270.
31. Ibid., *Just and Unjust Peace*, 257.
32. Sparks, *Tomorrow Is Another Country*, 131.
33. Mandela, "Response to the Speech by the State President."
34. CODESA: Opening Statement by State President F. W. de Klerk, December 20, 1991; available at http://www.anc.org.za/show.php?id=3976. Accessed May 31. 2015.
35. Mandela, "Response to the Speech by the State President."
36. Ibid.
37. De Klerk, *The Last Trek*, 241.
38. Ibid.
39. Carlson and Dee, "My Hands Are Clean." See more on the interaction between De Klerk and Boraine in Chapter 3.
40. De Klerk, *The Last Trek*, 169.
41. Mandela, "Address at the European Parliament."
42. Tutu, *No Future without Forgiveness*, 17.
43. Quoted in O'Malley, *Shades of Difference*, 523.
44. Mandela, *The Struggle Is My Life*, 210.
45. Padraig O'Malley, *Ramaphosa and Meyer in Belfast*, 18.
46. "A Document to Create a Climate of Understanding," forwarded by Comrade Sipho (Nelson Mandela) to F. W. de Klerk on 12 December 1989, quoted in Padraig O'Malley, *Shades of Difference*, 523–5.
47. De Klerk, quoted in Soko and Villa-Vicencio, *Conversations in Transition*, 44.
48. See De Klerk, "CODESA: Opening Statement." In his opening speech at CODESA, De Klerk specifically mentioned: i) the protection of the established economic interests of investors, landowners, businessmen, professional people, and salaried workers against demands for better living conditions for the less-privileged; ii) participation by minorities, and their protection from domination against demands of the majority (however constituted) for democratically obtained power; iii) the recognition and accommodation of diversity against the

need for a single nation; and iv) the need for education to be linked to language and culture against demands for a single educational system.

49. Philpott, *Just and Unjust Peace*, 269.

50. See, for example, South African History Online, "How SA Emerged as a Democracy"; and *Roca Report,* "New Political Force Formed."

51. Constand Viljoen, telephonic interview.

Chapter 2

1. Talks followed by formal negotiations were taking place from 1987 to 1993. Political power changed hands in 1994, and South Africa adopted its new Constitution in 1996. Yet, the Truth and Reconciliation Commission (TRC) was arguably the last of the transitional mechanisms that had as its sole mandate to address some of the issues outstanding from the negotiations processes, including how political violence would be dealt with before and during the transition.

2. Of course, this does not imply a denial of the importance of top leadership, but, even the famed Mandela–De Klerk axis depended heavily on many less-prominent individuals and organizations *before, around, and after* them that painstakingly helped to translate the ideal of reconciliation into viable political strategies.

3. It is vital, too, to acknowledge the key role played by the TRC—an institution that a majority of South Africans regard as having helped avert a civil war. See, for example, Gibson and Macdonald, *Truth Yes, Reconciliation Maybe* as well as the discussion in Chapter 3.

4. In similar vein, Mahmood Mamdani has compared the CODESA process with the TRC; see Mamdani, "Historic Significance of the Post-Apartheid Transition."

5. See Consultative Business Movement, "A Submission." The Consultative Business Movement aimed to bridge the growing gap between business and politicians.

6. To keep matters as low-key as possible, and to avoid politicking in the runup to the event, arrangements were kept secret. Eventually, twenty organizations confirmed their willingness to attend. The major ones included COSATU, the South African Communist Party, the ANC, the Azanian People's Organisation, the Pan African Congress, the NP, the Democratic Party, and the IFP. Meanwhile, 336 people died in political violence in May 1991 alone, making it the deadliest month since Mandela's release.

7. The Conservative Party, the Afrikaner Weerstandsbeweging, and the Herstigte Nasionale Party were the three organizations that boycotted the event on the principle that negotiations of any kind were unacceptable.

8. For a deeper analysis of the NPA, see Collin Marks, *Watching the Wind*; and Gastrow, *Bargaining for Peace*.

9. Peter Gastrow, a former National Chairperson of the liberal Progressive Federal Party who played a key role during the formation of the NPA, remembers that: "Delegates were asked to list issues that were obstacles to peace or issues that caused political violence. Instead of the many issues that were raised by delegates being debated, these were all simply written down on flipcharts stuck on the wall. During the tea break someone then grouped the numerous points that were raised under a few headings. Following a discussion of the headings and the way forward, a preparatory committee was appointed to take the initiative forward by establishing working groups that would address the issues that had been grouped under five or six headings. No details were discussed on 22 June and no drafting was done; that all happened later, and was done by the working groups under the auspices of the preparatory committee." Personal communication.

10. For a brief description, see the insert by Theuns Eloff in Christopher Saunders's chapter "Engaging the Other," 79. Eloff played a crucial role in enabling this meeting to succeed.

11. Gastrow, personal communication.

12. Personal communication.

13. For an exposition on reconciliation as trust, see De Greiff, "The Role of Apologies," 120ff.

14. With the insights offered by the TRC's findings, it is possible to identify at least three forms of ongoing violence that were interspersed with one another. First, public violence

between political factions engaged in turf wars was sometimes mischievously stirred up by "third force" provocateurs. Second, clandestine dirty-tricks campaigns were carried out by apartheid hit squads. And third, a series of disjointed right-wing terrorist incidents, including assassinations, bomb attacks, and intimidation, took place. On at least two occasions (in June 1991 and again in June 1992) the ANC broke off talks, accusing the government of orchestrating public violence through so-called third-force activities.

15. O'Malley, *Ramaphosa and Meyer in Belfast*, 23–24. Ramaphosa was then the ANC's secretary-general and chief negotiator, and was thus Meyer's counterpart. The Record of Understanding is available at http://www.anc.org.za/show.php?id=4206&t=Tranistion%20to%20Decmocracy. For more information, see also "Record of Understanding Is Agreed to by the SA Government and the ANC." http://www.sahistory.org.za/dated-event/record-understanding-agreed-sa-government-and-anc (accessed May 2015).

16. See Waldmeir, *Anatomy of a Miracle*, 200, 201; see also Sparks, *Tomorrow Is Another Country*, 182, 183.

17. For more information, see https://www.nelsonmandela.org/omalley/index.php/site/q/03lv02039/04lv02046/05lv02097/06lv02099.htm. Subcouncils were constituted in seven areas where the Transitional Executive Council would have real power, namely law and order, stability and security; defense; intelligence; foreign affairs; the status of women; finance; and regional and local government and traditional authorities.

18. Of the twenty-six negotiating partners, nineteen were represented on the Council.

19. O'Malley, *Ramaphosa and Meyer in Belfast*, 27.

20. Ibid., 33.

21. Ibid., 14.

22. The IFP, for one, remained a fringe player, never sure of whether or not they would participate fully. Some of the more extremist groups on both sides also chose not to participate, including elements in the Afrikaner right wing who refused to accept the leadership of Constand Viljoen, and cadres in the liberation forces who rejected the ANC, such as the military wing of the Pan Africanist Congress.

23. Quoted in Villa-Vicencio, *Walk with Us*, 66.

24. O'Malley, *Ramaphosa and Meyer in Belfast*, 14.

25. Ibid., 21.

26. Fanie du Toit, *Negotiation, Transition, and Freedom*, 11.

27. For a discussion of the antecedents to the TRC's amnesty regime, which dates back to efforts to address political violence during the CODESA process, see Doxtader, 2003, 121.

28. For a discussion of the first indemnity bill, see Sparks, *Tomorrow Is Another Country*, 123, 124. On the second indemnity bill, see Adam and Moodley, *The Negotiated Revolution*, 155.

29. Boraine, *A Country Unmasked*, 11.

30. See Doxtader and Salazar, *Truth and Reconciliation in South Africa*, 81–83.

31. Ibid., 83.

32. Boraine, *A Country Unmasked*, 14.

33. Roelf Meyer, interview.

34. Lederach and Appleby, "Strategic Peacebuilding," 25.

35. Based on the acceptance of an interdependent future, the MPNP was less a linear process than a succession of spaces to which negotiators could return to develop sufficient consensus on a shared framework that would encapsulate future aspirations of all South Africans. Growing awareness of political and other modes of interdependence across enemy lines, together with significant civic oversight and presence, may help to elucidate some of the conditions crucial to agreeing on a concept like "sufficient consensus" as a mechanism for imbuing reconciliation with the necessary forward momentum. The sense of "having to succeed" became a rationale that drove parties to widen inclusivity and deepen credibility, and to keep these crucial normative criteria carefully in balance, even when they appeared to contradict one another, as with the potentially explosive issue of dealing with the past, as explained in the next chapter.

Chapter 3

1. Desmond Tutu, interview.
2. The significant role played by the constitution-making process itself is discussed in more detail in Chapter 4.
3. For a description of the destruction of documentation, see the TRC's *Final Report*, Vol. 1, 202ff.
4. See Harris, *Between a Rock and a Hard Place*, 10. Harris identifies as a "first lesson" that "violence in and through transition displays continuities and changes with its past expression, patterns and forms."
5. Indeed, transformation of the judicial system would become of one of South Africa's most enduring new challenges, and one which remains unfinished more than twenty years after the advent of democracy.
6. South Africa National Unity and Reconciliation Act (No. 34 of 1995), quoted in Doxtader and Salazar, *Truth and Reconciliation in South Africa*, 13.
7. As TRC investigator Piers Pigou explained, "there was an overlap between the tail end of the human rights violation hearings and the beginning of the amnesty hearings. There should have been a much clearer synergy between these processes, especially as the revelations in amnesty applications and hearings were the biggest source of new primary data relating to violations. Yet the human rights violations process and investigative units largely did not benefit from this. The first five volumes of the *Final Report* were published in 1998, after the human rights violations hearings had concluded and before the bulk of amnesty process was underway. Volumes 6 and 7 were published as a codicil in 2003, and do not provide a detailed overview of what emerged during the amnesty processes. Although it may have been unrealistic to expect the report to provide more than an overview, its lack of detail does underscore the need for follow up, and for access to the TRC's records to be made available on an ongoing basis." Personal communication. The seven volumes of the TRC's *Final Report* can be accessed at http://www.justice.gov.za/trc/report/index.htm.
8. Pigou commented: "it was always going to be a tall ask to get an appropriate mix. The commission was dominated by individuals who had opposed apartheid and a number were close to the ANC, but a significant number were not." Personal communication.
9. See the TRC, *Final Report*, Vol. 7, 1–2.
10. Perpetrators of gross human rights violations would be given a window period in which to apply for amnesty on condition that they revealed the full extent of their complicity in crimes they had been involved in. The Amnesty committee would then decide, based on agreed criteria, whether or not to grant amnesty. Perpetrators who did not come forward risked prosecution.
11. Doxtader and Salazar, *Truth and Reconciliation in South Africa*, 295.
12. A Priority Crimes Litigation Unit was established in 2003 to, among other things, take TRC cases forward, but of the three hundred names put forward by the TRC, only twenty-one were found to be ready for prosecution. However, purportedly because of insufficient resources, very few cases were pursued, and the most important one, concerning three security police who were denied amnesty for the murder of three activists, stalled. In November 2005, new policy guidelines were issued for apartheid-era prosecutions, but again no actual prosecutions took place. Subsequent amended guidelines, based on the TRC criteria for amnesty, were challenged legally by a group of NGOs and subsequently rejected by the Pretoria High Court. In November 2007, then-president Thabo Mbeki issued a Special Dispensation for Presidential Pardons, which proposed establishing a Pardons Reference Team consisting of representatives of political parties who could advise the president on pardons for political crimes. However, victims were granted no rights to render testimony or challenge decisions, and proceedings were to be held in camera. When Mbeki rejected approaches by civil society organizations to offer input on these measures, and indicated that he would go ahead with this dispensation, a coalition of NGOs sought and won an urgent court interdict to stop the process, arguing that it would violate the spirit and intent of the TRC. The government, together with several right-wing prisoners, took the decision on appeal to the Constitutional Court. The highest court in the land found upheld the judgment of the lower court finding that "the

decision to exclude the victims from participating in the special dispensation process was irrational". It is important not to conflate the TRC's amnesty process with these presidential pardons: while both sought to deal with apartheid-era political crimes, their legislative and political contexts were very different. The TRC envisaged neither an extended amnesty nor a pardon process beyond its own mandate.

13. Wilson, *Politics of Truth and Reconciliation*, 230.
14. Crocker, "Truth Commissions," 108.
15. Garton Ash, "True Confessions."
16. Freeman, *Necessary Evils*, 10.
17. Gutmann and Thompson, "The Moral Foundations of Truth Commissions," 32–33.
18. Ignatieff, "Articles of Faith," 112–3.
19. Crocker, "Retribution and Reconciliation," 5–6.
20. Liberal arguments on reconciliation are discussed in more detail in Chapter 6.
21. Wilson, *Politics of Truth and Reconciliation*, 228.
22. Thus, it was argued that South Africa's leadership has to be judged, in retrospect, as deficient, if not misguided, in the ways it fostered and brought about reconciliation. Not only was the process undemocratic and illiberal but it was also irresponsibly utopian.
23. The liberal critique of the TRC has also fed into liberal views on reconciliation more broadly. I deal with this in more detail in Chapter 6.
24. Esterhuyse, *Endgame*, 144–5.
25. Mac Maharaj, interview. Maharaj, who, together with Fanie van der Merwe (then director-general of prisons and De Klerk's chief constitutional adviser) was in charge of managing the CODESA talks, tells of an urgent late-night session during which he and Van der Merwe drafted the now-famous postscript with its equally famous amnesty clause. Afterwards, he asked Van der Merwe if "his side would be able to live with it," to which the answer was positive. Maharaj, in turn, indicated that he believed the formulation would be acceptable to the ANC.
26. See, for example, Du Bois-Pedain, *Transitional Amnesty in South Africa*; and Villa-Vicencio and Doxtader, *The Provocations of Amnesty*. See also Sarkin, *Carrots and Sticks*; and Mark Freeman, *Necessary Evils*.
27. Professors Annette Seegers and André du Toit, both from the University of Cape Town's Department of Political Studies, are working on this topic.
28. See Doxtader and Salazar, *Truth and Reconciliation in South Africa*, 5.
29. Ibid.
30. Mac Maharaj, interview.
31. Ibid.
32. Seegers is a professor in the Department of Political Science at the University of Cape Town, and a co-drafter of the South African Constitution.
33. During the negotiations, Joe Modise, a founding member of the ANC's military wing and later South Africa's first post-apartheid minister of defense, reportedly assured top generals in the South African Defence Force that they would be given amnesty, but he was unable to deliver on this; see Frankel, *Soldiers in a Storm*, 22–25.
34. Seegers, "Amnesty in South Africa," 37.
35. Personal communication, April 6, 2014.
36. Asmal, *Victims, Survivors and Citizens*.
37. Boraine, *A Country Unmasked*, 30.
38. Ibid., 37.
39. Ibid.
40. Hansard, May 27, 1994, col. 187, quoted by Boraine in *A Country Unmasked*, 41.
41. Ibid., 44.
42. Ibid., 44–45.
43. For a description of this period, see Boraine, *A Country Unmasked*, 2000, 47ff.
44. The IFP expressed grave concern, notably about the idea that amnesty would be linked to public hearings "under the spotlight of the press." Constand Viljoen proposed that the exact wording of the Interim Constitution be retained as it related to amnesty, which, he argued, called for a general amnesty. He criticized the "moralist" and "sentimentalist" contributions

of NGOs to the debate, whose high ideals (presumably of the rights of victims and accounta-bility) could result, he argued, in some form of fanaticism.

45. Hansard, May 17, 1995, col. 1339, quoted in Alex Boraine, *A Country Unmasked*.

46. Doxtader, *With Faith in the Works of Words*.

47. These principles were drawn up by Carl Aage Norgaard to be used in the Namibian transi-tion to help define political crimes, and required proportionality between the crime and the political motive for committing it in order to qualify as a political crime; see Sarkin-Hughes, *Carrots and Sticks*, 63.

48. Hendricks, "Jettisoning Justice."

49. Boraine, *A Country Unmasked*, 298.

50. Kritz, "Where We Are and How We Got Here," 34.

51. The IJR's South African Reconciliation Barometer project conducts applied social research on reconciliation in South Africa and other post-conflict societies in Africa. The primary data, re-search findings, and publications produced by the Reconciliation Barometer since 2003 have become an established resource for governments, civil-society organizations, and researchers involved in developing policies, encouraging national debates and broadening the theory and the study of reconciliation. For more information, visit www.ijr.org.za.

52. See David Backer's interviews from 2002/2003 and 2008 with 153 victims selected using the TRC criteria: Backer, "Watching a Bargain Unravel?," 450, 452, 455, 456.

53. Pigou, personal communication.

54. Wilson, *Politics of Truth and Reconciliation*, 97.

55. Ibid., 119.

56. Ibid., 230.

57. Krog, *Country of My Skull*, 152. Krog wrote this after hearing that Tutu had been diagnosed with prostate cancer at a critical juncture in the life of the commission.

58. TRC, *Final Report*, Vol. 1, 17.

59. When pressed for an apology during his failed attempt to apply for amnesty at the TRC, Clive Derby-Lewis, who murdered Chris Hani, retorted that he was not legally obliged to provide an apology. Moreover, he added that one cannot apologize for an act of war.

60. Among many other accolades, Tutu had received the Nobel Peace Prize in 1984.

61. As quoted in Boraine, *A Country Unmasked*, 101.

62. Tutu made an impassioned plea to Winnie Mandela to "say sorry" after crimes associated with her football club had been revealed to the TRC, a pressure to which she did not yield. However inappropriate such moments may have appeared to those steeped in the strict sepa-ration of private and public morality (a separation that itself may be questionable during po-litical efforts to deal with a past that injured personal dignities so deeply), they were decidedly *not* reflective of how the TRC or Tutu operated most of the time.

63. As Piers Pigou commented, "the process itself—however painful—powerfully illustrated the suffering and humanity of the victims, and the humbling (by and large) of perpetrators . . . in a contained and essentially dignified process that did not result in deteriorating social/race relations. A series of taboo issues were exposed and publicly examined and the country did not collapse. . . . This seems to correlate closely with Tutu's notion of cleansing wounds as a prerequisite for sustainable healing." Personal communication.

64. Gish, *Desmond Tutu*, 83.

65. Mandela appointed judges Hassen Mall and Andrew Wilson as chairperson and vice-chairperson respectively and Judge Bernard Ngoepe as the third member. Commissioners Sisi Khampepe and Chris de Jager were appointed as committee members. After passing away due to ill health, Mall was replaced as chairperson by Wilson. Acting Judge Denzil Potgieter was appointed vice-chairperson; see TRC, *Final Report*, Vol. 6/1, 17.

66. Tutu, *No Future without Forgiveness*, 235.

67. See Kritz, "Where We Are and How We Got Here," 34.

68. See Sarkin, *Carrots and Sticks*, 2004.

69. See Dyzenhaus, *Judging the Judges*, 150.

70. The prosecutor in the Malan case, Tim McNally, was accused of sabotaging the prosecu-tion, while the actions of Judge Hartzenberg in the Basson trial drew sharp criticism, raising questions of bias and competency.

71. Boraine, *A Country Unmasked*, 146, 147. The TRC rejected a suggestion by deputy-presidents De Klerk and Mbeki to invite major political parties to outline their views of the history of apartheid in a joint forum, instead of having individual hearings. According to its proposers, such a forum would build confidence in the process of truth recovery, specifically between former armed forces from all sides. Boraine claimed that this was a manifestation of the notion of "collective responsibility" as proposed by General Viljoen, and that agreeing to it would have threatened the integrity of the TRC. He maintained that "the Commission should be victim-centred rather than institutionally focused."

72. Peter du Preez, 107.

73. Seventeen civil-society organiztions, including the South African Council of Churches, issued a statement stating the following: "It is ironic that the NP demanded an apology from Archbishop Tutu for this questioning and comments on their testimony when the vast majority of South Africans feel that the NP should be apologizing to the nation. It appears as if the court case is being used to gain media coverage in a desperate attempt to rescue the Party's degenerating social profile. It seems likely too, that the NP will use any judgment in the case to discredit the final report of the Commission. Finally, the court case may be yet another way for the NP to avoid taking responsibility for the actions of its security forces and to make a contrite apology." See "Who Should Apologise to Whom?" Public Statement on the National Party Court Case against the Truth and Reconciliation Commission: Endorsed by 17 Organisations, September 4. 1997 http://www.csvr.org.za/wits/articles/prtrcnat.htm (accessed November 17, 2014). The ANC responded to the NP presentation as follows: "The National Party and its leader F. W. de Klerk have once more shown a total and callous disregard for the pain and suffering caused to millions of our people by the system of apartheid. The National Party's submission to the TRC shows no remorse but instead rides roughshod over the goodwill and spirit of reconciliation shown by victims of the very crime against humanity for which the National Party government was responsible." See http://www.m2.com/m2/web/story.php/1997852568440080DDE88025683A0031A31F (accessed November 17, 2014).

74. Quoted in Boraine, *A Country Unmasked*, 159.

75. Ibid., 161.

76. Wessels, "Statement Given at the TRC," 321.

77. Steven Ratner and Jason Abrams remind us that the relationship between individual and collective responsibility is indeed vexed: "the more difficult issue has turned on determining which violations of human rights and humanitarian law entailing state (civil) responsibility also leads to individual criminal accountability"; see Ratner and Abrams, *Accountability for Human Rights Atrocities*, 14. Boraine implied that collective responsibility was something the TRC deliberately avoided by focusing on individual responsibility when he noted: "The argument for 'collective responsibility' as held by General Viljoen and as proposed to us by De Klerk and Mbeki, was flawed: we decided that individual accountability was the focus of the Truth and Reconciliation Commission"; see Boraine, *A Country Unmasked*, 187. But was this in fact the case? How does one make sense of political guilt ascribed in many of the TRC findings as anything other than some form of collective responsibility? Viljoen's argument was that different individuals, perhaps even entire organizations, would take responsibility *together* for specific wrongdoings. The TRC argued that this would dilute accountability and rob victims of a specific perpetrator to engage with (thereby undermining the TRC's model of interpersonal reconciliation). Boraine's argument, by contrast, suggested that De Klerk, *as an individual,* should take political responsibility for crimes committed by others under his command. Collective responsibility has been analyzed in terms of different models: hierarchical responsibility (blame the person at the top), collective responsibility (blame no one in particular, but the group as a whole, because "so many hands handled the issue"), or personal responsibility (investigating each individual, irrespective of office, in terms of causal responsibility and volitional responsibility—acknowledging that few war crimes are carried out in ignorance or under compulsion). At the very least, collective responsibility should take individual agency and organizational constraints into account, as well as arguments that no one is above the law. In these terms, De Klerk is personally and morally guilty if his actions were the cause of the wrongdoing (by commission or omission), if he was under no obligation to act

the way he did, and if he did not act, or refrain from acting, as a result of ignorance. De Klerk continued to claim ignorance at the TRC.

78. This point is supported by Du Bois-Pedain, "Communicating Criminal and Political Responsibility," 73.
79. Sarkin, *Carrots and Sticks.*
80. See Doxtader and Salazar, *Truth and Reconciliation in South Africa,* 28.
81. Ibid.
82. Quoted in Doxtader and Salazar, *Truth and Reconciliation in South Africa,* 30.
83. Ibid., 28.
84. Ibid, 28.
85. Doxtader and Salazar, *Truth and Reconciliation in South Africa,* 30.
86. Ibid.
87. Ibid., 31.
88. Ibid.

Chapter 4

1. Parts of this chapter was published as Fanie du Toit, "A Broken Promise? Evaluating South Africa's Reconciliation Process Twenty Years On," *International Politics Science Review,* March, 2017.
2. Underlying this discussion is the broader question of how one engages with one's enemies in ways that make a truly new and just beginning possible; how to set an entirely new and more equitable course for relationships not only between opposing political elites but also for citizens at every level of society. How does one engage in a way that foreshadows alternative, and materially more equitable, future situations when such a future seems counterintuitive, even unimaginable, and where very few precedents exist?
3. Kairos Theologians, *Kairos Document.*
4. This argument has recently been revisited and reworked in Allan Boesak and Curtiss DeYoung, *Radical Reconciliation.*
5. Quoted in O'Malley, *Shades of Difference,* 525.
6. Ibid.
7. Ibid.
8. Mandela, "I Am Not Prepared to Sell the Birthright of the People."
9. Quoted in Fazila Farouk, 'Whites Must Make Sacrifices.
10. Soyinka, *The Burden of Memory,* 83.
11. Ibid., 17.
12. Ibid., 83.
13. Ibid., 25.
14. Ibid., 26.
15. Ibid., 27.
16. Ibid., 75.
17. Through race, settlers were identified as beneficiaries of injustice, and through ethnicity, natives were identified as victims of, and outsiders to, the privileges of citizenship.
18. Mamdani, "When Does Reconciliation Turn into a Denial," 8.
19. Mamdani, "Historic Signficance," 12.
20. By "design" I mean the broad constitutional framework that was negotiated, and formed the basis of the mandate given to key institutions that were tasked with implementing the vision of the Constitution. By "implementation," I have in mind actual policies, and how these were implemented by political leaders. Given this distinction, one can argue (as Mamdani and Soyinka do) that the constitutional agreement itself compromised social justice because of its commitment to political reconciliation. Alternatively, one can accept the constitutional agreement as distributively just, but criticize the policy choices that followed and the leadership subsequently shown. For example, the Mandela government's stance on education and housing, the Mbeki government's controversial HIV/AIDS and GEAR policies, and the Zuma administration's public-order policing and judicial-reform policies have all been roundly condemned.

21. Mamdani. "Reconciliation without Justice."
22. Former ANC intelligence minister Ronnie Kasrils has criticized ANC leaders for making what he alleges was a "Faustian Pact" with big business; see Kasrils, "ANC's Faustian Pact."
23. FCI, "Business Charter," 68–74. For further commentary see Wessels, *Negotiating for Human Rights*, 28.
24. Wessels, *Negotiating for Human Rights*, 33.
25. Quoted in Wessels, *Negotiating for Human Rights*, 33.
26. The principles can be found online at: http://www.anc.org.za/centenary/show.php?id=35 (accessed October 10, 2014). Quoted in Asmal et al., *Legacy of Freedom*, 82.
27. Wessels, *Negotiating for Human Rights*, 24ff.
28. Neil Kritz, director of the Rule of Law Program at the US Institute for Peace, explained that "by 1993, the parties had negotiated an interim constitution which set out the basic ground rules for the process of adopting a permanent constitution and provided for the basic functioning of a 'Government of National Unity' throughout the constitution-making period. Under the interim constitution, the final constitution was to be adopted by a constituent assembly on the basis of a two-thirds vote and no constitutional commission was created. Election to the assembly was supervised by an independent electoral commission and governed by a proportional-representation list system laid out in the interim constitution. The constituent assembly, in addition to drafting a permanent constitution for the country, would also function as a parliament in the interim period. In addition, the interim constitution in South Africa set out 32 substantive principles which had to be followed in the drafting of the permanent constitution." Kritz, "Constitution-Making Process."
29. Constitution of the Republic of South Africa, Act 200 of 1993, Article 26, Chapter 3. https://peaceaccords.nd.edu/site_media/media/accords/Constitution_of_South_Africa_Act_200_of_1993.pdf (accessed 7 March 2014).
30. For more on these groundbreaking documents, see Asmal, et al., *Legacy of Freedom*, 2005.
31. As one observer noted, "the educational effort included a media and advertising campaign using newspapers, radio and television, billboards, and the sides of buses; an assembly newspaper with a circulation of 160,000; cartoons; a web site; and public meetings; together these efforts reached an estimated 73 percent of the population. From 1994 through 1996 the Constitutional Assembly received two million submissions, from individuals and many advocacy groups, professional associations, and other interests." See Hart, *Democratic Constitution Making*, 8.
32. Yacoob, *Drafting the Final Bill of Rights*, 51.
33. Yacoob, *Drafting the Final Bill of Rights*, 51; see also the Bill of Rights in the Constitution of the Republic of South Africa, *Government Gazette* No. 17678, 1996.
34. Constitution of the Republic of South Africa No. 108 of 1996, Chapter 2, Article 25.
35. Ibid.
36. Ibid.
37. Other important Chapter 9 institutions are the Public Protector, the Auditor General, the South African Human Rights Commission, the Electoral Commission, and the Commission for the Promotion and Protection of the Rights of Cultural, Religious and Linguistic Communities.
38. Corder, *Human Rights in Practice*.
39. Mamdani, 'Historic Signficance of the Post-Apartheid Transition," 12.
40. Soyinka, *Burden of Memory*, 35.
41. Mani, "Dilemmas of Expanding Transitional Justice."
42. De Greiff, "Transitional Justice."
43. On 30 November 1973, the UN General Assembly adopted the International Convention on the Suppression and Punishment of the Crime of Apartheid, which defined the crime of apartheid as "inhuman acts committed for the purpose of establishing and maintaining domination by one racial group of persons over any other racial group of persons and systematically oppressing them."
44. That its *Final Report* would be contentious was evident from the start, not least because of strong disagreements among members of the TRC itself. Differences about how to interpret its mandate led to one commissioner (Wynand Malan) to issue a statement reflecting his "minority position," which was included in the *Final Report*. Malan felt that by explicitly

endorsing the UN's view of apartheid, the TRC had overstepped its mark and alienated important constituencies. He argued that: "The question is whether such an unqualified finding
does not create a double-edged sword in terms of the objectives of national unity and reconciliation." The fact that Malan felt so strongly about this is telling of how seriously the TRC
debated the issue of structural violence and social justice; see TRC, *Final Report*, Vol. 5, 449.
45. Gibson and McDonald, "Truth Yes, Reconciliation Maybe."
46. Gibson, *Overcoming Apartheid*, 329
47. TRC, *Final Report*, Vol. 5, 210.
48. De Klerk took offense, challenged the evidentiary base of this finding, and succeeded in
forcing the TRC to issue their report with the page (containing the findings against him) formally blacked out. However, the TRC also equated the human rights abuses committed on
both sides, holding that a human rights violation can never be anything other than a crime, no
matter who commits it or which cause it supposedly supports. Mbeki, in a move that arguably
underscored the TRC's independence more than any other, took offense to the findings that
held the ANC morally responsible for the violations the liberation movement had committed,
and sought an urgent court interdict to prevent the report from being released; he claimed it
criminalized the struggle. Unlike De Klerk, Mbeki lost his bid, and it was determined that the
report could be released.
49. TRC, *Final Report*, Vol. 1, 61.
50. Ibid., 64, 65.
51. Doxtader, *With Faith in the Work of Words*, 5.
52. TRC, *Final Report*, Vol. 1, 55.
53. See Gibson and Macdonald, *Truth Yes, Reconciliation Maybe*.
54. Rabkin, "'Political Interference' Blocked TRC Prosecutions."
55. TRC, *Final Report*, Vol. 6, 144.
56. Galtung "Cultural Violence," 294, 295.
57. While Galtung's basic distinction between "negative" and "positive peace" has been widely
accepted, both in the peace studies movement and more widely in the conflict resolution literature, it has proved much more difficult to reach any kind of agreement on the more specific
meaning of "positive peace." Galtung defined "positive peace" in terms of another controversial distinction between "structural violence" and "cultural violence." According to Galtung,
"positive peace" entails the removal of both "structural" and "cultural" violence as the main
underlying causes of internal war. "Structural violence" concerns the way power is organized
in society in ways so as to inflict "avoidable insults to basic human needs, and more generally
to life, lowering the real level of needs satisfaction below what is potentially possible." Galtung
"Cultural Violence," 292, 294, 295.
58. Galtung "Cultural Violence," 295.
59. TRC, *Final Report*, Vol. 1, 1998, 17.
60. The term "mass violence" refers to the mass violation of individual dignity.
61. Louise du Toit, "Feminism and the Ethics of Reconciliation."
62. The ways in which the TRC failed to make gender a systematic part of the analysis have been
documented and discussed at length. See, for example, Fiona Ross, *Bearing Witness: Women
and the Truth and Reconciliation Commission in South Africa*; Njabulo Ndebele, *The Cry of
Winnie Mandela*; and Rubio-Marín, *What Happened to the Women?*
63. Emdon heads the Gender Desk at the IJR.
64. Backer, "Watching a Bargain Unravel?"
65. Lehohla, *Poverty Trends in South Africa*. In April 2014, Lehohla, South Africa's statistician-
general, announced that poverty levels had decreased over the period 2006 to 2011. His report
was based on metric data collected through the Income and Expenditure Surveys conducted in
2006 and 2011, and on the 2008/09 Living Conditions Survey. The food-poverty line of R321
a month, the lower-bound poverty-line (R433 a month for food and clothing), and the upper-
bound poverty line (R620 a month for food, clothes and shelter) have all been challenged as
unrealistic. Nevertheless, Lehohla reported that from 2006 to 2011, despite the global finan-
cial crisis costing South Africa close to a million jobs, the number of people living below the
food-poverty line declined from 27 in 100 to 20 in 100, whereas the lower-bound poverty line
declined from 42 in 100 to 32 in 100 (about 16.3 million out of total population of approximately

51 million) in 2011. Four million fewer South Africans were living in poverty as measured by the upper-bound poverty line in 2011—that is, 23 million as compared to 27 million in 2006. Nevertheless, this means that, in 2011, 46 in 100 South Africans were living in poverty as compared to 57 in 100 in 2006. But while poverty shrank, inequality, as measured by the Gini-coefficient, remained largely unchanged at 0.69 (if marginally better than the 0.72 measured in 2006) and still one of the highest recorded figures anywhere in the world. Of course, in many of the poorest areas in the world, these statistics are simply unavailable, which makes it difficult to confirm with absolute certainty that South Africa deserves to be known as the world's most unequal society. In addition, poverty statistics have become a source of controversy in South Africa, with critics claiming that South Africa's official figures paint a rosier picture than is in fact the case. Even so, the statistics given by Lehola are sufficient to the analysis I am seeking to develop.

66. See for example, ANC, "We Have a Good Story to Tell." For a more formal version of the same narrative, see: The Presidency, *Twenty-Year Review*.

67. Boraine, *What's Gone Wrong?* In a similar vein, see Calland, *The Zuma Years*; Max du Preez, *A Rumour of Spring*; Mashele and Qobo, *The Fall of the ANC*. Whereas these authors focus mainly on the ANC's maladministration and corruption as the main source of the current malaise, there are others who focus more on wrong policy choices made by the government in attempting to address apartheid's structural imbalances; see, for example, Habib, *South Africa's Suspended Revolution*.

68. The IJR's Reconciliation Barometer project is South Africa's largest and longest-running public-opinion survey on the issue of reconciliation. From 2003 to 2013, the surveys were conducted annually via face-to-face interviews, in six languages, with about 3,500 individuals from all nine provinces of South Africa. The survey questionnaires contained approximately a hundred questions. For details of the annual survey's sampling and methodology, see IJR, *Reconciliation Barometer*, 12.

69. Whereas 40.6 percent of South Africans mistrusted those from another race group in 2004, by 2014, this number was down to 28.1 percent; IJR, *Reconciliation Barometer*, 7.

70. IJR, *Reconciliation Barometer Survey* 2014, 7.

71. Ibid, 7.

72. Gibson, "Apartheid's Long Shadow."

73. Ibid.

74. Lehohla, 2014.

75. IJR, 2014.

76. In 2003 around 50 percent of whites supported state-funded redress for victims of apartheid human rights abuses. By 2013 this figure had dropped to around 33 percent for whites, but was reported as being at just under 70 percent for black and Asian South Africans.

77. IJR, *Reconciliation Barometer Survey*, 19.

78. Van Vuuren, *Democracy, Corruption, and Conflict Management*.

79. A Report of the Public Protector of South Africa, "Secure in Comfort."

80. Lekalake, "South Africans Increasingly Dissatisfied with Their Elected Leaders' Performance."

81. Adriaan, Bsson and Pieter, du Toit, "Enemy of the People—How Jacob Zuma stole South Africa and how the people fought back," 2017.

　　Jacques, Pauw, "The President's Keepers—Those Keeping Zuma in Power and out of Prison," 2017.

82. Msimang, 2015.

83. See, for example, Khayelitsha Commission, *Towards a Safer Khayelitsha*.

Chapter 5

1. This is not to say that reconciliation first appeared in South Africa. As a literary concept it has a varied history, and it figures prominently in various sources of the three major Abrahamic faiths, in different strands of philosophy (Friedrich Hegel's idealism, for example), and throughout political history. However, there are good reasons to view the studies of political reconciliation that have emerged since the South African case as a relatively coherent subset, not only because they tend to be in conversation with one another, but because they all use the relatively recent rise of the notion of transitional justice as a crucial point of

reference. In addition, the studies I refer to deliberately offer comparisons, rather than focus on one specific case; they include, but are not limited to: Brouneus's *Rethinking Reconciliation*; Bloomfield et al., *Reconciliation after Violent Conflict*; Eisikovits, *Sympathizing with the Enemy*; Lederach, *Moral Imagination* and *Building Peace*; Murphy, *A Moral Theory*; Philpott, *Just and Unjust Peace*; Rigby, *Justice and Reconciliation*; Schaap, *Political Reconciliation*; Shriver, *Ethic for Enemies*; Tutu, *No Future without Forgiveness*; Verdeja, *Unchopping a Tree*; and Villa-Vicencio, *Walk with Us*.

2. According to Weber, "an ideal type is formed by the one-sided *accentuation* of one or more points of view" according to which "*concrete individual* phenomena . . . are arranged into a unified analytical construct"; see Weber, "Objectivity in Social Science," 90. The notion of ideal types was an important tool that Weber used to organize and elucidate his sociological method. One of his fundamental premises was that diverse actions develop into "social action," which in turn congeals into patterns or types of actions. These patterns then delineate group boundaries, since they resist or react to other behavior patterns. Ideal types thus indicate patterns of action. As Stephen Kalberg wrote, "ideal types conceptualise as groups the patterned meaningful action shared by persons"; see Kalberg, "Perpetual and Tight Interweaving," 275.

3. For a provocative analysis of transitional justice as a "non-field," see Bell, "Transitional Justice"; see also Arthur, "How 'Transitions' Reshaped Human Rights."

4. See Weber, "Objectivity in Social Science," 90.

5. It is important to note that the phrase "within the framework of . . ." shifts in meaning across the next three chapters. In some cases, there is a virtual identification between reconciliation and the particular theory within which it is framed; in other cases the relationship is not of identification, but rather of mutual influence. In other words, the degree of influence that reconciliation, as a coherent concept, has on each theory differs across the three theoretical types.

6. Krog, *Country of My Skull*, 143.

7. For a historical account of this event, see Meredith, *Diamonds, Gold and War*, 207ff.

8. Molefe made this remark at an IJR workshop on August 1, 2014.

9. Volf, *Exclusion and Embrace*.

10. Remnick, "Vladimir Ilyich Lenin," 43.

11. Schaap, *Political Reconciliation*, 85.

12. Volf, *Exclusion and Embrace*.

13. USIP, "Social Reconstruction." As another example, USIP describes social restoration (which they equate with reconciliation) as "a condition in which the population achieves a level of tolerance and peaceful co-existence; gains social cohesion through acceptance of a national identity that transcends individual, sectarian, and communal differences; has the mechanisms and will to resolve disputes non-violently; has community institutions that bind society across divisions; and addresses the legacy of past abuses . . . simply put, reconciliation is a process through which people move from a divided past to a shared future, the ultimate goal being the peaceful co-existence of all individuals in a society . . . reconciliation programs seek to promote tolerance and mutual respect, reduce anger and prejudice from the conflict, foster intergroup understanding, strengthen nonviolent conflict resolution mechanisms, and heal the wounds of conflict."

14. Taylor, *Hegel*; see also Doxtader, "The Faith and Struggle"; and Verdeja, *Unchopping a Tree*.

15. Taylor, *Hegel*, 152ff.

16. A similar emphasis on a "politics of difference" drove the efforts of Will Kymlicka, also a Canadian, to come to terms with the phenomenon of minority groups within Western democracies. In Kymlicka's view, liberal democracies ought to accept the idea of "multicultural citizenship," based on a wide range of group-differentiating rights for national minorities and ethnic groups, without sacrificing their core commitment to individual freedom and social equality; see Kymlicka, *Multicultural Citizenship*, 126.

17. Fanon, *Wretched of the Earth*, 43.

18. Taylor, "Politics of Recognition," 38.

19. Schaap, *Political Reconciliation*, 42.

20. What distinguishes right-wing Hegelians from left-wing Hegelians is the desire to derive and formulate synthesis—the dialectical process produces "the third definite synergy." For

left-wing Hegelians, the dialectical process is never resolved; so recognition does not end but remains a calling, a vocation.

21. As quoted in the *New York Times*, October 19, 1984.

22. This implies accepting not only the other who is a potential friend, but also the other who is an enemy.

23. Volf, *Exclusion and Embrace*, 147.

24. Taylor, "Irreducibly Social Goods," 127ff.

25. In religious and cultural discourse, calls to establish or uphold moral communities are well known, and feature in expressions such as *"ummah wahida," "*one holy Catholic Church," "the holy land," or *"itai doshin."*

26. Volf, *Exclusion and Embrace*, 143.

27. Ibid.

28. See Philpott, *Just and Unjust Peace*, 79.

29. Ibid., 58.

30. See Gobodo-Madikizela, *A Human Being Died That Night*. In a similar vein, Harvard psychology professor Herbert Kelman described reconciliation as "mutual acceptance of the other's identity and humanity"; see Kelman, "Reconciliation from a Social-Psychological Prespective," 16. Kelman's view of reconciliation as "identity change" is in line with Taylor's communitarian approach in "Politics of Recognition" and involves mutual acknowledgment of the other's nationhood and humanity, confrontation with history, acknowledgment of responsibility, and the establishment of patterns and institutional mechanisms of cooperation. These initiatives aim to break, if possible, what Cypriot-born psychiatrist Vamik Volkan calls the transmission of intergenerational trauma. See Volkan, "Transgenerational Transmissions"; see also Kalayjian and Paloutzian, *Forgiveness and Reconciliation*; and Potter, *Trauma, Truth, and Reconciliation*.

31. Gobodo-Madikizela, *A Human Being Died That Night*.

32. Gobodo-Madikizela, "Radical Forgiveness," 37–38.

33. Philpott does not reject liberalism but redefines it in terms of social restoration without sacrificing those values that liberalism holds dearest, namely: human rights, the rule of law, and democratic participation.

34. Zehr, *Changing Lenses*, 181.

35. Minow, *Between Vengeance and Forgiveness*, 17.

36. It is also true, however, that in transitional-justice contexts restorative justice is often still seen as a "second best" option if "full justice" (prosecution) is not available. Restorative justice advocates challenge this assumption and point, for example, to the very low rehabilitation rates in prisons in post-conflict societies such as South Africa. In fact, South African prisons are often blamed for further corrupting young offenders, and for inducting them into formalized and highly influential crime networks when many land in jail for relatively petty crimes. By contrast, in São Paulo, authorities are experimenting with restorative justice as an intrinsic part of community development in the hope that this has a better chance of rehabilitating young offenders within the social reach of the community, rather than in a hostile prison environment far away from where the crime was committed. In this context, reconciliation between the criminal and the victim has a real chance of succeeding.

37. Gutmann and Thompson, "Moral Foundations," 32–33.

38. Weinstein, "The Myth of Closure."

39. The notion of modesty in this context was first put forward by Villa-Vicencio in his book *Walk with Us*, 171–2.

40. Verdeja, *Unchopping a Tree*.

41. Verdeja, *Unchopping a Tree*. Philpott and Verdeja are colleagues at the Kroc Institute for International Peace Studies at the University of Notre Dame in Indiana, USA. They have taken up this debate within the discipline of political studies, developing reconciliation theories that respond to the liberal charge of moral overreach without losing the main tenets of social restoration. Their theories represent related yet different attempts to conceive of reconciliation as social restoration. They have in common an attempt to rethink liberalism from a restorative-justice angle, but also to challenge some conventions within restorative-justice theory by positioning their arguments in close proximity to international liberalism.

Essentially both attempt to move toward a position more acceptable to classic liberalism, but from a social restoration position. Both regard liberalism as making important contributions toward a systematic theory of reconciliation, and they acknowledge the large measure of "overlapping consensus" that seems to exist within the international community on liberal democracy as the preferred outcome of political transition, but also on reconciliation as a means toward such an outcome.

42. Verdeja, *Unchopping a Tree*, 3.
43. Ibid., 21.
44. See Philpott, *Just and Unjust Peace*, 111.
45. Schaap, *Political Reconciliation*, 54.
46. The risk is entrenching oppressive identities just as political reconciliation begins to challenge and overcome theses. This is precisely the debate in many South African organizations that have adopted affirmative action or black economic empowerment as part of their human resources policies. Reserving positions for members of communities that were systematically disadvantaged by apartheid seems necessary. Yet many young South Africans who have grown up with, at least officially, a measure of non-racialism speak of their confusion at still being classified along racial lines if they apply for university or a job in the civil service. But for communitarians such as Taylor ("Politics of Recognition"), the risk of identity reification is worth taking. He argues that a liberal denial of identity leads to a superficial politics of reconciliation. If identity is fundamental to politics and to the art of living together peacefully, and if identity is essentially relational, it follows that restoring relations is a crucial task of reconciliation.
47. I am indebted to Barnard-Naude, "Forgiveness as Happenstance" for important input into this analysis.
48. Derrida and Roudinesco, *For What Tomorrow*, 161.
49. Derrida, "On Forgiveness," 45.

Chapter 6

1. Brody, "Justice."
2. Amy and Dennis, "Moral Foundations of Truth Commissions," 22. Such a moral defense would require that a TRC should be moral "in principle"; that is, it should offer sufficient moral reasons for forgoing criminal justice. It should also be moral in perspective; that is, inclusive of as many people seeking social cooperation. Finally, it should be moral in practice; that is, it should practice what it preaches and be manifestly fair and consistent in its operations. Gutmann and Thompson identified three possible responses to this "moral burden" of having to sacrifice prosecutorial justice, namely the realist, compassionate, and historicist responses, all of which they find wanting. In their view, Tutu's "compassionate" approach overemphasized Christian forgiveness.
3. My specific focus means therefore that general discussions of liberalism, including the well-trodden debates between liberals and communitarians, for example, are beyond the scope of this discussion.
4. Philpott, *Just and Unjust Peace*, 19, 70.
5. Ibid., 19, 70–72.
6. The rejection by some of the Palestinian legislative election results in 2006, when Hamas won a majority, can be seen in a similar light.
7. Andrieu, "Political Liberalism," 85ff.
8. Philpott, *Just and Unjust Peace*, 9.
9. Kymlicka and Bashir, *Politics of Reconciliation*, 16.
10. Definitions of the "rule of law" proliferate. A popular definition is that those making the law also live under it. Lon Fuller identifies the following eight principles of legality that, according to Colleen Murphy, capture the essence of the rule of law:

> (i) Laws must be general by specifying rules prohibiting or permitting behavioor of certain kinds. (ii) Laws must be widely promulgated and publicly accessible. (iii) Laws must be prospective, specifying how individuals ought to behave in future rather

than focusing on past behavior. (iv) Laws must be clear to citizens. (v) Laws must be noncontradictory; one law should not contradict another. (vi) Laws must not ask the impossible. (vii) Laws should remain relatively constant. (viii) There must be congruence between the written laws and how officials enforce them. See Fuller, *Morality of Law*, 39; Murphy, *A Moral Theory*, 43.

11. This is also true of the more recent and variously opaque theories of political economy associated with neoliberalism and the so-called Bretton Woods institutions.
12. Nevertheless, the critique I develop here *does* in fact apply to theories of reconciliation built on Rawlsian or, indeed, other liberal arguments. The trend toward accommodating communitarian concerns within once staunchly liberal positions becomes clear in Rawls's restatement of his position in his book *Political Liberalism*, which is commonly known as "the new Rawls"; for more on this, see Mulhall and Swift, *Liberals and Communitarians*, 1–33.
13. Arendt, *Human Condition*.
14. Locke, "Concerning Toleration," 44; see also Schaap's extended argument in this regard in *Political Reconciliation*, 32ff.
15. Arendt, *Human Condition*, 30.
16. Bonino, *Doing Theology*, 121. ANC intellectual Pallo Jordan pins liberals' rapid shift (in the eyes of some) from the left to the right of the political spectrum in South Africa on "their perceived betrayal of the principles that they claim to uphold." Jordan, "Disdain for Liberals." Communitarians, too, accuse liberals of a kind of egotistic individualism that shuns community and, in the name of security, makes society a competitive and socially hostile place. Utilitarians, who measure political success by the whether the greatest good is accrued by the largest number of people, are also critical, accusing liberals of raising the interests of (empowered) individuals above that of the common good.
17. Schaap, *Political Reconciliation*, 33.
18. Shklar, "Liberalism of Fear," 23. I am indebted to Andrew Schaap for drawing my attention to this quote, which also appears in his book *Political Reconciliation*, 26.
19. Locke, "Concerning Toleration," 26, 53.
20. Murphy, *A Moral Theory*, 28.
21. De Greiff, "The Role of Apologies," 120–37.
22. See as one example Hall, "Question of Cultural Identity." Hall usefully distinguishes between three conceptions of identity: the "Enlightenment subject" (corresponding roughly to what I call the "liberal subject"); the "sociological subject" (which corresponds roughly to social restoration's idea of "dialogical" identity); and the "postmodern subject" (which can be understood as having no fixed, permanent, or essential identity). He explains that the Enlightenment subject is "based on a conception of the human person as a fully centered, unified individual, endowed with the capacities of reason, consciousness, and action, whose 'center' consisted of an inner core which first emerged when the subject was born, and unfolded with it, while remaining essentially the same—continuous or 'identical' with itself—throughout the individual's existence," 597.
23. See www.ictj.com.
24. See Holkeboer and Villa-Vicenzio, "Rights and Reconciliation."
25. The result, over the past decade, has been a targeting of those who, although powerfully destructive in their own contexts, are relatively powerless internationally.
26. For example, Jendayi Frazer, US assistant secretary of state for African affairs from 2005 to 2009, wrote that "the ICC indeed has fallen far from the high ideals of global justice and accountability that inspired its creation." Frazer, "ICC Has Fallen." Meanwhile, in 2013 the African Union debated a continent-wide withdrawal from the ICC. Although the pressure to withdraw was led by Kenya, and strongly supported by Ethiopia, the African Union decided instead to ask the UN Security Council to defer cases against sitting presidents. See Akande, "How Nigeria, Others Averted AU's Withdrawal from ICC"; and *Mint Press*, "As African Governments Threaten to Leave."
27. Of course, the notion of "people on the ground" can mean different things: it can refer to communities, or to officials tasked with designing and steering transitional justice processes, or, indeed, to the various institutions created for this purpose.

28. The declaration is available at http://www.peace-justice-conference.info/download/
    Nuremberg%20Declaration%20A-62-885%20eng.pdf (accessed December 19, 2012).
29. See the report at http://daccess-dds-ny.un.org/doc/UNDOC/GEN/N04/395/29/PDF/
    N0439529.pdf?OpenElement (accessed December 19, 2012).
30. Ojielo, 2009, 124.
31. Brody, "Justice."
32. Ban, *Rule of Law.*
33. Available at http://www.ohchr.org/EN/Issues/TruthJusticeReparation/Pages/Annual
    Reports.aspx (accessed October 16, 2015).
34. "Report of the Special Rapporteur on the Promotion of Truth, Justice, Reparation, and
    Guarantees of Non-Recurrence, Pablo de Greiff." Available at http://www.ohchr.org/EN/
    Issues/TruthJusticeReparation/Pages/AnnualReports.aspx (accessed October 16, 2015).
35. See, for example, the UNDP office in Cyprus's work related to the so-called SCORE meas-
    urement index for social cohesion. Available at http://www.cy.undp.org/content/cyprus/
    en/home/operations/projects/action_for_cooperation_and_trust/social-cohesion-and-
    reconciliation--score--index-.html (accessed May 22, 2016). Another example includes the
    UNAMI initiatives in Iraq. Available at: http://www.iq.undp.org/content/iraq/en/home/
    presscenter/pressreleases/2016/02/27/parliament-members-and-civil-society-come-
    together-to-promote-community-reconciliation-in-iraq.html (accessed May 22, 2016).
36. De Greiff, "The Role of Apologies," 120ff.
37. Ibid., 126.
38. Ibid., 126, 127.
39. Ibid., 15, 16.
40. Murphy, *A Moral Theory*, 8, 20.
41. Ibid., 22.
42. Ibid., 188.
43. Ibid., 189.
44. Garton Ash, "True Confessions," 37.
45. An example would be Philpott's *Just and Unjust Peace.* Presumably the aim of this type of
    theory is to describe ways in which communitarian practices (that try to address the deep
    wounds of a postwar society) can usher in a liberal democracy, but the value of liberal democ-
    racy as such remains uncontested.
46. Philpott, *Just and Unjust Peace*, 71.
47. Precisely how individual freedom is conceptualized remains an area of considerable debate
    within liberalism, and, as indicated earlier, is beyond the scope of this discussion.
48. Van Roermund, "Rubbing Off and Rubbing On," 187.
49. Villa-Vicencio, *Walk with Us*, 95, 96, quotes Govan Mbeki, South African struggle veteran and
    father of Thabo Mbeki, speaking of the need to balance "having" and "belonging" in the South
    African nation-building process and elsewhere.
50. Schaap, *Political Reconciliation*, 4.
51. Ibid., 35.
52. See Locke, *Two Treatises of Government*, 32.
53. For an introduction to this conversation, see Hirsch, "The Agon of Reconciliation," 2, 3.

Chapter 7

1. Alexander Hirsch reminds us that the term *agonism* is derived from the ancient Greek word
   agōn "signifying a brand of struggle and in particular an athletic contest between contending
   agents in the midst of a religious festival"; see Hirsch, "The Agon of Reconciliation," 3. Several
   philosophers, from Machiavelli and Nietzsche, to Hannah Arendt, Max Weber, Carl Schmitt,
   and Michel Foucault, all refer to some form of agonist politics as essentially conflictual.
   This contrasts with how others see struggle: for example, deliberative democrats seek consensus through democratic institutions while liberals "leave precious little space for initia-
   tory or expressive modes of political action" (Dana Villa, quoted by Hirsch in "The Agon of
   Reconciliation," 4.)
2. Doxtader, "Is It Reconciliation?"

3. Seminal works on political transition per se are O'Donnell and Schmitter, *Transitions from Authoritarian Rule*; and Huntington, *The Third Wave*.

4. As Tim Murithi writes: "By examining each African case individually one might be able to come up with a rational explanation of why all the current cases of the ICC are in Africa. One might even argue that, to a neutral observer, if one critically analyses the facts, it is possible to reach the conclusion that the ICC was established with the sole purpose of prosecuting cases from Africa. At the same time, though, one could also identify a combination of domestic and international political interests behind the submission of, for the time being, only African cases and behind UN Security Council referrals to the ICC." See Murithi, *The African Union*.

5. Goldmann, "Sierra Leone," 510.

6. Sierra Leone TRC, *Witness to Truth*, Vol. 2, Ch. 2, para. 568.

7. Quoted by Goldmann, in "Sierra Leone," 513. Goldman also quotes the following from a letter that Hinga Norman wrote to his legal counsel: *"I have long been in receipt of copy of your letter . . . expressing the inappropriateness for me (your client) to appear before the Truth and Reconciliation Commission while I remain an indictee before the Special Court. Well, I was arrested, charged and detained on the 10th March 2003, thinking that by now, 25th August 2003, my trial would have started long ago; but I thought wrongly. Since there is no news about the start of the trial and there are signs that the TRC may soon close its sittings, I would prefer to be heard by the people of Sierra Leone, and also be recorded for posterity, especially where my boss, the President of Sierra Leone, who appointed me and under whom I served as the Deputy Minister of Defence and National Coordinator of the Civil Defence Force (CDF/SL), has already testified before the Commission. As my solicitor, I am applying through you, and requesting you as a matter of urgency, to please inform the necessary parties of my willingness to appear and testify before the TRC without any further delay."*

8. Ogora, "The Rights of Victims," 15.

9. Irin News, "Uganda."

10. Ogora, "The Rights of Victims," 15. At the time, Ogora worked for the Justice and Reconciliation Project based in Gulu, Northern Uganda. For more information on the organisation's current programs, visit http://justiceandreconciliation.com (accessed May 22, 2016).

11. In addition to the Justice and Reconciliation Project, see also the Refugee Law Project, which has done outstanding work in this area. For more information on this work, visit http://www.refugeelawproject.org/ (accessed May 22, 2016).

12. Philpott, *Just and Unjust Peace*, 79.

13. See Philpott, *Just and Unjust Peace*, 111.

14. Maddison, *Conflict Transformation and Reconciliation*, 78.

15. Daly and Sarkin, *Reconciliation in Divided Societies*, 205; as quoted by Maddison, *Conflict and Transformation*, 78.

16. Arendt, *Eichmann in Jerusalem*, 1977. Arendt's well-known book, with its famously provocative subtitle (*A Report on the Banality of Evil*), explored German and Jewish relations in the aftermath of the Holocaust.

17. Arendt, *Eichmann in Jerusalem*, 268, 269.

18. Schaap, *Political Reconciliation*, 2.

19. Arendt, *Men in Dark Times*, 15.

20. Schaap, *Political Reconciliation*, 2 (emphasis added).

21. Arendt, *Men in Dark Times*, 4–5.

22. Schaap, *Political Reconciliation*, 4.

23. Maddison, *Conflict Transformation and Reconciliation*, 79. To develop this argument, Maddison draws on Wingenbach and Chantal Mouffe, who wrote that the aim is a pluralism "that valorizes diversity and dissensus" and recognizes the contests between diverse communities as "the very condition of possibility for a striving democratic life." Quoted from Wingenbach, *Institutionalising Agonistic Democracy*, 63; and Mouffe, "Democracy as Agonistic Pluralism," 44.

24. Schaap, *Political Reconciliation*, 80.

25. Maddison, *Conflict Transformation and Reconciliation*, 97.

26. Schaap, *Political Reconciliation*, 35.

27. Connolly, *Identity/Difference*, x.
28. Maddison, *Conflict Transformation and Reconciliation*, 78.
29. Schaap, *Political Reconciliation*, 61.
30. Arendt, *Human Condition*, 201.
31. Schaap, *Political Reconciliation*, 62.
32. Eisikovits, *Sympathizing with the Enemy*, 56.
33. Ibid., Eisikovits also recognizes three other theories of reconciliation, namely: Trudy Govier's notion of *reconciliation as trust* in the mold of social restoration that is developed through forgiveness and acknowledgment; Susan Dwyer's account of *reconciliation as weaving back together the narratives* of our lives after the traumatic disruption caused by mass violence; and Andrew Schaap's notion of *agonist reconciliation* (ibid, 25ff).
34. Schaap, *Political Reconciliation*, 92.
35. Chapman, "Truth Commissions as Instruments of Forgiveness and Reconciliation," 265, 273.
36. Schaap, *Political Reconciliation*, 101
37. Maddison, *Conflict Transformation and Reconciliation*, 116.
38. Schaap, *Political Reconciliation*, 87.
39. The never-again moment of reconciliation is its "world-delimiting" dimension, and its promise of a new beginning together, its "world-rupturing" dimension; political reconciliation consists of a "fragile holding together of the world-delimiting and world-rupturing moments of politics," *Political Reconciliation*, 87.
40. What animates political reconciliation is "not the anticipation of community as an absolute end according to which we ought to regulate our present relations. Rather it is the will that the present be remembered by a possible future community as the moment in which it originated," *Political Reconciliation*, 90.
41. Schaap, *Political Reconciliation*, 115.
42. Maddison, *Conflict Transformation and Reconciliation*, 227, 228.
43. Barnard-Naudé, "For Justice and Reconciliation to Come," 200.
44. Schaap, *Political Reconciliation*, 131.
45. Verdeja, *Unchopping a Tree*, 157.
46. Schaap, *Political Reconciliation*, 61, 77.
47. Ibid., 74.
48. Daly and Sarkin, *Reconciliation in Divided Societies*, 228–9.
49. Schaap, *Political Reconciliation*, 77.
50. I discuss Mamdani's critique in Chapter 5. Robert Meister's view is found in his book *After Evil: A Politics of Human Rights*.

Chapter 8

1. Eisikovits, *Sympathizing with the Enemy*, 23.
2. See Villa-Vicencio, *Walk with Us and Listen*, 152–5.
3. Schaap, *Political Reconciliation*, 2.
4. Tutu, *No Future without Forgiveness*, 31.
5. Gade, "What Is Ubuntu?" 484.
6. Nabudere, *Ubuntu Philosophy*.
7. The fundamental relationality of identity, rather than its self-containment, is ubuntu's point of departure. Ubuntu can thus be read as a critical theory of identity, challenging core liberal ideas in this regard.
8. Levinas works out this argument in *Totality and Infinity* and goes into greater detail in *Otherwise than Being*.
9. John Paul Lederach, *Building Peace*, 37ff. For a retrospective discussion of his intellectual journey with respect to developing the notion of "infrastructures of peace," see John Paul Lederach, "The Origins and Evolution of Infrastructures of Peace: A Personal Reflection," *Journal of Peacebuilding & Development* 7, no. 3 (2012): 8–13, available at https://undp. unteamworks.org/node/417406 (accessed August 15, 2015).
10. Lederach, "The Origins and Evolution of Infrastructures of Peace," 2.
11. Ibid., 4.

12. Ahmad Mouath Al-Khatib Al-Hasani, 2014.

13. Ebrahim Rasool, 2015, 86.

14. Clark, *The Gacaca Courts*.

15. The full text of Ahmadinejad's speech is available at *Fourwinds10.com*, uploaded September 24, 2012, http://www.fourwinds10.net/siterun_data/government/united_nations/news.php?q=1348577127 (accessed May 17, 2013).

16. Shmulovich, "Israel's UN Envoy Walks Out."

17. The neighboring countries I include here are the Democratic Republic of Congo, Burundi, Rwanda, Uganda, and, a little further afield, South Sudan and Tanzania.

18. UN Resolution 1012 of 28 August 1995, http://www.usip.org/library/tc/doc/charters/coi_burundi1995.html (accessed May 23, 2006).

19. UN International Commission of Inquiry Concerning Burundi: *Final Report*, par. 213. Members of the commission included Abdelali El Moumni of Morocco, Mehmet Güney of Turkey, Luis Herrera Marcano of Venezuela, Michel Maurice of Canada, and Edilbert Razafindralambo of Madagascar.

20. For example, gunfire erupted around the premises of its Bujumbura offices on December 6, 1995, forcing the commission to withdraw into a hotel to continue its work.

21. UN International Commission of Inquiry Concerning Burundi: *Final Report*, par. 490–1.

22. For an authoritative account of international benchmarks on what constitutes a just transition, see Van Boven, *United Nations Basic Principles*.

23. See Daly and Sarkin, who characterize reconciliation processes that lack fairness and credibility as "zero-sum games": "if she wins, then I am going to be losing, and the only way to ensure that I don't lose is to prevent her from winning," *Reconciliation in Divided Societies*, 254–5.

24. Note that I use the concept "inclusive" rather than "national" to avoid the well-trodden debates about nationalism and nation-building, and also to emphasize the inclusion of citizens outside the political elites, as well as interest groups across political divides. On comprehensive approaches to sustainable reconciliation that cut across both horizontal and vertical divisions, see Lederach, *Building Peace*.

25. This is often the case in the truth-seeking exercises that have become a staple of transitional justice processes the world over. Truth-seeking exercises are typically designed to add credibility to reconciliation processes through establishing a measure of accountability for those involved in perpetrating intense political violence. They correctly prioritize justice for victim communities but, in so doing, they risk alienating perpetrator groups, and thereby potentially limit political inclusivity. For a discussion of this tension in the work of the South African TRC, see Villa-Vicencio, *Walk with Us and Listen*, 95, as well as Villa-Vicencio and Doxtader, *Pieces of the Puzzle*, 94.

26. Little states that "if reconciliation is understood as part of a process of transformation whereby social relations change over time in negative as well as positive ways, then disappointment is a crucial dimension of the continued pursuit of conflict transformation."

27. This is why some political analysts accuse reconciliation of promising what it cannot deliver. See, for example, Weinstein, "The Myth of Closure."

28. For her theory on capabilities, Murphy relies largely on Amartya Sen's well-known work in this regard. See Sen, *Development as Freedom*.

29. Arendt, *Men in Dark Times*.

30. For a theological discussion of reconciliation as "radical", see Boesak and DeYoung, *Radical Reconciliation*.

31. Hofmeyr, *Africa Rising?*

32. Ibid.

33. Tim Murithi and Fanie du Toit, "Reconciliation as Framework for Realising Sustainable Peace," A United Nations Development Plan Concept Report, Addis Ababa.

34. UN Peacebuilding Support Office, NOREF, and KAIPTC, *Building Just Societies: Reconciliation in Transitional Settings*, 14.

35. Freud, "Remembering, Repeating and Working-Through,", 145ff.

36. Ricoeur, "Can Forgiveness Heal?" 31ff.; Ricoeur, *Memory, History, Forgetting*, 505–6. See also: Duffy, *Ricoeur's Pedagogy of Pardon*.

37. Boesak and DeYoung, *Radical Reconciliation*, 133.

38. Ricoeur, *Memory, History, Forgetting*, 505–6.

39. See Nietzsche, *Untimely Meditations*. Nietzsche's distinctions between "antiquarian," "monumental," and "critical" history delineate different "uses of the past" but do not specifically
focus on dealing with past atrocities. However, his distinctions can readily be adapted to the
concerns of transitional justice. For one attempt at this kind of adaptation, see André du Toit,
"The Truth and Reconciliation Commission." Du Toit argues that to be overcome, the past
must be remembered in appropriate ways (and this is even more so where political atrocities
have occurred). He suggests that whereas "antiquarian" history reveres and preserves the past
for its own sake, "monumental" approaches are typically concerned with "celebrating the
greatness and glory of the past," while "critical" history is concerned with "accountability for
the past." Of these, "critical" history is most suited to general conceptions of transitional justice, at least to the extent that this is shaped by human rights discourses. However, Nietzsche
claimed that "monumental history" also needs a place if the past is to be overcome. This
applies, for example, to the need to reconcile a post-conflict society through appropriate symbolism and memorialization, and by convincing opposing groups to accept a common new
symbolic order rooted in a celebrated past. Nietzsche described this as "an attempt to give
oneself, as it were a posteriori, a past in which one would like to originate, in opposition to
that in which one did originate—always a dangerous attempt because it is so hard to know the
limit to denial of the past" (quoted in André du Toit, 4).

40. Shriver, *An Ethic for Enemies*, 119.

41. Ricoeur, "Can Forgiveness Heal?" 32.

42. Susan Dwyer, "Reconciliation for Realists," 110.

43. Caitlin Spring, one of the initial members of the White Privilege Project, writes: "The Rhodes
Must Fall movement spurred some of the most violent online racism I have ever seen, ironically providing quintessential examples for the existence of a transformative movement in
South African universities. However, amidst all the hate and aggression, emphatic ignorance
was also evident. It became unfair for black students to continually answer the same questions
at discussions and in online forums. For example, the existence of institutional racism in
South African universities was consistently denied by some white students, who felt that,
after democratization, equal opportunities existed in South Africa for people of all races. To
attempt to counter this ignorance, The White Privilege Project, as it was then called, emerged.
The idea was for white students to educate each other, and grapple together, on issues of white
privilege, white responsibility and white identity in contemporary South Africa. While defining these terms and conscientising each other and ourselves, it was hoped that the burden
of educating white students and alleviating some racism would be placed on white students
who felt the moral responsibility." Caitlin Spring, 2015.

44. The standard work on denial in the transitional-justice literature is Stanley Cohen's *States of
Denial: Knowing about Atrocities and Suffering*. Cohen provides a psychologically oriented
analysis rather than one oriented to the politics of history and memory, like those of Nietzsche
and Ricoeur.

45. A similar attempt to arrive at "an understanding of the many blind spots in Rwanda's official memory" is offered by Lemarchand, who used Ricoeur's distinction between "thwarted
memory," "manipulated memory," and "enforced memory"; see Lemarchand, "The Politics of
Memory."

46. Mamdani, *When Victims Become Killers*, 267.

47. Nietzsche, *Untimely Meditations*, 64, 102, 109.

48. Ricoeur, "Can Forgiveness Heal?" 33.

49. See Beike and Wirth-Beaumont, "Psychological Closure."

50. Ricoeur, "Can Forgiveness Heal?" 33.

51. Ibid.

52. Ibid.

53. Ibid., 36.

Conclusion

1. For some examples of such educational material, see http://www.ijr.org.za/publications.php. Education, and specifically history education, is, however, essential to the agenda of healing after mass political violence. Of course, the dangers of erecting new forms of hegemonic philosophies that exclude a new set of victims, and thereby create the conditions for the emergence of new conflict down the line, loom large when a nation seeks to foster some form of shared appreciation of a difficult past. However, social transformation implies a measure of accounting from those who perpetrated the violence as to why, how, and to what effect violence was perpetrated, and why victims can expect it not to recur. For a discussion on how this has played out in post-apartheid South Africa, see Du Toit, "Teaching History as if People mattered." For a broader discussion, see Elizabeth Cole, *Teaching the Violent Past*.

2. One civic attempt to inaugurate such a discussion comprised a series of two national conferences hosted by the IJR in April 2006 and October 2008 to mark ten years since the TRC's first victim hearings, as well as the handing of the final report to President Mandela, respectively. The first was entitled "The TRC Ten Years On," whereas the second conference, entitled "Revisiting the TRC Recommendations," focused explicitly on the measure to which the report had been followed up mainly by government, but also the private sector. The largely disappointing findings were broadly published in the media but soon thereafter dropped off the radar of public debate. In the absence of public pressure, ongoing attempts by civics, notably through the South African Coalition for Transitional Justice, which includes the victim support group Khulumani, have largely fallen on deaf ears, forcing civics into a more adversarial stance including litigation on issues related both to government's failure to prosecute those the TRC recommended that it did, as well as its failure to pay adequate and timeous reparations, again failing to follow TRC recommendations. Unfortunately legal standoffs between government and the civics seemed, for the time being, to have stalled progress on both prosecutions and reparations.

3. Langa, "Transcending a Century of Injustice," 14ff. Langa made these remarks in 2000 as the keynote speaker at the launch of the IJR in Cape Town, South Africa. The gathering reflected on the recently concluded TRC process and discussed ways to further justice and reconciliation in South Africa.

4. Friedman, "SA Should Try Reconciliation."

5. Wale, "Confronting Exclusion," 26ff.

6. Langa, "Transcending a Century of Injustice."

BIBLIOGRAPHY

Adam, Heribert, and Kogila Moodley. *Imagined Liberation: Xenophobia, Citizenship, and Identity in South Africa, Germany, and Canada*. Stellenbosch: Sun Media, 2013.

———. *The Negotiated Revolution: Society and Politics in Post-Apartheid South Africa.* Johannesburg: Jonathan Ball, 1993.

———. *Seeking Mandela: Peace-Making between Israelis and Palestinians*. Johannesburg and Philadelphia: Temple University Press and Wits University Press, 2005.

Adriaan, Bsson, and Pieter, du Toit. *Enemy of the People—How Jacob Zuma stole South Africa and How the People Fought Back*. Johannesburg and Cape Town: Jonathan Ball Publishers, 2017.

Akande, Laolu. "How Nigeria, Others Averted AU's Withdrawal from ICC." *South African Foreign Policy Initiative News*, October 16, 2013. Accessed November 30, 2014. http://www.safpi. org/news/article/2013/how-nigeria-others-averted-au-s-withdrawal-icc.

Alexander, Karin, Dianne Batchelor, Alex Durand, and Tyrone Savage, "Truth Commissions and Transitional Justice: Update on a Select Bibliography on the South African Truth and Reconciliation Commission Debate." *Journal of Law and Religion* 20, no. 2 (2005): 525–65.

Alexander, Neville. *An Ordinary Country: Issues in the Transition from Apartheid to Democracy in South Africa*. Pietermaritzburg: University of Natal Press, 2002.

ANC (African National Congress). *The Africans' Claims in South Africa*. 1943. Accessed October 2014. http://www.anc.org.za/show.php?id=4474&t.

———. "We Have a Good Story to Tell." *ANC Bulletin* (July 2013). Accessed December 18, 2014. http://www.anc.org.za/docs/necbul/2013/julyw.pdf.

Andrieu, Kora. "Political Liberalism after Mass Violence: John Rawls and a 'Theory' of Transitional Justice." In *Transitional Justice Theories*, edited by Susanne Buckley-Zistel, Teresa Coloma-Beck, Christian Braun, and Friederike Mieth, 85–104. London: Routledge, 2014.

Arendt, Hannah. *Eichmann in Jerusalem: A Report on the Banality of Evil*. New York: Penguin Books, 1977.

———. *The Human Condition*. Chicago: University of Chicago Press, 1989 (first published 1958).

———. *Men in Dark Times*. New York: Harcourt Brace, 1968.

Arthur, Paige. "How 'Transitions' Reshaped Human Rights: A Conceptual History of Transitional Justice." *Human Rights Quarterly* 31, no. 2 (May 2009): 321–67.

Asmal, Kader. "Victims, Survivors, and Citizens: Human Rights, Reparations, and Reconciliation." Inaugural Lecture. Cape Town: University of the Western Cape, 1992.

Asmal, Kader, with David Chidester and Cassius Lubisi. *Legacy of Freedom: The ANC's Human Rights Tradition*. Cape Town: Jonathan Ball, 2005.

Backer, David. "Watching a Bargain Unravel? A Panel Study of Victims' Attitudes about Transitional Justice in Cape Town, South Africa." *International Journal of Transitional Justice* 4, no. 3 (2010): 443–56.

Ban Ki-moon. "An Age of Accountability." UN Secretary-General's Address to the Review Conference on the International Criminal Court, Kampala, Uganda, May 31, 2010. http://www.un.org/sg/statements/?nid=4585.

———. *The Rule of Law and Transitional Justice in Conflict and Post-Conflict Societies*. Report of the UN Secretary General to the Security Council, S/2011/634, October 12, 2011. Accessed December 19, 2012. http://www.unrol.org/files/S_2011_634EN.pdf.

Barnard-Naudé, Jaco. "For Justice and Reconciliation to Come: The TRC Archive, Big Business, and the Demand for Material Reparations." In *Justice and Reconciliation in Post-Apartheid South Africa*, edited by F. du Bois and A. du Bois-Pedain, 172–205. New York: Cambridge University Press, 2008.

Barnard-Naude, Jaco. "'Forgiveness as Happenstance': A Response to the Annual Reconciliation Lecture by Martha Minow Entitled 'Forgiveness, Law, and Justice'. Delivered on 24 February 2014, University of the Free State, Bloemfontein, South Africa.

Beike, Denise R., and Erin T. Wirth-Beaumont. "Psychological Closure as a Memory Phenomenon." *Memory* 13, no. 6 (2005): 574–93.

Bell, Christine. "Transitional Justice, Interdisciplinarity, and the State of the 'Field' or 'Non-Field'." *International Journal of Transitional Justice* 3, no. 1 (2009): 5–28.

Bishara, Marwan. "Sobering Up after Israeli Elections: The Main Challenges Facing Israel Are Historical Not Political." *Al Jazeera*, March 16, 2015. Accessed March 1, 2015. http://www.aljazeera.com/indepth/opinion/2015/03/sobering-israeli-elections-150316071219971.html;   http://www.aljazeera.com/indepth/opinion/2015/03/sobering-israeli-elections-150316.

Bloomfield, David, Teresa Barnes, and Luc Huyse. *Reconciliation after Violent Conflict: A Handbook.* Stockholm: IDEA International, 2003.

Boesak, Allan Aubrey, and Curtiss Paul DeYoung. *Radical Reconciliation. Beyond Political Pietism and Christian Quietism.* New York: Orbis Books, 2012.

Bonino, Jose Miguez. *Doing Theology in a Revolutionary Situation.* Philadelphia: Fortress Press, 1983.

Boraine, Alex. *A Country Unmasked: Inside South Africa's Truth and Reconciliation Commission.* Oxford: Oxford University Press, 2000.

———. *What's Gone Wrong? On the Brink of a Failed State.* Cape Town: Jonathan Ball, 2014.

Botha, Barry. *The Afrikaner's Emancipation: Freeing South Africans from Their Apartheid Mindset.* Bloomington: iUniverse, 2008.

Brody, Reed. "Justice: The First Casualty of Truth?" *The Nation*, April 4, 2001. Accessed February 27, 2013. http://www.thenation.com/article/justice-first-casualty-truth#.

Brouneus, Karin. "Rethinking Reconciliation: Concepts, Methods, and an Empirical Study of Truth Telling and Psychological Health in Rwanda." DPhil thesis, Uppsala University, 2008.

Calland, Richard. *The Zuma Years: South Africa's Changing Face of Power.* Cape Town: Zebra, 2013.

Callinicos, Luli. *The World That Made Mandela.* Johannesburg: STE, 2000.

Carlson, Meredith, and Jane E. Dee. "'My Hands Are Clean,' De Klerk Says at Central." *Hartford Courant*, April 24, 1997. Accessed February 27, 2014. http://articles.courant.com/1997-04-24/news/9704240226_1_klerk-african-national-congress-party-apartheid.

Chapman, A. R. "Truth Commissions as Instruments of Forgiveness and Reconciliation." In *Forgiveness and Reconciliation: Religion, Public Policy, and Conflict Transformation*, edited by R. G. Helmick and R. L. Petersen, 247–67. Conshohocken, PA: Templeton Foundation Press, 2002.

Clark, Phil. *The Gacaca Courts and Post-Genocide Justice and Reconciliation in Rwanda: Justice without Lawyers.* Cambridge: Cambridge University Press, 2010.

Cohen, Stanley. *States of Denial: Knowing about Atrocities and Suffering.* Oxford: Polity Press, 2001.

Cole, Elizabeth A. *Teaching the Violent Past: History Education and Reconciliation.* Lanham, MD: Rowman and Littlefield, 2007.

Collin Marks, Susan. *Watching the Wind: Conflict Resolution during South Africa's Transition to Democracy.* Washington, DC: United States Institute of Peace Press, 2000.

Connolly, W. E. *Identity/Difference: Democratic Negotiations of Political Paradox.* Minneapolis: University of Minnesota Press, 1991.

Cooper, D. (2005) 'Escaping Consultative Business Movement. "A Submission to the Truth and Reconciliation Commission." In *The Consultative Business Movement, 1988–1994.* Johannesburg: Unpublished, 1997.

Corder, Hugh. *Human Rights in Practice, 1994–2005: Constitutional Rights.* Turning Points in Human Rights Series. Cape Town: IJR, 2009.

Crocker, David. "Retribution and Reconciliation." *Philosophy and Public Policy* 20, no. 1 (2000): 1–6.

Crocker, David. "Truth Commissions, Transitional Justice, and Civil Society." In *Truth versus Justice: The Morality of Truth Commissions,* edited by Robert Rotberg and Dennis Thompson, 99–121. Princeton: Princeton University Press, 2000.

Daly, Erin, and Jeremy Sarkin. *Reconciliation in Divided Societies: Finding Common Ground.* Philadelphia: University of Pennsylvania Press, 2007.

De Greiff, Pablo. "The Role of Apologies in National Reconciliation Processes: On Making Trustworthy Institutions Trusted." In *In the Age of Apology,* edited by Mark Gibney, Rhoda E. Howard Hassmann, Jean-Marc Colcaud, and Niklaus Steiner, 120–36. Philadelphia: University of Pennsylvania Press, 2008.

———. "Transitional Justice: A Catalyst for Peace and Reconciliation." Paper presented at the Second International Conference on Transitional Justice in Zimbabwe, Johannesburg, October 9–11, 2013. Accessed May 31, 2015. http://www.ijr.org.za/publications/pdfs/ICTJ-II-Conference-Report.pdf.

De Klerk, F. W. "CODESA: Opening Statement by State President F. W. de Klerk," December 20, 1991. Accessed September 3, 2013. http://www.anc.org.za/show.php?id=3976.

———. *The Last Trek, A New Beginning: The Autobiography.* London: Macmillan, 1998.

Derrida, Jacques. "On Forgiveness." In *On Cosmopolitanism and Forgiveness,* translated by Mark Dooley and Michael Hughes. New York: Routledge, 2001.

Derrida, Jacques, and Elisabeth Roudinesco. *For What Tomorrow: A Dialogue.* Edited by Jeff Fort. Stanford: Stanford University Press, 2004.

Doxtader, Erik. "A Critique of Law's Violence Yet (Never) to Come: United Nations' Transitional Justice Policy and the (Fore)Closure of Reconciliation." In *Theorizing Post-Conflict Reconciliation: Agonism, Restitution, and Repair,* edited by Alexander Hirsch, 27–64. Oxford: Routledge, 2012.

———. "Easy to Forget and Never (Again) Hard to Remember? History, Memory and the 'Publicity' of Amnesty." In *The Provocations of Amnesty: Memory Justice and Impunity,* edited by Charles Villa-Vicencio and Erik Doxtader, 121–55. Cape Town: IJR, 2003.

———. "The Faith and Struggle of Beginning (with) Words: On the Turn Between Reconciliation and Recognition." *Philosophy and Rhetoric* 40, no. 1 (2007): 119–46.

———. "Is It Reconciliation If We Say It Is? Discerning the Rhetorical Problem in the South African Transition." Unpublished paper, 2002.

———. "The Potential of Reconciliation's Beginning: A Reply." *Rhetoric and Public Affairs* 7, no. 3 (2004): 378–90.

Doxtader, Erik. *With Faith in the Works of Words: The Beginnings of Reconciliation in South Africa.* Cape Town: David Philip, 2009.

Doxtader, Erik, and Philippe Joseph Salazar. *Truth and Reconciliation in South Africa: The Fundamental Documents.* Cape Town: New Africa, 2007.

Du Bois-Pedain, Antje. "Communicating Criminal and Political Responsibility in the TRC." In *Justice and Reconciliation in Post-Apartheid South Africa,* edited by Francois du Bois and Antje du Bois-Pedain. Cambridge: Cambridge University Press, 2008.

———. *Transitional Amnesty in South Africa.* Cambridge: Cambridge University Press, 2007.

Duffy, Maria. *Paul Ricoeur's Pedagogy of Pardon: A Narrative Theory of Memory and Forgetting.* New York: Bloomsbury Academic, 2012.

Du Preez, Max. *Pale Native: Memories of a Renegade Reporter.* Cape Town: Zebra, 2003.

————. *A Rumour of Spring: South Africa after 20 Years of Democracy.* Cape Town: Zebra, 2013.

Du Preez, Peter. "The Presidents, the Truth and Reconciliation Commission, and the End of Machiavellian Politics." In *Socio-Political and Psychological Perspectives on South Africa*, edited by Christopher R. Stones. New York: Nova Science, 2001.

Du Toit, André. "The Truth and Reconciliation Commission as Contemporary History." In *Toward New Histories for South Africa: On the Place of the Past in Our Present*, edited by Shamil Jeppie. Cape Town: Juta, 2004.

Du Toit, Fanie. "A Broken Promise? Evaluating South Africa's Reconciliation Process Twenty Years On." International Politics Science Review, March 2017.

————. "Introduction." In *Negotiation, Transition, and Freedom: Turning Points in History.* Vol. 6. Cape Town: IJR, 2004.

————. "Teaching the Past as if People Mattered: History Education as Peace Education in Post-Apartheid South Africa." In *Peace Education in Fragile African Contexts: What's Going to Make a Difference? Thinking about Effectiveness*, edited by Sylvester Bongani Maphosa and Alphonse Keasley. Pretoria: Africa Institute of South Africa, 2016.

Du Toit, Fanie, and Erik Doxtader, eds. *In the Balance: South Africans Debate Reconciliation.* Johannesburg: Jacana, 2011.

Du Toit, Louise H. "Feminism and the Ethics of Reconciliation." In *Law and the Politics of Reconciliation*, edited by Scott Veitch. Edinburgh Centre for Law and Society Series. Aldershot: Ashgate, 2007.

Dwyer, Susan. "Reconciliation for Realists." In *Dilemmas of Reconciliation: Cases and Concepts*, edited by Carol A. L. Prager and Trudy Govier, 91–110. Waterloo, ON: Wilfrid Laurier University Press, 2003.

Dyzenhaus, David. *Judging the Judges, Judging Ourselves: Truth, Reconciliation, and the Apartheid Legal Order.* Oxford: Hart, 1998.

Ebrahim, Hassen, and Laurel E. Miller. "Creating the Birth Certificate of a New South Africa: Constitution Making after Apartheid." In *Framing the State in Times of Transition: Case Studies in Constitution Making*, edited by Lauren E. Miller. Washington, DC: USIP, 2010

Eisikovits, Nir. *Sympathizing with the Enemy: Reconciliation, Transitional Justice, Negotiation.* Dordrecht: Martinus Nijhoff, 2010.

Elster, Jon. *Closing the Books: Transitional Justice in Historical Perspective.* New York: Cambridge University Press, 2004.

Esterhuyse, Willie. *Endgame: Secret Talks and the End of Apartheid.* Cape Town: Tafelberg, 2012.

Fanon, Frantz. *The Wretched of the Earth.* New York: Grove Press, 1963.

Farouk, Fazila. "Whites Must Make Sacrifices to Uplift SA's Poor." *Independent Online*, August 14, 2014. Accessed October 23, 2014. http://www.iol.co.za/business/markets/whites-must-make-sacrifices-to-uplift-sa-s-poor-1.1561858.

FCI (Federated Chamber of Industries). "Business Charter of Social, Economic, and Political Rights." First published 1986, reprinted in *Innes Labour Brief* 1, no. 4 (1990): 68–74.

Frankel, Philip. *Soldiers in a Storm.* Johannesburg: Westview Press, 2000.

Frazer, Jendai. "ICC Has Fallen from High Ideals of Global Justice, Accountability." *Daily Nation*, March 16, 2013. Accessed November 30, 2014. http://www.cmu.edu/cipi/news-events/pdfs/130316_Daily-Nation_ICC-has-fallen-from-high-ideals-of-global-justice-accountability.pdf.

Freeman, Mark. *Necessary Evils: Amnesties and the Search for Justice.* Cambridge: Cambridge University Press, 2009.

Freud, Sigmund. *Civilization, Society, and Religion.* Penguin's Freud Library, Vol. 12. London: Penguin. 1991.

————. "Remembering, Repeating, and Working-Through (Further Recommendations in the Technique of Psycho-Analysis II)." Vol. 12 in *The Standard Edition of the Complete Psychological Works of Sigmund Freud, 1953–1974.* London, 1914.

Friedman, Steven. "SA Should Try Reconciliation: For Real This Time." *Business Day*, July 30, 2014. Accessed May 18, 2015. http://www.bdlive.co.za/opinion/columnists/2014/07/30/sa-should-try-reconciliation--for-real-this-time.

Friedman, Steven, and Doreen Atkinson. *The Small Miracle: South Africa's Negotiated Settlement.* Johannesburg: Ravan, 1994.

Fuller, Lon. *Morality of Law.* Rev. ed. New Haven: Yale University Press, 1969.

Gade, Christian. "What Is Ubuntu? Different Interpretations amongst South Africans of African Descent." *South African Journal of Philosophy* 31, no. 3 (2012) 484–503.

Galtung, Johan. "Cultural Violence." *Journal of Peace Research* 27, no. 3 (1990): 291–305.

Garton Ash, Timothy. "True Confessions (The Truth Commission in South Africa)." *New York Review of Books,* 44 (July 17, 1997): 37–8.

Gastrow, Peter. *Bargaining for Peace: South Africa and the National Peace Accord.* Washington, DC: USIP Press, 1995.

Gibson, James, and Helen Macdonald. *Truth Yes, Reconciliation Maybe: South Africans Judge the Truth and Reconciliation Process.* Cape Town: IJR, 2001.

Gibson, James L. "Apartheid's Long Shadow: How Racial Divides Distort South Africa's Democracy." *Foreign Affairs* (2015). Accessed July 1, 2015. https//www.foreignaffairs.com/articles/south-africa/2015-02-10/apartheid-s-long-shadow.

Gibson, James L. *Overcoming Apartheid: Can Truth Reconcile a Divided Nation?* Cape Town: HSRC Press, 2004.

Giliomee, Hermann. *The Afrikaners: Biography of a People.* Reconsiderations in Southern African History. Cape Town: Tafelberg, 2003.

Gish, Stephan. *Desmond Tutu: A Biography.* Westport, CT: Greenwood Press, 2004.

Gobodo-Madikizela, Pumla. *A Human Being Died That Night: A South African Story of Forgiveness.* Cape Town: David Philip, 2003.

———. "Radical Forgiveness: Transforming Traumatic Memory beyond Hannah Arendt." In *Justice and Reconciliation in Post-Apartheid South Africa,* edited by François du Bois and Antje du Bois-Pedain. Cambridge: Cambridge University Press, 2009.

Goldmann, Matthias. "Sierra Leone: African Solutions to African Problems?" In *Max Planck Yearbook of United Nations Law,* Vol. 9, edited by Armin von Bogdandy and Rüdiger Wolfrum. Leiden: Brill, 2005.

Graybill, Lyn. *Truth and Reconciliation in South Africa: Miracle or Model?* Boulder, CO: Lynne Rienner, 2002.

Gutmann, Amy, and Dennis Thompson. "The Moral Foundations of Truth Commissions." In *Truth v. Justice: The Morality of Truth Commissions,* edited by Robert I. Rotberg and Dennis Thompson. Princeton: Princeton University Press, 2000.

Habib, Adam. *South Africa's Suspended Revolution: Hopes and Prospects.* Johannesburg: Wits University Press, 2013.

Hall, Stuart. "The Question of Cultural Identity." In *Modernity: An Introduction to Modern Societies,* edited by Stuart Hall, David Held, Don Hubert, and Kenneth Thompson. Oxford: Blackwell, 1995.

Harris, Bronwyn. *Between a Rock and a Hard Place, Violence, Transition, and Democratisation: A Review of the Violence and Transition Project.* Cape Town: Centre for the Study of Violence and Reconciliation, 2006.

Hart, Vivian. *Democratic Constitution Making.* Special Report 107. USIP, 2003.

Hendricks, Fred. "Jettisoning Justice: The Case of Amnesty in South Africa." In *Gathering Voices: Perspectives on the Social Sciences in Southern Africa,* edited by Teresa Cruz María e Silva and Ari Sitas. Social Knowledge Series: Heritage, Challenges, Perspectives, Vol. 10. Madrid: International Sociology Association, 1996. Accessed March 3, 2014. http://www.isa-sociology.org/colmemb/national-associations/en/meetings/reports/   Southern%20Africa/Chapter%207.pdf.

Hirsch, Alexander Keller, ed. *Theorising Post-Conflict Reconciliation: Agonism, Restitution, and Repair.* Oxford: Routledge, 2012.

Hofmeyr, Jan. *Africa Rising? Popular Dissatisfaction with Economic Management despite a Decade of Growth.* Afrobarometer Policy Brief No 2. IJR, Cape Town. 2013.

Holkeboer, Mieke, and Charles Villa-Vicencio. "Rights and Reconciliation." In *Pieces of the Puzzle: Keywords on Reconciliation and Transitional Justice*, edited by Charles Villa-Vicencio and Erik Doxtader. Cape Town: IJR, 2004.

Huntington, Samuel P. *The Third Wave: Democratization in the Late Twentieth Century*. Norman: University of Oklahoma Press, 1991.

Huyse, Luc. "Justice after Transition: On the Choices Successor Elites Make in Dealing with the Past." *Law and Social Inquiry* 20 (1995): 51–78.

Huyse, Luc, ed. *Traditional Justice and Reconciliation after Violent Conflict: Learning from African Experiences*. Stockholm: IDEA International, 2008.

Ignatieff, Michael. "Articles of Faith." *Index on Censorship* 25, no. 5 (October 1996): 110–22.

IJR. *South African Reconciliation Barometer Survey 2014 Report: Reflecting on Reconciliation; Lessons from the Past, Prospects for the Future (SARB 2003–2013)*. Cape Town: IJR, 2014. Accessed April 2015. http://ijr.org.za/publications/pdfs/IJR%20SA%20Reconciliation%20Barometer%20Report%202014.pdf.

Irin News. "Uganda: ICC Indictments to Affect Northern Peace Efforts, Says Mediator." *Irin News*, October 10, 2005. Accessed September 8, 2014. http://www.irinnews.org/report/56654/uganda-icc-indictments-to-affect-northern-peace-efforts-says-mediator.

Jacques, Pauw. *The President's Keepers—Those Keeping Zuma in Power and out of Prison*. South Africa: Tafelberg, 2017.

Jaspers, Karl. *The Question of German Guilt*. Translated by E. B. Ashton. New York: Dial Press, 1947.

Jordan, Pallo. "Disdain for Liberals Is Not Because of Intolerance." *Business Day*, November 23, 2012. Accessed January 15, 2013. http://www.bdlive.co.za/opinion/columnists/2012/11/22/disdain-for-liberals-is-not-because-of-intolerance.

Kairos Theologians. *The Kairos Document*. Johannesburg: Scotaville, 1985. Accessed May 30, 2014. http://www.disa.ukzn.ac.za/index.php?option=com_displaydc&recordID=boo19860000.026.009.354.

Kalayjian, Ani, and Raymond F. Paloutzian, eds. *Forgiveness and Reconciliation*. New York: Springer, 2009.

Kalberg, Stephen. "The Perpetual and Tight Interweaving of Past and Present in Max Weber's Sociology." In *Max Weber Matters: Interweaving Past and Present*, edited by David Chalcraft, Fanon Howell, Marisol Lopez Menendez, and Hector Vera. London: Ashgate, 2008.

Kasrils, Ronnie. "How the ANC's Faustian Pact Sold Out South Africa's Poorest." *The Guardian*, June 24, 2013. Accessed October 20, 2014. http://www.theguardian.com/commentisfree/2013/jun/24/anc-faustian-pact-mandela-fatal-error.

Kelman, Herbert. "Reconciliation from a Social-Psychological Prespective." In *Social Psychology of Intergroup Reconciliation: From Violent Conflict to Peaceful Co-Existence*, edited by Nadler Arie, Thomas Malloy, and Jeffrey D. Fisher. New York: Oxford University Press, 2008.

Khayelitsha Commission. *Towards a Safer Khayelitsha: Report of the Commission of Inquiry into Allegations of Police Inefficiency and a Breakdown in Relations between SAPS and the Community of Khayelitsha*. Cape Town, August 2014. Accessed February 15, 2015. http://www.khayelitshacommission.org.za/.

Kritz, Neil. "Constitution-Making Process: Lessons For Iraq's Congressional Testimony, 25 June 2003." Accessed October 21, 2014. http://www.usip.org/publications/constitution-making-process-lessons-iraq.

———. "Where We Are and How We Got Here: An Overview of Developments in the Search for Justice and Reconciliation." In *The Legacy of Abuse: Confronting the Past, Facing the Future*, edited by Alice H. Henklin. New York: New York University School of Law, 2002.

Kritz, Neil, ed. *Transitional Justice: How Emerging Democracies Reckon with Former Regimes*. Vols. 1–3. Washington, DC: USIP, 1995.

Krog, Antjie. *Country of My Skull: Guilt, Sorrow, and the Limits of Forgiveness in the New South Africa*. New York: Broadway Books, 2000.

Kymlicka, Will. *Multicultural Citizenship: A Liberal Theory of Minority Rights*. Oxford: Oxford University Press, 2000.

Kymlicka, Will, and Bashir Bashir, eds. *The Politics of Reconciliation in Multicultural Societies.* Oxford: Oxford University Press, 2008.

Langa, Pius. "Transcending a Century of Injustice." In *Transcending a Century of Injustice,* edited by Charles Villa-Vicencio. Rondebosch: IJR, 2000.

Lapping, Brian. *Apartheid: A History.* London: Grafton. 1986.

Lederach, John Paul. *Building Peace: Sustainable Reconciliation in Divided Societies.* Washington, DC: ISIP, 1997.

——. *The Moral Imagination: The Art and Soul of Building Peace.* New York: Oxford University Press, 2005.

——. "The Origins and Evolution of Infrastructures of Peace: A Personal Reflection." *Journal of Peacebuilding & Development* 7, no. 3 (2012): 8–13. Accessed August 15, 2015. https://undp. unteamworks.org/node/417406.

Lederach, John Paul, and R. Scott Appleby, "Strategic Peacebuilding: An Overview." In *Strategies of Peace: Transforming Conflict in a Violent World,* edited by Daniel Philpott and Gerard F. Powers. Oxford: Oxford University Press, 2010.

Lehohla, Pali. *Poverty Trends in South Africa: An Examination of Absolute Poverty between 2006 and 2011.* Pretoria: Statistics South Africa, 2014. Accessed April 2, 2015. http://beta2.statssa. gov.za/publications/Report-03-10-06/Report-03-10-06March2014.pdf.

Lemarchand, René. "The Politics of Memory in Post-Genocide Rwanda." In *After Genocide: Transitional Justice, Post-Conflict Reconstruction, and Reconciliation in Rwanda and Beyond,* edited by Phil Clark and Zachary D. Kaufman. New York: Columbia University Press, 2009.

Levinas, Emmanuel. *Otherwise than Being.* Pittsburgh: Duquesne University Press, 1998.

——. *Totality and Infinity.* Dordrecht: Kluwer Academic, 1991.

Little, Adrian. "Fear, Hope, and Disappointment: The Politics of Reconciliation and the Dynamics of Conflict Transformation." Paper presented to the International Political Science Association Panel on Reconciliation, Transformation, Struggle, Montreal, July 24, 2014. http://paperroom.ipsa.org/papers/paper_28872.pdf.

Locke, John. "A Letter concerning Toleration." In *John Locke: A Letter concerning Toleration in Focus,* edited by J. Horton and S. Mendes. London: Routledge, 1991.

——. *Two Treatises of Government.* Vol. 2. [1689].

Lodge, Tom. *Mandela: A Critical Life.* Oxford: Oxford University Press, 2006.

——. *South African Politics since 1994.* Cape Town: David Philip, 1998.

Maddison, Sarah. *Conflict Transformation and Reconciliation: Multilevel Challenges in Deeply Divided Societies.* Routledge Studies in Peace and Conflict Resolution. London and New York: Taylor and Francis, 2016. Kindle.

Mamdani, Mahmood. "The Historic Significance of the Post-Apartheid Transition in South Africa." Mapungubwe Institute for Strategic Reflection's Annual Lecture, March 18, 2013.

——. "Reconciliation without Justice." *Southern African Review of Books* 46 (December 1996).

——. "When Does Reconciliation Turn into a Denial of Justice?" Sam Nolutshungu Memorial Lecture, Human Sciences Research Council, Pretoria, 1998.

——. *When Victims Become Killers: Colonialism, Nativism, and the Genocide in Rwanda.* Princeton: Princeton University Press, 2001.

Mandela, Nelson. "Address by Nelson Mandela at the European Parliament." Strasbourg, June 13, 1990. Accessed April 1, 2015. http://www.mandela.gov.za/mandela_speeches/1990/ 900613_europarl.htm.

——. "I Am Not Prepared to Sell the Birthright of the People to Be Free." Statement read by Zinzi Mandela at Jabulani Stadium, Soweto, February 10, 1985. Accessed February 27, 2014. http://db.nelsonmandela.org/speeches/pub_view.asp?pg=item&ItemID=NMS013.

——. *Long Walk to Freedom: The Autobiography of Nelson Mandela.* Boston: Back Bay, 1995.

——. "Notes Prepared by Nelson Mandela for His Meeting with P. W. Botha, 5 July 1989." Documents and Reports compiled by Padraig O'Malley, hosted online at the Nelson

Mandela Centre of Memory, http://www.nelsonmandela.org/omalley/index.php/site/q/03lv01538/04lv01600/05lv01640/06lv01642.htm.

———. "President's Budget Debate Opening Address by President Nelson Mandela: 100 Days Speech." Cape Town, August 18, 1994. Accessed March 8, 2014. http://www.africa.upenn.edu/Govern_Political/Mandel_100.html.

———. "Response to the Speech by the State President, F. W. de Klerk." First Session of CODESA, World Trade Centre, Kempton Park, December 20, 1991.

———. "Statement by President Nelson Mandela on Receiving the Truth and Reconciliation Commission Report." October 29, 1998. Accessed March 14, 2014. http://www.anc.org.za/show.php?id=3072.

———. *The Struggle Is My Life*. Bombay: Popular Prakashan, 1990.

Mani, Rama. "Editorial: Dilemmas of Expanding Transitional Justice, or Forging the Nexus between Transitional Justice and Development." *International Journal for Transitional Justice* 2, no. 3 (2008): 253–65.

Mashele, Prince, and Mzukisi Qobo. *The Fall of the ANC: What Next?* Johannesburg: Picador Africa, 2014.

Meister, Robert. *After Evil: A Politics of Human Rights*. New York: Columbia University Press, 2010.

Mendez, Juan E. "Accountability for Past Abuses." *Human Rights Quarterly* 19 (1997): 255.

Meredith, Martin. *Diamonds, Gold, and War: The British, the Boers, and the Making of South Africa*. London: Simon & Schuster, 2008.

Minow, Martha. *Between Vengeance and Forgiveness: Facing History after Genocide and Mass Violence*. Boston: Beacon Press, 1998.

Mint Press. "As African Governments Threaten to Leave the International Criminal Court, Civil Society and Human Rights Groups Push Back." *Mint Press*, October 14, 2013. http://www.mintpressnews.com/au-countries-threaten-to-leave-icc/170459/.

Mouffe, C. "Democracy as Agonistic Pluralism." In *Rewriting Democracy: Cultural Politics in Postmodernity*, edited by E. D. Ermath. Aldershot: Ashgate, 2007.

Msimang, Sisonke. "The End of the Rainbow Nation Myth." *New York Times*, April 12, 2015. http://www.nytimes.com/2015/04/13/opinion/the-end-of-the-rainbow-nation-myth.html?_r=0.

Mulhall, Stephen, and Adam Swift. *Liberals and Communitarians*. 2nd ed. Oxford: Blackwell, 1996.

Murithi, Tim. "The African Union and the International Criminal Court: An Embattled Relationship?" *IJR Policy Brief* 8 (2013). Accessed August 15, 2014. http://www.ijr.org.za/publications/pdfs/IJR%20Policy%20Brief%20No%208%20Tim%20Miruthi.pdf.

Murithi, Tim, and Fanie du Toit. "Reconciliation as Framework for Realising Sustainable Peace." A United Nations Development Plan Concept Document. Addis Ababa.

Murphy, Colleen. *A Moral Theory of Political Reconciliation*. Cambridge: Cambridge University Press, 2012.

Nabudere, Dani. *Ubuntu Philosophy: Memory and Reconciliation*. An Occasional Paper. Accessed April 13, 2014. http://repositories.lib.utexas.edu/bitstream/handle/2152/4521/3621.pdf?sequence=1.

Nan, Susan Allen, Zachariah Cherian Mampilly, and Andrea Bartoli, eds. *Peacemaking: From Practice to Theory*. Vol. 1. Santa Barbara, CA: Praeger, 2012.

Nietzsche, Friedrich. *Untimely Meditations*, edited by Daniel Breazeale. Cambridge: Cambridge University Press, 1999.

Nino, Carlos Santiago. *Radical Evil on Trial*. New York: Yale University Press, 1996.

Ndebele, Njabulo S. *The Cry of Winnie Mandela*. Claremont, South Africa: David Philip, 2003.

OAU (Organisation of African Unity). "Harare Declaration: Declaration of the OAU Ad-Hoc Committee on Southern Africa on the Question of South Africa." Harare, Zimbabwe, 21 August 1989.

O'Donnell, Guillermo, and Philippe C. Schmitter. *Transitions from Authoritarian Rule*. Vol. 4, *Tentative Conclusions about Uncertain Democracies*. Baltimore: Johns Hopkins University Press, 1986.

Offe, Claus. "Disqualification, Retribution, Restitution: Dilemmas of Justice in Post-Communist Societies." *Journal of Political Philosophy* 1 (1993): 17–44.

Ogora, Lino Owor. "The Rights of Victims in the Context of the ICC Interventions and Community Reconciliation Initiatives." In *The ICC and Community-Level Reconciliation, In-Country Perspectives: Regional Consultation Report 2011*, edited by Tim Murithi and Allan Ngari. Cape Town: IJR, 2011.

Okello, Moses Chrispus, Chris Dolan, Undine Whande, Nokukhanya Mncwabe, Levis Onegi, and Stephen Oola, eds. *Where Law Meets Reality: Forging African Transitional Justice*. Nairobi: Pambazuka Press, 2012.

O'Malley, Padraig. *Ramaphosa and Meyer in Belfast. The South African Experience: How the New South Africa Was Negotiated*. An Occasional Paper, John W. McConnack Institute of Public Affairs, University of Massachusetts, Boston, June 1996. Accessed April 2014. https://archive.org/stream/ramaphosameyerin00omal/ramaphosameyerin00omal_djvu.txt.

———. *Shades of Difference: Mac Maharaj and the Struggle for South Africa*. New York: Viking, 2007.

Ojielo, Ozonnia. "Breaking with the Past: Transitional Justice in Sierra Leone." In *From Civil Strife to Peace Building: Examining Private Sector Involvement in West-African Reconstruction*, edited by H. Besada, 97–128. Waterloo, ON: The Centre for International Governance Innovation and Wilfrid Laurier University Press, 2009.

Philpott, Daniel. *Just and Unjust Peace: An Ethic of Political Reconciliation*. Oxford: Oxford University Press, 2012.

Philpott, Daniel, ed. *The Politics of Past Evil: Religion, Reconciliation, and the Dilemmas of Transitional Justice*. Notre Dame: University of Notre Dame Press, 2006.

Potter, Nancy Nyquist. *Trauma, Truth, and Reconciliation: Healing Damaged Relationships*. Oxford: Oxford University Press, 2006.

The Presidency, Republic of South Africa. *Twenty-Year Review: South Africa 1994–2014*. Pretoria: Office of the President, 2014. Accessed December 18, 2014. http://www.20yearsoffreedom.org.za/20YearReview.pdf.

Ramphele, Mamphela. *Laying Ghosts to Rest: Dilemmas of Transformation in South Africa*. Cape Town: Tafelberg, 2008.

Rasool, Ebrahim. "The Pharaoh Returns. The Politics of 'Order' and the Muslim Yearning for Freedom." In *The African Renaissance and the Afro-Arab Spring. A Season of Rebirth?*, edited by Charles Villa-Vicencio, Erik Doxtader, and Ebrahim Moosa. Cape Town: University of Cape Town Press, 2015.

Ratner, Steven R., and Jason S. Abrams. *Accountability for Human Rights Atrocities in International Law: Beyond the Nuremberg Legacy*. Oxford: Oxford University Press, 2001.

Rawls, John. *Political Liberalism*. New York: Columbia University Press, 1993.

Remnick, David. "Vladimir Ilyich Lenin." *Time Magazine*, April 13, 1998, 43.

Ricoeur, Paul. "Can Forgiveness Heal?" In *The Foundation and Application of Moral Philosophy*, edited by Hendrik J. Opdebeeck. Leuven: Peeters, 2000.

Ricoeur, Paul. *Memory, History, Forgetting*. Translated by Kathleen Blamey and David Pellauer. Chicago: University of Chicago Press, 2004.

Rigby, Andrew. *Justice and Reconciliation: After the Violence*. Boulder, CO: Lynne Rienner, 2001.

Roca Report. "New Political Force Formed in South Africa" Blog post no. 53, May 1993. https://rocareport.wordpress.com/2014/05/28/19930553-htm/.

Ross, Fiona. *Bearing Witness: Women and the Truth and Reconciliation Commission in South Africa*. London: Pluto Press, 2003

Rubio-Marín, Ruth. *What Happened to the Women?: Gender and Reparations for Human Rights Violations*. New York: Social Science Research Council, 2006.

Sarkin, Jeremy. *Carrots and Sticks: The TRC and the South African Amnesty Process*. Belgium: Intersentia Press, 2004.

Saunders, Christopher. "Engaging the Other." In *Turning Points in Transition*. Cape Town: IJR, 2011.

———. "Of Treks, Transitions, and Transitology." *South African Historical Journal* 40 (May 1999): 247–56.

Schaap, Andrew. *Political Reconciliation*. London: Routledge, 2005.

Seegers, Annette. "Amnesty in South Africa: 1985 to 1994." Paper presented to the 20th Anniversary Conference, Centre for the Study of Violence and Reconciliation, Cape Town, 2009.

Shklar, Judith N. "The Liberalism of Fear." In *Liberalism and the Moral Life*, edited by N. Rosenblum. Cambridge, MA: Harvard University Press, 1989.

Shmulovich, Michal. "Israel's UN Envoy Walks Out of Ahmadinejad Speech on 'Rule of Law.'" *Times of Israel*, September 24, 2012. Accessed May 17, 2013. http://www.timesofisrael.com/prosor-walks-out-of-ahmadinejads-rule-of-law-speech-at-un/.

Shriver, Donald. *An Ethic for Enemies: Forgiveness in Politics*. Oxford: Oxford University Press, 1995.

Sierra Leone TRC. *Witness to Truth: Final Report of the Sierra Leone Truth and Reconcilliation Commission*. Accessed August 15, 2014. http://www.sierraleonetrc.org/index.php/view-the-final-report/download-table-of-contents/volume-two.

Soko, Mills, and Charles Villa-Vicencio. *Conversations in Transition: Leading South African Voices*. Cape Town: David Philip, 2012.

South African History Online. "How SA Emerged as a Democracy from the Crises of the 1990s." Grade 12 resource. Accessed April 14, 2014. http://www.sahistory.org.za/article/negotiations-toward-new-south-africa-grade-12-2.

———. "Record of Understanding Is Agreed to by the SA Government and the ANC." Accessed April 14, 2015. http://www.sahistory.org.za/dated-event/record-understanding-agreed-sa-government-and-anc.

Soyinka, Wole. *The Burden of Memory: The Muse of Forgiveness*. Oxford: Oxford University Press, 1999.

Sparks, Allister. *Beyond the Miracle: Inside the New South Africa*. Johannesburg: Jonathan Ball, 2003.

———. *The Mind of South Africa: The Story of the Rise and Fall of Apartheid*. London: Arrow, 1989.

———. *Tomorrow Is Another Country*. Johannesburg: Struik, 1995.

Stover, Eric, and Harvey Weinstein, eds. *My Neighbor, My Enemy: Justice and Community in the Aftermath of Mass Atrocity*. Cambridge: Cambridge University Press, 2004.

Taylor, Charles. *Hegel*. Cambridge: Cambridge University Press, 1975.

———. "Irreducibly Social Goods." In *Philosophical Arguments*. Boston: Harvard University Press, 1997.

———. "The Politics of Recognition." In *Multiculturalism*, edited by Amy Gutmann and Charles Taylor. Princeton: Princeton University Press, 1995.

Teitel, Ruti G. *Transitional Justice*. Oxford: Oxford University Press, 2002.

Terreblanche, Sampie. *A History of Inequality in South Africa, 1652–2002*. Durban: UKZN Press, 2002.

Thompson, Leonard. *A History of South Africa*. New Haven: Yale University Press, 2000.

TRC (South African Truth and Reconciliation Commission). *Summary of Amnesty Decisions*. January 11, 2000. Accessed February 3, 2014. http://www.justice.gov.za/Trc/amntrans/index.htm.

———. *Truth and Reconciliation Commission Final Report*, Vols. 1–5. Cape Town: Juta, 1998. Accessed February 3, 2014. http://www.justice.gov.za/trc/report/index.htm.

Tutu, Desmond. *No Future without Forgiveness*. New York: Doubleday, 1999.

UN International Commission of Inquiry Concerning Burundi. *Final Report*. Posted by USIP Library on January 13, 2004, received from Ambassador Thomas Ndikumana, Burundi's Ambassador to the United States, June 7, 2002. Accessed May 2015. http://www.usip.org/sites/default/files/file/resources/collections/commissions/Burundi-Report.pdf

USIP (United States Institute of Peace). "Social Reconstruction." Accessed February 5, 2013. http://www.usip.org/guiding-principles-stabilization-and-restoration-the-web-version/social-well-being/social-reconst.

Van Boven, Theo. *The United Nations Basic Principles and Guidelines on the Right to a Remedy and Reparation for Victims of Gross Violations of International Human Rights Law and Serious Violations of International Humanitarian Law*. United Nations Audiovisual Library of

International Law, 2010. Accessed March 2015. http://legal.un.org/avl/pdf/ha/ga_60-147/ga_60-147_e.pdf.

Van der Merwe, Hugo, Victoria Baxter, and Audrey Chapman, eds. *Assessing the Impact of Transitional Justice: Challenges for Empirical Research*. Washington, DC: USIP Press, 2009.

Van Roermund, Bert. "Rubbing Off and Rubbing On: The Grammar of Reconciliation." In *Lethe's Law: Justice, Law, and Ethics in Reconciliation*, edited by E. Christodoulis and S. Veitch. Oxford: Hart, 2001.

Van Vuuren, Hennie. *South Africa: Democracy, Corruption, and Conflict Management*. London: Legatum Institute, 2014. http://www.li.com/docs/default-source/democracy-works/democracy-works---south-africa-conference-paper---democracy-corruption-and-conflict-management---by-hennie-van-vuuren-pdf.pdf?sfvrsn=2.

Verdeja, Ernesto. *Unchopping a Tree: Reconciliation in the Aftermath of Political Violence*. Philadelphia: Temple University Press, 2009.

Villa Vicencio, Charles. *Walk with Us and Listen: Political Reconciliation in Africa*. Washington, DC: Georgetown University Press, 2009.

Villa-Vicencio, Charles, and Erik Doxtader, eds. *Pieces of the Puzzle. Key Words on Reconciliation and Transitional Justice*. Cape Town: Institute for Justice and Reconciliation, 2004.

———. *The Provocations of Amnesty: Memory, Justice, and Impunity*. Cape Town: IJR, 2003.

Volf, Miroslav. *Exclusion and Embrace: A Theological Exploration of Identity, Otherness, and Reconciliation*. Nashville, TN: Abingdon Press, 1996.

Volkan, Vamik D. "Transgenerational Transmissions and Chosen Traumas." Opening address to the International Association of Group Psychotherapy XIII International Congress, August 1998.

Waldmeir, Patti. *Anatomy of a Miracle: The End of Apartheid and the Birth of the New South Africa*. New Brunswick, NJ: Rutgers University Press, 1997.

Wale, Kim. "Confronting Exclusion: Time for Radical Reconciliation." In *SA Reconciliation Barometer Survey: 2013 Report*. Cape Town: IJR.

Weber, Max. *Economy and Society*, edited by Guether Roth and Claus Wittich. Berkeley: University of California Press, 1978.

———. "Objectivity in Social Science and Social Policy." In *The Methodology of the Social Sciences*, edited by E. A. Shils and H. A. Finch. New York: Free Press, 1949.

Weinstein, Harvey M. "Editorial Note: The Myth of Closure, the Illusion of Reconciliation: Final Thoughts on Five Years as Co-Editor-in-Chief." *International Journal of Transitional Justice* 5, no. 1 (2011): 1–10.

Wessels, Leon. *Negotiating for Human Rights*. Turning Points in Human Rights Series. Cape Town: Institute for Justice and Reconciliation. 2009.

———. "Statement Given at the TRC State Security Council Hearings, 1997." In *Truth and Reconciliation in South Africa: The Fundamental Documents*, edited by Erik Doxtader and Philippe Joseph Salazar. Cape Town: New Africa, 2007.

Wilson, Richard. *The Politics of Truth and Reconciliation in South Africa: Legitimizing the Post-Apartheid State*. Cambridge: University of Cambridge Press, 2001.

Wingenbach, Ed. *Institutionalising Agonist Democracy: Post-Foundationalism and Political Liberalism*. Farnham: Ashgate, 2011.

Witwatersrand University and South African History Archive. *Traces of Truth: A Select Bibliography of the South African TRC*. http://www.saha.org.za/resources/docs/PDF/Projects/trc_bib.pdf.

Yacoob, Zac. "Drafting the Final Bill of Rights, 1994–1996." In *Constitutional Rights*. Turning Points in Human Rights Series. IJR: Cape Town, 2009.

Youngster [pseud.]. "How Mandela Sold Out Blacks." *News 24,* July 17, 2012. Accessed February 27, 2013. http://www.news24.com/MyNews24/How-Mandela-sold-out-blacks-20120717.

Zehr, Howard. *Changing Lenses: A New Focus for Crime and Justice*. Scottsdale, PA: Herald Press, 1990.

Interviews and Personal Communication

Ahmad Mouath Al-Khatib Al-Hasani, former president of the National Coalition for Syrian
    Revolutionary and Opposition Forces and a former imam of the Umayyad Mosque in
    Damascus, Doha, Qatar, 2014.

Scott Appleby, Professor of History and Director of its Keough School of Global Affairs, at Notre
    Dame University, South Bend, Indiana, USA, March 2012.

Pablo de Greiff, UN Special Rapporteur on the Promotion of Truth, Justice, Reparation and
    Guarantees of Non-Recurrence of Serious Crimes and Gross Violations of Human Rights,
    Skype conversation with IJR, Pretoria, South Africa, October 9, 2013.

Peter Gastrow, former National Chairperson of the Progressive Federal Party and member of the
    National Peace Accord Secretariat, personal communication, March 18, 2014.

Roelf Meyer, former chief negotiator for the South African government during the MPNP, inter-
    view, Pretoria, South Africa, April 2013.

Mac Maharaj, ANC leader, former joint secretary of the Transitional Executive Council and
    Presidential Spokesperson, telephonic interview, March 2014.

Piers Pigou, former TRC investigator, personal communication, April 6, 2014.

Caitlin Spring, University of Cape Town White Privilege Founding Group Member, personal
    communication, June 17, 2015.

Desmond Tutu interviewed on *Truth, Justice and Memory, A DVD Series on the South African Truth
    and Reconciliation Commission.* Cape Town: IJR, 2012

Constant Viljoen, Former Head of the South African Defence Force, telephonic interview, August
    25, 2013.

INDEX